The Soul's Perspective on How to Achieve Perfect Radiant Health:
A Compilation

THE SOUL'S PERSPECTIVE ON HOW TO ACHIEVE PERFECT RADIANT HEALTH: A COMPILATION

Dr. Joshua David Stone

Writers Club Press
San Jose New York Lincoln Shanghai

The Soul's Perspective on How to Achieve
Perfect Radiant Health: A Compilation
All Rights Reserved © 2001 by Dr. Joshua David Stone

No part of this book may be reproduced or transmitted in any form or by any means, graphic, electronic, or mechanical, including photocopying, recording, taping, or by any information storage retrieval system, without the permission in writing from the publisher.

Writers Club Press
an imprint of iUniverse.com, Inc.

For information address:
iUniverse.com, Inc.
5220 S 16th, Ste. 200
Lincoln, NE 68512
www.iuniverse.com

I want to officially state that I am not a medical doctor. I take no responsibility for healing. I am providing material only, and my own personal opinions and experience. Consult a qualified health care practitioner and/or medical doctor in matters of physical health when needed.

Much of the information in this book has been channeled through communication with the Ascended Masters. As with all this type of information, it is subject to the lens of the individual who is receiving the information. It is up to the discretion of the reader to determine what is valid for them.

ISBN: 0-595-17409-4

Printed in the United States of America

Contents

1 The Importance of Eating a Healthy Diet 1
2 How to Heal the Physical Body through the Power of the Mind . .7
3 How to Heal the Physical Body through
   the Power of Your Spirituality 18
4 The 250 Golden Keys To Creating Perfect Radiant Health
   in Your Physical Body from the Soul's Perspective 22
5 How to Overcome Spiritual, Mental,
   Emotional and Physical Fatigue 42
6 Developing A Good Spiritual, Mental, Emotional,
   Etheric, Physical, Environmental and Social Diet 49
7 Daily Spiritual Affirmations to Work With 59
8 How to Develop an Extremely High-Functioning
   Physical, Psychological and Spiritual Immune System 68
9 The Importance of Loving the Physical Body 80
10 How to Clear the Negative Implants,
   Elementals, and Astral Entities 91
11 Dr. Lorphan's Healing Academy on Sirius 122
12 The Fifty Point Cosmic Cleansing Meditation 141
13 How to Utilize the Unbelievable
   Power and Abilities of the Holy Spirit .145
14 Caring for the Temple of GOD 151
15 Healing from the Higher Dimensions .163
16 The Psychological Causation of Disease by Djwhal Khul 174
17 Integrating Traditional and Non-Traditional Modalities 192
18 The Use of Color and Sound in Spiritual Healing 197

19 The Issue of Spiritual Weariness and How to Overcome It 211
20 Practicing the Presence of GOD 219
21 Turning Lemons into Lemonade: A Millennium Perspective ..226
22 How to Clear Specific Diseases:
   From the Perspective of the Masters 232
23 GOD, My Personal Power, The Power of My Subconscious
   Mind and My Physical Body are an Unbeatable Team! 260
24 Physical Immortality 269
25 A New Species of Light and Higher Light Body Integration ...280
26 Eighteen Great Cosmic Clearings and Cleansings 282
27 How to Physically Ground Your Spirituality 295
28 How to Develop an Integrated Christ/Buddha Living Space ..323
29 Honoring and Sanctifying the Material Face of GOD 329
30 The Dr. Joshua David Stone Suggested
   Program for Dealing with Cancer 333
31 The Spiritual/Christ/Buddha Ideal and An Integrated and
   Balanced Approach to Physical Health, Prosperity and Life! ..336
32 The Importance of Removing the
   "Earth Crystals" From Your Subtle Bodies 342
33 Learning to Co-Create with Nature 346
34 The Soul's Perspective on Transition,
   Death, Separation and Grief 351
35 Crosses to Bear 354
36 A Battleplan as to How to Deal
   with Chronic Health Problems 359
37 The Issue of Living on Light 393
38 Dining with GOD 398
39 The Incredible Importance of Mastering, Loving and
   Taking Responsibility for the Earth and Earth Energies 408

40 What Does Spiritually Mastering the
    Earth and Earth Energies Really Mean? 418
41 The Importance of Loving and
    Enjoying the Earth and Earth Life! 430
42 The Soul and Mighty I Am Presence 21 Day
    Program for Mastering Bad Habits and Addictions 453
43 The Eight Point 21 Day Program for Creating
    Unconditional Self-love and Self-worth 472
44 The Negative Ego and the Return of the Divine
    Mother and the Goddess Energies to Earth 491
45 The Core Fear Matrix Removal Program 521
46 The 385 Ascension Activations and Cleansings
    of GOD to Ask for Before You Go to Bed Every
    Night for Yourself and Mother Earth 527
47 My Spiritual Mission and Purpose
    by Dr. Joshua David Stone 544
About the Author 561

1

The Importance of Eating a Healthy Diet

It is very important in regard to physical health to eat a really good physical diet! In previous books I have stayed away from speaking about this, however for this book I have decided to write a short chapter on this subject! This is actually difficult to speak about, for diet is very different for each person. One's age, Spiritual development, type of work, race, country, climate, body type, ray structure, and unique body chemistry all play a part. So any person who claims to self-righteously tell you that this is the only diet anyone should eat, does not know what they are talking about.

With this in mind I am going to make some suggestions which I think are very helpful. I do not claim to be a Medical Doctor or a professional Nutritionist. However, my unique Spiritual and Holistic Health background and attunement to this aspect of life may make me in some ways more qualified to speak than most. I am going to speak in general however!

What I would say is this: First off I would recommend following a diet that is rich in vegetables most of all. Especially green leafy vegetables. If you can handle more raw and fresh vegetables, all the better. However, if you have any digestive weakness then steam them. As much as 50 to 60% of what you eat should be vegetables. Make sure you get enough protein. Now I myself at this time am a vegetarian; however, I do not make a blanket rule that for Spiritual and/or physical reasons you should not eat meat. For some people's bodies this may be appropriate.

If you eat meat I would stick with chicken and hamburger or beef, and try to get it as fresh as you can. Protein should be about 20% of the diet. Then as far as starch goes, grain is a good source, especially white rice, brown rice, oatmeal, cooked rye cereal or rye bread! Starch should be around 15%. Don't overload on Starch. Protein is actually more important! Fresh fruit is good, but eat it fresh and don't have too much for there is a lot of natural sugar in it. Most people are allergic to dairy and I would not eat too much of it. Get a little bit of oil and fat in the diet as well.

Diet is extremely important especially the older you get! Do not over eat! You need much less food then society dictates. Eat to live, don't live to eat!

The other main rule I would highly recommend is to follow proper food combining! Do not mix starch and protein at the same meal! Eat fruit alone! Drink liquids 20 minutes before you eat to two to three hours after you eat! Eat melons alone! Do not eat a lot of nuts for they are very hard to digest! Trust me on this. Proper food combining is essential. You don't have to be neurotic about it, but generally follow this!

Drink lots of fresh water! If you can afford it I would highly recommend the "Water of Life"! Speak to me about this at the Academy if you are interested! As far as vitamins and minerals go it is a good idea for most people to do this. Get a food source vitamin however, do not use synthetic vitamins for they are poison to the body! Use only vitamins and minerals that are made from natural food sources. Any health food store can guide you in this direction. Don't overload yourself with vitamins, minerals and all these products, for in truth, your body honestly does not like 99% of them. Your mind may think it does, but your body elemental does not. The absolute ideal way to eat is to check everything you eat with a pendulum to see if your body really wants it. The problem is, however, most people do not know how to use a pendulum and if they do they may not have practiced enough to get 100% clear information!

Do not eat a lot before bed, the body should not be digesting a lot of food while you sleep. It should be healing, resting and regenerating.

This is important. Read the chapter on "The Issue of Living on Light!" I am not saying to stop eating, but to train your body to sustain on GOD's Light also!

Do not eat very much sugar, for it is not good for the body. Sugar is the medium in which bacteria is grown in laboratories. The less the better! Do not use artificial stimulants such as coffee, tea, ginseng, or anything else. Rely on GOD and the Masters for energy! If you are tired, sleep or take a nap. There is nothing wrong with this. Most people sleep around seven to eight hours a day. If you need more at times that is fine, and if you need less that is fine too. Take time for work and play! Do not drink soft drinks! Never take recreational drugs, and as much as possible try to avoid taking drugs from traditional doctors. There are, of course, exceptions to this. Try and rely on homeopathics and Herbs for all your healing! Find a good homeopathic doctor, naturopath, and/or Herbalist! If you ever have to take antibiotics then be sure to supplement with Acidophilus. There is a brand called Jaroophilus that I highly recommend. If you have to use a sweetener use honey, but don't eat too much of that. An occasional dessert is fine, just don't overdo it! Pray to GOD, the Masters and Angels to electrically rewire your body to help you live more on GOD's Light. This along with the good diet will give you all the vitamins and minerals you need! Get a purple plate as advertised in this book and always put your food on it for five minutes before you eat to clear and energize it! You can also put a clear quartz crystal in your water to energize it. In the past I have even kept mine in my water cooler! Try to eat only fresh food. Organic is better but you don't have to be neurotic! Do not eat processed food! Do not eat any preservatives! Be sure to wash your vegetables really well for they are filled with pesticides. Work with the Futureplex line of homeopathics that I speak of in this book.

I have a friend who has the top of the line radionics machine. This is a machine that thousands of people can be put on it. For $1000 dollars, a picture of yourself and a hair sample, they will put you on this machine 24 hours a day, seven days, a week 365 days a year, and run you on this, which is programmed to work on healing every aspect of your body! Anyone who needs a real up-grade might consider this. Contact me at the Academy and send me these things and I will personally make sure you are put on this program. I only do this for friends, and I am not going out of my way to advertise this service. I am a big believer in the power of radionics since I have two much smaller machines which I use for my personal use, and which I have been using for ten years! Radionics machines are hard to use so this alternative I am giving you is actually much better for you are on it for an entire year nonstop! If you need a major upgrade for your entire physical body you might consider this! Again, I recommend the Water of Life, for this will give you a lot of energy and will really help to cleanse your body!

Be sure to get some physical exercise at least three times a week. Walking is the best exercise! Be sure to get outside. Try to get 15 to 20 minutes of sun every day! This energy is actually stored in your etheric body! Stay away from mercury fillings! They sometimes leak and mercury is not the best thing for the body! Stay away from aluminum pans and aluminum foil! These Futureplex homeopathics I describe in this book can help cleanse a lot of these metals and chemicals out of your system!

Eat a lot of Bieler Broth. You make this by steaming zucchini, green beans, a little celery and a little parsley. The majority is zucchini and green beans. I would recommend eating this three times a week. Also fasting with it for a day once a month or even once a week. This will do absolute wonders for your physical body and health. It will totally clean out your liver. It is a liver rejuvenator. After the vegetables are steamed you just add the slightest bit of water from the steamer you just cooked it in and blend up the vegetables so it is a thick broth. Don't add too much water or it will not be thick enough. I have lived on this stuff for 20 years and there is nothing that has done wonders for me more than this. I have fasted on it for weeks at times. You can occasionally experiment and add other vegetables but this should be the foundation. Trust me, do this! It will rejuvenate you like nothing else. You will see it in your eyes, hair and skin!

The other type of fast I would recommend once a year is an apple fast! Just eat raw apples for three days. At the end have some olive oil as a type of laxative effect. Raw apples have the unique property of pulling toxins out of the system if eaten raw in a fasting situation! Only do this once a year if you feel so guided to and no more! The Bieler broth you can eat every day, the more the better! You can also eat the Bieler broth as an extra side dish with your protein and salad or whatever!

If you ever have a stomach ache and you need to eat something, eat a baked apple. A homeopathic doctor told me this, and the last 20 years if this would ever happen I would make a couple of baked apples that were cooked really well and this always healed it right up! Do not eat a raw apple for this purpose, only baked!

If you have health challenges, find a good Homeopathic Doctor and/or Naturopath who uses Homeopathics and Herbs, and get a whole detoxification and purification program. Try and get all the residual toxins out of your body. This will do wonders for your immune system! Taking extra vitamin C is a good idea as well! Call on the Masters to put a screen of protection around you when anyone around you is sick! This is just good preventive medicine, and the Masters will do this!

The most important thing, as well, is to have a good mental diet, emotional diet, energetic diet, and Spiritual diet! Good food, good thoughts, good feelings and emotions will do the trick! Always affirm you are in perfect radiant health! Tell yourself this ten times every day! Affirm you are invulnerable to catching any virus or bacteria, for you are the Christ, in truth! If you get sick, don't lay a trip on yourself and don't let others lay a trip on you. It is just a sign that you are cleansing and this is a good thing! Tap your thymus glad often to keep it activated! The more you achieve "Integrated Ascension," the more you will be filled with Spiritual current on all levels, and this and the Grace GOD and the Masters will help you to not get sick! Most of all pray constantly to GOD, the Masters and your Healing Angels for help in everything in your life including the maintenance of your physical body! They can do wonders to rejuvenate the physical and etheric vehicles! Ask them also to remove all your negative implants and negative elementals. This will also do wonders for your physical body! If you want help this one time call the Academy and I will set you up with a channel to clear these for you from all your past lives and this one! I would highly recommend this! Just as we want to get rid of all negative thoughts, all negative feelings and emotions, all negative energy, we also don't want to put any poisonous or toxic food into our bodies and we want to remove all imbalanced energies that are within the four body system and/or with the Mental, Emotional, Etheric and Physical body! If you keep your Spirit, mind, heart, feelings, energy body and physical body completely pure, only putting pure energies into each of these bodies, it will be impossible for disease of any kind to grow there. Do remember that some physical health stuff is Spiritual mutation not physical health problems. The more accelerated your Spiritual Path, Ascension Process, and Initiation Process the more the physical body will have to adjust to the higher frequencies of energies which often does cause physical health lessons. In some cases it just goes with the territory and no matter how healthy a person is this will occur!

In conclusion, follow these simple tips and you will find your health greatly improving!

2

How to Heal the Physical Body through the Power of the Mind

It is important to understand that we each have a conscious, subconscious and superconscious mind. The subconscious mind, as you know, functions like a computer and has an enormous number of abilities but needs a computer programmer to properly utilize those abilities. That is the function of a healthy conscious mind. One of the most important functions of the subconscious mind is that it completely runs the physical body. Anything you program it to do, good or bad, in regards to the body, it will do. If you program it to create perfect radiant health it will do this. If unconsciously you allow negative thoughts in your mind if can also create deleterious health.

One of the most remarkable stories that bears repeating is a true story that my father told me about a man who had been diagnosed with terminal cancer. He was taken to a friend of my father's who was a cancer specialist who recommended exploratory surgery to remove the cancer if they could. On the day of the surgery he was given anesthesia and they cut him open and the cancer, to the doctor's concern, was so extensive and pervasive that he just sewed him right back up and told his wife that to try to remove all of the cancer would kill him on the operating table. It was better to let him live the rest of his days in peace. Now the cancer patient's wife, for some strange reason, never told her husband what the doctor said. The cancer patient went home thinking that the cancer had all been surgically removed. Three months later the man returned to the doctor for his checkup and they took x-rays and the man had no cancer in his body. The doctor was totally flabbergasted. He asked the former cancer patient what he had been doing, for the doctor had never seen such a remarkable recovery. The former cancer patient replied, "What are you talking about? You removed the cancer three months ago." The doctor replied, "Didn't your wife tell you? I did nothing of the sort! The cancer was so pervasive I would have killed you if I tried to remove all of the cancer in your body." The patient replied, "You mean you didn't remove the cancer three months ago?" The doctor said, "No." Three months later the cancer had totally returned again and the man was dead.

This, my friends, is the power of the mind. Anything that you think, image or visualize and impress upon your subconscious mind will manifest within the physical body. The science of hypnosis and self-hypnosis clearly proves this also. Women using such techniques have scientifically been proven to grow larger breasts using just the power of the mind and imagery. We have seen hypnosis stage shows where a man was asked to lay horizontally on top of two chairs two or three feet off the ground and was given the suggestion that his body was rigid like steel. Once the subconscious mind accepted this suggestion this is exactly what happened. A person in a conscious state could not possibly have done this. We have read miraculous reports of people walking over hot coals, which has been called "firewalking." I know for a fact that it can be done because my mother and sister did it. We hear of remarkable reports of Indian saints lying on beds of nails or being buried under the ground for long periods of time and then coming up out of the ground perfectly fine. I saw a report of a man in Russia who could literally stay under water for twenty minutes. There are reports of people who can live without eating physical food and live on God's light. Doctors constantly speak of spontaneous remission. Even the medical profession speaks of the powerful effects of the mind in scientific terms when they speak of the placebo effect. One person is given a specific type of medication and another person is given a sugar pill but thinks it is medication. If you believe you are taking medication, even if you are not, the subconscious mind will make the body believe that it has.

One other fascinating example of this is how doctors in Japan will often not tell their patients when they have life-threatening diseases. They will treat them with the proper remedies, but will not tell them of the actual serious illness that they have. This is because they realize that if the patient holds this thought or image it will counteract all of the help that they can give them. This may be a little controversial but the thinking behind it does have some validity. If someone is diagnosed with AIDS, but in truth doesn't really have it, they can develop all of the symptoms of AIDS just by the power of suggestion. Parmahansa Yogananda, the great Indian saint, used to say that even if you're ninety-nine years old and on your deathbed the only thought you should be affirming in your mind is that you are in perfect radiant health.

If a person believes that they are going to die at a certain age they probably will even if the physical body is capable of living longer. We all understand and know that the will to live is the most important factor in health crisis of any kind. If a person does not have a strong will to live, no medication or natural remedy will help.

So far we have been talking about the power of the mind on a subconscious level. There is also the power of the mind on a superconscious level. The superconscious mind, also known as the soul, oversoul, higher self, Mighty I Am Presence and/or monad, is also capable of introducing miraculous healing potentialities. The key to perfect radiant health is the proper use of affirmations, positive visualization, positive self-suggestion, positive self-talk, and prayer. Of course, honoring physical means is important as well. Things such as diet, physical exercise, sunshine, fresh air, proper recreation, and proper sleep habits. Now there are some schools of thought such as the Christian Scientists who try to deal with all physical health lessons just on the mental plane. I mean this as no judgment but this is not right. GOD has four faces: spiritual, mental, emotional and physical, and all must be honored, sanctified, and integrated properly. Why disown a level? It's when all four levels are working together in perfect harmony and balance that perfect health potentiality is most accelerated.

So prayer and/or invocation are the terms for calling in the superconscious mind for help and its powers are in the miraculous realm. Along with calling in the superconscious mind for help in physical health issues I also recommend calling in the angels and inner plane ascended masters. In some religions this is referred to as the saints. Their healing powers are also profound and miraculous in nature. We often hear of stories of people calling on the Virgin Mary and having miraculous healings. A great many of the great religious leaders in Earth's history were not only great spiritual teachers, but were also great healers. The Master Jesus' healing abilities were legendary. The same is true of a present day avatar currently living in India known as Sai Baba. He has been known to raise people from the dead on numerous occasions. All the great saints who have passed on to the spiritual world are still available through the power of prayer. In our culture today the archangels and angels are having a resurgence of popularity. My friends, these are not figments of our collective imagination. They are real and their healing powers are awesome if you will just call on them. The law of the universe is that your superconscious mind and the inner plane spiritual masters and angels are not allowed to help unless you ask. Ask and you shall receive. Knock and the door shall be opened. If you read the chapter in this book on Doctor Lorphan and his healing academy on Sirius, many of the tools and techniques for calling on the superconscious level are revealed. Try them and I guarantee that you will have immediate, tangible results that are unmistakable. The great channel of the universal mind, Edgar Cayce said, "Why worry when you can pray?" I would like to update this great message and say, "Why be concerned when you can pray and do affirmations and positive visualizations?"

I had a personal example of the power of the mind that was shown to me over twenty years ago. I used to be an avid jogger and long distance runner. At around the age of twenty-four I developed a leg injury and I could not jog. At first it was diagnosed as a calcium deficiency which made total sense because I was not eating any diary or calcium at the time in my diet. I started taking calcium and my leg definitely improved, however I had had the injury for almost a year prior to this so I unconsciously had formed a mental habit of having this injury. In a joint meditation with a friend of mine I consulted my superconscious mind as to why I could not shake this leg injury. My superconscious mind told me that it was all in my mind that there was nothing wrong with my leg. I strongly protested saying that every time I started to jog I was in serious, excruciating pain. My superconscious mind told me that this was because I was constantly telling people that I had a bum leg, At that time I was just beginning to fully understand how the subconscious mind worked and so I started telling myself many several times a day that my left leg had like steel-like strength and power, and was powerful, healed and whole. When people asked me about my jogging or my leg I would tell them my affirmation. Son of a gun, two weeks later I started trying to jog again and after almost three years of not being able to run, my leg was fine. I continued the affirmations and have never had a problem since.

Often, my friends, our conscious mind is holding one thought but our subconscious mind is holding another and we are not aware of it. The key is to get the conscious mind to only hold thoughts taught to it by the superconscious mind and for the subconscious mind to only hold thoughts taught to it by the conscious mind. In this way, the three minds function as one mind. It is not enough just to pray, for it is not the job of the superconscious mind to control your thinking. That is the job of the conscious mind.

It also is not enough to just do affirmations and positive visualization and/or treatments. Science of Mind, which is wonderful, focuses on this level and this is great and fantastic. It is also necessary, however, to ask for help and not just affirm it. Treatments, affirmations and visualization do not replace prayer. A treatment is not a prayer either, even if it is focused on spiritual matters. There is a difference between a request or call for help. A call for help does not have to imply weakness or lack. The idea is to call for help from full personal power.

Spiritual psychology teaches us to always remain in the perfected state. So anytime you experience imperfection in your physical body or anywhere else in your life, this just means it is time to pray and affirm and visualize the truth of GOD's perfected ideal which is our ideal because GOD created us. All imperfection, hence, is immediately transformed into perfection by the power of your consciousness.

Now the next point is a real key to this whole process. It is not enough just to do prayer, affirmations and visualizations. Some of you may say, "How can this be?" What I mean by this is that you could be praying, affirming and visualizing all day long, however, if your basic thinking, inner self-talk, interaction with others, and deeds do not demonstrate this perfected ideal then you are affirming negative thoughts into your subconscious mind, without even realizing it.

Let me give some examples. If you do not own your personal power in your life, inwardly and outwardly, even though you constantly pray and do affirmations and visualizations your subconscious mind will be filled with negative thoughts. The same is true with self-love. Another key is learning to place a golden bubble of protection around yourself every morning that keeps out the negativity from other people. If you do not do this, other people's negativity and hypnotic suggestions will go right into your subconscious mind, even though you are constantly praying, affirming and visualizing.

Another example is what I call self-talk. We are constantly dialoging with ourselves through the process of what I call self-inquiry. His Holiness The Lord Sai Baba has said that 75% of the spiritual path is self-inquiry. This is the simple process of just monitoring your thoughts, emotions and impulses on a moment to moment basis and choosing which ones you are going to allow into your mind and which ones you are going to keep out. Most people on this planet live way too much on automatic pilot and are not vigilant enough over their thinking. Spiritual psychology teaches us that our thoughts create our reality, including our feelings and emotions. Proper thinking is the key to inner peace and happiness. The world is a projection screen for our thoughts and we are experiencing our own movie by how we interpret life. There are, in truth, only two ways to interpret life. We either interpret life from the Christ/Buddha attitude system or from the Negative Ego/Lower-Self/fear-based attitude system. Sai Baba has said, "The definition of GOD is that GOD equals man minus ego."

To fully realize GOD and achieve self-realization we must keep all negative ego thoughts out of our mind. This is one of the number one keys to achieving perfect physical health. Again, we can be praying, affirming and visualizing all day long, however, if we are not doing the fundamental work of keeping the negative ego thoughts out of our mind on a moment to moment basis we are deluding ourselves. Most people in the world do not truly understand spiritual psychology and the difference between negative ego thinking and spiritual thinking. I say to you, my friends, that this is the single most important lesson on the spiritual path. I cannot recommend more highly that you read my books *Soul Psychology* and *Integrated Ascension,* which are available through the academy that I founded. Many of my other nineteen books speak to this issue and I highly recommend calling the Academy for a free information packet.

Every thought that comes from another person or our own subconscious mind is either a negative ego thought or a spiritual thought. Said in another way, it is a thought of fear or a thought of love; it is a thought of oneness or a thought of separation. The job of a healthy functioning conscious mind is to deny any thought that is not of GOD to enter your mind, and to immediately switch your attention and your thinking to the spiritual and/or Christ/Buddha thought that contains the perfected ideal. One key monitor for determining how you are doing in this process is to examine if you have negative feelings and emotions and if you live in a state of love, joy, evenmindedness and inner peace. If you do not, and this is not a judgment; it is just a gift and a sign that there are some attitudinal adjustments you need to make. This is the purpose of this book and many of my other books. To help my readers understand this process and to give them the tools to easily remedy this. It does not take twenty years of therapy. It only takes twenty-one days to cement any new habit into the subconscious mind.

Every thought you allow into your conscious mind from your own subconscious mind and from others is an affirmation and visualization. If you are allowing negative ego thinking in, from either level, this is unconsciously affecting your physical health, immune system and energy level.

Many very sincere lightworkers pray constantly to GOD and the Masters for protection and yet are sabotaged by negative energies from inner and outer levels and cannot understand why. They think that GOD and the Masters are supposed to provide all of the protection. This is not true. They will do their share, however, the key responsibility lies in this process of healthy self-inquiry having to do with being vigilant on a psychological level. It is not the job of GOD and the Masters and your superconscious mind to control your thoughts and this point cannot be emphasized enough. This is your job! It is why you have incarnated. How can you possibly become a Master in your own right if you expect higher inner plane forces to do all of the work for you?

In another wonderful book called *A Course in Miracles* it is stated in one of the lessons that "sickness is a defense against the truth." What this means is that GOD created us and as the Bible says we are made in His image. We each are Sons and Daughters of GOD, or apprentice Christs. Our true identity is the Christ, or the Buddha, if you prefer. The words we use do not matter, for all religions teach the same thing. Our true identity is that we are gods/goddesses made in the image of our Creator. We were not created in sin; we were created in perfection. GOD does not catch colds or a flu bug and in our ideal state neither do we. So, sickness is a defense against the truth because the truth is that all negativity, suffering and illness stems from the negative ego, which in essence is fear and a belief in separation from GOD. The law of the mind is that whatever you believe is the reality that you live in. If you believe in the illusion of negative ego thinking you will experience this reality, however, this does not make it true. The truth is the negative ego does not exist and neither does separation from GOD. Negative thinking or emotions also do not exist in GOD's reality and neither does physical sickness or financial poverty. It is the job of the healthy functioning conscious mind that is attuned to GOD and one's higher self to affirm only truth and not illusion.

So, sickness, on a physical level, is a defense against the truth of GOD's true reality. It is our job to keep our attention on this reality and think and imagine and pray for only this reality. And this will program our minds to only think Christed thoughts, which will create only Christed, Buddha-like feelings and emotions. This will also create only Christed, Buddha-like actions and only Christed, Buddha-like physical health. This will also magnetize and attract only Christed, Buddha-like people and experiences. When "negative" things do occur in this type of consciousness they will not be looked at as "negative", but rather as spiritual tests, lessons, challenges and opportunities to grow.

Physical health lessons are a gift, my friends, and are just teaching us that there is another level of purification that is needed on a thought, emotional, physical and spiritual level. They should not be judged, but looked at as more of a cleansing process and teacher. They are very often, in spiritual people, a sign of accelerated spiritual growth; for every time one moves to a higher level or frequency another level of cleansing needs to take place.

Lastly, it must also be understood that some physical health challenges are karmic in nature and are for the glory of GOD. Some people are meant to have them so they can demonstrate the power of the spirit of

GOD and the will of GOD and the love of GOD in physical form. Mother Theresa had severe heart problems yet served. St. Francis was wracked with health lessons, yet was one of the most famous saints of this last millennium. Physical health lessons are a part of physically incarnating into this earthly school. It is important not to coddle oneself, yet also to take proper care of the physical vehicle. You do not have to have perfect health to achieve ascension and you do not have to have perfect health to serve and make a difference in this world. Those with chronic health lessons must learn to own their personal power and remain evenminded even though the physical vehicle is not functioning perfectly. Anger or depression over chronic physical health lessons is a waste of time and energy. Acceptance and focusing on what you can do instead of what you can't do is the lesson of the day. Most importantly, do not judge self for having health lessons and do not judge others for you have not walked in their moccasins and you do not know the divine reasons why things are as they seem. Many lightworkers give pat or generalized, stereotypical answers that they read in a book that they think applies to all lightworkers. This is illusion and self-righteous, and verifies that a little knowledge is sometimes a dangerous thing. I repeat again, in spiritual people it is often those who have the most health lessons who are making the most progress on their spiritual path. Accelerated spiritual growth demands higher and higher and more refined levels of purification. This will often manifest as physical health lessons, which is not a sign that you are doing anything wrong, but, in truth, a sign that you are doing something right. I am not saying here that you should try to get sick; I am just saying it is almost impossible, if not impossible, to incarnate into a physical body and be on an accelerated spiritual growth process and never experience physical health symptoms. Even Sai Baba, who is a universal avatar, when taking on karma of his students, has had to run it through his physical vehicle and at times has gotten extremely ill. Being an avatar this is a unique situation, being able to actually take on heart attacks and strokes of others, but this shows that even a universal avatar, which he is the only one on the planet, is not completely free of all physical laws. However, I must say he is the closest to achieving the transcendence of all physical laws in terms of an incarnated being on Earth. I am not saying this to push anyone in the direction of being a student of Sai Baba necessarily. I am just reporting as an objective reporter, so to speak, who, in truth, is involved with all spiritual teachers and all spiritual paths, since I follow a path of synthesis and eclecticism. If you do not know much about Sai Baba I recommend that you read the chapter that I wrote about him in my first book.

In conclusion I wish you all positive Christed thoughts and perfect radiant health!

3

How to Heal the Physical Body through the Power of Your Spirituality

In the last chapter we spoke of how to heal the physical body through the power of the mind. In this chapter I am focusing on how to heal the physical body through integrating your spirituality. The essence of the Spiritual path, the ascension process and completing one's seven levels of initiation, has to do with first merging with one's higher-self and/or soul. This is firstly termed the completion of one's third initiation. The later merging with one's spirit, Mighty I Am Presence and/or monad culminates with the completion of the seventh initiation.

The merging with one's soul and/or higher-self on Earth has a tremendous healing affect on one's physical body. When one merges with one's soul and/or higher self, by definition they are moving towards living out of higher self thinking rather than lower-self thinking. Values such as unconditional love, forgiveness, nonjudgmentalness, service, co-operation, harmlessness and brotherhood becomes predominant. The merging with one's soul opens the heart chakra, which is connected to the thymus gland. The thymus gland being the key to your immune system. As you become more unconditionally loving your immune system functions more effectively, hence your thymus gland is more stimulated.

The higher your level of initiation and the more love and light quotient you carry in your aura have an extremely positive effect on the physical body. Love and light protects you from disease and actually feed the body and cells. This light also serves as protection from negative energies.

As you open more and more to your soul and spirit they merge deeper and deeper into your mental body, emotional body, etheric body (energy body) and finally fully into the physical body. When the Mighty I Am Presence and/or monad are fully anchored, your physical body becomes electrified with light in the most positive way. It is literally pouring out of your cells. The spirit of God is literally living in every cell of your body.

This makes the mind gravitate to only Christed thinking rather than negative ego thinking which further electrifies the body with light.

As one strives to live out of the Christ/Buddha consciousness rather than the negative ego consciousness this serves to completely spiritualize the emotional body and/or vehicle. As one fully embraces their soul, spirit and Spiritual path you learn to completely let go of all negative emotions. Negative emotions are not of God. They are of the negative ego and fear based thinking. As the soul and spirit fully integrate into the emotional body unconditional love reigns supreme and negative emotions such as anger, worry, depression, sadness, upset, impatience, disappointment, lack of self-love, lack of self-worth and jealousy, to name a few, begin to disappear. They are replaced with a spiritualized emotional body filled with unconditional love, forgiveness, nonjudgmentalness, personal power, self-love, healthy boundaries, co-operation, joy, happiness, acceptance, looking at things as lessons and spiritual tests, self-worth, high self-esteem and Christ consciousness.

These spiritualized emotions not tainted by negative ego thinking have an enormously exhilarating affect on the physical body. These emotions fill the cells and the aura with even more light and love. How can a God-filled cell get sick? The answer is it can't.

Negative emotions have an extremely deleterious affect on the physical body. Too much anger can cause liver problems and stomach problems. Too much worry can cause ulcers. Too much depression and sadness can totally debilitate the physical vehicle and basically de-energize it.

My friends, every negative thought you think and every negative emotion you allow to manifest lodges somewhere in your organs, glands, cells and bones. They can be seen in your aura by a clairvoyant and will be reflected in your dream life while you sleep.

My beloved readers, you would not drink "physical poison" or eat "spoiled food." Allowing negative ego thoughts and/or emotions into your consciousness is like eating mental and emotional poison and it affects the physical body in a similar but subtler way.

The good news is that every spiritual thought and spiritualized emotion you create also manifests in every organ, gland, cell and bone in your body. These spiritualized thoughts and emotions electrify the body with perfect radiant health.

Sickness or illness is not a bad thing but rather a signal that further purification of the mind, emotions, energy body and physical diet is needed. This cleansing and purification also is needed in lifestyle, physical health habits and relationships. Physical health lessons should be looked at as a gift not a negative thing. Every time we move to a higher level of frequency, initiation and vibration another level of purification is needed. Lightworkers often focus their purification on a spiritual level and not enough on the psychological and physical levels.

We must pay our rent to God on all levels. Everything in God's universe is governed by laws. These laws operate on a spiritual, mental, emotional, etheric, physical and material level. When you are disobedient to these laws you suffer. This is not God doing this to us, but rather we doing it to ourselves. God teaches us to become Masters and understand His universal laws through this process. Life is a constant process of learning and making adjustments. The higher one goes spiritually, the more straight and narrow the path becomes. To become self-realized and to become a spiritual master one must demonstrate self-mastery and self-discipline in a consistent manner on all levels in service of love. When we get off the path we will experience suffering which is God's gift to help remind us to get back on the path.

As we open more and more to our soul and spirit and let them ground fully into our four body system all the higher chakras open. When we live out of only the personality and not the soul we live out of the lower three chakras. As the upper four chakras open, as one opens spiritually, much more light and love is allowed to flow to us from Source. This further electrifies the physical body with good health.

As one continues to evolve spiritually higher chakras begin anchoring into the seven primary or basic chakras, or energy centers. There are actually over 330 chakras going back to the Godhead. As one evolves these higher chakras spiritually become anchored into the etheric and physical vehicle and fill the body with unimaginable light frequencies. The health benefits are exponential.

Adding to this as one opens up spiritually you have the help of your soul, Mighty I Am Presence, Angels and inner plane Ascended Masters who will help you with all physical health concerns if you will just pray and ask for help.

So, my beloved readers, I think you can see that if you want good health opening to your spiritual life is essential. You should open to your spiritual life because this is the sole purpose of life; however, one of the side benefits of doing so is greater and greater levels of perfect radiant health.

4

The 250 Golden Keys To Creating Perfect Radiant Health in Your Physical Body from the Soul's Perspective

- Physical diet
- Physical exercise and fitness
- Fresh air
- Sunshine
- Deep breathing
- Health affirmations (See chapter in this book on affirmations)
- Health prayers
- Stretching
- Yoga
- Aerobic exercise (walking, jogging, bicycling, swimming, rowing)
- Strength training (weights)
- Fasting (three day raw apple fast, or green vegetable juice fast with a little bit of carrot juice or water)
- "Water of Life" is available from Academy for cleanings, energizing and balancing chemical balance in physical body! Highly recommended!
- Have your implants and negative elementals removed by a trained initiate at The Academy.

- Channeled Ascension clearing session (Call the Academy).
- Using a pendulum to test your food.
- Purple energy plates to energize and cleanse food.
- Read this book
- Find a good homeopathic, herbalist, and or naturopathic doctor!
- Have your mercury fillings removed!
- Buy and work with my Ascension Activation Meditation Tape called "The 18 Point Cosmic Cleansing Meditation" available from the Academy.
- Call forth an "Axiatonal Alignment", three times a day!
- Call forth a "Golden Net" from your own Mighty I Am Presence, three times a day!
- Call forth from Archangel Michael and Faith, and your own Mighty I Am Presence, every day to start your day, a "Golden Dome" and/or a "Tube of Light of Protection!"
- Call Forth from the Lord of Arcturus for the Arcturian liquid crystals to be poured into your energy field to deactivate any and all negative energy!
- Call to Djwhal Khul for the anchoring of the "Prana Wind Clearing Device" to cleanse your meridians, nadis, and energy fields!
- Call to your Healing Angels to work on you every night while you sleep!
- Call forth help for Healing from Dr. Lorphan and the Galactic Healers from the Great White Lodge on Sirius!
- Call forth for the inner plane "Acupuncture Team" to do etheric Acupuncture on you!
- Find a good holistic Medical doctor you trust!
- Work with Bach Flower Remedies
- Always keep a good "Positive Mental Attitude!"
- Spiritualize all your negative feelings and emotions to positive ones!
- Find a good "Laying on of Hands" type of Healer for emergencies.
- Occasionally get a Chiropractic Adjustment.

- Especially read chapters; "How To Remove Implants," "Dr Lorphan's Healing Academy On Sirius" and "Developing A High Functioning Immune System On All Three Levels", in this book!
- Do positive creative visualization for five minutes every day for perfect radiant health!
- Work with Radionics to cleanse and balance energy fields (See Academy Website)!
- Eat a diet based on Principles of Proper food combining (See local health food store booklets).
- Eat lots of green leafy vegetables, vegetables, protein, starch.
- Drink lots of water.
- Ask Spirit and the Masters to run Spiritual Current through you to start every workday!
- Call in Etheric surgeons to repair your etheric body from any past life or child trauma!
- Call in Healing Angels to repair any holes or leaks in your Aura.
- Work with my 13 audio Ascension Activation Meditation Tapes on a daily basis to Spiritualize and Electrify your energy fields with Spiritual Current!
- Only allow yourself to eat a very small amount of sugar!
- Stop using all artificial stimulants except on special occasions or emergencies
- Never use recreational drugs!
- If possible try to use homeopathics and herbs, instead of drugs, for healing!
- Take extra Acidolphilus if you ever have used or use antibiotics.
- Get enough sleep every night!
- Take a good food source vitamin and mineral supplement after meals every day (no factory made supplements, only natural food source)!
- Work with Aromatherapy.
- Ask Spirit and the Masters to Balance Your Chakras and Energy fields every day or even twice a day!

- Ask your Mighty I Am Presence to fully Anchor and Activate your Monadic Blue Print Body into your Four Body System!
- Call to the Holy Spirit to undo and heal the cause of any physical health problem you are suffering from!
- Love your physical body and talk to it, for it has a form of consciousness!
- A Homeopthic Company called Futureplex has a number of homeopathic products for bacteria, viruses, immune system booster, and environmental detox. They are called "Bacterotox, Virotox, Envirotox, Prototox." You can read about these in my book! Call Homeopathic Pharmacy in Los Angeles to order them (818) 905-8338.
- Never ever use Microwave ovens, it puts holes in the aura of the food!
- Create a Science of Mind Treatment for your health or have a Science of mind practitioner create one for you to say for your health, which you can say once a day!
- Say a prayer to Spirit and the Masters to remove all energy of disease from your mental body, emotional body, etheric body and physical body!
- Call to the Lord of Arcturus and the Arcturians to clean and clear all energy of cancer from your mental, emotional, etheric and physical bodies!
- Go for an affirmation walk doing physical health affirmations the entire time!
- Put your Health Affirmation on tape and play them as background music while you are just working around the house!
- Put your Health affirmations on an endless loop tape or endless play tape recorder and play it softy in the back ground all night while you sleep!
- Have a dialogue with your physical body in your journal to see if there is anything it wants or is trying to tell you!

- Realize GOD works through the physical body and if you have a health lesson GOD is trying to teach you something.
- Talk to the physical as you would a good friend and form a positive relationship to it and thank it for all its good work on your behalf, for the physical body needs love, honor, friendship and respect as well. There is a form of consciousness within it called the "body elemental!"
- Twenty times throughout the day give yourself a "Thymus Tap" to increase functioning of Thymus Gland which is your immune system!"
- Never use Aluminum Foil, or Aluminum pots and pans, for you can get aluminum poisoning.
- Do not over indulge in sexuality for it can drain your energy!
- Moderation in all things!
- Call in Spirit and the Masters to remove all Core Fear Programming, negative ego programming, and poor health programming from your subconscious mind and four-body system!
- Ask Spirit and the Masters to clear your Genetic line of any health problems or weakness!
- Ask Spirit and the Masters to clear all your Past Lives from health challenges, lessons or problems that may be affecting you now!
- Ask Spirit and the Masters to clear, cleanse and detach you from any health lessons being caused by bleed through from one of your 144 Soul Extensions from the your Monad and Mighty I Am Presence!
- Ask your Soul and Mighty I Am Presence to help you create Perfect radiant health everyday!
- Call to Mother Mary and Archangels Raphael to have the Golden Angels live in any area of your body on a permanent basis that is chronically weak!
- For any person who is dealing with Chronic Health Lessons, it is absolutely essential that you read my books *Soul Psychology, How To Release Fear-Based Thinking and Feeling: An In-depth Study of*

Spiritual Psychology and *The Golden Book of Melchizedek: How To Become An Integrated Christ Buddha In This Lifetime!*
- Ask Spirit and the Masters for the Lower aspect of all your Rays to be cleansed from your energy fields!
- Ask Spirit and the Masters for the lower aspect of all your 12 major Archetypes to be cleansed from your energy fields!
- Ask Spirit and the Masters for the lower aspect of all 12 signs of the Zodiac to be cleansed from your energy fields!
- Once a month do burning pot in each room of your home to cleanse the Spiritual, mental, emotional, and etheric atmosphere in your home!
- Be conscious, for Healing, of the color of clothes you wear each day!
- Use Colored lights for Healing!
- Play sleep tapes at night for Healing!
- Buy Subliminal Music tapes for Healing!
- Read all my books in my Ascension Book Series to be completely transformed and to Achieve Spiritual Mastery on a Spiritual, Psychological and Physical/Earthly level!
- Find the appropriate work/play balance!
- Ask Spirit and the Masters to bath you in any Color or Sound Resonance you need for healing!
- Call to Dr. Lorphan and the Galactic Healers to repair any chakras that may be damaged from past lives or this life!
- Call to Spirit and the Masters to completely cleanse and clear your 12 Body System, energy fields, aura and all your Chakras!
- Call to Melchizedek, The Mahatma and Archangel Metatron for a Viral Vacuum or Bacterial Vacuum any time there is any virus or bacterial energy in your system!
- Call to Spirit and the Masters to Place an impenetrable golden bubble of protection around you if there is anyone who is sick around you, and ask that they be placed in the Golden bubble as well and helped to heal!

- Fast on Beiler Broth as much as possible (Steam zucchini, green beans, and a little parsley and celery). Then blend it up and drink it! It is the panacea for all health concerns.
- Call to the Lord of Arcturus and the Arcturians to clear all energy of cancer from your mental, emotional, etheric and physical bodies!
- Go for an affirmation walk doing physical health affirmations the entire time!
- Put your Health Affirmations on tape and play them as background music while you are working around the house!
- Put your Health Affirmations on an endless loop tape or endless play tape recorder and play it softly in the background all nigh while you sleep!
- Have a dialogue with your physical body in your journal to see if there is anything it wants or is trying to tell you!
- Realize GOD works through the physical body, and if you have a health lesson then GOD is trying to teach you something.
- Talk to the physical as you would a good friend and form a positive relation-ship to it. Thank it for all its good work on you behalf, for the physical body needs love, honor, friendship and respect as well. There is a form of consciousness within it called the "body elemental!"
- Twenty times throughout the day give yourself a "Thymus Tap" to increase functioning of the Thymus Gland, which is you immune system!
- Never use aluminum foil or aluminum pots and pans, for you can get aluminum poisoning.
- Do not over indulge in sexuality, for it can drain your energy!
- Moderation in all things!
- Call in Spirit and the Masters to remove al Core Fear Programming, negative ego programming, and poor health programming, from your subconscious mind and four-body system!
- Ask Spirit and the Masters to clear your Genetic line of any health problems or weakness!

- Ask Spirit and the Masters to clear all your Past Lives from health challenges, lessons or problems that may be affecting you now!
- Ask Spirit and the Masters to clear, cleanse and detach you from any health lessons being caused by bleed through from one of your 144 Soul Extensions from your Monad and Mighty I Am Presence!
- Ask you Soul and Mighty I Am Presence to help you create Perfect radiant health everyday!
- Call to Mother Mary and Archangel Raphael to have the Golden Angels live in any area of your body that is chronically weak!
- Pray for a miracle healing every day from Spirit and the Masters!
- Be sure to stay grounded!
- Clean your house once a week!
- Keep really good hygiene!
- Ask Spirit and the Masters that all past or present diseases or health problems to be cleansed from your aura!
- Do not be a hypochondriac!
- Be open to traditional and nontraditional forms of healing!
- Six almonds a day is a cancer preventative (Edgar Cayce)!
- Enjoy and Love Earth life!
- Take time to rest!
- Ask Spirit and the Masters to fully anchor and activate your Mayavarupa body! (It is the Ascension Body – See my book *The Complete Ascension Manual*!)
- Forgive your physical body for not working well at times!
- Call Spirit and the Masters to remove all improper Soul Fragments and to bring back all Soul Fragments that do belong to you, as GOD would have it be!
- Call to Archangels Michael and Faith to cut all energetic cords with people in this life and past lives that are Spiritually inappropriate and draining your energy!
- Call to Spirit and the Masters to Cleanse and purify all your Karma!

- Try to keep your legs and arms uncrossed as much as possible, for it keeps the flow of electrical current from flowing smoothly through the body!
- Work with Crystals and Gemstones!
- Honor your body's natural Body rhythms!
- Live in the Tao and conserve your energies!
- Keep proper self-boundaries!
- Keep a proper selfish and selfless balance!
- Study holistic health!
- Clear your spouse of implants and elementals as well! (See Revised edition of *Soul Psychology* on how to do this!)
- Clear your pets of all negative implants and elementals!
- Take catnaps if you are tired!
- Cosmic Cellular Cleansing (See my book, *Cosmic Ascension!*)
- Be sure to look at everything that is going on with your physical body and everything in your life as a Spiritual Test!
- Be sure to learn how to fully be grounded at all times! (See book, *Empowerment and Integration Through The Goddess* available from the Academy!)
- Strive and affirm for physical immortality!
- Strive and pray for Physical Ascension!
- Pray to Spirit and the Masters to have your 144 Soul extensions cleansed, cleared and integrated within your being! (See my book *Cosmic Ascension!*)
- Sit in Ascension Seats of GOD! (See my books, *The Complete Ascension Manual*, *Beyond Ascension* and *Cosmic Ascension*, for this can greatly increase health and vitality as well!)
- Ask Spirit and Masters to help you fully establish your Antakarana to your Higher Self, Mighty I Am Presence and back to GOD!
- Ask Spirit and the Masters to Widen your Antakarana to allow more Spiritual Current to flow through!

- Pray to Spirit and the Masters to increase the amount of Spiritual Current that is coming in!
- Pray to Spirit and the Masters for an increase in energy any time you need it!
- Learn to fully honor and sanctify the Material Face of GOD! (See my books *The Golden Book of Melchizedek* and *Empowerment and Integration Through The Goddess,* which are available from the Academy!)
- Create a Huna Prayer for Perfect physical Health!
- Take time to "Be", instead of always being so active!
- Spend time in nature!
- Spend time meditating leaning up against a tree!
- Take time to smell the flowers!
- Pray to Spirit and the Masters to deactivate and clear any electrical or geopathic energy imbalances in your home!
- Do not keep your feet too close to a color television, for your feet chakras will soak up the radiation!
- For any Health Problem for self or others, send prayer requests to the Academy and I will place them on our "Interdimensional Prayer Altar" for this purpose!
- Call to Spirit and the Masters twice a day for a Love and Light Shower to cleanse your energy fields and aura!
- Call to Saint Germain for the Violet Transmuting flame, to transmute any health concerns!
- Ask Spirit and the Masters to remove any gray fields in your aura!
- Call to Spirit and the Masters to remove any astral dross, mental dross, or etheric dross from your aura and energy fields!
- Call to the Lord of Arcturus for the "Golden Cylinder" to remove any and all negative energy from your energy fields!
- Get a massage occasionally, professionally or from a friend!
- If you are sick, definitely go and get a colonic, for it will do you wonders!

- Take a lot of extra vitamin C every day!
- Call Spirit and the Masters to remove all negative thoughts and emotions from your energy fields that may be causing you to have health lessons!
- Ask Spirit and the Masters to remove all "etheric needless, darts and/or bullets" from your organs and energy fields from people who have sent you negative energy and anger in the past!
- Be sure at all times to have a really good physical, mental, emotional, energetic, and Spiritual diet!
- Anchor and Activate all your "Higher Light Bodies and Higher Chakras into your energy fields"! See *The Complete Ascension Manual, Beyond Ascension, Cosmic Ascension, Revelations of a Melchizedek Initiate,* and *The Golden Book of Melchizedek,* all available from the Academy! Doing this will enormously increase your physical health and vitality!
- Ask Spirit and the Masters to implement all the ideas and suggestions listed in this chapter, at night while you sleep!
- When you start to worry about your health, "pray instead!"
- To all health lessons, be they temporary or chronic say, "Not my will but thine, thank you for the lesson!"
- Some health lessons of a chronic nature may be "For the Glory of GOD," so don't give your power to your body and live your life thanking GOD for this Spiritual Test!
- Use sage in your home and a little incense to cleanse atmosphere!
- Anchor the Secret Rods of GOD in your four-body system and chakras (See my book *Golden Book of Melchizedek: How To Be An Integrated Christ/Buddha In This Lifetime!*)
- Do not give your personal power to your physical body!
- Be sure to wash your vegetables well, to cleanse all pesticides!
- Ask a homeopathic doctor or homeopathic pharmacist for homeopathics to remove all heavy metals and chemicals from your body! Furtureplex has some products for this as well!

- Ask Spirit and the Masters to place you in "Color Baths," on the inner plane!
- Pray to Spirit and the Masters to clear and cleanse the lower aspect of all 12 Sephiroth in the Cosmic Tree of Life!
- Ask Spirit and the Masters to balance your feminine and masculine aspects within self!
- Ask Spirit and the Masters to balance your Heavenly and Earthly Aspects!
- Ask Spirit and the Masters to help you to master, balance and integrate all Seven Rays, and Ray attributes and qualities!
- Ask Spirit and the Masters to help you develop a Full Spectrum Conscious-ness Vision and Perspective!
- Ask Spirit and the Masters to cut any etheric cords in regard to people who are currently draining you!
- Ask Spirit and the Masters to cut any etheric cords of people who you have had past sexual involvement with from this life or past lives that need to be cut or that are causing you to be drained of any energies!
- Ask Spirit and the Masters to remove any and all unwanted entities from hanging around your energy fields that are not of an Ascended Master nature, if this prayer be in harmony with GOD's Will!
- Ask Spirit and the Masters to help you to learn to always think and feel only from your Spiritual/Christ/Buddha Consciousness and never from your negative ego/fear-based/separative mind!
- Ask Spirit and the Masters to help your stay balanced and integrated at all times!
- Call on Mother Mary and Archangel Raphael any time you need healing help!
- Call on Sai Baba any time you need healing help!
- Call on Sananda any time you need healing help!
- Call on the Lord of Arcturus and the Arcturians any time you need healing help!

- Call Melchizedek, the Mahatma and Metatron to establish an impenetrable wall of protection around you at all times!
- Pray to and ask for help from Djwhal Khul with his Holographic Computer for help with any Health lessons and challenges!
- Call to the Lord of Arcturus and the Arcturians for Balancing and/or tightening your grids if necessary!
- Call Forth from Archangel Metatron for the anchoring of any fire letters, key codes and sacred geometries needed to accelerate healing!
- Call to the 14 Mighty Archangels for healing!
- Call to the Archangels for sound tones of healing!
- Ask for Healing to be given to you at night while you sleep!
- Pray to Spirit and the Masters to imprint programs of perfect radiant health into your subconscious mind at night while you sleep!
- Pray to Spirit and the Masters to imprint the "Virtues and Qualities of GOD into your four-body system while you sleep!"
- Pray to GOD, Christ and the Holy Spirit for help with any Health problems you have!
- Pray to Spirit and the Masters to remove all glamour, maya and illusion from your being!
- Pray to Spirit and the Masters for guidance and more ideas on how you can heal your self!
- Ask to be fully merged and integrated with your Higher Self and Monad on Earth!
- Be sure to breathe deeply!
- Practice Tai Chi, Qui Gong, or Aikido
- Repeat the Names of God, Mantras and Words of Power, to increase physical health and vitality!
- Practice self-hypnosis to give suggestions of perfect health!
- Give suggestions of perfect health to subconscious after Meditations!
- Give suggestions of perfect health to subconscious at night while you sleep if you wake up, or as you are falling asleep or just waking up!

- Pray before you eat your physical food, and ask GOD and the angels to bless it and cleanse it of all energetic impurities!
- Pray to Spirit and the Masters to increase your light quotient so you have more energy in your energy and light fields to heal with!
- See your true identity as God, The Christ, the Buddha, and the Eternal self and realize that Sickness is a defense against the truth! You are God and Christ and hence cannot get sick! Affirm this!
- Realize most health crisis are cleansings which are good!
- Also realize a great many health crisis are signs of accelerated Spiritual Growth and the physical manifestation of the Ascension process!
- Practice Ecology!
- Be sure to manifest your Spiritual Mission on Earth in a physical sense, which will help run more Spiritual current through you physically!
- Do not be afraid of asking your Brothers and Sisters for help, for that is what we are here for. Remember, we are all just incarnations of GOD, so this would just be God helping God!
- Do not accept pat answers in regard to physical health lessons, for the physical body and health lessons are a way to multifaceted and multidimensional, and again some are just Spiritual Mutational symptoms and signs of Spiritual refinement in the physical, so don't let people lay trips on you! Keep your Golden Bubble of Light up at all times and let their trips slide off you like water off a duck's back!
- Be compassionate towards others who are sick, but not empathetic where you take on their stuff. Pray to Spirit and the Masters to clear it if you have done this or are doing this!
- Occasionally take time to sleep separately from Spouse or mate if you feel a need to regenerate your energies!
- Fulfill your Spiritual puzzle piece on Earth, this will help your health!

- Work with my Meditations in *The Golden Book of Melchizedek* to anchor and activate the "72 Higher Light Bodies of GOD" and to anchor and activate your "Love/Light and Power Bodies of GOD!"
- Use the 25 programming techniques in my book *Soul Psychology*, to pro-gram the subconscious mind to create perfect radiant health in the physical body!
- Grow your own vegetables if possible!
- Buy organic vegetables if you can!
- In my book *How to Achieve Perfect Radiant Health,* study the first chapter, which is about eating a good physical diet. It will give you hundreds of excellent physical and Spiritual suggestions on diet that I have practiced and gathered together from all my studies and work in Holistic Health. From suggestions on diet from Spirit and the Ascended Masters. You won't find this information in any physical health book on this planet! That is why I have called this book *How To Achieve Perfect Radiant Health From The Perspective of the Soul*! This is the Soul and Spirit's perspective on physical health not the personality or just mind! Tell all your friends who need a major health upgrade about it! It is available at this time only from the Academy!
- Develop a Christ Buddha Living Space in your Home!(see *The Golden Book of Melchizedek*)
- Consider having a Feng Shui expert come to your home!
- Play music in the background that you find healing to your physical body and soul!
- Have your "Earth Crystals" removed! See *The Golden Book of Melchizedek*!
- Call to Spirit and the Masters for the full anchoring and activation of your Higher Adam Kadmon Body!
- Call to Archangel Metatron to program your Gematrian body with all the codes for Perfect Radiant Health!

- Call to Archangel Metatron to program your Electromagnetic body for perfect radiant health!
- Call to Spirit and the Masters to fully anchor and Activate your Anointed Christ Overself Body, your Zohar Body of Light and your Overself body, which will bring more Light and perfect blueprint bodies into your field!
- One of the best things you can do for your physical health is to develop a Psychology, Philosophy and Belief System that perfectly matches that of GOD, Christ, The Holy Spirit, your Mighty I Am Presence, your Higher Self and the Inner Plane Ascended Masters. This can be achieved by carefully reading and studying my books *Soul Psychology* and *How to Release Fear Based Thinking and Feeling: An In-depth Study of Spiritual Psychology*. These two books will have an enormous impact on your physical health as well!
- The other key to increase physical health is to develop Self-Mastery and Self-Realization on the Spiritual Level, which will then have an imprinting effect on the etheric and physical level. To achieve this, study my books *The Complete Ascension Manual, Beyond Ascension, Cosmic Ascension, The Golden Book of Melchizedek: How to Become and Integrated Christ/Buddha in this Lifetime, Revelations of a Melchizedek Initiate, The Golden Keys to Ascension and Healing!*
- Call to Spirit, the Masters and Angels to imprint, at night while you sleep; thoughtforms, images, and suggestions of perfect health!
- Every night before bed, ask and pray to Spirit and the Masters, to all night long, work on your physical body for healing in whatever area you need it. The key is in the asking, for they are not allowed to help unless you ask and pray!
- Going to a Health Farm for a week as a gift to the physical body.
- Taking an Epson Salt bath.
- Taking a bath with Water of Life products.
- During all the hours you are consciously awake, call and pray to Spirit and the Masters for help any time, you have any symptoms,

be they energetic or physical, and they will come and instantly begin working on you!
- Get acupuncture treatments from a trained doctor!
- Call to Spirit and the Masters to fully repair the electrical system in your etheric and physical body!
- Master your mind and emotions! (See *How to Release Fear-Based Thinking and Feeling: An In-depth Study of Spiritual Psychology* and *Soul Psychology*) Available from the Academy!
- Be sure to take responsibility for "Mastering the Earth, Earth Energies and fully Integrating the Material Face of GOD!" (See *The Golden Book of Melchizedek* available from the Academy!)
- Be sure to integrate the God/Goddess aspects of self (See new book *Empowerment and Integration of the Goddess* available from Academy!)
- Learn to "Dine with GOD!" (See *The Golden Book of Melchizedek*)
- Learn how to call on Spirit and the Masters to help you eat a good physical diet but also live on Light as a dietary supplement!
- Pray to Spirit and the Masters for etheric vitamin and mineral shots!
- Pray to Spirit and the Masters to etherically give you any medicine you need that GOD also wishes you to have for help in your healing!
- Read chapter in *The Golden Book of Melchizedek* on health lessons caused by "Spiritual Mutation and Ascension Acceleration process!"
- Read my book *Ascension and Romantic Relationships* to make sure that you are 100% clear on relationship issues. Make sure that you are not improperly bonding in your Romantic or any other type of relationships that may be pulling on your energies inappropriately!
- Call to Spirit and the Masters to clear and cleanse any energy from group karma, racial karma, planetary karma, and ancestral karma!
- Ask GOD, Christ, the Holy Spirit, to cleanse and purify your Oversoul, Monad and entire being, all the way back to your original Covenant with GOD!

In extreme health cases, if you do all these things and you are still not recovering go to a skilled Spiritual Channel, Spiritual Psychic, Clairvoyant and/or Intuitive Medical practitioner and see if they can pick up any karmic reasons or any other psychological lessons that need learning. I will say, however, if you do all the things I have mentioned in this chapter and in my books; *How to Achieve Perfect Radiant Health from the Soul's Perspective, The Golden Book of Melchizedek: How to be an Integrated Christ/Buddha in this Lifetime, How to Release Fear Based Thinking and Feeling: An In-depth Study of Spiritual Psychology* and *Soul Psychology, Revised Edition*, that in 99% of the time, in my humble opinion, you will be able to create with the help of GOD, Christ, the Holy Spirit, the Masters, the Archangels and Angels, and the Christed Extraterrestrials, the healing, balancing and repair of just about any and all health lessons on a Spiritual, mental, emotional, etheric and physical level! In this program and outline that Spirit, the Masters and I have set up for you is one of the most comprehensive health programs ever put forth in any book on physical health, for it is not just focusing on the physical level, it is also focusing on the Spiritual level, Mental level, Emotional level, Etheric level, Physical Earthly level and Interpersonal or Relationship level. It is only when you approach Healing from this "Integrated Health Full Spectrum Prism" approach from the Soul and Spirit's Perspective that physical health can really even be understood! My Beloved Readers most doctors and practitioners approach Health from a purely physical level, which is great! It needs to be understood, however, that 90% of all health problems and concerns have their origins and initial cause in the mental body, emotional body and etheric body! The program here that Spirit, the Masters and I have set up for you, along with a little extra reading on your part to insure full training is achieved on a Spiritual, Psychological and Physical/Earthly Level, will completely purify, cleanse and heal, not only your physical body, but the etheric, emotional, mental and all your Spiritual bodies! This will not only cause a much greater increase in your health and overall vitality, but Spirit, the Masters and I are also helping you to achieve God Realization and Integrated Ascension! This, my Beloved Readers, is why you have the health lessons you have! It was GOD, Christ, the Holy Spirit, your Mighty I Am Presence and Higher Self's way of motivating you to seek truth, so that you would see that achieving God Realization and Integrated Ascension is the key to achieving Perfect Radiant Physical Health as well! My Beloved Readers, trust in the guidance and suggestions that Spirit, the Masters and I have given you here for I tell you that these suggestions work! If you follow the guidance given in this chapter, this book, and in the few books I have mentioned, you will become a "Crystal Clear Diamond of GOD" on a Spiritual, Mental, Emotional, Physical and Physical/Earthly Level! When you are this purified and refined on every level there will be no place for disease or health lessons to manifest! If they ever do manifest because of some lessons that need to be learned for there is no judgement in this and this is part of the Spiritual Path, you will have the Spiritual Knowledge and tools as contained in this chapter, book, and books I have mentioned, to heal yourself of any and all health concerns on a Spiritual, Psychological and Physical/Earthly level!

My Beloved Readers, did not that Bible say, "Seek ye the Kingdom of GOD and all things shall be handed unto thee? This includes, my Beloved Readers, "Perfect Radiant Health!" In those very few cases where the health lesson is karmic, I will teach you through my books how to use whatever health lessons you have "For the Glory of GOD!" Spirit, the Masters and I will show you how to maintain 100% inner peace regardless of any health lessons you have! For your physical body does not cause your reality, your thoughts do! In those extremely rare instances where a health lesson is karma, Spirit, the Masters and I will show you how to enormously increase your overall physical health and be at total inner peace with any health challenges you do have! So all will achieve the 100% inner peace they seek! If you follow this overall program as Spirit, the Masters and I have presented in this chapter, book and small set of books I have recommended, you will I humbly suggest, achieve "an inner peace and overall general good health and Spiritual vitality that passeth understanding," regardless of what health lessons you are dealing.

So let it be Written! So let it be Done!

5

How to Overcome Spiritual, Mental, Emotional and Physical Fatigue

One of the lessons a great many people and lightworkers are dealing with is Spiritual, Mental, Emotional and Physical fatigue. My inner guidance has asked me to write a chapter on this subject to help people and lightworkers remain highly energized on all levels, at all times. I will begin here by explaining what causes these levels of fatigue and what lightworkers can do to reverse this process and have it never return.

The number one reason why people feel fatigued is not from a physical level, it is from a psychological level. The number one reason for fatigue is most people, and that includes lightworkers, do not fully own their personal power at all times. When you don't own your personal power at full strength, it drains your energy battery.

The second reason is that people are not fully demonstrating self-mastery over their mind and emotions, which causes them to be victims of themselves and of life instead of Masters and causes of their reality. This completely drains one's energy battery. Instead of mastering life, life beats down the individual. The third reason people get exhausted is they don't love themselves and forgive themselves for their mistakes.

The fourth reason people get exhausted and fatigued is they think too much with their negative ego mind instead of interpreting life from their Christ/Buddha Mind. This completely debilitates one's energy system because the mind has too many negative thoughts and hence creates and builds too many negative feelings and emotions.

All these above mentioned psychological lessons cause one to not be right with self and right with GOD. This causes untold numbers of conflicts and imbalances in relationships, which again totally drains the energy body.

All the negative thoughts and emotions also debilitate the physical organs and glandular system, which creates even more fatigue.

The fifth reason why people get fatigued is they do not psychospiritually protect themselves properly each morning to start their day. This causes them to be victimized by other people's negative energy and to be hypnotized by other people's negative suggestions. It also allows other people to become the computer programmers of their emotional life. This is incredibly exhausting and debilitating to the energy body.

The sixth reason people get fatigued is they do not pray enough. They do not realize the incredible powers that GOD, Christ, the Holy Spirit, the Ascended Masters, Archangels and Angels, Elohim Masters, and Christed Extraterrestrials can bring to bear on a daily basis. They get fatigued because they try to create life themselves, instead of co-creating life with GOD and the Masters. Each person must cause their own reality, but part of doing this effectively is constantly calling on GOD and the Masters for help, for everything.

The seventh reason people get fatigued is they don't do enough positive affirmations and visualizations along with attitudinal healing. Every time something doesn't go your way, one should always do a prayer, affirmation, visualization or attitude adjustment to bring that situation back to the perfected state. This way one's consciousness always remains in a state of healing the situation in an assertive manner, which keeps one incredibly energized.

The eighth reason people become fatigued is that they allow themselves to be run too much by the emotional body instead of recognizing that one's thoughts create one's emotions. Once one sees and demonstrates this self-mastery over the emotional body by learning to cause and create only positive Christ/Buddha emotions, they will become much more energize. This incredibly energizes the etheric and/or energy body as well as the subconscious mind.

The ninth reason why people get fatigued deals with the physical level. A great many people use too many artificial stimulants for energy. In the short term this helps, however, in the long term it exhausts the physical body. Artificial stimulants should be used in emergencies only, not on a regular basis. People also do not eat a good diet and enough vegetables and protein. This over time will deplete the physical body chemically and nutritionally.

The next reason for fatigue is people do not get enough physical exercise on a regular basis, which makes the body very sluggish. They also do not get enough fresh air and sunshine.

People must also be sure to get enough sleep and not over-work or under-work. They must also take time for play and recreation.

The eleventh reason why people get fatigued is they have not found their Spiritual Service work, puzzle piece, and Spiritual Mission. Too many people work at jobs that do not have meaning for them and/or they do not have the proper attitude of service at that job. When one takes the attitude of Spiritual service in whatever job they are doing in life, then work becomes joy. As the Master Jesus said, "True pleasure is serving GOD." I personally can't wait to get up every morning. It doesn't matter what kind of work I have to do. To me work is incredibly enjoyable. If someone gave me a billion dollars I would be doing the exact same thing. When one finds one's Spiritual mission and service work, then every thought, word, and deed becomes energized because you are doing it to serve GOD and one's fellow Sons and Daughters of GOD.

The twelfth reason people get fatigued is another physical one. People eat too much food. Too many people live to eat instead of eating to live. Most people do not need half the food they are eating. The body does not require seven course meals. The improper combining of foods and eating too much, drains one's energy and makes one tired.

The thirteenth reason people don't have as much energy as they want, is that they do not fast enough. Some kind of fast once a week or once a month for one to three days will do wonders for the body's energy level.

The fourteenth reason people do not have enough energy is they do not drink enough water. The drinking of water will keep your body clean and free of toxins.

The fifteenth reason people do not have as much energy as they would like is, that they do not spend enough time in nature and connecting with the Earth Mother. Enormous sustenance and energy can be acquired from remaining grounded and connected and attuned to the Earth. It must be understood that energy can be gained from the Earth, from a proper psychology, and from Spiritual levels. It is essential to take advantage of all three. If anyone is rejected or disconnected it will have a short circuiting effect on the other levels. This is why I call the sixteenth key to becoming more energized "Integrated Ascension". It is essential on your Spiritual Path to integrate Spirit in a balanced and integrated manner in all four bodies. The doing of this will have a very energizing affect on your entire system.

The seventeenth key to energizing your system is to not eat too much sugar, junk food, processed food and food with too many chemicals and preservatives. The doing of this just fills the body with too many adverse chemicals and toxins. Sugar on occasion is fine, however too much will toxify the body and facilitate the growth of bacteria and viruses, which are depleting to the immune system and the body's energy system.

The eighteenth key to becoming more energized is to not be a workaholic. This is because pushing yourself too hard will, over time, exhaust your adrenal glands. The adrenals will then be pulling energy from the other glands and organs.

The nineteenth key to energizing your system is stopping your bad habits such as smoking, certainly drugs, too much alcohol and other lower-self addictions. These over time can drain the body of energy.

The twentieth key to energizing your system is to cultivate the psychospiritual quality of enthusiasm. One should ideally be enthusiastic at all times. This is the use of personal power with the emotional body engaged. Your feelings and emotions lie within the subconscious mind, which is the real storehouse of energy within your being. When you own your personal power with feeling and enthusiasm, this activates the subconscious storehouse of energy.

The twenty-first is to be sure to breathe. Most people do not breathe enough. They take breathing for granted hence they do not breath deeply enough. When you breathe in fresh air, you are breathing in Prana and Vital Force. This Prana and Vital Force then is stored in the etheric body for later use. This is also why aerobic exercise is essential. Breathing also allows more oxygen into the cells, organs, and glands, as well as the blood stream.

The twenty-second key to having more energy is to supplement your diet with extra natural food source, vitamins and minerals. I am not going to list all the possible supplements one can use, for I leave that up to your own intuition and personal knowledge. This is essential in our society because of all the pesticide use and low grade food we eat, because of the chemicals and lack of relationship to the Nature Spirits, Nature Devas, and Elemental Kingdom. If we worked with these Kingdoms more, our food and vibrational frequency would be at a much higher level. This is why nutritional supplementation is a good idea for most people.

The twenty-third key to energize your system is to always be optimistic and never be pessimistic. Pessimistic thoughts and feelings will deplete your energy. Optimistic thoughts and feelings will energize your system. Most people do not realize the incredible effect our attitude and feelings have on our energy system.

The twenty-fourth key to energizing your system is to ask GOD, Christ, the Holy Spirit, your Higher Self, your Mighty I Am Presence, the Ascended Masters, Archangels and Angels, Elohim Masters, and Christed Extraterrestrials for more energy. It sounds simple, but it is really that easy. The key to life is asking. "Ask and you shall receive." Ask for more energy and GOD and the Masters will give you more energy. Why rely on artificial stimulants when you can rely on GOD, the Masters, your personal power, your positive attitude, the power of your subconscious mind, the laws of the physical body and the Earth and the Earth Mother, to energize you. You can even ask the Earth Mother to give you energy through your feet chakras so you will be receiving energy from Spirit, the Earth, and you will be creating it yourself through your personal power, self-mastery, and causal mental attitude.

The twenty-fifth key to energizing your system is to remain focused on your path of Ascension and God Realization at all times. Keep your attention always focused on GOD and your Higher Self. Never allow yourself to give in to your lower self-desire. If you do, just forgive it, learn the lesson, move forward and do not look back. The higher and more advanced you become in your Initiation level and path of Ascension, the more light you will carry in your Light Body, which of course, is more energizing. The higher your Initiation level the more electrical frequency you will hold, and the more energized your system will become. The higher your level of initiation the more you will fully embody your Mighty I Am Presence, which is also incredibly energizing. If you demonstrate your Spiritual Path in an integrated and balanced way, your entire 12 body system will become an absolute "Lightening Rod" of energy on a Spiritual, Psychological and Physical/Earthly level.

The twenty-sixth key to energizing your system is to not over indulge in sex, but do not necessarily underindulge either. This is not to say that you need sex for energy, for the path of celibacy can actually build energy and build what is called in the East "Ojas." This is sexual energy that is brought up the Chakra column to build Brain Illumination. This might be called Brain Orgasm! I brought up not underindulging in sex only because sexual involvement does not have to be energetically depleting if done properly. If done too much or from lack of love it can be. Also if done with the wrong people. So it is not sex, it is how sexual energy is used. Tantric sexuality can also be incredibly energizing.

The twenty-seventh key to energizing your system is to hang around people and form friendships with people who are energizing. Also, be sure to never give your power to others, and to be unconditionally loving towards others at all times!

The final key to be energized at all times is to, in every situation of life and every moment of life in thought, word, and deed to always choose GOD instead of ego. Every moment of our life, we are confronted with this choice. It occurs with every thought we think, every feeling we create, every action we take. Every time you choose GOD, you will become re-energized. Every time you choose the ego, your energy will drop a bit. The nice thing about this process is that everything is forgiven and everything is a lesson, so in the next moment you can always choose GOD again!

6

Developing A Good Spiritual, Mental, Emotional, Etheric, Physical, Environmental and Social Diet

We all recognize the importance of eating a good physical diet. This is essential to keeping the physical chemistry of the body in proper balance and providing the fuel we need for outputting energy. Most people on the Earth, however, and even lightworkers at times, do not pay as much attention to the diet of their other bodies. Let us begin here with the mental body!

Love, Light and Power workers need to be much more conscious and vigilant over the thoughts they allow into their consciousness from within and without. This may be the single most important aspect of one's entire Spiritual path. The reason this is so is because it is our thoughts that create our reality. Our thoughts create our feelings, emotions, behavior and what we attract and magnetize. Every moment of our lives we are choosing either to think with our Christ/Buddha mind or our negative ego, separative mind. If we do not control our mind we cannot have mastery over our emotions and we will not be right with self, right with GOD or right with any relationship in our lives. Far too many people in this world live too much on automatic pilot and do not realize how incredibly powerful the mind is. It is not only important to be joyously vigilant over the thoughts rising up from within self, but also to be joyously vigilant over the thoughts that come from other people in the form of words, letters, books, magazines and newspapers. It is essential in life to learn to respond rather than to react. It is essential to be a master rather than a victim. It is essential to have a certain involved detachment so you can choose what you will allow in and what you push out. A lot of people think that denial is a bad thing. What people do not realize is that there is negative ego denial and Christed denial. To attain GOD realization and inner peace it is imperative that you deny all negative thoughts from entering your consciousness from within and without. This is why every day before you start your day you should put on your mental armor or mental protection. I suggest a golden white semi-permeable bubble that allows in positive thoughts and feelings and keeps out negative thoughts and feelings. People put on physical clothing every day but they do not think of the importance to put on mental and emotional clothing.

In my humble opinion, lightworkers and people in general should be much more discerning about the books, magazines, and newspapers they read, and the television and movies they watch. If you read a trashy novel this just fills your mind with garbage and your sub conscious mind and liver need to process it. As Edgar Cayce said, "Thoughts are things." When you go to a movie that is scary or filled with violence and lower-self energy, this lowers your vibration and frequency, and is like eating spoiled food and it takes its' toll on the other vehicles. It even creates toxicity in the physical vehicle. Engaging in negative conversations can do the same thing. Being too much in hypnosis while watching the news or television in general can literally hypnotize you with negativity.

Be aware, my friends, you are in a state of hypnosis every time you lose your joyous vigilance and every time you fall into automatic pilot. I use the term here "joyous vigilance" to emphasize the point that you can have self-mastery and self-discipline and be happy simultaneously. When you are watching television, for example, and some commercial comes up for some horror film, my suggestion is to mute the TV and do not watch those images. When you are watching television and there is a talk show and someone is spewing their negative ego agenda, shut of the TV or change the channel. When you are standing in line at the market do not fill your consciousness with tabloid journalism. You could be spending that time chanting the names of GOD. Every moment of out lives, in truth, we are choosing GOD or negative ego. Just because we achieved a certain level of initiation doesn't mean that this stops. The negative ego is very seductive and tricky and must be guarded against at all times.

If you remain on automatic pilot and do not keep your protection up, other people's negative thoughts, words, and the negativity that is so pervasive in our world, will bring you down if you let it. The spiritual path is really a test every moment to see if you can maintain your GOD Self in all situations of life on a consistent basis. It is also a test to see if you can forgive yourself for your mistakes and learn from your mistakes and do better the next time.

In terms of your emotional diet, the process is very similar to what I have been discussing above. If you are listening to the radio in the car, be more joyously vigilant over the kind of songs and lyrics you allow yourself to listen to. Whenever we are in a receptive state we are in hypnosis, and the lyrics and the feeling tones will program your subconscious mind without you even realizing it. At all times we strive to be the cause of our reality and not the effect.

Be more joyously vigilant over the people you spend time with. Emotionally negative people should be avoided if it at all possible. If you do have to be with emotionally negative people in your family or at your job, keep your bubble of protection up. I have provided you in this book one of the most profound protection meditations ever created to help defend you against such people.

If you go some place like a party or a store or a person's house and it doesn't feel good, give yourself permission to leave. So often in life we just flow or follow the line of least resistance instead of choosing every moment the path of our highest spiritual realization. If you go to the movies and you don't like how you feel watching it, don't just stay there just because you spent six dollars, get up and leave. Watching violent and lower-self movies is not only an insult to your emotional body; it is an insult to your soul and spirit, which in truth is what you are.

It is important to keep up this joyous vigilance even when you are by yourself. Most people when they are by themselves let down their mental and emotional vigilance. I am here to tell you that this is a 24 hour day and night job, even while you sleep. If you are dreaming and you don't like your dreams, change them and/or wake yourself up. To most people it does not occur to them that they can actually co-create in their dreams while sleeping. This is called lucid dreaming. If you do not like the dreams while you are in them or when you wake up, go back and change them. This will profoundly change your reality for the better.

Getting back to this point of being joyously vigilant while by yourself, do not go on automatic pilot when alone and give in to negative ego daydreaming. This can manifest as just negative thinking, or playing out negative ego emotional reactions with people. For example this might be fantasizing that you are cussing out someone or reading someone the riot act in a negative ego manner. A great many people who live on Earth are being negative a great deal of the time and they don't even realize it. Do not give in to negative thoughts or emotions in your inner actions with people or when you are home alone. I have a little tool I use when I am laying in bed getting ready for sleep. If my mind starts going to a negative thought or negative ego agenda or just something that doesn't feel good, I immediately open my eyes, which I have set up with myself as a type of reset. The opening of my eyes resets my consciousness back to a positive place.

During the daytime I am constantly changing the channel of my mind so to speak. The second it starts going in a negative direction I stop it and direct it elsewhere. This can be done just by stopping it or by choosing to think another thought. It can be done by doing an affirmation, a positive visualization, saying a prayer or repeating the name of GOD. It can also be changed by doing some new physical activity.

This whole process is especially important before going to sleep for where one's consciousness goes at the time of the sleep is determined by what you are thinking about. If you are watching the news before going to sleep you may end up in Bosnia. You may think I am joking but I am not. If there is a low grate of negative thinking or feeling you are going to end up at the astral plane while sleeping which may not be so pleasant. Also, we all like to have good positive dreams while we sleep and not nightmares or negative dreams. 98% of our dreams are nothing more than a symbolic representation of our thinking and feeling during that day. So if you want to have good dreams at night, then think and feel positively during your day. This is actually the purpose of dreams, to give us feedback in visual form of how we have been thinking, feeling and acting that day.

One more aspect of this whole subject of keeping a good spiritual, mental, emotional and etheric diet is the issue of what is going on on what I call the psychic plane. Take for example, you are by yourself and you are angry at someone at work or a family member, and you are playing out some angry confrontations in your mind and feeling body. This all seems to most people very innocent. Well my friends, I am here to tell you that it is not. Especially when you become more advanced in your spiritual path and initiation process. The anger that you are thinking about on the psychic plane can be seen as arrows and darts shooting towards the subject of your thoughts. If their aura is not strong it will penetrate their field and probably lodge in their liver or someplace else. The more evolved you are spiritually, the more power your thoughts, images and feelings will have on the inner plane.

Also realize that when you think of someone they telepathically receive it. All of creation is just GOD, and we are sons and daughters of GOD, and, in truth we are al one. If people indulge in lower-self sexuality or fantasizing this affects the other person. Our daydreams effect other people. This is nothing to feel bad about, for we have all had negative daydreams and played out untold numbers of scenarios in our mind. Most people have a strong enough physical, psychological and spiritual immune system to not be affected very much. At a lower state of initiation these scenarios we play out in our mind don't have much power and of course everything is forgiven and everything is a lesson. I bring up this issue just to make everyone more aware of the responsibility and accountability that is needed on all levels to truly become a full fledged self realized being, and full fledged Ascended Master.

On an etheric level it is important to be joyously vigilant in terms of just energy. Again this could be walking into someone's house and not feeling comfortable with the energy in the room. You may come home at night and feel some strange energy in the house and not know what it is. Learn to trust this and ask GOD and the Masters to clear it. You may feel some strange energies in your auric field when waking up from sleep. Do not be passive and leave strange energy in your field. Immediately call for a platinum net, or for the prana wind-clearing device from the inner plane Ascended Masters, and it will blow all the negative energy out of your field. Another tool would be to call forth the violet transmuting flame to transform your etheric and energy body.

On a physical body level maintain your joyous vigilance. Don't eat when you are not hungry. Don't eat junk food just because you are tired. Drink lots of water. Do not eat too much sugar. An occasional desert is fine, but be moderate in all things. As described in another chapter in this book, call on the inner plane Ascended Masters for help maintaining your physical vehicle. Try not to overeat and it is a very good idea to be careful of your food combining. Be sure to get enough protein in your diet and don't over indulge on starches just because they taste better. Use homeopathics and herbs instead of drugs when at all possible. Get physical exercise every day if you can, as well as some fresh air and a little bit of sunshine. Stay away from relying on artificial stimulants and rely on your own natural energy and the infinite energy of GOD and the Masters. Adding good dietary supplements is a good idea also. Pray over your food before eating it and if possible get some kind of positive energy plate to place your food on for 5 minutes before eating it. I recommend the purple energy plates that many of you are familiar with. This will clear all the energetic toxins from your food. Eat as many vegetables as you can in your diet, as well as the proper ratio of other foods that works best for you. If you have any skill working with the pendulum, test the foods that are really the best for your body elemental and not just the one's that are the best for your taste buds. You can also do this by muscle testing. Do not use food as a replacement for love. If you need love give it to your inner child, receive it from the inner child and allow yourself to fully receive it from GOD and the Masters. Once a week or once a month go on a one or two day fast to give your body a rest from eating and let it clean itself out. This can be done with vegetable juice, fruit juice, vegetable soup or broth. Vegetables are better because they contain less sugar.

On a social level, choose friends that are spiritually uplifting. At earlier and even intermediary stations of the path the people you spend time with may be one of the single most important factors in your spiritual path. If your friends do get negative at times in their thinking or feeling do not allow yourself to catch their psychological disease. Maintain a strong psychological immune system, and help them to become more positive rather than you sinking to their level. There is no such thing as a contagious disease on a psychological and on a spiritual level. There are only people with weak psychological and physical immune systems. Maintaining joyous vigilance is integrally connected to maintaining a strong physical, psychological and spiritual immune system.

On an environmental level it is important to keep a good diet as well. People do not often think of keeping a good diet in an environmental sense however it is extremely important. For example, try to keep your living space clean and organized. Make your living space aesthetically and artistically beautiful. Have beautiful pictures at the wall, have lots of plants. Light incense and/or aromatherapy oils. If you are spiritually inclined create spiritual altars in different places in your home with pictures of the Masters. Play beautiful inspiring music in the background, or meditation tapes. Make your home pleasing to the senses and uplifting to the soul.

It might be worth your while to invest in a Feng Shui session. This is the Chinese art of spiritual design or organization of a house or home. When I had this done. It was recommended that we get a fountain in our living room. Certain closet doors were to be covered. Certain rooms were for business, certain ones for romance, and certain ones for learning. The woman who did the session was incredible, and we followed a great many of her suggestions. It changed the vibration and physical harmony of our household in a very uplifting manner.

Be sure to do burning pots at least once a month to clean the physical atmosphere of your home. This is done by getting a small cooking pot and placing it on the floor with a plate under it. Place a half an inch of Epsom salt in the pot covered by an inch of rubbing alcohol. Then light a match to it. I call this the New Age campfire. This will clean whatever room you put it in 100% of all etheric, astral and mental negative energies. These energies will appear clairvoyantly as dark or gray clouds in your house. You could be living in these clouds for years and not even realize it. When people come over, they will sense this energy and you will sense it in their homes as well. For example, you may have had a fight with your spouse and that negative energy may be still be floating on the ceiling of your living room. Incense or even sage will not necessarily get rid of it. The Masters can help with their platinum nets, however even they recommend the burning pots for some of these energies get very physicallized in the house. I recommend doing this in every room of your house at least once a month or more if you feel a need. If you ever move into a new house or office this is absolutely essential. It is also a good idea to give your physical home a good physical cleaning every once in a while and especially when you are moving into a new home. You must understand that thoughts, feelings and energy get lodged in walls of your home. A burning pot will help, however a good scrubbing of the walls and floors with a good cleaning agent will also do wonders for the raising of the vibration of the aura of the house.

Also in terms of your environmental diet, don't just rely on air conditioners and heaters. Try to open the windows and get fresh air into the house and lots of sunshine. Be sure to clean the filters at least once a year so you are not recirculating dust that blocked and clogged filters. Part of having a good environmental diet is giving good consideration of where you physically live. Every country, state and city has a particular aura and ray frequency. Every city has a certain level of psychological and spiritual evolution. Every city has an astral body, mental body, etheric body, physical body and spiritual body. Some cities are more evolved and more clear than others are. Most third dimensional people think of smog or physical pollution on just a physical level. There is also such a thing as astral smog, etheric smog, mental smog and emotional smog. When you choose a city to live in you are choosing to live in the aura and energy field of that collective consciousness. An interesting perspective that most people do not consider when looking at their environmental diet. Also to be considered is the amount of nature as well as the air pollution, sound pollution, smell pollution, electrical pollution, water pollution, pesticide pollution to name just a few. All these things must be processed by your different bodies. There is a wonderful homeopathic product called Envirotox made by Futureplex. It is specifically designed to remove environmental toxins from your body that accumulate from city dwelling. For those living in a big city it might be a product that would be useful to you. Your neighborhood homeopathic pharmacy will probably have it or an equivalent.

In conclusion, when you consider all the different negative energies in the world it is amazing that our physical bodies remain as strong as they do. We live at a time in Earth's history, however, when people have weakened immune systems. A great deal of the cause of this has to do with the lack of joyous vigilance on a spiritual, mental, astral, etheric, psychic, physical, social and environmental level. The lack of this joyous vigilance allows toxins at each of these levels to enter our aura in a very subtle way, which at first glance doesn't seem to be a lot. However, when you add all these different bodies together, and over many years, these many level toxins begin to run down your five major bodies, and take a toll on your organs and glandular system. This usually results in some form of disease, chronic health problems, lack of energy and vitality, lack of joy, lack of love and lack of spiritual enthusiasm. The good news is no matter how much depletion has taken place the physical body and all your bodies are very resilient. By using the insights and tools that I have outlined in this book and in my other books, in a very short period of time you can build yourself back into tiptop shape with GOD and the Masters help. If you will do your part and keep joyous vigilance on all the levels I have spoken of in this chapter, GOD and the Masters will do their part through the invocation and utilization of the tools I have provided, to completely resurrect and rebuild your twelve body system into a well oiled, finely tuned spiritual vehicle and vessel for the "Integrated Christ" you are in truth. GOD and the Masters will help you do this not only for the joy, happiness and love it will build within yourself, but also so that when made completely whole, healthy and revitalized, they may use you as channels, instruments and vehicles of service for the great many of our brothers and sisters who need our help on this planet!

7

Daily Spiritual Affirmations to Work With

One of the most important and effective tools to maintain self-mastery, reprogram the subconscious mind, and keep one's consciousness in Spiritual/Christ/Buddha Consciousness at all times, is doing affirmations! The affirmations I have provided here are specifically created and designed by Spirit, the Masters and myself to do the trick like no others!

The absolute keys to Psychospiritual health are:
- Learning to own your personal power.
- Developing unconditional self-love and self-worth.
- Developing Spiritual attunement and faith!
- Keeping up your golden bubble of protection.
- Maintaining good physical health.

The following affirmations are the best I have ever found to help you achieve and maintain the above listed qualities! I recommend doing them three times a day for a minimum of 21 days, and to pick out your favorite ones and keep them with you to use any time you need a little pumping up, so to speak, in your mental and emotional body! I know you will enjoy working with them!

Affirmations

Personal Power and Becoming a Creative Cause

- I am the power, the master, and the cause of my attitudes, feelings, emotions, and behavior.
- I am 100% powerful, loving, and balanced at all times.
- I am powerful, whole, and complete within myself. I have preferences but not attachments.
- I am 100% powerful and decisive in everything I do.
- I have perfect mastery and control over all my energies in service of a loving spiritual purpose.
- I am the master and director of my life, and my subconscious mind is my friend and servant.
- I am a center of pure self-consciousness and will, with the ability to direct my energies wherever I would have them go.
- I am powerful, centered, and loving at all times.
- I am powerful and centered at all times and nothing in this external universe will I allow to knock me off balance or center.
- I have 100% personal power and I vow never to give it to my subconscious mind or other people ever again.
- I have perfect self-control and self-mastery in everything I do.

Self-Love Affirmations

The following are self-love affirmations for reprogramming your conscious and subconscious thinking:

- I love and forgive myself totally for all my mistakes, for I now recognize that mistakes are positive, not negative.
- I now fully recognize that I have worth because God created me, and I do not have to do anything to have it.
- I now recognize that I am a diamond, not the mud on the diamond.

- My worth is unchangingly positive because it is a spiritual inheritance. It is not increased by my success nor decreased by my mistakes.
- I realize now that I have total worth and value as a person whether I learn my lessons in life or not.
- I now recognize that everything that has ever happened in my life has been positive, because it all contained lessons I needed to learn.
- I choose to live in the "now" and not hold the past against myself.
- I hereby choose to approve of myself, so I do not have to go around seeking approval from others.
- I deserve love because God created me, and my mistakes are not held against me.
- I realize that everything that happens in life is a teaching, a lesson, a challenge, and an opportunity to grow.
- I now realize that I am the "I" person, chooser, consciousness, and spiritual being and that this part of me deserves unconditional love at all times.
- I am the light and not the lampshade over the light.
- I deserve love because my true identity is not what I do in life. I am the chooser of what I do.
- I now understand that I am here to learn lessons and grow in life, but if I make mistakes I am still totally lovable and unchangingly worthy.
- I hereby choose the attitude of being very firm with myself and unconditionally loving.
- I am the master of my life and I choose to be my own best friend instead of my own worst enemy.
- I choose to love me as God loves me unconditionally.
- I now choose truly to understand that I want to be perfect, with the understanding that the mistakes are positive and part and parcel of the growing process.
- I now realize on the level of my true identity being the "I", the chooser, the person, the spiritual being, the soul. I am a perfect equal with every other person in the world.

- I now choose to awaken and recognize that it was only the faulty thinking of my ego that has caused me not to love myself.
- I now choose to undo all the faulty thinking society has programmed into me and replace it with self-love.
- I choose to recognize that I deserve love and so do other people.
- I choose to recognize that I am guiltless and sinless, because all mistakes are just lessons and opportunities to grow. Mistakes, in reality, are golden nuggets of wisdom and are positive.
- I now realize that God does not hold my misuse of free choice against me, so why should I?
- I love me. I forgive me. I approve of me, and I commit myself from this moment onward to treating myself in a spiritual manner rather than in an egotistical manner. I now fully realize that the way in which I think is the reality in which I live. I have been living in my own self-created hell of faulty thinking. I now choose to and will live in my self-created heavenly state of consciousness. It is really that simple.
- I unconditionally love me because I am a son/daughter of God, and my misuse of free choice or faulty thinking is not held against me.
- Could what God created not be lovable and worthy?
- I love me because I am innocent and not guilty.
- The only thing in this infinite universe that says I do not deserve love is my "ego." I hereby reject my ego and its false attitude and get back in tune with my true spiritual attitude and self.
- I now, once and for all, release the ego's game of *"having to do"* in order to deserve love and worth. I now fully recognize I have always been lovable and worthy and will always be so.

My Favorite Affirmations: Guaranteed to Make you Feel Better if said with Regularity and Enthusiasm!!!

- Mental strength, physical strength, spiritual strength!!!
- Personal power, positive anger, mental strength!!!
- I am the power, I am the Master, I am the cause.
- I'm mad as hell and I'm not going to take it anymore.
- Get thee behind me, Satan!!!
- I have perfect faith and trust in God!!!
- Personal power, positive anger, eye of the tiger and faith, trust and patience in God!!!
- Personal power, causality, steel-like mastery!!!
- The power of my three minds makes me the omnipotent force in this universe!
- God, my personal power and the power of my subconscious mind are an unbeatable team.!!!
- My mind power and spirit power are an unbeatable team!!!
- Be still and know that I am God.
- Father, I thank you for the miraculous healing of my...
- Water off a duck's back, water off a window pane, invulnerability, invincibility, rubber pillow, filter...
- God, God, God, Christ, Christ, Christ, Jesus Christ, Jesus Christ, Jesus Christ!!!
- Absolute total supreme mastery!!!
- Tough love, tough love, tough love!!!
- Mental power, physical power, spiritual power!!!
- Faith, trust, patience in God!!!
- Fake it 'til I make it, fake it 'til I make it...
- Every day in every way I am getting stronger and healthier!!!
- God is my co-pilot!!!
- With my power and God's Power and the power of my subconscious I cannot and will not be stopped!!!

- All out war against Satan, and for God and love and positivity!!!
- I will be more powerful from this moment forward than I have ever been in my entire life!!!
- As God is my witness, I will not be stopped!!!
- The Force is with me and I am with the Force!!!
- The Source is with me and I am with the Source!!!
- I am sustained by the Love of God!!!
- I can do all things with God, Christ, and my higher-self who strengthens me!!!
- As God is my witness, I will never give my power to anyone or anything ever again!!!
- God, my personal power, and the power of my subconscious mind!!!
- Not my will, but Thine, thank you for the lesson!!!
- I may lose a few battles, but I am going to win the war!!!
- I declare all out joyous vigilance to get my life together!!!
- I am going to be the absolute master of my life from this day and moment forward!!!
- God goes with me wherever I go!!!
- I love God with all my heart and soul and mind and might, and I love my neighbor as myself.

Read the affirmations again and this time say them with enthusiasm!!!
Read each affirmation from three to seven times!

Emotional Invulnerability

- I am 100% invulnerable to other people's negative energy. Other people's negative energy slides off me like water off a duck's back.
- I am the cause of my feelings and emotions—not other people. I will not give them this power over me ever again.
- Other people's negative energy bounces off me like a rubber pillow.
- I hear what other people have to say to me. However, I internalize only that which "I choose" to internalize.

- The only effect other people's negative energy has is the effect I let it have. I choose not to be affected ever again.

Trust and Patience Affirmations

- I have perfect faith, trust, and patience in my Higher Self.
- I have perfect faith and trust that God is now providing for my every need.
- I hereby surrender all problems and challenges into God's hands.
- Why worry when I can pray?
- With God helping me I will succeed for sure.
- I have perfect faith in my own power as well as perfect faith and trust in God's power.
- I have invited God's help and I know his invisible hands are now working in my life to answer my prayers.
- I have invited God's help and I have perfect faith, trust, and patience He will provide me with what I want, or something better.
- I have asked and I know I shall receive.
- I know God will answer my prayer, in His time not mine, and I will have perfect faith, trust, and patience until that time comes.
- If my prayer isn't answered in exactly the way I want, I know that this is a lesson He would have me learn.
- I have perfect faith, trust, and patience that God will answer my every prayer.
- Prayer, personal power, and affirmations and visualizations are an unbeatable team.
- I have perfect faith, trust, and patience in my self, my superconscious mind, and the power of my subconscious mind, to attract and magnetize to me everything I need.

Physical Health Affirmations

- My physical body is in perfect radiant health.
- My physical body now manifests the health and perfection of Christ.
- Every day in every way I am getting better and better.
- I am physically fit with an abundance of energy.
- I sleep soundly and deeply every night and wake up fully rested and refreshed early every morning.
- Father, I thank You for my long and healthy life in your service.
- Father, I thank You for my unlimited increase in the power and energy of my physical battery.
- God, my personal power, and the power of my subconscious mind are now healing, energizing, and strengthening my physical body.
- My physical body is now healing with Godspeed.
- God, my personal power, and the power of my subconscious mind are now returning my body to perfect radiant health.
- Be still, and know that I am God, and my physical body now manifests the health and perfection of Christ.
- Father, I thank You for my unlimited increase in the functioning of my glandular system.
- My glandular system is now operating at its full Christ Potential.
- My thymus gland and immunity system are now operating at their full Christ Potential.
- I am a son or daughter of God, so I cannot possibly be sick.
- God, my personal power, and the power of my subconscious mind are now revitalizing, recharging, and awakening my physical body.
- I am in love with physical exercise, and I am now being filled with an abundance of physical energy.

Affirmations of Saint Germain through Godfre Ray King from The I AM Discourses Books

- Be still and know I Am God!
- I Am God living in this body as (your name).
- I Am a fully liberated God living in this body as (your name).
- I Am the Mighty I Am Presence!
- I Am the Ascended Master (your name)!
- In the name of the Beloved Presence of God, who I Am.
- By the power of God, who I Am.
- The Mighty I Am Presence is my real self!
- I Am the resurrection and the life.
- I Am the truth, the way and the life.
- I Am the embodiment of divine love.
- I Am the open door which no man can shut.
- I Am God in action!
- I Am the Scepter of Dominion, the Quenchless Flame, the Dazzling Light and Divine Perfection made manifest!
- I Am the revelation of God.
- I Am the baptism of the Holy Spirit.
- I Am the ascended being I wish to be now.
- I Am the realization of God.
- I Am an open door to all revelation.
- I Am the Light that lights up every room I enter.
- I Am the Presence of god in action this day.
- I Am That I Am!
- I Am the eternal liberation from all human imperfection.
- I Am a perfect channel and instrument of God.
- I Am the presence filling my world with perfection this day.
- I Am an invincible body of Light.
- I Am the Light that lights everything that comes into the world.
- I Am the victory in the Light!
- Forgive them Father, they know not what they do.
- I Am the cosmic flame of cosmic victory!

8

How to Develop an Extremely High-Functioning Physical, Psychological and Spiritual Immune System

My beloved readers, one of the most important understandings every light worker needs to incorporate in order to achieve Integrated Ascension is how to develop an extremely high functioning immune system physically, psychologically and spiritually. In my personal opinion the four keys to achieving Integrated Ascension are learning to fully own and claim your personal power, developing your semi-permeable bubble of light, developing unconditional self-love and self-worth, and maintaining an attunement to your Higher Self, Monad, the Ascended Masters and GOD at all times. These four principles are the psychological foundation of your entire spiritual life. If any one of these are not functioning properly your entire life will be off-kilter. In other sections of this book I speak of the importance of personal power and self-love. The issue of attunement to your Higher Self, Monad, the Ascended Masters and GOD fill all the pages of this book and all the other books of mine you have read, so it is unnecessary to explore this aspect further in this chapter. The issue that I do want to explore in this chapter is the revolutionary concept that we have actually three immune systems, not just one.

In the mass consciousness or common language, when we think of the words "immune system" we think of physical health. Our physical immune system is what protects us from disease. As I think all of you, my beloved readers, know there is no such thing as a contagious disease. This is an illusion and stems out of a belief in victim consciousness which is also an illusion. We are all masters not victims. We are causes not effects. This applies to the physical immune level as well. There is no such thing as contagious disease, there are just people with compromised immune systems. This last statement is not a judgment but rather a simple statement of fact.

Our Physical Immune System

My beloved readers, the first question that we must ask is how do we develop a high functioning immune system and what causes a physical immune system to be compromised? This is a very multi-faceted subject. The answer to the question of how to develop a high functioning physical immune system lies in a proper physical diet, getting a good night's sleep, proper physical exercise, getting enough fresh air and sunshine, removing all of the residual toxins in the organs, glands, cells and blood which I speak of in the chapter on spiritual healing tools for the physical body. Other factors that affect the physical immune system are your work/play balance and stress factors in your work and personal life. Other factors are past life karma, speed of spiritual growth, inherited genetic weakness, and overall balance or lack of balance in your life. Other factors that can affect the immune system are living in cities and on a planet that is filled with pollution, receiving vaccines as children, and seeing doctors that prescribe drugs like candy and who have no understanding of holistic naturopathic or homeopathic remedies that are not toxic to the human body.

Other factors are residual toxins such as mercury fillings, pesticides, metal poisoning, chemical poisoning, and preservatives in our food.

Sugar addiction, eating too much processed food, bad food combining, over eating, not drinking enough water, under eating, and lack of life force in our food because the nature kingdom deva's and plant spirits have been driven from our gardens as a result of pesticides and Humankind's rejection of their existence, which are more factors that affect the physical immune system. Other factors are depletion of the rainforests causing lack of proper oxygenation of the planet, and burning of too much fossil fuels instead of using natural spiritual forms of energy. The gaping hole in the ozone layer that is allowing certain ultraviolet rays in that we should be protected from. The pollution in our rivers and drinking water, the use of aluminum cookware causing aluminum poisoning, all the electrical power lines in big cities and electrical equipment in our houses, and the use of microwave ovens which places actual holes in the aura of the food. The rampant use of recreational drugs as well as pharmaceutical drugs instead of using homeopathics and herbs. Using factory and synthetic made vitamins and minerals instead of using natural forms of these sub-stances in our vitamin/mineral supplements. Also the new practice of the FDA of allowing markets to irradiate our fruits and vegetables with toxic radiation. Also the radiation contamination from being too close to color TVs and microwave ovens. All the low grade electromagnetic toxicity from electrical appliances in our home. Just living in a big city is compromising to the immune system. Using cell phones too much and/or sitting in front of a computer without proper energetic protection, which can easily be obtained from your local New Age homeopathic pharmacy or bookstore.

These, my beloved readers, are just a few of the physical toxins that compromise our immune system. Is it any wonder people get sick so much in our world? Three quarters of the things I have mentioned, traditional doctors have no knowledge of. Just going to a traditional doctor compromises our immune system. It is close to impossible to get well in a hospital there is so much negative energy imbedded in the walls. Ronald Beasley, the famous spiritual teacher from England who passed on a number of years ago, said that hospitals should be burned down every five years. The tests that traditional medicine uses to diagnose disease are often extremely invasive. They fill you full of dyes, poke holes in your spine, fill you full of radiation, and give you blood transfusions or organ transplants, which are spiritually totally poisonous to lightworkers.

I do not mean to get down on traditional medicine because it definitely has its place and in a certain sliver of understanding it is even brilliant. From a full spectrum prism perspective it is extremely fragmented in its understanding. Fifty years from now much of what they do will be viewed as barbaric and as being a product of the Dark Ages. In the future, testing and diagnoses will be done through energetic means, not physical means.

So, my beloved readers, is it any wonder that so many people are sick and have compromised immune systems? Most people aren't exposed to the information that I have shared here until their adult life. By this time all these factors have taken a great toll on the physical vehicle. It is almost a given if you incarnate into this world that your immune system is going to be very stressed. What I have spoken of so far, my beloved readers, is just the physical toxins that affect the immune system. I have not even begun to speak of the psychological factors, or spiritual and energetic factors that affect our immune system on all levels. The crux and final point of this that I would like to make is for all of us to be much more compassionate, loving, and understanding to our fellow brothers and sisters who have health lessons of one kind or another. For the truth of us all is that "But for the Grace of GOD go I" and "By the Grace of GOD go us all."

We have all been born into a world that is extremely lacking in New Age understanding and very backward in many ways. This again is not a criticism but a fact. This makes incarnating into this mystery school called planet Earth an extremely courageous proposition. We should all develop great compassion for ourselves for making such a gallant decision. It is our job as lightworkers to raise the consciousness of the planet so our children do not begin learning these lessons in adult life rather than in the early stages of schooling where this information should be taught. This is the new wave of spiritual education that is reforming every aspect of our society in politics, spiritual education, economics, the arts, the sciences, religion, business, medicine, psychology and spirituality.

Our Psychological Immune System

My beloved readers, equally important to developing a high functioning physical immune system is developing a high functioning psychological immune system. In truth, developing a high functioning psychological immune system is even more important to developing a healthy physical immune system than even a great many of the physical factors. This is true because our thoughts create our reality. Even if you do everything right on the physical level, if the psychological immune system is not functioning properly this will compromise your physical immune system. So let us now explore what I mean by developing a healthy psychological immune system.

This begins with each morning with getting up and claiming your personal power and putting on your mental, emotional and spiritual armor, love and attunement. Just as we put on physical clothes every morning we must also put on mental, emotional and spiritual clothes each day. This begins with putting on your personal power, then your semi-permeable bubble of protection, then your unconditional self-love and self-worth, then your attunement to your Oversoul, Monad, and Ascended Masters and GOD. Then you must put on your overall Christ attitude and consciousness, which could also be called your positive mental attitude.

Some of the other most important attitudes to put on are: having preferences instead of attachments, looking at things as lessons, non-judgmentalness, and forgiveness to name just a few. The other most important attitudes to claim is that you are the cause of your reality by how you think. Part of this understanding is to fully own that every feeling and emotion you have is caused by how you think and not by any person or circumstance outside of self. Your thoughts not only create your feelings and your emotions but also your behavior and what you attract, magnetize and/or repel in your life.

It is this attitude of being a cause rather that being an effect, a master rather than a victim that also makes you invulnerable. When you fully own your mental and emotional invulnerability and that you cause your reality and can demonstrate this in your daily life then you have a healthy psychological immune system. Through the process of self-inquiry this means every time a negative ego thought tries to enter your conscious mind you push it out and deny it entrance and instead replace it with a Christ/Buddhic attitude and/or feeling. The negative ego in your own subconscious mind is like a thoughtform virus or thought-form bacteria. If you let the negative thoughtform into your mind you will be mentally and emotionally sick and hence have a weakened psychological immune system. If this continues to happen over time this is the initial cause for actual physical viruses and bacteria to form as well.

The same principal applies to negativity coming from other people. This is why it is essential every morning upon arising to affirm and visualize that you have a semi-permeable bubble of light around you that protects you not only from other people but also gives you a certain degree of detachment and protection from your own subconscious mind. So this semi-permeable bubble of light protects you from your own subconscious mind and from other people and outside negativity. The bubble is semi-permeable because it allows in positive energy but keeps out any and all negativity.

This is the proper masculine/feminine balance that is needed to stay psychologically centered. When negativity comes towards you when your psychological immune system and bubble is intact, it hits your bubble and slides off like water off a duck's back and/or bounces off like a rubber pillow. My beloved readers, do you see the profundity of this concept? The semi-permeable bubble of light gives you the needed protection and detachment both inwardly and outwardly to not become victimized and not to react. The ideal is not to react, but to respond without victimization taking place. Then one can respond out of calm, loving, rational observation, spiritual discernment and nonjudgmentalness. Children even understand this when they say "…sticks and stones may break my bones but names can never hurt me." They are affirming their psychological and/or emotional invulnerability.

Now it is important to understand here that when I say you are invulnerable I'm speaking of this on the mental, emotional and spiritual level, not the physical level. Obviously none of us are invulnerable physically, for another person can kill, maim, or hurt our physical vehicle. Even though this may be the case no one has any control over our thoughts, emotions or spirit. Our spirit and soul, as you all obviously know, is indestructible and eternal. The ideal is to make your mind and emotions reflect this aspect of self rather than being overidentified with the physical vehicle which, in truth, is the definition of what the negative ego thought system is about.

When your thinking and emotions are attuned to the Christ consciousness you will not only be in your power at all times and in your bubble at all times, you will also be in unconditional love, joy, even-mindedness, equanimity, and inner peace at all times as well. The only thing in truth that takes you out of this is your own thinking. There is no judgment when this happens, however when it does it is important to know where the truth lies.

It is inevitable for everyone to lose their happiness, joy and inner peace at times, however, by practicing the science of attitudinal healing, over time one can have longer and longer periods of total unchanging inner peace, joy and love. Any time you have negative emotions in you it is a sign attitudinal healing is needed and with no self-judgment you should make the needed attitudinal and emotional corrections. We don't always have control over what happens in our outer circumstance in life, however we do have total 100% control over the attitude we take towards outer circumstances. Herein lies the secret to inner peace, happiness and joy.

The Master Jesus gave the ultimate example of this in his life on Earth 2000 years ago. He was whipped, beaten, crucified and had nails stuck in him, yet he still demonstrated not only his mastery over outer circumstances but also mastery over his physical body when he said, "Forgive them Father, for they know not what they do." Even though his physical body was tortured and ultimately killed, he retained his Christ consciousness. He set this example for you and I, my friends. If he could do it in such an extreme circumstance, then certainly we can do it in all the spiritual tests, lessons and worldly tribulations we confront in our daily lives.

Just as when you have a virus or bacterial infection you are sick physically, when you have negative ego thoughts and emotions you are sick psychologically. My beloved readers, can you see what havoc to your physical immune system and psychological immune system you will cause if you don't own your own personal power, semi-permeable bubble of light, unconditional self-love and self-worth, attunement to your Higher Self, Monad, Ascended Masters, GOD and your Christ consciousness and positive attitude? I know many lightworkers who eat good diets and do all the right things physically, however their physical immune systems are in terrible shape predominately from having unbelievably weak psychological immune systems. To be healthy physically, in truth, all three levels of immune systems have to be functioning properly.

Having a healthy psychological immune system in order to not catch the psychological diseases (moodiness, anger, depression, fear, unhappiness, upset, judgementalness, meanness, self-pity) is essential not only for physical health, but also essential for spiritual health, the achievement of GOD-Realization, the passing of your initiations and Integrated Ascension. Most people on this planet have very compromised psychological immune systems which is affecting their physical immune systems as well as their spiritual purpose for being on this planet. This again is not a judgment but just a point of observation and insight, which this chapter is hoping to correct and remedy or at least lead one in the proper direction. For those who have lessons involving a weakened psychological immune system I again highly recommend reading my books *How To Clear The Negative Ego, Soul Psychology, How To Release Fear-Based Thinking and Feeling: An In-depth Study of Spiritual Psychology* and *The Golden Book of Melchizedek: How To Become An Integrated Christ/Buddha In This Lifetime.*

One last point I want to make on the psychological immune system is in regard to the issue of unconditional self-love and self-worth. If this psychological work is not achieved, the lightworker will seek the self-love and self-worth outside of self instead of within self and from GOD. This will psychologically cause a hole to be created in one's bubble of protective light from the inside. In truth, every improper negative ego attitude will do this, unconditional love and self-worth being so important to a healthy psyche. The real keys to Integrated Ascension lie within personal power, self-love, self-worth, your bubble and attunement to GOD. Ponder on this.

If you don't own your personal power this will also sabotage your semi-permeable protective bubble of light, for by not owning the power you are automatically giving it to your subconscious mind, emotional body, inner child, lower self desire, negative ego, and/or other people. A healthy psychological immune system begins for most with owning your personal power. Your bubble of protection, self-love and self-worth, and attunement to Higher Self, Monad, Ascended Masters and GOD won't hold if you don't do this. In truth, all four of those keys are totally interdependent on each other. Lack of self-love and self-worth will sabotage the other three. Lack of your semi-permeable bubble of light will sabotage the other three. Lack of attunement to Higher Self, Monad, Ascended Masters and GOD will sabotage the other three. The work begins with owning your personal power, however all four plus an overall

Christ consciousness and positive mental attitude must be maintained in an integrated and balanced manner for psychological equilibrium and homeostasis to be maintained.

Our Spiritual Immune System

The third and final immune system that needs to be developed is what I call the spiritual immune system. My beloved readers, I am happy to say that this is the easiest level of immune system to develop if you will follow my simple instructions. What I am about to share with you is truly a Divine dispensation which has been given in other forms before but not as succinctly and precisely as what I am going to share with you now.

The key to developing a high functioning spiritual immune system is to, in this moment as you read this book, call forth His Holiness Lord Melchizedek, the Mahatma, and Metatron, and request that they anchor and activate the semi-permeable wall of light around your twelve-body system. Ask in this moment that this semi-permeable wall of light be anchored permanently.

This is a most profound and wonderful gift given forth by these three Cosmic, wise, and loving Masters. This semi-permeable wall of light is the spiritual counterpart to the semi-permeable bubble of light that I mentioned was so essential to your psychological immune system. The second that it is asked for it will be installed and given. This is a personal promise from Melchizedek, the Mahatma, and Metatron Forevermore this semi-permeable wall of light will protect you.

It is slightly different from normal spiritual protection for it is semi-permeable in nature, which means it will allow in all positive, loving energy, however, it will keep out all negative energy. What is also unique about this gift is that it is being permanently installed not just in this moment or just for today. Thirdly, what is unique about this gift is that it is made of platinum white energy. As I've told you before, platinum is the highest frequency color available on the Earth. This means there is no negative energy in the universe that can penetrate its frequency of protection. You never have to request this again after this one time for its effectiveness is eternal.

What this semi-permeable wall of light will do for you is to filter out all personal and impersonal negative energies trying to enter your field of an energetic, astral, mental and ethereal nature. This is a great blessing to have this protection.

Now it is very important to understand that this spiritual, semi-permeable wall of light will not replace or take the place of your semi-permeable psychological bubble and will not replace the need to keep physical toxins out of your body. *Each immune system must do its part.* The spiritual immune system is incapable of doing the work of the psychological immune system.

This is the big mistake that many lightworkers make. For example they call forth to Archangel Michael for protection and Archangel Michael gives it unfailingly. Lightworkers don't understand why they may continue to be attacked by dark forces, negative extraterrestrials, their own subconscious mind and other people. The answer is quite simple. If we as lightworkers do not maintain our own psychological immune system this creates gaping holes in our aura that even the cosmic Masters cannot remedy. It is not their job to think for us or create our emotions for us. If they did so they would be defeating the prime directive of noninterference with our free choice and in truth would be taking the lessons away from us that we incarnated to learn. If we as light workers do not own our personal power, maintain our bubble, develop unconditional self-love and self-worth, stay attuned to GOD, and maintain a Christed and positive attitude, we can pray from here to kingdom come and the protection we seek will not be forth coming. It is not because it is not given, for it is always given and is always given one hundred percent. The key lesson here being that the spiritual immune system will not suffice to replace the psychological immune system.

So again, my beloved readers, we come back to the concept of Integrated Ascension. Just as each mind in our spiritual constitution (subconscious, conscious, superconscious) has its part to play, the same is true of the these levels of our immune system. The spiritual immune system by the 3 M's will work wonders and will be an incredible support as long as we as lightworkers take responsibility for operating our own psychological immune system, and also take responsibility for keeping toxins out of our physical vehicles. When all three immune systems are integrated in this manner it is then and only then that someone can develop a fully functioning physical immune system and can achieve Integrated Ascension. It is my sincere hope and prayer that this discussion has brought greater light and understanding to this most fascinating subject!

9

The Importance of Loving the Physical Body

It is very important, as part of your Spiritual Path, to love not just GOD, the Heavenly Father/Mother, your Brothers and Sisters, your self and your inner child, it is also very important to Love your physical body and GOD's Physical body! GOD's Physical Body is the Infinite Material Universe. So this makes your physical body, a microcosm of GOD's Macrocosmic Physical body! As I have said in other chapters, there are Four Faces of GOD (Spiritual, Mental, Emotional and Material)! All are equally important! You must integrate them all equally, and love them all equally too fully Realize GOD! God is as much in the Material Universe as He is in the Mental, Emotional or Spiritual dimensions of reality!

This chapter is focused on loving your physical body, which is a part of GOD's physical body! We each are Sons and Daughters of GOD and incarnations of GOD living in physical bodies! The physical body as we know is our Temple! Just as the infinite material Universe is GOD's Temple! Many lightworkers look on the physical body, the Earth, and/or the infinite Material Universe as being inferior or less than the Spiritual worlds! This, my Beloved Readers, is illusion! The Material Universe is one of GOD's Seven Heavens! It is one of the many mansions of GOD! Matter is densified Spirit, and Spirit is rarified matter! There is no separation my Beloved Readers, it is just all one energy which is GOD! Matter is not even dense in reality! It just appears dense to us. There are enormous amounts of space between electrons, neutrons, protons, etc.

Adding to this discussion, the physical body has consciousness. As with all matter, it is created by the elemental kingdom and elemental beings. Elemental Beings are the microcosmic version of the Mighty Elohim or Co-creator Gods, who help GOD create the infinite Material Universe! There are tiny elemental beings who help the angels create a flower and there are Elohim who help GOD create Universes! My Beloved Readers, there are elemental beings that live in our physical body that have helped to create it! This has been known esoterically as the "body elemental"! Everything in GOD's Infinite Universe has Consciousness. That is why it is possible to communicate with our animals, a tree, a flower, a shrub, a pea plant, or a mineral. It is possible to communicate with the Spirit that inhabits that life form and it is possible to communicate with the Elemental consciousness that has helped to create that form. It is also possible to communicate with the angelic forces that overlight that form!

So there is consciousness in the physical body! It is possible to communicate with the body elemental! I have recommended using a pendulum in my books, for example, to say what the body elemental really wants to eat. A great many people eat from their mind and not from what the body elemental really wants and needs. They think they need, for example, all these supplements and products that come out on the market, however, if they really tuned in to the body elemental they would find nine out of ten times they don't. They just think they do. Or if they do want the products it might be only one tenth of the amount the are taking! The same thing occurs with food. They may eat for example, tons of tofu, but their body elemental may be allergic to tofu. However, they read in a book that tofu is supposed to be healthy. It can be the same thing with certain vegetables. The body elemental may resonate with certain kinds of vegetables and not with others. However we are taught through our minds that all vegetables are good. All supplements are good! Nothing could be farther from the truth. Every body is different. What is good for one body could be poisonous for another.

This is why most nutritionists, with no judgement intended, don't know what they are talking about. They do their work from book knowledge instead of really tuning into the body elemental and seeing what it really wants!

The same can occur from listening to your feelings. The question is, are your feelings coming from your personality, lower-self, desire body, or are they truly coming from the body elemental. A lot of lightworkers think that if it is coming from my feelings it must be what my body wants. Again this is not always the case my friends! Again what is the source of the feelings? The body elemental or the personality, desire body, astral body, or lower-self? We must really train ourselves to get back in touch with the body elemental, for our up bringing in this world trains us to lose attunement to it! If people really under-stood what the body elemental really wanted, compared to what most people do, they would be shocked. This is why people get sick so often as well as get tired and don't have as much energy as they want!

Then there is the issue of the symptoms that the physical body often has. When we have symptoms in the physical body this is GOD teaching us some-thing. For everything in GOD's infinite Universe is governed by laws. There are Spiritual laws, Mental Laws, Emotional Laws and Physical Laws. Part of the purpose of life is to learn these laws on all levels and become obedient to them. When we are not, we create suffering for ourselves on the different planes of consciousness. Many people get angry or frustrated when they get sick or when the physical body has health lessons or chronic symptoms. This is GOD teaching you some-thing. The mind often wants to override the physical body and push it unmercifully. The mind often does not want to give it enough sleep, proper diet and nutrition, proper exercise, fresh air, and sunshine. The mind often wants to fill it full of drugs, or just not respect it or love it as it does Spiritual things or outer things and people. Eventually the body may break down for periods of time! This is GOD saying you are not loving and respecting your physical body! You are out of the "Tao" of your Heavenly and Earthly balance! Your mind may want to do things this way, but it is overriding the physical body and the physical body is part of GOD's plan as well! You must pay your rent to all your bodies including the physical. It is not a lesser body or a less intelligent body. It just has a different kind of intelligence than Spirit, mind or feelings! You will only truly realize God when all four are properly integrated and balanced! When the body gets sick or goes haywire this just means there is some lesson you need to learn. It is not a judgement! You must just adjust your consciousness and lifestyle to work with the wants and needs of the physical body! So instead of fighting the body, we need to work embrace the body and work with it! Even learn from it!

The physical body is the instrument and vehicle of the Soul, which is you! It has consciousness, but it is not meant to run your life! You are meant to run your life. I have seen at times some lightworkers give it too much intelligence as well, or more than it really has! It must be integrated, loved and honored, but just as with your other bodies, you are meant to be the captain of your own ship and make all your bodies (Spiritual, mental, emotional, etheric, and physical) serve you!

Now the etheric body is the blueprint for the physical body! If you are having any problems with the physical body, it is always a good idea to say a prayer to GOD, the Masters and the "Etheric Inner Plane Healing Team" to repair the Etheric body from any past life or present live trauma or damage. It is also a good idea to call Spirit and the Masters to have them anchor your "Perfect Monadic Blueprint Body!" This will insure that your physical body is operating off a perfect copy to repair itself. Sometimes people don't recover from health lessons because their Etheric body has been damaged and so no matter what they do physically it will not repair itself until the Etheric Body has been repaired and until the Perfect Monadic Blueprint Body has been anchored and activated!

Now the other interesting thing about the physical body is that the physical body is also run by the subconscious mind. This can be clearly proven by the use of hypnosis. We see in stage shows how people are able under hypnosis to do the most amazing physical feats that they could never do in a million years in a conscious waking state! This is because the subconscious mind runs the physical body. The problem is that the subconscious mind is a non-reasoning mind. So if you tell it or allow other people to give it improper suggestions it can make you sick! For example you could be feeling perfectly fine and a friend comes up to you at the store and sees you and says you don't look well you look a little sick! You may feel fine, however if you allow that suggestion to lodge in your subconscious mind you will start feeling sick! Now this is a very profound understanding for it has enormous implications. This is why doctors in Japan often will not tell their patients they have serious illnesses. For if they patient thinks they do, their mind thinking this will implant this idea into the subconscious and their minds will create worse symptoms than the actual illness. There is some interesting considerations to this practice. The same thing occurs to people with AIDS or cancer.

Let's take this one step further. How about people who do not love themselves! What does this do to program the subconscious in terms of how it affects the physical body? Now let's take it one step further. How about people who let their minds, their feelings and emotions run them too much. How about people who let their negative ego minds, lower self, desire body, run them too much! How does this program the subconscious mind to affect the physical body? Let's take this understanding one step further! Every thought you think lodges someplace in your aura and affects the physical body! Every feeling and emotion you feel affects the physical body. The subconscious mind is the seat of your feelings and emotions. You can't feel anger, for example, without this affecting your liver and organs! People often get ulcers from worrying! My Beloved Readers, are you seeing the incredible connections between Spirit, mind, feelings and your physical body! If you are too ungrounded and spend too much time out of your body, your body will be more exhausted. If you are not grounded and integrating your physical body and the Earth and Earth life, you will not have any energy in your lower chakras which will cause the physical body to malfunction! Adding to this, every thought you think manifests through one of your seven basic chakras. If any of the chakras are under or over activated this affects the seven major glands. For each chakra is connected to a gland! If your consciousness is not integrated and balanced this can have an enormous affect on how your glandular system is operating! This of course affects the flow of your hormones! So we see again how much consciousness affects the physical body!

Then we must look at our thoughts, beliefs and the images we hold in our mind about our body! If we think we are sick or worry about getting any given illness, if we think this long enough, even unconsciously, this can eventually make you either get that illness or have symptoms of it. The subconscious is a computer and it can be programmed to create perfect radiant health or to be sick! It all depends on the thoughts, images and feelings you program it with! This is why it is so important to always tell ourselves that we are in "Perfect Radiant Health!" This is why Parmahansa Yogananda said that even when we are 99 years old and are on our deathbed we should be telling ourselves that we are in perfect radiant health!

Now another important lesson regarding the physical body and maybe the most important, is that we should never give our Personal Power to our physical body! I am amazed how many lightworkers do this! The second they get tired physically, there goes their Personal Power! The second they get sick, or have any symptoms, there goes their Personal Power. You must love the physical body, honor it, but not give it your Personal Power and do not "Coddle yourself and become a hypochondriac" which many lightworkers do! Health lessons are just part of living in this world and if we become dysfunctional every time we have a health lesson we are not going to accomplish very much! So I don't want to confuse love and coddling! We also must have a certain mental toughness in life. Mother Theresa had a terrible heart condition but did her mission. The Dalai Lama had hepatitis but does his mission! So toughness and love must be balanced! People can make themselves sick by coddling themselves and being hypochondriacs! So Personal Power and Unconditional love must be balanced in relationship to the proper care of the physical body! You must develop self-mastery over your mental, emotional, and physical body! If you don't also learn to master the negative ego, it will not only misprogram your thinking, it will misprogram all your feelings and emotions which will cause your subconscious mind, energy body and hence physical body to be misaligned! All illness begins on the mental, emotional and etheric realm first. It is also our consciousness that tells us what foods we are going to put in our physical bodies!

A Course in Miracles states that "Sickness is a defense against the Truth!" This is because each of our true Identity is the Christ or the Buddha! Just as GOD doesn't get sick, we will not get sick if we fully identify with GOD on all levels! First, we must see ourselves and others as the Christ and the Buddha to realize this. Secondly, as I said earlier, to realize this we must also Realize and be obedient to GOD's Laws Spiritually, mentally, emotionally, etherically and physically! This book and my other books are teaching you these Laws and principles! If we learn and practice them, then we learn by Grace! If we don't, we learn by Karma. Karma is suffering! Karma is not bad or a judgement! It is just a more severe lesson to help give us a stronger signal or reminder that we are not in harmony with GOD's Laws on some level! So you see, if the physical body or any body for that matter is having a symptom or lesson, this is not bad. This is good! This is a sign that that there is a lesson to learn! The physical body can be one of the best teachers of all to help you become attuned to what true God Consciousness is. Enormous numbers of lightworkers often fight the physical body instead of recognizing that GOD is working through the physical body teaching you Spiritual lessons. Your mind may want to go fast, but your physical body is saying

I need to rest, sleep or just be! The Mind is not always right my friends! We must honor the Tao of our physical bodies regardless of what plans the mind has! The mind must learn to honor, love and respect the Divine Intelligence of the physical body and the Earth for that matter! This is part of the honoring of the Divine Mother and the Goddess energies as well!

The body is also incredibly affected by the mind and emotions. Its energy level and how well you sleep at night is 100% affected by your consciousness. My Beloved Readers, Spirit, mind, feelings, and the physical body are all one! They are integrated, whole, synergistic and one! The are made of the same energies! There is no separation between them! One is not better than another! If you think Spirit is better than matter you have disowned a part of GOD and have taken the first step to imbalance, having weakened physical energy and potential seeds for future health lessons! You are not loving the physical body and not loving properly the Material Face of GOD!

Your mind and emotions can also even change the physical structure of the body. Through hypnosis it is a fact that women have been able to grow larger breasts! If you hold a very Christ/Buddha-like thought, image and feeling sense of self this will actually make you look more handsome and beautiful. It will actually affect the structure of your physical body to a certain extent!

When you learn to keep a good "Psychological Immune System" that keeps out the negative thoughts, and feelings of others and the outside world, this will actually greatly strengthen your physical immune system! Indeed here we have the Hermetic law, "As Within, So Without! As Above, So Below!

So my Beloved Readers, if you don't love your physical body, or even don't like or hate your physical body as some people do, you can imagine the adverse affect it can have on the physical body! This is not to mention the fact that it is a part of GOD's body in a microcosmic sense! To not love your physical body is to not love a part of GOD! Adding to this, as

I have already made clear, your physical body has consciousness and intelligence! To not love your physical body is to not only to not love the substance of GOD, but is to not love the consciousness and intelligence that has created the form and is constantly maintaining the form!

One last story I would like to share in regard to the power of loving the physical body. This was a type of study that was done! It was called the "X Factor in Healing!" In this one hospital, they found that certain patients were healing much faster than others were and they were trying to figure out why. After a very close study of all the factors and some experiments that were done what they figured out is that the "X Factor in Healing" is "Love!" The Patients that healed the quickest were the ones who were treated by nurses and doctors who gave them the most love! This is a true story and a true study!

So my Beloved Readers, can you see now why so many people in this world are tired so much, and physically weary? Can you see why so many people have weakened immune systems? Can you see why people get sick so much? Can you see why so many people have cancer! Cancer is "disintegration" of the physical, which is a product of a "disintegrated consciousness on some level"! The important thing is to see that physical disease can be one's greatest teacher. It is just the karmic push people need to fully realize God and their Spiritual Path! If we didn't have physical health lessons people would just continue in their imbalanced ways and never choose to fully get on their Spiritual Path. Thank GOD for the Wisdom of our physical bodies! It may be one of our greatest Spiritual Teachers of all! It may often break up a lot of the mind's plans! However, I have a little secret for you. This is often times just what the Doctor (Spirit) ordered! It is not that the mind is bad or negative, it is not! Just sometimes it tries to override the physical body in its exuberance and this is the only part of the mind, which of course is the negative ego mind, that must be controlled. The Spiritual mind will always create in harmony with the physical body and in harmony with the physical body of the World! It is the Perfect Integration of all Four Bodies (Spirit,

Mind, Feelings and Physical Body) working together in perfect harmony that allows full God Realization to take place!

In conclusion, my Beloved Readers, this chapter has been written as a deeper understanding of the importance of totally loving, honoring, and sanctifying your physical body! It is even more than just a Temple for the God you are! It is a consciousness and integral aspect of GOD's Wholeness and Four Faces! It is time for all separation and overidentification and underidentification to be removed! It is time to see that Spirit and Matter are one, just as Feminine and Masculine are one! They must all be balanced, integrated and sanctified! We must pay our rent to all of them! God Realization will not be achieved unless you love your physical body and you love the Earth, the Material Universe and Earth Life as well! Embrace and love your physical body and the Earth and Earth Energies! My Beloved Readers, when you fully do this you will find a most incredible surprise! You will find GOD smiling at you from the Earthly realm as much as He does from the Spiritual Realm! This will enhance your God Realization and Spirituality enormously! Each Face of GOD is so incredibly rich! Don't short change yourself! Honor, sanctify and learn from the Material Face of GOD! Love your precious physical body! Talk to your physical body for it has consciousness and intelligence! Tell it how much you love it, just as you tell yourself and your inner child! Embrace it as part of your God Team! Be Friends with it, Love it, Care for it, Learn from it, Honor it, and remember as well to maintain Self-Mastery over it as with all the bodies! This is the balance and integration to strive for to achieve full God Realization and Perfect Radiant Health! If you love and honor your physical body it will honor and love you! It will be a faithful servant! It will help you to truly understand a great many of GOD's Laws on the physical level! It will teach you in a great many ways how to live in the "Tao"! How to live in perfect harmony and balance with yourself, your physical body and with nature! Trust in your physical body's intelligence, for in truth, it is GOD speaking to you through your beloved physical body! I conclude here saying that the Master Jesus said the whole law could be summed up in the words, "Love the Lord thy GOD with all your Heart and Soul and Mind and Might, and Love your Neighbor as you Love Yourself!" No more perfect words may have ever been written! I would like to suggest to also remember to love your physical body, the Material Universe, and the Earth Mother as well! For in so doing, we our loving GOD's physical body and our physical body, which, in truth, are one!

10

How to Clear the Negative Implants, Elementals, and Astral Entities

In my second book in the series called *Soul Psychology*, I went into incredibly great detail in explaining soul and spiritual psychology and how it is different from traditional psychology. I personally believe that this book is one of the clearest and most comprehensive writings on this subject. I also spent a great deal of time in this book discussing the difference between negative ego versus spiritual thinking, which is probably the single most important lesson lightworkers need to understand and practice to realize God.

This has to do with the difference between the psychological level and the psychic level of soul and spiritual psychology. I cannot tell you how excited I am to share this new information with you. I again repeat that this is some of the most important information I have ever come across, so I ask you to be patient as I attempt to unfold this understanding to you.

There are three levels that need to be mastered to achieve Self-realization. These three levels are the spiritual level, the psychological level, and the physical level. All three need to be mastered, and are separate levels of understanding. Very few lightworkers are developed in all three. Usually they are developed in two of them and weaker in one. The physical level deals with ones physical body and ones physical environment and keeping healthy, purified and clean.

The spiritual level is what most lightworkers are most focused on and is the key to the ascension process and the passing of one's initiations. It is the focus of working with one's Higher Self, Mighty I Am Presence, and the Ascended Masters, building light quotient, and anchoring light technologies.

The psychological area deals with the conscious mind's relationship, not so much with the superconscious as much as with the subconscious mind, and the four-body system (physical, mental, emotional, and spiritual). This level is about how one deals with thoughts, feelings, emotions, intuition, sensations, instincts, relationships, balancing of the four bodies, integrating the three minds (conscious, subconscious, and superconscious), balancing the chakras, and so on.

In my opinion, the psychological level is the most important one because it is the foundation of one's psychic house, so to speak. It is most important because it is your thoughts that create your reality. There are many people who have taken advanced levels of initiation but who are still victims and are totally run by their negative egos, which is like a psychological cancer to their whole program.

The Psychic Level of Spiritual Psychology

In *Soul Psychology*, I addressed the psychological level in great detail. Now I am going to address the psychic level of spiritual psychology, which is the final piece in the puzzle. Both of these aspects of spiritual psychology are of equal importance. People on the Earth cannot be healed of psychological and physical disease, and achieve ascension and Self-realization without addressing both of them. The psychic level of spiritual psychology deals with principles that most of humanity are not aware of. It is completely ignored in the area of traditional psychology, and in most cases ignored or not understood in most spiritual practices.

What I have been leading up to this entire chapter is how to clear negative alien implants, negative elementals, astral entities, etheric mucous, parasites, negative imprints, toxic astral energies, gray fields, etheric wounds, holes in the aura, and extraterrestrial possession, to name a few. This is an area of work that is usually addressed by psychic healers only and/or those who are clairvoyant, and even most in this group do not have a very good understanding of how to deal with this level.

A person can do all the psychological clearing work in the world, but if this psychic level of spiritual psychology is not addressed the person will never fully recover from their physical or psychological problems. On the other side of the coin, a person can work on this psychic level of spiritual psychology and clear all these aspects I have listed, but if they don't do the psychological work I have described in the *Soul Psychology* book, they will not recover completely and achieve full Self-realization. This might be described as the work of the mystic and the work of the occultist that needs to be blended and combined.

What I am about to share with you, which is so incredibly exciting, is a method by which you can clear both levels yourself without necessarily having to rely on other people to help you. My *Soul Psychology* book was written in a way to help you do this on the occult side of spiritual psychology.

The purpose of this chapter is to give you the tools and information to clear and heal the psychic level of spiritual psychology. Most people rely on other practitioners to help them on this level, which is fine. The ultimate goal, however, is to be able to do it yourself. This is what Djwhal Khul, Vywamus and the Synthesis Ashram is now offering all lightworkers regardless of what ray type or inner plane ashram you are connected to.

An Overview of the Work

The first step in this process is to call forth from Djwhal Khul and Vywamus a golden seal, or golden dome of protection for all the work you will be doing. Step number two is to call forth again from Djwhal Khul, Vywamus and your own Mighty I Am Presence that a corridor be set up between you and the Interdimensional Synthesis Ashram of Djwhal Khul. Step three is to request to be taken in your spiritual body into the ashram for healing, clearing, and ascension activation work.

You will be coming to the Interdimensional Synthesis Ashram for many specific types of clearing work. At each session you will request specifically what type of clearing and purification you require. In one session you might request that your negative extraterrestrial implants be cleared. In another session request removal of any astral entities. In a third meditation request from Djwhal Khul and Vywamus that they clear your negative elementals and/or parasites. In another session still, request that they remove all negative imprints from past lives. This chapter will describe in great detail all the different negative psychic debris that must be cleared from your physical, etheric, astral, mental and spiritual bodies.

I want to emphasize here that you do not need to be clairvoyant, clairaudient, or psychic at all to do any of the work I am discussing in this chapter. That is what is so beautiful about this. If you are clairvoyant or clairaudient all the better, however it is completely inconsequential to the process. It is just a matter of allowing the Masters to do the work for you upon your request. All they need is an invitation. Everyone can feel energy. You will feel lots of energy sensations going on in your head and throughout your bodies as this is going on.

What I am sharing with you now is a new dispensation that has been given to mankind in recent times. You don't even have to completely understand the process to take advantage of it. The main point is to get purified and cleaned out from these unwanted negative aspects. In this chapter I will attempt to give you in intricate detail a greater understanding of what it is you are clearing and purifying.

It is also a very good idea to request this as you are going to bed every night. This will allow the Masters to work on you and clear you while you sleep. It is a lot less expensive than traditional therapy or going to a psychic healer. I am not putting down spiritual counseling or psychic healers for I am one myself. I am just pointing out the classic story of why give a person a fish to eat when you can teach them to fish. This is the first time in my entire life I have come across a method by which lightworkers can, in both an occult and mystic fashion clear themselves. The Ascended Masters don't even charge money. You can't beat that.

It must be understood that all physical diseases or physical problems as well as all psychological problems have these negative implants, negative elementals, parasites, negative astral aspects, etheric mucous, or etheric damage, connected to it. In the future medical doctors will work with psychic spiritual healers as a team.

Psychologists and spiritual counselors will be trained in this work as well, or work with a specialist in this area to achieve a complete healing. I emphasize here again, you can obtain mastery of your mind, emotions, and body and still have negative implants, astral entities, parasites, negative imprints, etheric mucous and negative elementals in your field. This applies to all lightworkers.

The amazing thing, however, is that it is not that big of a deal to get rid of all these things, and this is the purpose of this chapter. I will also discuss later how you can do this work with other people, such as students, family, friends and even people who are not consciously open to this level of understanding.

Much of this toxic psychic energy was implanted in childhood, and in past lives. The negative extraterrestrial implants exist in all the bodies, (physical, etheric, astral, mental). Negative imprints are a result of past life traumas. For example, you may have been stabbed by a sword in a past life, and that sword on a psychic level is still stuck in you. This needs to be removed. Sometimes it gets complicated because as you move toward the third initiation and merge with your soul, you begin to also connect with your eleven other soul extensions from your soul family. Sometimes you will begin clearing your soul extensions' past life imprints, which are like parallel lives. As you move higher in the initiation process into the monadic level or spirit level, which exists beyond the soul level, you can begin clearing imprints from your monadic family of 144 soul extensions' parallel lives.

All this astral and psychic debris is often the core cause of many viruses and bacterial infections. Medical doctors are only dealing with the physical or material level and not addressing the true cause. When we are implanted by negative extraterrestrials, usually during a traumatic event like an accident, depression, divorce, drugs, any physical or psychological imbalance, this usually allows the negative elementals, also called parasites, to create more havoc as well. The negative elementals are negative thoughtforms that attach themselves to different parts of our physical and metaphysical bodies.

They are what then often allows viruses and bacteria to enter first the etheric body, then the emotional body and eventually the physical body. The physical body has a natural defense mechanism that fights this; however the metaphysical body doesn't. The parasites or negative elementals go through the openings in the molecules and attach themselves to places in the body that are most vulnerable. Any area of weakness that you have in your physical, emotional and/or mental bodies is guaranteed to have parasites and negative extraterrestrial implants.

This is nothing to be afraid of, for everybody on Earth has them and we have had them for all of our past lives. As one moves upward in their path of initiation it is important to clear them. This process of going to the Interdimensional Synthesis Ashram of Djwhal Khul allows you a way to clear yourself on a daily or weekly basis.

It is important for lightworkers to understand that even if someone has cleared their implants, they can and do come back. I used to be under the assumption that once they were cleared I was free. I know for absolute fact that is not true. All these things can and do at times get back in, although not to the same degree they once did. That is why it is essential that you have a tool and method for constantly re-clearing yourself that does not cost thousands of dollars. Everyone should learn to do this themselves.

This brings me to the discussion of protection. If lightworkers would make a habit of placing protection around themselves religiously three times a day, every morning upon getting up, every afternoon, and before bed, this negative invasion would be avoided to a great extent, though not necessarily completely. Weekly clearing regardless of your level of initiation is pretty much standard procedure for living in this world. The fact is also that it is no big deal getting rid of all this stuff with the tools and information I am supplying you in this chapter.

Psychic Holes In the Aura

Wherever we have psychic holes in the aura, this allows an opening for astral energies. I remember I once saw a psychic healer many years ago who told me there was a small torpedo like hole in my aura in the front my body. She said it came when I was a child. I was able to trace it to when my parents were having a major fight and about to split up. It was the worst fight my parents ever had. The negative energy from this fight, even though I was in the other room, blasted a hole in my aura that I carried with me for thirty-five years. The psychic healer patched it up. You can request the Masters and etheric healing team to repair any holes or leaks.

Raising the Energies into the Light

The very interesting thing that the Masters do with all these negative psychic aspects is to bring light into them, dissolve them, raise them into the Light and back into the Central Sun, and then bring that same energy back into your four-body system in a reclassified manner. I personally find this fascinating. No energy is wasted. The same energy that was causing illness and weak-nesses is transformed and brought back for the opposite purpose. As the different negative psychic energies are removed this allows the etheric body to return to its perfected form. Most people don't realize that the etheric body or blueprint body can be damaged. This is why many people who have chronic illness never get better no matter what they do. If you are operating out of a tainted mold, so to speak, how can you possibly heal? After all the negative psychic aspects are removed, request that your etheric body be repaired.

Sensing Implants

Negative implants can be seen clairvoyantly, however, your clairvoyance must be turned to them. Most people don't realize that there are hundreds of levels and degrees of clairvoyance. Just because a person is clairvoyant doesn't mean they will see the implants. Some see certain kinds and don't see others. One way to help in this process is by calling the Universal Light from Vywamus. This Universal White Light helps one to see them. The implants often look like pods or swollen seeds or spidery forms, or as some kind of technical device. They tend to pulsate and feel warm to those who are more clairsentient.

There are common places in the body where implants can usually be found. The throat and glands are very common, and in the lymph nodes. Any growths on the physical body will contain them along with elementals. The third eye is a common place for implants as well as the sinuses, and the heart. The implants in the heart tend to block the functioning of the immune system. The upper chest is another place, along with the underarms. The solar plexus is where negative elementals (parasites) are often found as well as the glands, nerves and genitals. Usually the more abuse in childhood, the more the implants and parasites.

Pets and Implants

Your pets can have negative implants also. Bring your pet into the ashram and call forth the Inner Plane Healing Masters to clear your animal friends, asking for permission from their Higher Self. Permission must be obtained first.

AIDS and Psychic Attachments

Djwhal Khul said in his training that parasite removal and this type of over-all clearing can have an enormous benefit. The key here as with all disease is to what extent has the psychic attachments damaged the physical vehicle. This would apply to cancer also. If you can catch it early enough, profound shifts can take place. Physical regeneration is still possible no matter what the stage, however, as we all know, the physical body is the slowest to recover once damage has occurred. Regardless of what stage, clearing should be done immediately. Even if the person dies from AIDS or cancer the clearing achieved will allow a much greater passing to a higher level on the inner plane.

No matter what kind of disease you are dealing with; be it schizophrenia, multiple personalities, anorexia, or bulimia, it will be connected to parasites and probably negative implants. Where there is a physical, emotional or mental weakness or vulnerability, these psychic infestations will be there.

Gray Field

People who have chronic neurosis or phobias often have a "gray field" around them which is a by-product of chronic attack from these types of implants, elementals and astral entities or negative astral aspects. For a complete healing every person on Earth must be cleared not just physically or psychologically, but also etherically and astrally. All disease is caused in this astral level first and then moves to the other bodies.

The Psychological Level and Negative Elementals

When a person doesn't do their psychological work of clearing the negative ego and all negative emotions and qualities of judgment, anger, superiority complex, violence, abusiveness, inferiority, to name a few, these negative qualities, especially the emotionally loaded ones, attract negative elementals to them. This is why both the psychological and psychic astral levels must be cleared simultaneously, or one will defeat the other.

It also must be understood that there are positive elementals of love, joy and inner peace which are of a beneficial nature and that will help to build this positive type of habit.

One of the basic requests that everyone should ask for when doing healing with self or others is to ask that the physical, emotional, and mental bodies return to the Light of the soul. For it is in the soul or Higher Self that all work is done. This may sound silly to ask such a simple thing. I assure you it isn't. Until one takes the third initiation they are not really fully connected with the soul and/or Higher Self yet. The third initiation is the soul merge initiation. It is not until the fourth initiation that this merger is complete. The Higher Self basically does not pay attention to the incarnated personality until the incarnated personality pays close attention to the soul. This is why we find some people in this world doing all kinds of criminal and sociopathic types of things, which a person who is connected to their soul can't possibly understand.

Djwhal Khul has stated in this training that there are three basic aspects to this process when working with self or others. The first is to help the personality to realign with the soul. The second is to help the person make the connection to the Interdimensional Synthesis Ashram. The third is facilitating the removal and transmutation of all toxic astral energies.

The Rays and The Purification Process

Another way of working to clear this astral and etheric debris is to call on the rays. The seventh ray of Saint Germain is the violet transmuting flame and can be of great help in this work. Another ray that is extremely helpful is the eighth ray, which is the violet and green flame, and is especially used for "cleansing purposes."

The Fear Matrix Removal Program

One of the keys to removing all of the psychic attachments as I mentioned earlier is the matrix removal program. Call upon Djwhal Khul and Vywamus especially to do this work. After calling it forth it will appear as a network of golden white light strands that will superimpose themselves over a person's light grid and through all the chakras. This serves to make all irregular etheric parts visible. The matrix removal program serves not only to remove the core fear from your four-body system but to also remove implants and then parasites.

You should start in your first meditation with core fear removal. This can take a while because you are removing fear from not only this life but all your past lives, and at times even your soul extensions. Then move to focusing on removing all alien implants. This can take up to an hour or longer. Then move to parasites or negative elementals. Then you can move down the rest of the list I gave you such as negative imprints, etheric mucous, repairing etheric damage, astral entities and so on.

This three-stage process could be done in one session if it is done with a team of healers. If it is being done by one person or for yourself it is better to break it up into three sessions. The Hierarchy wishes to get as many lightworkers cleared as possible, so please share this book and its information with as many people as possible.

Your New Monadic Blueprint Body

As mentioned earlier, most people's etheric body has been tainted from traumas in this life or past lives. It is good to have it repaired and it is even better to call forth the anchoring and activation of your new monadic blueprint body. This is much like your Mayavarupa body, which is a perfect blueprint body of your Mighty I Am Presence. By calling forth to Djwhal Khul and Vywamus for this body you will be assured to be working with a perfect mold prior to ascension.

Self-Inquiry

On the psychological level you always want to be vigilant over every thought you think for it is your thoughts that create your reality. It is your thoughts that create your feelings, emotions, behavior, physical body and what you attract or repel in your life. This being the case you constantly want to be vigilant for God and His kingdom. This means to deny any thought that isn't of God to enter your mind. It means to push all negative thoughts out of your mind and to turn your attention like a channel changer to only positive spiritual thoughts. It is just a matter of where you put your attention. Keep your attention on the Christ attitude, not the negative ego thoughts.

Lightworkers are not vigilant enough in this regard. There is the tendency to go on automatic pilot too easily. Negative thoughts will lead to negative feelings, emotions and the attention of negative elementals, parasites and lower astral entities. Sai Baba has called this process Self-Inquiry, and says it is 75% of the spiritual path. Negative ego is the cause of all problems. There is no other problem. You don't want to give it your attention. This is also why Sai Baba says that the definition of God is, "God equals man minus ego."

Negative Emotions

Negative emotions come from negative egotistical thinking. This is a fact!!! A great many lightworkers don't realize this. Practice self-inquiry with your negative emotions also. Another even better term is attitudinal healing. When a negative emotion comes up immediately reinterpret the situation with your Christ Mind which will instantly release the negative emotion. For further explanation read the *Soul Psychology* book if you haven't read it already. There is also a time and place for catharsis or in other words giving it expression as a form of release. As you get more mastery of the process of attitudinal healing you will need to rely on catharsis less and less. You will more and more, and for longer periods of time, remain in a state of consciousness of love, joy, even-mindedness, inner peace, and forgiveness.

Physical Illness

It is always important to work on all three levels: spiritually, psychologically, and physically. Do not give physicalness your power. Know in truth that it is an illusion, for Christ can't be sick. As Yogananda said, even on your death bed you should be affirming you are in perfect radiant health. Whatever you think is programming the subconscious to create that in your physical body. Work with homeopathics, herbs, good nutrition, fresh air, sunshine, daily exercise. Drink lots of pure water to clear out as much of the physical toxins as you can. Finding a good homeopathic doctor can be extremely helpful in this regard. The removal of physical toxins will help strengthen your immune system on the physical level just as removing all the psychological and psychic toxins will strengthen your psychological immune system.

Periods of Rest

When your initial psychic clearing meditations are over it is a good idea to rest. Much of this work is like psychic surgery. Don't have the Masters remove all your implants and then go to a wild party. A lot of the work being done in this chapter takes place in hours that past disciples took many lifetimes to do.

Releasing Astral Entities

These astral entities are attracted though gross traumas that have brought misalignment of the energy field. They are also attracted from lower-self thinking rather than thinking only from your Higher Self. A person living a low life existence will attract low life entities. Drug addiction is another guaranteed way to attract them, as well as alcohol abuse. Sometimes these negative entities are carried over from past lifetimes. This may occur when a soul has chosen to reincarnate too quickly. In extreme cases such as this there are usually massive holes in the aura and many negative elementals.

In working with yourself or another person in this process it is very important to request the full force of Djwhal Khul, Kuthumi, and Lord Maitreya's ashram to surround the entity and ask that it be dissolved, consumed and/or removed immediately. Some entities are of a psychic nature, and some are confused souls. When working with another person invite them into the Synthesis Ashram with you. Get their permission, either directly or on a spiritual level for this work to be done. In working with another person be sure you are sealed in a ball of golden light. In super extreme cases you can call forth the Karmic Board for consultation and help. All negative energies associated with this process are transformed into Light and brought back cleansed and purified.

Animals and Astral Energies

Animals have a spiritual mission in this lifetime also. They will often take on the problems of their owner in an attempt to burn off karma for them. There is very often a mirroring process between your pet's health and your health. Some animal's missions are to act as a sacrificial karma clearer and others to just transmute. For this reason you should work on your animals like you would with your self, again call the inner plane Healing Masters to keep them healthy and to remove implants, astral entities, and negative elementals.

Djwhal Khul's Light profiles

Djwhal Khul keeps Light profiles of the lightworkers he works with. It is like a computer screen that shows the aura and overall development of each student he is working with. Even though Djwhal Khul is a second ray Ascended Master almost all students of all seven rays spend time training in his ashram because of his unique focus of spiritual education which is the key element of the second ray. Through these Light profiles he studies brainwaves, thinking, emotional life, physical health, service work, initiation level, light quotient level, and ascension readiness of all he meets.

More on Extraterrestrial Implants

The negative Extraterrestrials use the implants for many reasons. One is that the energy from your body can be siphoned off at night while you sleep. The implants serve as a type of energy sucker. Another function of these negative implants is as a tracking and/or monitoring device. Another function is information gathering, and blocking of Light Forces. There are a great many on this planet who are almost completely taken over by these devices.

Positive Implants

There are what might be called positive implants that are placed by the Ascended Masters, or higher cosmic beings and more advanced ascended extraterrestrials such as the Arcturians or the Ashtar Command. One example of this is the microtron by Metatron, which I have spoken of in my other books.

The Prana Wind Clearing Device

One other very useful tool given to Djwhal Khul's ashram by the Arcturians is the Prana Wind clearing device. It is like a fan that's anchored in your solar plexus which serves to blow away all the negative etheric mucous, and to blow energy through all the meridians and nadis to clear your whole field. This is something that could be used everyday when coming home from work, or whenever there is any sense of contamination. Just request that it be anchored by Djwhal Khul, Vywamus, and/or the Arcturians and it will instantly be done. Even if you can't clairvoyantly see it, you will feel it.

Core Love

Whenever you are doing this work, when you are done it is a good idea to call in core love which, of course, is the opposite of core fear. Any time you give fear it tends to feed the implants and negative elementals and negative astral entities, core love does the opposite. Perfect love casts out fear. When the core matrix fear removal program is called in, you can release any fear that comes up for you. The Masters just suck it out like a vacuum cleaner. It is rather extraordinary. In the case of implants, the matrix removal program will surround the implant with a very fine filament of golden white light and simply dissolve it along with any negative elementals.

Astral Disease

All physical or psychological disease appears in the astral or emotional body first, before moving into the physical body. Call to the Masters and request all astral or etheric disease be removed from your four-body system and not allowed to enter your physical body. Can you imagine if this was taught in school and all school children practiced this everyday, through all grade levels. This is true preventative medicine. All forms of disease, cancer, tumors, growths, malignancies could be dissolved before manifesting into the physical as adults.

Self-Love

If there is one thing that might be called a panacea of life, it is self-love. If a person doesn't develop a healthy self-concept and self-image and self-love, much of what we are a talking about is in danger of returning. If this is a lesson for you, work with the affirmations in the soul psychology book. Study the information I have shared on the subject and work with other tools, and this problem can be easily remedied. It is as easy to self-love as it is to self-hate. It is just a matter of thinking and programming your computer in a different way than how your parents or society has programmed you. Any new habit can be created in 21 days.

The Divine Plan

After you have been cleared of implants, core fear, negative elementals, astral entities, negative imprints, etheric mucous, you will find and see your etheric grid reconnecting and coming back into proper alignment. All ingredients are now in place for the perfect unfoldment of your personal Divine Plan and service mission, and the way is made clear for the completion of your seven levels of initiation.

Soul Fragments

In Djwhal Khul's training there is also one other interesting discussion on the understanding of soul fragments. Occasionally fragments of the Self, sometimes called fragments of the soul or personality parts that the soul builds through the lifetime, can scatter because of trauma and become attached to an individual and be carried along in a piggyback fashion. Djwhal Khul said that sometimes this is carried in the form of another personality, and if it is severe enough creates a psychosis or multiple personality situation. Ask Djwhal Khul and Vywamus to remove all soul fragments that don't belong to you, and to help you call back all soul fragments that do belong to you in Divine Order under the guidance of your monad, and Mighty I Am Presence.

This soul fragment is of course different from a walk-in situation, which is a positive thing. It is also different from a soul braid, or the integration of several parts of the Self from the oversoul, or the future Self that is wishing to embark and become a part of the known person.

Other Consequences of Implants

One of the other consequences of negative Extraterrestrial implants is that they drain energy away, which causes the etheric weave in the etheric body in that spot to collapse. This in part makes a person prone to disease in that area of the body. It also serves to disrupt the proper chemistry in the body and in that area. This causes a weakening of the entire immune system and also tends to tax the liver and lungs, because of greater toxicity that is created. Astral parasites and/or negative elementals are attracted, and this then creates a whole complex of problems that need to be lifted from the body. This complex web creates etheric mucous that is literally squeezing out the life force.

Eventually this whole process moves into the physical tissue, and is one reason why there is so much physical disease in our culture. Add to this negative thinking, negative emotions, stress, bad relationships, bad nutrition, pollution, environmental toxicity and you see why there is such a massive breakdown of the immune system in our culture. It is amazing, actually, that we do as well as we do.

The good news is that much of this can be transformed rather easily as I have been explaining in this chapter. The second piece of good news is that you can do it yourself on a daily or weekly basis. The third piece of good news is that you can take your friends and family with you. You can do this consciously with another person, or you can do it without their conscious permission. If you do it without their conscious permission, you must get permission from their Higher Self to do the work. This is helpful, for example, if you have a mate who is not open but you want them cleared anyway. Most of the time the Higher Self will say yes. However there are times when it won't. Make the request and ask the Masters to do the work if it is okay with their Higher Self and then just let go. Even If you are unclear what the answer is just put the whole affair into the Master's hands and let them work.

Fatigue

Fatigue is another factor that makes one vulnerable to implantation. This is a lesson we all deal with at times and is why it is a good Idea to clear once a week. If you are overtired or run down or sick, request extra protection from Archangel Michael.

More on Attached Astral Entities

I want to make it clear that astral entities are not just confused or earthbound souls. There are a great many other kinds of astral entities of a more psychic nature which are not incarnated personalities that come under this umbrella. This occurs most often from one's parents when one was a child, usually when the parent is disturbed and in a rage, or an alcoholic, or sexual molestation occurs. Some aspect of the parental energy field will attach itself as an entity to the child. An energy that the parent is carrying will transfer partially or wholly to the child. This will cause the child's behavior to change dramatically.

It is a type of possession. This type of entity is most probably from the elemental kingdom. This is an etheric form that bonds with the mineral based body and the etheric body of a child or person. It begins to form an interfering system of psychological response, and interferes with normal development and growth. Most criminals involved with violence have this type of attached entity.

There are other types of elemental entities that are not Earth based but rather psychologically based. They can attach to the brain, mind and nervous system of a child or adult. They mimic whatever they are given as stimulation. If they are given the example of mistreatment, they will mimic that state of consciousness. This will increase the harmful messages going through the individual's consciousness. This forms a type of tape loop and positive messages are screened out. All positive emotions can also be screened out in extreme cases. At times in life we all see individuals who are in this type of sorry state and we wonder how could they get so fouled up. Understanding some of these mechanisms that were installed in childhood can give us greater compassion for those tragic souls.

In many cases a co-dependency is created by the individual with these entities even though it is of a disturbed nature. There is a saying that a person would rather stay in negativity than change, for change is scary. They have no experience as to what positive support is. So negative support is better than the unknown. It seems to me that many people stay in bad marriages for the same reason.

A third type of astral entity is an Extraterrestrial attachment of a lower nature. This again is not a walk-in situation, or a soul braid. The extraterrestrial astral entity has lost connection with its own source and rides piggyback in a vain attempt to feed itself. This type of connection is again made during some kind of trauma such as a life threatening illness, car accident, or separation, where the individual on Earth felt afraid and wanted company. He/she reached out but without conscious discrimination and this is what walked through the door, so to speak.

Djwhal Khul has suggested that all parents teach their children from the earliest possible age to understand prayer, and to talk to their guardian angel, and angels in general. The earlier a child can form this spiritual connection the better.

There could also be entities from other lifetimes or entities that jump into the energy field because of death in a war. Even worse would be a combination of the aforementioned astral entity possessions. The most important thing here is that all these can be removed in a matter of twenty minutes in Djwhal Khul's Interdimensional Synthesis Ashram.

Having Others Help You with This Process

There is nothing wrong with having someone help you with this process. If you want help call me and I will provide you with that help in some form or another. If you need help in the beginning that is fine. It is just a matter of developing the confidence in yourself that you can do this.

Irritations, Spots, and Leaks

One other thing you might ask Djwhal Khul and Vywamus to do is repair and heal any spots or irritations in your etheric, astral, and/or mental body. This can also be addressed to the Inner Plane Healing Masters. Also request that all leaks in your four-body system be repaired.

Repatterning

It is also important that once this work is done there be a procedure of positive repatterning. This is similar to what I said earlier about bringing in core love. Once you remove core fear, you must replace it with something or there is a void. The opposite of core fear is core love. This is why it is helpful to put yourself on an affirmation and prayer program for 21 days. Use the affirmations, meditations and prayers in my *Soul Psychology* book, in *Beyond Ascension*, and in *The Complete Ascension Manual*, especially the meditation at the end of the book. This will cement the new habit, which takes 21 days to solidify.

Motives

One other golden key is to examine with devastating honesty your motives for doing all that you do. Are your motives coming from the negative ego or your Christ Consciousness and soul? The negative ego can be very tricky, and very selfish. Really be honest with yourself in this regard. Clearing negative ego motives may be the single hardest lesson on the entire spiritual path. It is very easy to pass what I am saying over and say, "Oh I mastered that in the Spring of '72"!!! This is an area we all need to be constantly vigilant about!!!

Visiting Other Planets between Lives

Many souls obviously do not achieve their ascension, which is the movement into the fifth dimension. This leaves them, of course, in the reincarnation process. This is no judgment but rather just part of the process of evolution. While spending time between incarnations in the fourth dimension it is also possible to visit the other planets. What most people don't realize is that other planets have other dimensional bodies, as does the Earth. Vywamus spoke of nine different levels of Earth and I am sure it is the same for other planets.

I bring this subject up because often in visiting these other fourth dimensional planets in our solar system between lives people also pick up implants. As you remember, this was also why Melchizedek recommended not going to the ascension seats on these planets, because they are fourth dimensional in nature. Once in the fifth dimension you are above the implanting process; something to consider in your ever evolving cosmic journey!!!

Requesting Dispensations from The Karmic Board

In the practice of doing your healing work in service of the Divine Plan in whatever form you are working in, on occasion you will come across certain clients that are more difficult than others. It is possible at these times to call forth to the Lords of Karma for special dispensations on their behalf. One example of this might be after clearing all their negative implants, elementals, and astral entities, ask that a greater merger now occur between the client's personality and soul and monad, with a special dispensation to help the person disengage from their lower self, if this prayer is in harmony with God's Will!!!

The Golden Cylinder

Another phenomenal method for removing implants, elementals, and a varied assortment of negative energies is called the Golden Cylinder of Lord Arcturus. I would recommend using this once you have done a massive matrix removal clearing. Once you have been cleared, the Golden Cylinder can be used as a very quick method of clearing. What I am sharing with you here is an absolute gold mine, so please have the eyes to see and the ears to hear. This is one of the most phenomenal tools I have ever shared. I personally have been using it every day or every other day just to purify and refine my field. The Arcturian technologies are so fabulous they are beyond description.

All you have to do is call to the Lord of Arcturus and the Arcturians to anchor the Golden Cylinder, just as you would the Prana Wind clearing device. It comes in and just sucks all the negative energies out. You can ask for implants, negative elementals, and negative energy to be removed. It is a very quick way to clear your field whenever you need help. Try it, you'll like it!!!

Universal White Light

One other method for removing alien implants is to call in the Universal White Light. This type of Light serves to highlight the imbalanced energies lodged in one's field. They often cannot be seen without this Light. Just because a person is clairvoyant doesn't mean they are even seeing one tenth of what is really going on in the inner plane. There are levels and degrees of clairvoyance. Most clairvoyants do not even see alien implants, and if they do they can see only a small fraction of the ones that are there. Using this Universal White Light, which is like a white mist, can help in this regard.

The Crystal Light Technology of The Arcturians and Melchizedek

Experience yourself in a crystal cave. Ask the Arcturians and Melchizedek to send down a projection of crystal. You sit right underneath this crystal that is like a feeder tube. A liquid crystal is siphoned into the crown of the head. You are now receiving a treatment of crystal energies. Drink and absorb this in. It is knitting the bones into the structure of the perfect body to carry the Light. It creates a structure and foundation for your Light body physically.

Feel the crystalline structure of your own form. This crystal light technology is another road to healing on many, many levels. Melchizedek told us the liquid crystal has the effect of "neutralizing" all imbalanced energies within the physical, etheric, astral, mental, and spiritual bodies. What he recommends is that after you sit for a while in the crystal cave and absorb the liquid crystal, call forth the Golden Cylinder of the Arcturians to pull out and vacuum up any and all negative energy that has now been neutralized.

This Arcturian crystal light technology will also neutralize all alien implants, which is another enormous advantage. When you are done you must ask to remove the neutralized energy. This is very important.

So this technology is a two-step process. All of the various Arcturian technologies can be divided into two aspects. The first is the "neutralizing" effect, and the second is activational.

Next call to Lord of Arcturus to place a crystal in each chakra. Breathe deeply and allow this process to take place. Ask him to then activate these crystals. You will feel them begin to spin in each chakra in a clockwise manner. Feel the expansion from front to back and back to front in each chakra. This creates a feeling and reality in your chakras of one unified chakra. Breathe deeply and allow this to be incorporated through your whole body system. These crystals are very light but very strong. They are gifts from the Masters that you must go out into the world with and share the Light that they help to intensify!!!

Crystal Technology for Healing Etheric Wounds

Call to the Lord of Arcturus and the Arcturians to come forth with their liquid crystal technology to cauterize any etheric wound on all levels. This is done from the furthest reaches within, traveling outwards until healed. Call forth to Vywamus to reweave the etheric webbing upon request. This creates a true healing, for the etheric wound will no longer be present. It brings all the bodies back to their original state.

Crystalline Protection for Children

This next tool is specifically designed for children, not for adults. It is a new technology designed to help New Age children who are very vulnerable when young. This tool is for the purpose of providing extra protection as the healing is going on. Call forth to Djwhal Khul, Lord Maitreya, Vywamus, and the Lord of Arcturus for a crystalline web of golden screening protection. It is placed around the field of the child, enfolding it and creating a barrier until the child is able to hold the healing totally within themselves. This is available to any and all children of your own or children you work with. Just ask.

Ascended Master Organ Beam

When dealing with a weak organ, ask the Ascended Masters to send an energy beam into that organ for five days to strengthen it.

Bach Flower Remedies

Bach flower remedies are a wonderful tool for healing. The Futureplex line has products, three of which are: biofield protection, anger release, and fear release, which really work. As an added support you might try this most effective tool.

Aromatherapy

Aromatherapy can be another extremely helpful tool in your overall healing. Healing can come through smell, taste, touch, sight, hearing, the mind, emotions, physical body or spirit.

The Spiritual Faucet

One of the healing techniques that you might request if you are having weak-ness with an organ such as the liver, pancreas, spleen, gallbladder, or kidneys, is the Spiritual Faucet or Spiritual Spigot technique.

Usually there is a cloud of etheric mucous that surrounds an organ having trouble. Request of the Inner Plane Healing Masters to install a faucet into the organ on an etheric level. Whenever the etheric mucous starts to build up this faucet will automatically drain it. When you are feeling symptomatic in that organ, you can also make a request to the Masters and your etheric body that the faucet be opened to that organ to drain the negative energy.

Etheric Needles, Bullets, and Darts

In the process of living on Earth, every person here runs into the anger of other people. This may be a spouse, relationship, family member, child, business partner, friend, or acquaintance. What most people don't realize is that when a person is angry, this sends etheric needles, bullets, and darts into the other person's field. These become lodged in the etheric body. Earlier in my life I was involved with a lady who did not have a great deal of control over her emotional body and negative ego, even though she was a major lightworker.

Upon our breakup she was creating a great deal of anger within her own consciousness. This was not something that was unique to me, however, in that moment I seemed to be the brunt of her focus. I was not engaging her in this behavior. After our breakup, I was doing "Spring cleaning" on my four-body system and the Masters told me that my liver was filled with needles or darts, like a porcupine, from the anger of this person.

A lot of this had occurred on the psychic or inner plane level and not overtly. I had been having liver symptoms and this is what was poisoning my liver. This, of course, is a universal phenomenon and is something that all Lightworkers should ask the Inner Plane Healing Masters to remove. They had to pull these darts and needles out one by one being careful not to poison my system in the process. I felt much better after having them removed. A number of them had also lodged in my pancreas.

The main lesson here is to not attack even if attacked. Lesson number two is if you are being attacked or have been attacked in the past, ask the Masters to remove this stuff from your etheric body wherever it may be lodged. A lot of time we don't realize it, but we have been carrying these needles, darts, pins and bullets for many, many years and sometimes many lifetimes.

Summation of Things to Request Djwhal Khul and Vywamus Clear from Your Field

Alien Implants
Astral Entities
Negative Elementals
Parasites
Core Fear
Imprint Removal
Physical Illness
Etheric Damage
Gray Fields
Irritations, Spots, and Leaks in the Four-Body System Aura
Negative Thoughts
Negative Emotions
All Negative Ego Programming
Removal of Improper Soul Fragments That Belong to You
Repair Bodies
Clear and Repair Chakras
Clear Archetypes

Review of the Process

- Either sit up or lie down.
- Request the Golden Dome of Protection.
- Ask to be connected with and to be taken to the Synthesis Ashram of Djwhal Khul in a bi-location experience.
- Call forth Djwhal Khul and Vywamus and the Matrix Removal Program.
- One by one request the removal of the aforementioned list of psychic attachments.

- Relax and become passive and let the Masters work on you without moving around.
- Do one meditation for each psychic attachment on the list for the big ones, and two at a time for the more generalized and easier ones to clear.
- Do a clearing once a week or every couple of weeks, or whenever you feel the need.
- Clear your pets simultaneously, for the Masters can work on many beings at the same time. If necessary, call in other Masters.
- Call in friends and relatives and students once you are accustomed to the process, however, always ask permission of the person's Higher Self and the Masters when working with others.

An Even Deeper Body Cleansing

When this aforementioned process is completed then I recommend an even deeper physical body cleansing. For example, ask to have your liver cleansed and cleared by Djwhal Khul, Vywamus and the Inner Plane Healing Masters. The liver may have dark spots in it from past life or present life abuse! For area of weakness ask for it to be cleared and cleansed. Some possible examples of this type of clearing might be requesting a cleansing and clearing of:

Liver
Pancreas
Kidneys
Gall Bladder
Lymph System
Bloodstream
Nervous System
Bones
Glandular system
Spleen

Heart
Lungs
All Toxins
All Obstructions
Genital System
Muscular System
Colon
Small and Large Intestines
Brain
Stomach
Upgrading the Immune System

It is probably best here to focus on the inner plane Healing Masters. Go to the Synthesis Ashram healing seat for a truly preventative type of medicine. This clears the dark spots that could eventually manifest in the physical tissue.

A Complete Clearing

After you have gotten used to being worked on in the Synthesis Ashram and make it part of your regular routine, you can eventually shorten the process by just going into the Ashram and calling for the Matrix Removal Program for Djwhal and Vywamus and/or the Inner Plane Healing Masters and then requesting a complete clearing. At first you can read the list through quickly. In the future, after the routine in established, you can just say you want a complete clearing.

Doing this is kind of like taking your car in for its 50,000 mile overhaul and tune-up. Call forth the Matrix Removal program in the Synthesis Ashram anytime you feel your fields getting contaminated and run down by the lessons of Earth Life. I think we all agree that the planetary mystery school called Earth Life can be a tough one.

The Synthesis Ashram of Djwhal Khul and the Matrix Removal Program can be an absolutely invaluable tool for keeping yourself clear. Perhaps you can now see why in the beginning of the chapter I said that this healing seat in Djwhal Khul's ashram is as important as the ascension seats. See you in the Ashram!!! Namaste.

11

Dr. Lorphan's Healing Academy on Sirius

My beloved readers, it brings me great joy to begin this particular chapter. It is a common belief among many lightworkers not to value the physical body as much as the emotional, mental and spiritual bodies. It is very important for lightworkers to understand that the physical body is one of GOD's bodies as well. Everyone on the spiritual path has to deal with health lessons in one form or another. No one escapes this. Some people's physical bodies may be weaker than others, however, other people may have weaker emotional bodies, mental bodies, spiritual bodies or psychological selves. Everyone who is on an accelerated spiritual path will have physical health lessons to contend with. This is not necessarily from being sick or ill or from doing anything wrong, but from the accelerated speed of growth in the spiritual vehicle, mental vehicle, emotional vehicle and the etheric vehicle. Every time these bodies take a leap in spiritual evolution the physical body must catch up in vibration. I'm reminded of an incident at one of the Wesak Celebrations where Sai Baba and the Ascended Masters were giving a shaktipat through me as I touched people's third eye with Sai Baba's amrita or Divine nectar. I did this for three or four hundred people, which served to increase their vibrational frequencies. A couple of hours later, one woman reported that after she received the shaktipat from Sai Baba that she lost the vision in one of her eyes, partially. This again was just a quantum leap in the octave of light she was holding, which the physical vehicle was trying to catch up with. I called in the Ascended Masters to help in the situation and her physical eye lesson quickly recovered and she was fine. I share this story to only point out how even people in perfect health on a physical level are going to have health lessons from accelerated spiritual growth. When planetary spiritual energies are pouring in many lightworkers get wiped out for many days. This would be another example.

Other lightworkers might have physical health problems from doing too much meditation, or too many ascension activations. Other lightworkers develop physical health problems because of emotional lessons that are going on in their subconscious mind. Other lightworkers may develop health lessons from doing too much mental or spiritual work. Other lightworkers still develop health lessons from being too heavenly and hence not being physically grounded enough. One of the main points I'm making here is that physical health lessons are not bad. They are part and parcel of the spiritual path. Often light workers are very judgmental and self-righteous when dealing with people who have health lessons often making the person feel bad by intonating that the person is doing something wrong and that they should figure out the cause immediately.

I'm here to tell you, my beloved readers, that their physical health lessons may be a sign that they're doing something right. It just may be a sign that they are growing spiritually at a very accelerated rate. It may also be a sign that they are doing a cleansing to reach a more purified level of GOD Realization. If they weren't focused on their spiritual life this may not even be happening. They also might be cleansing planetary karma as an act of service on some level. It might be a past life cleansing or cleansing an integration of a soul extension from one's Oversoul and Monad.

Other lightworkers may be given health lessons by GOD to balance certain past karma and it is not because they are doing anything wrong in this lifetime. So, my friends, the possibilities are endless and there is not one of us on the planet that does not live by the axiom "But by the

Grace of GOD go I." We all need to be much more compassionate and understanding with our fellow brothers and sisters who are dealing with physical health lessons.

As we evolve spiritually we also take on spiritual leadership and much greater responsibility. We also take on great responsibility for many students and clients. All these things can take a toll on the physical vehicle no matter how evolved you are. The physical vehicle reflects every thought we think, every emotion we feel, every energy we channel, the food we eat, and every action we take. The more evolved we become the quicker our karma. The more evolved we become the more refined and sensitive our vehicles become.

Living in a dense, unrefined world doing service work will put stress on the physical vehicle no matter what level of initiation. I have just been speaking here of all the spiritual reasons why the physical body has ailments. I have not even begun to get into all the physical reasons why the physical body breaks down such as diet, accidents, pollution, lack of physical exercise, bacteria, viruses, poor sleep habits, job stress, relationship stress, weakened physical immune systems, digestive problems, and genetic inherited weakness. The list is endless.

Let me end this section by saying again let us all be very compassionate to ourselves and others. When we are going through health lessons it is common for lightworkers to think that we are the only ones. I am here to tell you that is not true. All lightworkers have to confront physical health lessons for it is just the nature of living in this planetary mystery school called Earth and inhabiting physical vehicles. Let us also remember the Biblical quotation, "After pride cometh the fall." I can't help but remember a channeling that Edgar Cayce gave to a gentleman who I believe was paralyzed. In the reading he was told that his physical ailment stemmed from a past life where he had an Adonis type of physical body and he used to criticize others for not being as healthy and handsome as he was. This should give us all pause to think and to ignite the compassion of Lord Buddha and Quan Yin.

Personal Sharing

My beloved readers, I have had my share of health lessons as well and because the traditional medical establishment I found to be a waste of time for me personally I explored the more holistic, naturopathic, homeopathic, New Age forms of physical healing as I'm sure all of you have as well. I want to be clear here that I'm not putting down traditional medicine for it definitely has its place. I am just saying for me, personally, and the very subtle subclinical and spiritually induced physical lessons I was dealing with, traditional medicine was a total waste of time and money. It all depends on what kind of physical health lessons you're dealing with. My entire four-body system being so refined and purified, the taking of any drugs or invasive tests would be totally poisonous to me. As one medical doctor said to me one time, "You slipped through the cracks of Western medicine." I was dealing with such a level of spiritual subtlety that they didn't have a clue what to do with my particular health lessons at the time.

I found the entire holistic, naturopathic, homeopathic and New Age forms of healing and medicine to be fascinating and spent many years of my life cleansing residual toxins of the most refined nature. Things such as mercury fillings, vaccines, past antibiotics, metals, chemicals, parasites, vaccines, fungus, environmental toxins, past drugs used for healing, any mind altering drugs, disease toxins on a subclinical level (tuberculosis, cancer, Epstein-Barr, hepatitis are a few examples), caffeine, nicotine, lead (from paint), aluminum toxicity (from aluminum cookware), copper toxicity (copper pipes), radiation (too close to color T.V. and microwave), low grade electromagnetic disturbances (from all the electrical equipment in the home), alcohol, preservatives and toxins from poor diet and/or junk food to name a few. What I would recommend is finding a good New Age homeopathic practitioner and bring in this list and tell him or her that you want to cleanse all these things from your system. If you can't afford to do this, or you can't find one, then go to your nearest homeopathic pharmacy and they can recommend certain generic homeopathics that help cleanse these residual toxins from the organs, glands and blood.

Doing this cleansing of these residual toxins will do wonders for upgrading your immune system and increasing your vitality and overall health and energy. I also recommend taking homeopathics specifically for immune system building and organ cleansing. For greater emotional balance, I would recommend exploring Bach Flower Remedies taken in homeopathic form. For more information on this, I would recommend reading my book *How To Clear The Negative Ego*. Just as one wants to remove the mental toxin of negative ego from the mental body, one also wants to remove emotional toxins in the form of negative emotions from the emotional vehicle. One also wants to remove energetic toxins from the etheric vehicle. One also wants to remove physical toxins from the physical vehicle.

There are many New Age cutting-edge technologies for detecting these subtle toxins that have remained lodged in our organs and cells since childhood. The cleansing of all these residual toxins through the use of homeopathics and herbs was a very spiritual experience for I felt like I was spiritualizing my physical vehicle to a very great extent. This also went along with eating an extremely pure diet. I do not recommend that people become fanatical on this level, however, for me personally, because of my unique lessons and path, it was essential that I be very disciplined in this area. The combination of removing all the residual toxins and eating such a pure diet has kept my immune system working at a very good level. Taking the time to spiritualize the physical vehicle in this manner is well worth one's time, energy and even financial investment.

One thing I have learned in my life is that if the physical vehicle is not supporting me, it is very difficult to do all the spiritual and service work that I love to do so much. So again it is important to pay one's 'rent' to GOD on all levels (physical, etheric, emotional, mental and spiritual).

The physical body is as much GOD as is the spiritual body. All faces of GOD must be honored and sanctified.

The Continuing Journey

As time went on in my evolutionary journey of initiation and ascension I began moving more and more away from physical forms of healing, and physical cures and began relying much more on Spirit and energetic cures. Now I want to say here I am not recommending my particular path to my beloved readers. I feel the best path for most people is the balanced, integrated path. There is a time for Western medicine, a time for holistic New Age medicine, and there is a time to rely on Spirit and the Ascended Masters for help. Because of my incredibly refined and purified nature, system and mission, and incredibly subtle health lessons that were more energetic and electrical in nature, at one point in my life I stopped even taking herbs, homeopathics, vitamins and going to traditional medical and holistic New Age practitioners completely. I was so purified on those levels that it was a waste of time and my body no longer wanted to take any kind of physical substance of that kind. Again I emphasize I am not recommending this to other people, but for me personally it was the 100% right path.

I began relying much more on radionics which is the science of sending energy to my self from those substances such as homeopathics and herbs rather than taking the physical form itself. For me personally this worked much better and I found it to be much more effective. I went through a phase of getting laying on of hands treatments which for a period of my life was extremely helpful but eventually even that level became too gross for me. Now, my beloved readers, this whole process worked in conjunction with my initiation process. The higher I went in my initiation process and the more light I was carrying electrically the more I relied on Spirit for all my physical healing. This process also correlated with eating less and less amounts of food. At this stage of my life I still eat food in small amounts, however, in truth I am 90% now living on light. The amount of food I eat is so minute no third dimensional person would think that one could survive. Again I do not recommend this to my readers except in extremely rare cases for I think it is much better that people be balanced on all levels and eat normally. For me personally, because of my unique health lessons and mission this was the 100% right path for me to follow. I also have done this very slowly over many years and have waited to live on light predominately until almost my twelfth initiation. So I do not recommend stopping eating 'cold turkey' for there are a handful of people on this planet that this is their destiny and not eating very physical food and living mostly on light seems to be my destiny. To be honest this is not something that I necessarily want to do it is just something that just progressed in this direction because of my unique health lessons, mission and destiny. I will say here that I feel stronger physically on this path than I did eating a normal diet and that is why I'm on this path. I also asked Melchizedek, the Mahatma and Metatron to program my twelve body system through certain fire letters, sacred geometries and geometrical codes so I wouldn't lose weight and even though I still do eat some food and plan to continue this small amount of eating the rest of this incarnation I am not losing weight. The light is somehow being transformed into physical mass.

The Healing Academy of Dr. Lorphan

At this stage of my life having taken the twelfth initiation I completely rely on Spirit, Melchizedek, the Mahatma, Metatron, Dr. Lorphan, the Galactic Healers, Sai Baba, Archangel Raphael, the Platinum Angels, Sananda, Djwhal Khul, a group of Masters called the Core 7, the Lord of Arcturus, my Monad or Mighty I Am Presence, the Divine Mother and Lady Masters, the 7 Chohans and the Core 21 for all my healing needs.

Let me begin by introducing Dr. Lorphan who is my doctor. So, my beloved readers, I still have a doctor and the humorous thing about it is that he doesn't live on Earth, he lives in the Great White Lodge on Sirius. He is the finest doctor in the entire galaxy and he is the director and head trainer of all the healers in the Great White Lodge on Sirius. This is not the physical planet of Sirius but rather the etheric spiritual capitol of our planet, which Shamballa is an outpost for. Masters travel throughout the galaxy to train with him and his wonderful staff of galactic healers. My beloved readers, I am introducing him and his staff to you now so he may become your doctor as well. I recommend that you keep your traditional earthly physician, and New Age holistic practitioners, and now add Dr. Lorphan and his team of galactic healers to your team healing approach. Even though I only rely on Spirit, I want you, my beloved readers, to take advantage of all levels of healing support that are available to you. This is important in the concept of Integrated Ascension and synthesis, which my work is totally based upon. My unique mission to rely completely on Spirit allows me to bring this level of physical healing to you, my beloved readers, in a most unique and creative fashion. Because I rely so completely on Spirit for my physical health I am uniquely qualified to bring through this information for it is my personal experience. Maybe GOD has chosen this path for me for just this purpose. Most light workers don't realize the amount of help Spirit can provide even dealing with the dense physical vehicle. Remember, everything in the universe is just energy at different octaves of density. A dense ice cube when placed on the hot pavement melts into water and then steam. Spirit is like steam and the physical body is like the ice cube. All are just energy. The inner plane Ascended Masters are masters of energy transformation.

Healing Tools of Dr. Lorphan and His Healing Team

Let me begin by saying that Dr. Lorphan has asked me to write this chapter to let each of you know personally that he and his staff are willing to help any sincere lightworker with any and all physical health lessons that you are dealing with. The same offer applies to all the Ascended Masters, who are also incredible healers themselves. I personally use both Dr. Lorphan and his healing staff and many of the Ascended Masters who you are familiar with. I also call on the Archangels and Angels as well and certain extraterrestrial groups who have certain advanced technologies in this regard. On this note let me begin by describing some of the spiritual healing tools I use which I share for the sole purpose of making them available to you, my beloved readers. I am purposely describing these tools in a very succinct and concise manner to make them easy to access and apply. In the following chapter I will take more time to elaborate in more detail upon some of the more important ones. The purpose of this chapter is to just make them available to you in the most efficient, concise, practical way possible. On this note I will now unfold the revelation of these most Divine spiritual healing tools.

The first tool I use is actually one of Melchizedek's, the Mahatma's and Metatron's. It is called the Golden and/or Platinum Net. It is a net that you can call forth from Spirit, which filters and strains out any imbalanced or negative energy. I would recommend that you request this at least twice a day. I would also recommend that you ask that the Platinum Net be placed in all the doorways and archways in your home on a permanent basis. This way every time you walk through an archway or a doorway you are automatically cleansed. Ask for this for your family in terms of the Platinum and Golden Net and your pets. It will also serve to clear negative implants and elementals. Also ask the 3 M's to bring forth the Platinum Net four times a day (morning, noon, early evening and before bed) every day without even having to ask. These beloved Masters will do this for you if you ask them to. Their love and compassion is unfathomable, as is their dedication to service.

Whenever you are sick or someone in your family is sick ask for a screen of protection so that their bacteria or virus cannot enter your field.

Whenever you sense any kind of bacteria on a subclinical or clinical level enter any of your subtle bodies, call the three M's (Melchizedek, the Mahatma and Metatron) and Dr. Lorphan and his healing staff and call forth the Cosmic Bacterial Vacuum. These Masters will actually suck the bacteria out of your field like a vacuum cleaner.

Whenever you sense viral energy in your subtle or physical vehicle on a subclinical or clinical level call forth from the 3 M's, Dr. Lorphan and his healing staff to bring forth the Cosmic Viral Vacuum. This again will suck out the viral energy like a vacuum. Trust me, my beloved readers, it really does work. You still must be obedient to the other levels of Divinity and GOD's laws on those levels, however this process will lend tremendous support.

Call to the etheric healers for help in repairing your etheric vehicle. The etheric body can be damaged from past lives and/or past trauma in this life. Your etheric body is your blueprint body, which your physical body works off of. If it is damaged, your physical body will never recover. This is easily remedied by asking the etheric healers to repair it.

Call to the Ascended Masters of your choice and also ask that your monadic blueprint body be permanently anchored into your field as well as your mayavarupa body, which are your higher perfect blueprint bodies. This will greatly accelerate physical healing.

Call to the 3 M's or any other Cosmic Masters of your choice to permanently anchor their energy through you 24 hours a day, 7 days a week, 365 days a year. This is what I have done with the 3 M's and this is the food that sustains my physical vehicle to a large extent. It can be yours as well for the asking. The law of the universe is you must ask, for these great and noble Masters are not allowed to give you these blessings without your request for they are not allowed to interfere with your free choice. My job, my beloved readers, is to humbly guide you what to ask for and the blessings of the cosmos shall be yours as long as you are sincere in your efforts to serve GOD and your brothers and sisters in Christ.

I have also asked the 3 M's to provide vitamins and minerals in the 3 M's cosmic light that they are constantly downpouring. I think this is part of the reason why I feel so sustained by the light. The color of the energy from Melchizedek is the highest purity of gold. The color of the energy from Metatron is platinum. The color of the energy from the Mahatma is rainbow white light. My beloved readers, do you see all the vitamins and minerals in this energy?

I've also asked the 3 M's to program my gematrian body and entire twelve body system with the fire letters, key codes and sacred geometries to partially live on light. So the ideal here is to live on food but also to live on light.

If you want to gain weight request to the 3 M's and Dr. Lorphan to program those fire letters, key codes and sacred geometries. If you want to lose weight make the same prayer except in reverse.

If you have an area in your physical and etheric body that is especially weak call to Metatron and the Platinum Angels or Golden Angels to 24 hours a day, 7 days a week, 365 days a year live in that area. For example, I often get strained vocal chords from all the talking, counseling, lecturing and phone calls. The Platinum Angels live in my vocal chords and throat lining to keep it soothed and also to keep any negative bacteria out for any place there is a weakness in the body bacteria and viruses tend to take hold. This can be easily remedied with this spiritual healing tool. I have the Platinum Angels now also living in my digestive system and have invited them into my entire body. The color of platinum is the highest frequency color available to Earth. The only frequency higher is the energy of GOD at the 352nd level of Divinity, which has no color.

For really tough health lessons I would recommend calling forth the inner plane acupuncture team under the directorship of Dr. Lorphan. Share with them your physical health concern and they will place etheric needles in your etheric body which you will not even be aware of which will greatly activate the chi in your system in those areas needed.

When you feel your whole system being energetically clogged or just having too much cloudy astral, etheric and mental energy call forth the prana wind clearing device from the Lord of Arcturus. This beloved Master will anchor this etheric fan into your third chakra, which will blow out all the energy through all your nadis, meridians, veins and arteries. Try it, it will do you wonders.

When you are fatigued I recommend calling forth to the Lord of Arcturus who will use the advanced technology on his mother ship to revitalize and energize your system if you ask him to. It is better than a cup of coffee and you don't fill your physical vehicle with the two hundred known toxins that coffee contains. Try not to rely on artificial stimulants. Why use artificial stimulants when GOD and the GOD Force can be your source of energy?

When you are overworked and your energies are all out of balance and too top heavy I like to call the Lord of Arcturus and the Arcturian temple workers to balance my meridians. You will feel an immediate rush of energy through your meridian system.

Another wonderful Master to call on that specializes in healing is Archangel Raphael and his Healing Angels. Certain angels are given certain assignments in GOD's Kingdom. Archangel Raphael was created by GOD to do physical healing. Call on him and his Healing Angels whatever the health lesson.

Two other Masters that are incredibly proficient in healing are His Holiness the Lord Sai Baba and Sananda. Sai Baba, being an incarnated universal avatar, has enormous shakti, and being omnipotent, omniscient and omnipresent can help with any problem you have, including physical ones. Sananda, I have found to be an extremely effective healer as well. Sometimes I like to call on other Masters for healing just as a change of pace and to also merge and attune with their energies. These two Masters would definitely reside in this category.

One of the most effective healers of all which lightworkers forget to call on is their own Monad and/or Mighty I Am Presence. Who knows your body better than your own Monad, and who has more motivation to help heal it than your Monad who is your true self? Call on your Monad for help in this area and you will be amazed at the energetic support that it can provide.

Call to the 3 M's, Dr. Lorphan and the Galactic Healers once a week for an implant and negative elemental removal of all these imbalanced energies from all your subtle bodies. It is really as simple as just asking.

Clairvoyantly and/or intuitively I have often sensed certain crystallization developing in some of my joints on a very subclinical, etheric level. This sometimes develops from too much time spent doing office work, typing, computer work and the likes. I have asked my dear friend the Lord of Arcturus to keep this crystallization removed from my system at night while I sleep whenever I need it. He has graciously agreed to perform this service for me.

Whenever you are feeling out of balance emotionally and even mentally call to Dr. Lorphan and the Galactic Healers to rebalance your emotional and mental bodies which will also aid in the healing of your physical body.

Before starting your work each day be it counseling, typing, computer work, desk work, driving a truck, piloting a plane, administering to patients, call in the 3 M's and/or the inner plane Ascended Masters of your choice to run their energies through you throughout the day. I do this religiously and I find my stamina and energy level is literally increased one hundred fold and I find that my physical vehicle has a hundred times more durability. The idea is to run GOD and the GOD Force's energy while you work and not your own. Why use your battery when you can use GOD's battery?

When you have very serious or stubborn health lessons sometimes one Master is not enough. At these times I call on a whole group of Masters to work on me simultaneously. This might be, in my case, the entire Core 21, which are the Council of Masters I work with. A sub group of this is the Core 7. Another sub group is the Divine Mother and the Lady Masters who are wonderful healers and bring forth a feminine healing that is so often needed. I also call on the 7 Chohans who work extremely effectively as a unit. Try this particular spiritual healing tool when your health lessons are very stubborn.

In certain rare instances when great planetary world service is involved and I haven't been feeling well physically the 3 M's have actually completely stepped in and taken over my body in a way that I can only describe as how Lazarus must have felt when Jesus and Lord Maitreya raised him from the dead. In certain instances of great spiritual planetary importance I have been amazed by the incredible healing abilities that they have at their disposal. From really not feeling well I felt instantly healed to do the planetary world service work that I needed to do.

For those of you who have a special attunement to Djwhal Khul as I do, Djwhal can be very helpful at times with certain health lessons. What I do is ask him to hook me up to his holographic computer in his office in his Ash-ram on the inner plane and through this most advanced holographic computer he can make very minute and finite energy corrections to balance the energy fields.

Another request I often make in a similar vein to Dr. Lorphan and the Galactic Healers and to the Lord of Arcturus and his Arcturian helpers is a request to just rebalance my energy fields.

I also take advantage of all the services of these most wonderful healers at night while I sleep. If there is an area in my physical etheric body that is a little electrically weak, I request before bed that for example the Lord of Arcturus run his Arcturian mother ship computerized energy all night long to strengthen that area. I find this to be extremely effective. The Arcturians have said that there is no physical health problem that they could not help to heal over time.

One other Arcturian tool for physical healing is to ask to be taken to the mechanism chamber in one's soul body at night while one sleeps in a bi-location type of sense. The mechanism chamber is specially constructed to work on physical health lessons.

Another very important spiritual healing tool is to call to Dr. Lorphan and the Galactic Healers to heal up any leaks, spots, tears, and/or irritations in the aura and in all five bodies (physical, etheric, astral, mental and spiritual). This tool is extremely important because any tears or holes in the aura will cause a leakage of energy almost like bleeding in a physical body, but this type of bleeding can occur on a etheric, astral and mental level.

Another preventative tool which probably is worth while to everyone to use every once in a while is to have Dr. Lorphan, the Lord of Arcturus and the Galactic Healers remove any cancerous energy that is starting to develop in any of the subtle bodies or in the physical body. These energies always begin in the subtle bodies and then move to the physical. This type of prayer request nips this in the bud.

Another very helpful spiritual healing tool for keeping the physical body in good working order is to request each day for Dr. Lorphan and the Galactic Healers to balance your chakras. This will keep your glandular system functioning properly as well as your organs.

If ever you are physically sick with some kind of immune system process call to Dr. Lorphan and the Galactic Healers to give you etheric vitamin C shots. Remember, my friends and beloved readers, everything is just energy.

One other extremely important healing tool is to call forth to the 3 M's and Dr. Lorphan to clear your genetic line of all imbalanced energies. My beloved readers, we do not have to be a victim of anything in life and that includes our genetic heritage.

Call to Dr. Lorphan and the healing group to clear from your four-body system all etheric disease, astral disease, mental disease, spiritual disease and lastly physical disease. "Ask and you shall receive, knock and the door shall be opened."

Call to the Ascended Masters of your choosing as well as to Dr. Lorphan and his healing group to bring forth the Core Fear Matrix Removal Program and to pull out of your subconscious mind all thoughtforms, images and negative feelings connected with poor health. After letting the Masters work on you for 15 to 20 minutes with this process then request that they place into your subconscious mind thoughtforms, feelings, images and attributes of perfect health in every aspect of your physical body.

Another extremely helpful spiritual healing tool if you have a weak organ or area of your body, is to request from the 3 M's or any Cosmic Master of your choosing, to place a permanent energy beam from them to the particular spot in your physical body that is weak. Once this area of your body is healed and strengthened this energy beam can be removed or placed in a different area of your body.

One other very unique spiritual healing tool is to call to one of the Masters you are most connected with and request that he or she imprint their etheric body onto your physical body in a type of energetic telepathic battery hook up. I did this with Sai Baba at a time when I had a weakness in certain areas of my physical vehicle. My sense was this definitely gave me added energy and power source to those slightly weakened areas.

Earlier I suggested calling to the etheric team to repair the etheric body. Also call to Dr. Lorphan and the Galactic Healers to repair any damage from past lives or this life to your astral and mental bodies. This will greatly strengthen your etheric physical vehicle as well.

If you are aware of any residual physical toxins in your body that need cleansing you can call to the Lord of Arcturus and his Arcturian helpers to cleanse those toxins with help from the Arcturian technology. An example of this that I used one time was I was eating a lot of vegetables, however the vegetables I had bought were not organic and I could tell there were a lot of pesticides on them. I asked the Masters about the pesticide level in my body and they said it was too high. I asked the Lord of Arcturus about bringing that level down and about cleansing those particular toxins. He graciously agreed to help me do this. I also facilitated this process by putting a particular homeopathic on my radionics machine that also helped. I would also recommend to you, my beloved readers, to take homeopathics or herbs specifically designed for this purpose. Go to your neighborhood homeopathic pharmacy and they can guide you to what homeopathic is best for that. Again working on both levels, spiritual and earthly, is the most effective method in all these tools. I use the example here of pesticides but you could apply the same concept and principle to removing mercury from your system from leaking mercury fillings, or even smog from living in a city. Be creative.

One other very effective spiritual healing tool for physical healing is to call to the Lord of Arcturus to anchor and activate his liquid crystals which serves to deactivate any imbalanced energy going on in the five body system (physical, etheric, astral, mental and spiritual). I personally find this tool to be extremely effective.

Call to the 3 M's and the Ascended Masters of your choice to make sure you are not taking on any physical health karma from your eleven other soul extensions from your Oversoul. Also request that you not take on any physical health karma from the 144 soul extensions from your twelve Oversouls and/or Monad. Part of this process is also to affirm this in your own mind that you are not going to allow this to happen. This must be done on both levels to be effective.

The possibilities of requesting help from Dr. Lorphan, the Galactic Healers, Raphael, the Platinum and Golden Angels, the Lord of Arcturus and the Ascended Masters is infinite. The most important thing is to remember to pray and ask for help and to ask these Masters very specifically as to your health concerns. If you do not get the results you desire keep asking. In my personal experience I find each of these different Masters I talk about do healing in a different way. I call on different Masters for different physical symptoms for in the process of trial and error certain Masters are more effective than others in regards to certain health problems. If it's a very serious health crisis you must be realistic and not expect to be instantly cured. This can happen, however it is not the norm. Keep rotating and trying out different Masters and groups of Masters to see which ones are most effective for you. Your intuition will guide you in this process.

One of the nicest things about working with Dr. Lorphan, the Galactic Healers, the Ascended Masters, Angels and extraterrestrials for healing is that they are available 24 hours a day, seven days a week, 365 days a year. You do not have to make an appointment in advance and they don't charge any money. It is their honor to serve.

Short Cut

One of the short cuts in this process that I have worked out with the Masters is first to give them all a blank check open invitation to work on me 24 hours a day, 7 days a week, 365 days a year without me having to ask each time. I want to be clear about this that I still ask all the time, however they are constantly working on me without me having to ask as well which I really appreciate.

I've also worked out some codes with them, which I will share with you, my beloved readers, to make this process even easier. I don't like having to go through these long-winded prayers each time I want them to come in. So I worked out a deal with each of the individual Masters for a short code word that calls them forth. For example, my code for the Lord of Arcturus is "Call Arc," then I state the place in my body that needs work. So this would be "Call Arc vocal chords." So with all the Masters I just say the words call and then their name and then the body part and they instantly come in and begin working on it. To have a code like this is helpful for sometimes I am standing in line at the bank or in the market or at a workshop and I just telepathically or whisper to myself saying those three words of the Masters name and the body part and it's quick, easy and efficient. If you want to set this up with them just tell them you want to set up a similar system to what Joshua has and they will happily oblige.

Summation

In conclusion, I am sure you, my beloved readers, can feel the power and profundity of these spiritual healing tools for enhanced physical health. Again you must be obedient to GOD's laws on all levels and you can't expect to eat a terrible diet, get no exercise, allow your negative ego to run rampant and be filled with negative emotions and expect the Ascended Masters to keep you physically healthy. These spiritual healing tools only support the good works you are doing on these other levels. If you will do your part GOD and the Masters will do theirs. These spiritual healing tools are available to everyone regardless of your level of initiation. Everyone is deserving, no matter what you are doing on your spiritual path. All that is requested by the Masters is that you are consciously moving forward on your spiritual path to the best of your abilities and mistakes are O.K. Take advantage of this Divine dispensation of health from Dr. Lorphan, the Galactic Healers, the 3 M's, the Ascended Masters, the Arcturians, and the Angels. They are there to help you not only physically, but on all other levels as well. It is their joy to serve and help and they but await your call and invocation!

12

The Fifty Point Cosmic Cleansing Meditation

Close eyes, let us begin by all taking a deep breath – exhale.

We call forth the Entire Planetary and Cosmic Hierarchy for help in implementing this meditation for the entire group.

We call forth a Planetary and Cosmic axiatonal alignment.

The meditation we are about to do is extremely in-depth and will foster enormous ascension acceleration, so I want you all to just completely relax and be like a sponge, and let the Masters do their Divine handy work.

We call forth Lord Michael, to establish a golden dome of protection for all in attendance.

We call forth Vywamus and the Archangels to bring forth their golden hands as a Net, to cleanse any and all negative energies in the field of each person individually, and in the collective group body.

We call forth from Melchizedek, the Mahatma and Metatron, for the anchoring of the Platinum Net to cleanse the energy fields of each person in attendance in even a deeper fashion now.

We now call forth to the Lord of Arcturus and the Arcturians for the anchoring of the "prana wind clearing device" individually, and in our collective group body.

See this prana wind clearing device as a type of fan that is anchored into the solar plexus, and blows and clears all unwanted energies out of the etheric body system.

Feel the Prana Wind Clearing Device now being lifted out of your field by the Lord of Arcturus and the Beloved Arcturians.

We now call forth from Djwhal Khul, the Seven Chohans, Lord Maitreya, Allah Gobi, Lord Buddha, and the Cosmic Masters, for the anchoring of the core fear matrix removal program.

See this as a latticework of light that is anchored into the four-body system, and hence highlights any negative energies or blockages in your energy fields.

We begin by calling forth the removal of all fear programming and blocks to every person in this room achieving their ascension at the highest possible level.

See this fear programming as black roots intertwined in your energy fields' now being pulled out like a vacuum cleaner through your crown chakra by the Masters.

Planetary and Cosmic Hierarchy, please now remove all separative thinking from the four-body system.

Please now do remove all judgmental programming from the four-body system.

Please remove all lack of forgiveness from the four-body system.

Feel these negative aspects again being pulled out of your energy fields through the crown chakra like unwanted weeds being removed from a beautiful garden.

Planetary and Cosmic Hierarchy, please remove all impatience and negative anger.

Please remove all negative selfishness, self-centeredness and narcissism.

Please remove any negative thoughtforms, negative feelings and emotions, and/or imbalanced archetypes from the four-body system.

Please remove all superiority and inferiority thinking created by the negative ego.

Please remove all aspects of guilt and shame consciousness created by the negative ego.

Please remove all negative ego and fear based programming in a generalized sense.

Please cleanse and remove all extraterrestrial implants and negative elementals.

We call forth the cleansing and removal of all unwanted astral entities.

We call to Melchizedek, the Mahatma and Metatron, for the Cosmic viral vacuum, to remove and pull out any clinical or subclinical viruses currently existing in any of our energy fields.

Please also remove and pull out all negative bacteria with the Cosmic bacterial vacuum program.

We call to the Archangels and the Elohim, to remove all disease energy from the physical, etheric, astral and mental vehicles.

We call forth each person's personal Inner Plane Healing Angels, to now heal, repair, and sew up any irritations, spots, and/or leaks in the aura.

We call forth to Melchizedek, the Mahatma, Metatron, Archangel Michael and the Archangels, for the removal of all improper soul fragments.

We also ask for the retrieval of all the soul fragments from the universe that belong to us, in Divine order.

We call forth each person's etheric healing team, and now request that the etheric body be repaired and brought back to its perfect blueprint now.

We call forth the anchoring now of each person's perfect Divine Monadic blueprint body, and/or Mayavarupa body, to use from this moment forward to accelerate healing and spiritual growth on all levels the rest of this lifetime.

We call forth a complete cleansing and clearing of our genetic line and ancestral lineage.

We call forth the Lord of Arcturus to now bring forth the Golden cylinder to remove and vacuum up any and all remaining negative energy in our collective energy fields.

We call forth a clearing and cleansing of all past lives and future lives.

We now call forth the integration and cleansing of our 144 soul extensions, from our Monad and Mighty I Am Presence.

We now call forth a clearing and cleansing of all karma. As you all know, one needs to balance 51% of their karma to take the beginning phase of their Planetary ascension.

We ask for the greatest possible cleansing of our karma now.

We call forth from Melchizedek, Mahatma and Metatron, for the anchoring of a match stick worth of the Cosmic Fire to very gently burn away all astral, mental and etheric dross and gray clouds from our fields.

We now request a complete clearing and cleansing of our entire Monad and Mighty I Am Presence itself.

We now call forth the greatest cleansing process this world has ever known, from Melchizedek, Mahatma, Metatron, Lord Michael, the Archangels, the Elohim Councils and from GOD.

We now call forth the Ultimate Cosmic Cleansing and Clearing, back to our original covenant with GOD, upon our "Original spiritual creation"

We will take a few extra moments of silence to receive this Blessing and Grace.

We now call forth from all the Cosmic and Planetary Masters gathered here a downpouring and light shower of "core love" and the "Christ/Buddha/Melchizedek attributes" to replace all that has been removed and cleansed, by the grace of GOD and the Cosmic and Planetary Hierarchy.

We call forth Archangel Sandalphon, Pan and the Earth Mother, to help us now become properly integrated and grounded back into our physical bodies.

We call forth our personal Inner Plane Healing Angels to now perfectly balance our chakras and four-body system.

When you are ready, open your eyes and enjoy the tremendous sense of well being and crystal clear clarity in your energy fields.

13

How to Utilize the Unbelievable Power and Abilities of the Holy Spirit

One of the great untapped secrets of the Universe which lightworkers and people of the Earth have not taken full advantage of are the incredible powers, love and grace of the Holy Spirit. Now, when I bring up the Holy Spirit I am not saying here that you need to be a Christian. I personally am a Christian, a Buddhist, a Hindu, a Jew, a Muslim and a follower of all Spiritual Paths and Mystery Schools and no one Religion, Mystery School or Path. To me they are all one. This again is the Path of Synthesis, my friends. Even though this is the case I know in my heart of hearts and soul of souls of the living, breathing existence of GOD, Christ, and the Holy Spirit. I know and believe in this, just as I recognize in the same way the existence of the Buddha in Buddhahood and the Atma in Hinduism, YHWH in Judaism and the Kabbalah and Allah and the Prophet Mohamed in the Muslim faith.

I do not just believe in the existence of the Holy Spirit; I know the Holy Spirit. It is interesting to me that so many people in the New Age Movement work with the Inner Plane Ascended Masters, the Archangels and Angels, the Elohim Masters, the Christed Extraterrestrial Races, their Mighty I Am Presence and Monad, their Higher Self, their Soul; however, very rarely or not that often do I hear people talking about the Holy Spirit.

In some ways the Holy Spirit is the Ultimate Spiritual Master, for it is the aspect that GOD created right out of Himself to, in essence, be the "Answer" to all our challenges and lessons in life. It is wonderful to go to the Ascended Masters, the wonderful Archangels, the Elohim, however, you can also go directly to GOD and the voice of GOD is the Holy Spirit.

When we pray to GOD, the Godhead does not come Himself but rather has divided Himself into three aspects. This is the Trinity of GOD. GOD being the Godhead or the Creator of everything at the 352nd level of Creation. GOD is in part unfathomable, and yet on another level is also quite personal. We think of how big our Universe is or how big the Melchizedek Universe is on a multi-dimensional level. Well, consider that GOD is made up of infinite number of Universes. It is true that we are made in his image, however, there is one big difference. GOD created us; we did not create GOD! This is why *A Course In Miracles* says that "awe" is an appropriate response to GOD but not an appropriate response to a fellow inner plane Ascended Master no matter how high their evolvement. The proper response to a very evolved inner plane Ascended Master is "respect". It is the respect of an elder Brother or Sister so to speak, but not awe. Awe is only appropriate for GOD who is unfathomable, but is also incredibly personally knowable.

At the Annual Wesak Celebrations I actually do Ascension Activation Meditations where GOD actually participates. Many think that GOD should be kept separate, however, this is illusion; it is possible to have a direct personal relationship with GOD. There are many kinds of relationships to GOD, the most profound being the state of "Revelation".

Now the second aspect of the Trinity is the Christ, which is the intermediary so to speak between GOD and His Creation. What many lightworkers and people do not realize is that there are many levels to the Christ. When Jesus realized the Christ 2000 years ago, he was realizing it on a Planetary level. What you must realize is that there is also a Solar level to the Christ, a Galactic level, a Universal level, a Multi-Universal level and a full Cosmic level of the Christ.

The initiation process, of which in truth there are 352 levels of initiation, takes you through all of these to fully realize the Christ in the fullest sense of GOD, at the highest possible level. No one on Earth has done this. The most evolved realization of Christ on Earth is His Holiness the Lord Sai Baba in India. He is demonstrating on Earth the realization of the Christ at the Universal level. He has not however, realized the multi-universal Christ or the Cosmic Christ status of a Cosmic Ascended Master. He is, however, the most advanced realization of the Christ on Earth that the Earth has yet known.

Lord Maitreya, who is head of the Spiritual Hierarchy, holds the position of being a Galactic Christ for our Planet. Master Kuthumi is preparing to take over this position in the Spiritual Government of the Planetary Christ, which is a Galactic level realization.

I want to make it clear here that no one can skip levels, and if you think you can this is the negative ego talking and illusion. Everyone must go through the initiation process through each level, and must demonstrate their Divinity and serve at each level before advancing. Demonstration of GOD on an on going basis, and service at each level is the key. So as we evolve we come to know and realize greater and greater levels of the Christ. The Master Jesus is working on fully realizing the Galactic Christ at a very high level along with Master Kuthumi and a great many of the well known other Ascended Masters of our Planetary Hierarchy. In their initiation process they have not as yet begun the realization of their initiations of becoming a Universal Christ. Most lightworkers on Earth are focusing on realizing the Planetary Christ.

So as we see here, it is also possible to have a very close relationship to the second aspect of the Trinity, which is the Holy Christ Presence. I am not talking about Jesus here, for he is just one man who realized this integration and unification on a Planetary level. Since his life as Jesus 2000 years ago, he has also done so on a Solar level and Galactic level. He is still in a state of evolution through the 352 levels of initiation as well. The most important point being that it is 100% possible to have a continuing ongoing personal relationship with the Holy Christ Presence, which keeps expanding as we evolve spiritually.

The third aspect of the Trinity is the Holy Spirit. The Holy Spirit is an aspect of GOD that he has placed within us as the answer to all our problems. In truth, all problems are created by the negative ego or separative mind. All answers and solutions come from the Holy Spirit. The Holy Spirit speaks for the "Atonement" or the "At-one-ment." To atone means to undo. Of the many profound gifts of the Holy Spirit and the infinite wisdom, knowledge, love and power it possesses; the most profound ability it has in my humble opinion, is its ability to undo past mistakes and negative interactions and situations.

My beloved Brothers and Sisters, listen very closely to what I am about to share with you, for in my humble opinion, this is one of the most profound Esoteric Secrets of GOD's infinite Universe, which has unbelievable importance and significance to your life. The Holy Spirit has the ability to atone for, or stated more clearly "undo," the ramifications of any mistake that you have made in your life. The Holy Spirit can not only undo it in your subconscious and unconscious minds and auric field, it can also undo the effects that your mistakes may have caused to other people or other situations.

My beloved readers, I cannot tell you how many times in my life when I have made a mistake or even when I didn't make a mistake, and I have gotten myself into some sticky situation, that I have called on the Holy Spirit to undo the causes that have gotten me there. I have called on the Holy Spirit to undo health lessons. I have called on the Holy Spirit to undo mistakes I have made and the negative results that came from them. I have called on the Holy Spirit to undo negative actions with people even when the negativity was coming from someone else and not me. I have called on the Holy Spirit to undo situations in my life that need fixing. I have called on the Holy Spirit to undo literally everything that is not going 100% according to my preferences. Again, it is funny a lot of lightworkers are so busy on calling on the Masters and Angels that they forget that they can call on GOD and the Trinity of GOD and especially the Holy Spirit.

The Holy Spirit has powers and abilities that are so multidimensional and Cosmic in nature that, in truth, it would be impossible to explain how the Holy Spirit is able to do what I am telling you. All I know is that the Holy Spirit can and will do this for you if you ask. There is no situation in life that it cannot undo or rebuild if you call upon it. There is no situation in life that it does not have the answer for. Definitely continue calling on the Ascended Masters, the Saints, the Archangels and Angels, the Elohim Masters and the Christed Extraterrestrial groups such as the Ashtar Command and the beloved Arcturians, however, do not forget to call on the Holy Spirit. The Holy Spirit is the Ultimate Cosmic Master that GOD has placed inside of you to be the answer to all your challenges and lessons, and the Ultimate Power in the Universe to undo obstacles on every aspect of life. This applies to the physical level, the etheric level, the astral level, the mental level, and the Spiritual level. There is not one time in my life that I have called on the Holy Spirit that it has not been able to do as I requested. As long as your requests are sincere and pure and are not negatively ego motivated, it will help you and it is literally the arm of GOD. Do an experiment and try out what I am saying and see if every word I have told you is not the truth!

With GOD's help, the help of your own Mighty I Am Presence and your own Higher Self, the Ascended Masters help, the help of the Archangels and Angels, the help of the Elohim Masters, the help of the Christed Extraterrestrial Races, the help of your own personal power and will, the power of your own subconscious mind which can be utilized through creative visualization and creative affirmations, and the help of GOD, Christ and the Holy Spirit, how can you fail? If you utilize in your life all of these levels of power, love, and wisdom there is no force in GOD's infinite Universe that can stop you!

There are, in truth, only two voices in life; the loud irrational, unloving, separative, fear based voice of the negative ego and lower self, and the other "still small voice within" of unconditional love, forgiveness, grace, omnipotence, omnipresence and omniscience. As you learn to deny and quiet the negative ego mind, and learn to think and feel only from your Christ/Buddha Mind, which is the mind of the Holy Spirit, you will live and move and have your being in GOD's Grace, Grandeur and Love at all times. If ever you begin to slip out of this "Holy Instant" on any level, call upon GOD, the Masters and the Holy Spirit for help and the infinite Love, Power and Wisdom of GOD's infinite Universe will come leaping to your aid! There is no problem, challenge or lesson on any level that GOD, the Godforce and the Holy Spirit cannot solve to bring you peace of mind.

Your job, my beloved readers, is to be joyously vigilant for GOD and His Kingdom against the negative ego and to deny any thought not of GOD to enter your mind. If you do this, there is only one other voice that will hence be present, and this is the sweetest voice of all creation. It is the Voice of GOD, also known as the Voice of the Holy Spirit!

14

Caring for the Temple of GOD

A Healthy Diet

This golden key, which was a major one in my healing, was staying on a strict diet. The key for me here was seeing a psychic nutritionist in Los Angeles named Eileen Poole. In my opinion, she is the finest psychic nutritionist on the planet. All of her work is done through channeling and not by book knowledge. Following Eileen's recommendations, using a pendulum to test all of my food and a purple Positive-Energy Plate to energize my food, has had a highly energizing effect on body.

Because of my past health history, I had to be more disciplined than most with my diet. Being very disciplined in my eating greatly increased my energy and strengthened my immune system. Although I had some digestive weakness, I was rarely sick. A healthy diet also served to lighten the atomic structure of my physical vehicle, which made me more sensitive to subtle energies. I am a big proponent of a healthy diet. I also drink lots of pure, fresh water.

Food-Combining

Another golden key I have found to be extremely helpful is following the laws of food-combining. I feel that this is a highly efficient way to eat and that it conserves energy.

The basic laws of food-combining are to eat protein with vegetables and starch with vegetables, but not protein and starches together. The other food-combining law is to eat fruit alone. Charts are available in health food stores that provide more detail, but these are the basic guidelines. I swear by this way of eating. My system seems to run more efficiently this way.

Fasting and Cleansing Diets

Another practice I have found to be of great value is fasting or going on cleansing diets. The fast I have enjoyed and used the most has been green vegetable juice with a little carrot juice mixed in.

The one I currently use the most is something I learned about from Eileen Poole, called Bieler broth. This was made famous by her mentor, Henry Bieler. He wrote a wonderful book called *Food Is Your Best Medicine*. To make Bieler broth; steam zucchini, green beans, celery and parsley in a large pot. Then put the steamed vegetables in a blender with an equal amount of water. It forms a thick soup, which I find delicious. It is a most wonderful substance to fast and cleanse on. It is specifically designed to be a liver rejuvenator, and it does work.

Over the years, I have varied the recipe to use other types of vegetables and it works just as well. I consume this every day. By fasting on this for one to three days, or even for a meal, I can see the results in my eyes, skin, hair and aura. I swear by this stuff. I have been eating it for fifteen years and never get tired of it. It has been one of the golden keys for healing and maintaining my physical body.

Avoid Artificial Stimulants

The next golden key has been a vow to refrain from using artificial stimulants including coffee, caffeinated teas, drugs, and even herbal stimulants. I was a big coffee drinker in my younger years. What I have come to realize in my maturing years is that the goal is to be even-minded in all things. This applies to one's thoughts, emotions and physical body. It is not good to live a roller coaster of extreme highs and lows.

Avoid Drugs

The next golden key has been a strict rule to stay away from all drugs. As an adolescent, I experimented with them like most people from my generation. The Masters state emphatically that the use of drugs is not for high-level initiates. There are few points on which I am very firm, but this is one.

Those disciples and initiates who fool around with drugs have been seduced by the lower self and negative ego. They should forgive themselves and retain no guilt, but they should stop immediately. Altered states of consciousness should be obtained from meditation, not from substances that poison the liver. The smoking of pot also puts holes in the aura.

Lightworkers also should stay away from prescription drugs and use herbs and homeopathics. These are more effective and contribute to the health and wellbeing of the physical body. There are emergency exceptions to this, of course, but as a general rule there should be no conflict about it. In the not-too-distant future, I believe that many of the current practices of Western medicine will be abolished. Doctors of the future will work with energy in a variety of ways. Disease will be seen as imbalance, so there will be a shift to treating the cause of imbalance, which often lies in the subtler bodies, mind, and emotions.

Purple Positive-Energy Plates

This golden key has been of inestimable value in terms of my physical wellbeing. This is the use of a purple Positive-Energy Plate. I cannot recommend this more highly. The purple plate is a New Age technology in which the atoms and electrons of the aluminum have been altered so that the plates resonate with the basic energy of the universe. The plates create a field of positive energy that penetrate any substance. This energy is beneficial to all life: plant, animal and people. I know from personal experience that these plates work, and I have checked this out with the ascended masters and my pendulum, as have many of my friends.

I would venture to guess that 90 percent of the foods we obtain, even health food, have a negative or neutral spin. You can check this out with a pendulum. This can be caused by pesticides, by the deterioration of the food in the refrigerator or on the shelf, by the people who handled the food or by the scanners at the grocery store checkout counter. The possibilities of energy contamination are endless.

For this reason I always pray over my food and use my purple energy plate. They come in different sizes. I have the large ones, which cost around $40. Small ones costs about $12. I conscientiously place all my food on this plate. My purple plate is my placemat. Leave food on the purple plate for five to seven minutes before eating. The plates can also be used to energize homeopathic remedies, herbs, and supplements.

If you check the food with a pendulum both before and after it has been on the plate you will see the difference. The plate puts a positive spin on the food. This will guarantee that you are getting the proper energy even if you are not always able to obtain the best food. If you are going to have a dish of ice cream, at least put it on the purple plate to deactivate the negative energy and create a positive energy spin. I have tested it out and it is much more effective than even Hanna Kroeger's Soma Board, which was created for the same purpose. To order, see information at the end of this chapter.

Radionics

The next golden key for the healing of my physical body has been radionics. I have two radionics machines, one called SE5, and another I refer to as the black box. I began using these radionics machines to send myself the energy of substances that I needed rather than taking the actual pills. This is not necessarily for everyone, but with the combination of my radionics machines and the Ascended Master tools, I have been able to keep myself in excellent health.

I don't claim to understand fully how these machines work. But somehow, by simply putting my hair sample or picture on the machine and a substance or numerical code on another plate, the radionics machine knocks out any virus, fungus or other problem I am dealing with. It also saves me a lot of money because I use the same homeopathic over and over again without having to ingest them. I keep them energized by storing them on one of my purple energy plates. I use radionics as a preventive health care tool. I run the radionics machine 24 hours a day to send myself supplements, homeopathic remedies, immune boosters and the like. I love the idea of working with pure energy and spirit for my healing. The ideal here would be to use both physical and energy methods according to your inner guidance. Radionics is most definitely a science of the future.

Protection against Electromagnetic Pollution

The next golden key relates to counteracting electromagnetic pollution. There are many products on the market for minimizing the effects of electromagnetic energies. The one I have found most helpful has been the Teslar watch, invented by Nikola Tesla. When you wear the watch, a force field is placed around your energy field that prevents electrical frequencies from entering your field. The watch has a pulse synchronized to the pulse of the Earth and the human body that is totally unique.

I always have disliked wearing watches, for I felt that they interfered with the natural flow of energy through my acupuncture meridians. Testing has been done on the Teslar watch, and it has been proven to be effective in bolstering the immune system on subtle levels. It also keeps good time. I am not sure where to obtain the Teslar watch at this time. But if you are motivated, contact people who are involved with radionics or check the ads in New Age magazines.

Avoiding Microwave Ovens

This golden key has been to stay away from microwave ovens. Contrary to popular opinion, nuking your food is not a New Age form of cooking. Microwave ovens put holes in the etheric field of your food, which has a very deleterious effect on your physical body. Long-term use of a microwave oven can have a very negative effect on your health if you are not careful.

Balanced Exercise

The next golden key in manifesting health has been balanced exercise. It has been said that there are three aspects to physical exercise; stamina, flexibility and strength. The stamina I currently get is from walking, which Edgar Cayce has proclaimed to be the best exercise. I used to be a long distance runner and jogger, but now I find this too jarring to my system. I like walking better. Walking helps oxygenate my system.

In terms of strength, for many years I went to the gym and lifted weights. I don't feel the need to do this now, but it is a good thing for those inclined toward it.

Yoga and Stretching

The next golden key has been doing hatha yoga and stretching. The yoga and stretching are wonderful for the flexibility aspect of balanced exercise. One of the keys to perfect health is keeping the spine flexible. The nexus of nerves connected with the spine serves every cell, nerve, organ and gland in the body. Yoga can be used as a type of meditation or simply as a physical exercise.

The Thymus Thump

The next key has been a simple practice of doing what is called the thymus thump. Simply tap your fingertips on the center of your upper chest maybe two or three times a day. Thymus thumping stimulates the thymus gland, which is the heart of your immune system.

Chakra Zips

The next key has been giving myself chakra zips. To do a chakra zip, cup your right hand just below the first chakra. Sensitize yourself to the energies for a moment and then slowly raise your cupped hand up through all of your chakras, bringing your hand up over your head. Do this three times very slowly, about one inch away from your physical body. Doing this opens the chakras and spins them in the proper direction.

I do this whenever I get tired or when my energy system feels a little out of balance. It immediately realigns your energy. It seems like a very simple thing, but I can't tell you how much this has helped me.

Keep Your Legs and Arms Uncrossed

This next golden key is not crossing your legs, feet or arms. This inhibits the flow of energy though your meridians and chakras. It is a very hard habit to break, bit I have conscientiously tried to do this so that my energy could flow freely.

Keep the Chakras Spinning Correctly

The next golden key is to ask the Arcturians and the inner plane healing masters several times during the day to keep my chakras open and spinning in the proper direction. The lessons and challenges of life can often throw this process out of whack as we all know.

A Complete Ascension Clearing

The next golden key has been to give myself a complete ascension clearing about every three months just in case any imbalanced energies have gotten in and lodged themselves in my energy field. If any of my readers are interested in such a clearing, give me a call and I will set you up with a session the first time. After that, I recommend that you do it on your own.

Wear Gems and Amulets

The next golden key has been wearing certain gemstones or amulets to increase my energy or add a certain vibration. For many years I wore a crystal pendant that I felt greatly expanded my aura and served to bolster my immune system. For many years I carried in my pocket the amulet that Sai Baba materialized for me. I have gone through phases of wearing other amulets that have had a very powerful effect. Every gemstone, as we know, has a specific vibration, so there is no guidance I could give to people other than to use your own intuition as to what feels right. There are also many wonderful books on the use of crystals and gemstones. At times, I have also gone through phases of not keeping any amulets or gemstones on my person when that felt right.

Honor Your Body's Natural Rhythms

This golden key has been learning to trust the rhythms of my own physical body. My natural rhythm is to sleep only about five or six hours a night and then take a catnap in the late afternoon. This is what my physical body likes. However, each person is different and must find his or her particular body rhythm. I have a seventh ray body, but others with different ray bodies and missions will operate differently. Trusting my own natural rhythms has been an important key to my overall effectiveness. In South America and Mexico, afternoon siestas are the norm for the entire population. I must have been Mexican in a past life, for I love my siesta.

Conserve Energy

The next golden key has been what I call conserving my energies. This is something that my physical body has taught me. In my early years I tried to be superman. I had to learn to set better boundaries, to be selfish and say no. I had to learn to ask for help and delegate responsibility. Now, with increased leadership responsibilities I focus on the most essential things. I had to develop the leadership skills to see the wisdom in asking for help and delegating responsibility.

My physical body has taught me to become a master at conserving my energy and to regard my energy as extremely precious. Conserving energies means looking at how and with whom I spend my time. It means not being a slave to my phone and setting boundaries for how long I remain on the phone. It means doing my prayers and invocations in the simplest manner possible and with the least expenditure of energy. It means having priorities and clearly defined goals and objectives, and then creating the "battle" plans for achieving these.

Spend Time in Nature

The next golden key has been spending time in nature. Now I admit this was not the easiest thing to do growing up in Los Angeles. After working most of the day though, it was essential for me to get outdoors and walk in the fresh air and sunshine, even if this was just walking in a park with some trees and green grass. My physical body would crave this as well as my spirit. I am sure all of you can relate to this.

Have Fun

This golden key is having fun and not being too serious. It is important to have fun and joke around and take time for pleasure and recreation, such as going to movies, watching certain television shows and engaging in sports. Spend time with friends and enjoy earthly life as well as the heavenly worlds. The spiritual path is one of having the best of both worlds. As you can tell, I am about as committed, self-disciplined and focused as they come. Even though this is the case, I greatly enjoy Earth life. I stop to smell the roses. I enjoy the process as well as achieving the goals I set for myself. If you are not experiencing joy on your spiritual path, something is wrong and needs to be corrected. Having fun is an important part of living a balanced life.

Holistic Care

The next golden key has been working with holistic health care practitioners, including homeopathic, naturopathic and bioenergetic practitioners and doctors of oriental medicine. Many of the practitioners I have worked with use advanced machines such as the Vega machine that can test for subclinical substances that can be poisoning and weaken the immune system. This type of work has been instrumental in the building of the strength of my physical body and keeping my immune system in excellent shape.

Through working with these machines, I was able to clear the subclinical toxins from my body. I cleared out such things as mercury from leaking amalgam fillings, aluminum from cooking utensils and foil, parasites, subclinical bacteria, viruses, fungi, vaccines, radiation from television sets, electromagnetic toxicity, chemicals, drugs that I had been given as a child, pesticides, and other environmental poisons. This list is just the tip of the iceberg, but it gives you an idea of what you are dealing with and how to proceed.

Homeopathic Remedies

The next golden key has been a line of homeopathic products that I think are incredible. They are called Futureplex. They were created by Roy Martina, who is considered one of the finest homeopathic and bioenergetic practitioners in the country. Following is a description of some of the products:

Bacterotox: My experience is that this gets rid of 90 percent of all bacteria-related infections. I feel it is far better than taking antibiotics, which I never use.

Acute Virotox and Post Virotox: I have found that these two products get rid of 90 percent of all viruses. Western medicine has no cure for viruses.

Immune Energy: I have found this product to be a powerful immune system enhancer. It helps to rid the body of many unwanted microorganisms by boosting the immune system.

Lymphotox: This is another wonderful product that is extremely helpful in cleansing the lymph system.

Envirotox: I have found this product to be extremely helpful in ridding the body of environmental toxins.

Gentle Drainage: This product has been very helpful in cleansing my system when it gets a little clogged.

Adrenal Pep: This gives me a boost of energy when I am a little tired. It is much better than drinking coffee or caffeinated tea.

Cellular Recharge: This helps recharge my cells when they are rundown.

Revitalization: This product is very helpful in revitalizing my whole body when I have become overtired or a bit rundown.

For legal purposes I will state that I am not a medical doctor. However, these homeopathic products are one that I have found extremely helpful in my life. I run them on my radionics machine along with certain vitamins and minerals 24 hours a day and, by the grace of God, I never get sick anymore. The combination of running such a high light quotient, merging with my mayavarupa body, eating a healthy diet that is in harmony with my particular body, drinking lots of pure water, exercising every day, and working with my radionics machine and these homeopathic remedies seems to do the trick.

It is certainly fine to take these products orally under the tongue. I don't do this only because, for my system, radionics seems to work better. I can't recommend these products more highly. I have no financial involvement with the company, so I recommend them to you from the perspective of wanting to help you achieve excellent health. These products have been a godsend for me over the last ten years. They are not sold in most homeopathic pharmacies, however, so I have listed a few resources where you can order them.

To order the Positive-Energy Plates, contact Susan Bryant and Sandy Burns at:

Earth Elementals
P.O. Box 31149
Flagstaff, AZ 86003-1128
Ph.: (520) 527-1128

Source for Futureplex Homeopathic Remedies:

Capitol Drugs
4454 Van Nuys Blvd.
Sherman Oaks, Ca 91403
Ph.: (818) 905-8338
Fax: (818) 905-8748

Eileen Poole:
Earlier I mentioned Eileen Poole, the psychic nutritionist I have been seeing for fifteen years. She does not work over the phone, but if you are ever traveling in Los Angeles, she is well worth seeing. Her phone number is (310) 440-9976.

15

Healing from the Higher Dimensions

Arcturian Technologies

The Arcturians are a godsend. Working with them has been a major key to the resurrection of my physical body, and they have had an enormous effect on the acceleration of my ascension. Following are some of the many wonderful love and light technologies that have come forth from the Arcturians. They use the highly advanced computers on their ships to do this work. Once your are on line, so to speak, in the computer banks of the Arcturian ships, the slightest request is instantly answered. I have found that the Arcturians technologies have produced more healing for my physical body than anything else I have used. It is as if I have my own private healers available anytime I need them. I am much indebted to Lord Arcturus and the Arcturians for their help.

Increase Your Light Quotient and Strengthen The Physical Body

This golden key has been so indispensable in my manifestation that I use it every day. I call to Lord Arcturus and the Arcturians for a 100 percent light quotient increase, along with a healing and strengthening of whatever parts of my physical body need attention. Other times I request strengthening of my vocal cords or immune system. At still other times

I ask for help in balancing all the meridian flows in my body. I do this sometimes before bed and find I sleep better. I also do it after typing for four or five hours. You all know the feeling of how the body can ache after typing or sitting at a computer for a long time. I make this request and usually within fifteen to thirty minutes I feel my entire etheric system come back into balance.

Call on the Arcturians In Extreme Situations

This golden key is for people with chronic health problems. For those of you with this spiritual challenge, I recommend running the Arcturian energies 24 hours a day on a consistent basis. Keep praying to the Lord of Arcturus and the Arcturians for a 100 percent light quotient increase and healing of the physical body part that you're having trouble with. If the energy doesn't feel strong enough, ask them to increase the frequency. Keep asking over and over again for an increase until they do it to a level at which you can really feel yourself percolating, so to speak.

If you feel yourself beginning to fade and not feel well again, call them back in and ask for more light and healing in that area. Call in the Arcturian liquid-crystal technology every day followed by the golden cylinder a half hour later. This will keep your field clear and energized.

In extreme situations when I am not feeling well, I will ask to go to the physical healing chamber on the Arcturian ships to be worked on. When I am extremely fatigued and in emergencies, I ask the Arcturians for a total revitalizing and energizing of my physical body. I have found this to be an invaluable tool. I also meditate or take a catnap when I feel tired. In extreme situations you also can call upon Dr. Lorphan and the galactic healers (see Golden Key 66).

Arcturian Liquid-Crystal Technology

This Arcturian tool is their liquid-crystal technology. Upon request, the Arcturians will siphon into your four-body system and chakras a type of liquid crystal that will immediately deactivate any and all negative energy. Often I will use this process first and then call in the golden cylinder.

The Arcturian Golden Cylinder

The Arcturian golden cylinder can be called for directly from Lord Arcturus, and it will be lowered down over your four-body system. It will remove all kinds of toxic energies, and I have used it to remove unwanted implants, elemental, etheric mucous, parasites and any other imbalances on any level. It is like a huge magnet that draws out impurities then as the cylinder is lifted up off the body, it pulls out any remaining residue. I have found that combining this with the liquid-crystal technology completely clears my field every time. These tools have been a godsend in the healing of all my bodies. They are also ascension accelerators. I use these tools especially during the sleep state anytime I feel myself getting unclear or becoming contaminated from involvement with life lessons.

The Arcturian Prana Wind Machine

This golden key is their prana wind machine. I have found this tool to be invaluable. Call for the Arcturians to anchor this into your energy field. It is a fan that is lowered into the heart chakra, and it blows all negative energy right out of your energy field. It realigns and clears your nadis, or etheric wiring, and your whole etheric light grid. It also helps to clear your veins and arteries. It has a very strengthening effect on my physical vehicle. I use this anytime I feel any negative energy in my energy field.

The Arcturian Joy Machine

Their joy machine is another amazing Arcturian tool. It has a wonderfully beneficial effect on the emotional body. Anytime I feel emotionally low, I call for the Arcturian joy machine. I'll make you a bet. If you call right now to the Arcturians for their joy machine to be activated, I will bet you ten light quotient points that you will not be able to stop smiling and even laughing. I have shared this with friends and they have been completely blown away. The Arcturians will send you pure ninth ray joy, and you will not be able to be depressed even if you want to. Nothing is more healing than joy. Ascension, joy and love are all connected. Use this tool to help cultivate this Christ/Buddha quality in your daily life.

Arcturian Voltage Increase

The next golden key has been the use of the Arcturian voltage-increase technique. Often when I'm standing in line at he market or post office and want to utilize the time I will whisper to myself or telepathically say, "Lord Arcturus and Arcturians, increase the voltage." I will feel an increase in the flow of spiritual current running through my body. It is simple, effective and can be done quickly in the midst of any activity.

The Arcturian Plating System

This is a key dispensation I received from Lord Arcturus. This was an anchoring of the Arcturian plating system into my chakra system. Lord Arcturus said that this advanced technology could, metaphorically, mail a letter in 18 seconds that normally would take the chakra system three months. These advanced technologies, which one by one were anchored in over time, literally resurrected my entire being.

Arcturian Reprogramming of Your Etheric Biochemical Makeup

The next golden key is to ask Lord Arcturus and the Arcturians to reprogram your biochemical etheric makeup to make sure it is in accord with your physical body structure. In my case, at one point my spiritual, mental and emotional bodies were evolving faster then my physical vehicle, so the Arcturians had to upgrade my etheric biochemical makeup to create consistency within my four-body system.

Higher Dimensional Healing Teams and Temples

The Inner Plane Healing Masters

The next golden key is working with the inner plane healing masters. These healers have been the other major key to the resurrection of my physical body. When calling forth this group of inner plane healers, invoke your Christ self and your monad along with the inner plane healing masters. I call them in or feel myself in one of their healing chambers anytime I'm not feeling well, no matter what the symptoms or cause. When I needed them the most, I would call them in many times a day. After you call them in, tell them what you want them to work on. Lie down and rest or meditate and let them work on you for up to an hour.

Following are some special requests that you can make of the inner plane healing masters:

Request a complete cleansing and repairing of all of your vehicles: spiritual, etheric, mental, emotional, and physical. This includes asking them to repair any leaks or holes in your aura.

Request to be given shots on the etheric level of the substances you need such as vitamins, minerals, hormones and so on under the guidance of the Ascended Masters. This is like giving these to yourself radionically or like the request for etheric acupuncture. It works because everything is energy.

I used to get a lot of healings from other practitioners until I realized that nearly everything I needed I could access on my own. This is the finest group of healers available to humanity. The Inner Plane healing Masters and the Arcturians are an awesome one-two punch for staying in good health on all levels.

Restore Your Divine Blueprint

The next golden key was asking the etheric healing team to repair my etheric damage from past lives and this life. This is most important, because otherwise the physical body is working from an imperfect blueprint and complete recovery cannot occur. Call this team in and ask them to repair your etheric body and bring it to a state in which it outpictures only your perfect monadic blueprint. Working with this team, in conjunction with calling for the anchoring of my monadic blueprint body and my mayavarupa body, greatly accelerated both the healing of my physical vehicle and my ascension.

The Acupuncture Healing Masters

This golden key is to ask the Ascended Master acupuncture healing team to put etheric acupuncture needles in your body to help correct any physical health problems you are having. Ask them to remove the needles when you are complete.

Dr. Lorphan and The Galactic Healers

An invaluable golden key in my healing was with Dr. Lorphan and the galactic healers. This is a highly advanced group of healers you can call upon in extreme health situations. Because my health lessons were so severe I called on Dr. Lorphan, and he did wonders with recircuiting my energy field. I use Dr. Lorphan and the galactic healers in serious situations when I need resources in addition to the wonderful healing gifts of the Arcturians and the Inner Plane Healing Masters.

Color Baths in the Inner Plane Healing Temples

With this golden key, request to go to the healing temples on the Inner Plane and bathe in the color baths. These are pools of liquid light and color. They are the most glorious healing spas. Call to your angels of healing and request to have a healing bath in a healing pool of whatever color you desire. This is a wonderful thing to do before bed because it is so relaxing and rejuvenating.

Healing on All Levels

Healing Must Be Done on All Levels

This golden key is to remember that physical healing cannot be completely manifested without first healing the etheric body, emotional body and mental body. Use the tools I have provided in this book to heal these bodies, which are the cause of all disease in the physical body.

Clear Using the Fear Removal Program

This golden key, the program for removing your core fear, has been a godsend. This technology is a process whereby all of the core fears you have stored in you four-body system, from this lifetime and all of your past lives can be removed with help from the ascended masters. Call forth Djwhal Khul and Vywamus to anchor this latticework technology into your energy field, and request their help in removing your core fears. This can be done in regard to overall fear or with specific fears.

This matrix also can pull out all astral entities, astral disease, gray fields and mental and/or etheric disease and help to mend and realign your etheric light grid with the help of the holographic computer in DK's ashram.

Over a period of about nine months I had enormous amounts of core fear removed from my four-body system. Clearing and removing all of these black weeds from my system catalyzed a resurrecting and regenerating effect on me. In just one weekend workshop that I led, the masters removed 45 percent of my core fear for my entire life. This is quick therapy! This technology is available to all. I go into this in more detail in a chapter in *Beyond Ascension*.

Remove Etheric Toxic Debris

The next golden key in my healing was to request the removal of all etheric darts, needles and bullets. These negative aspects have usually been deposited from past lives, but they can also be acquired from this life. I was involved in one relationship where the person has a lot of anger and at one point it was directed at me. Dr. Lorphan and the Inner Plane Healing Masters had to spend two days pulling out the darts and needles lodged in my liver.

Every time people attack or get angry at others, they are sending them psychic darts such as this. All this stuff needs to be cleansed and removed. You can see now why people get so sick and why there are so many diseases relating to a breakdown of the immune system, such as cancer. To a great extent it is because all of this Inner Plane stuff has not been cleansed and removed. This is why conventional medicine is so ineffective with chronic diseases. They deal with just 10 percent of reality and are missing 90 percent of what is going on in the rest of the twelve-body system.

Clear the Etheric Filter Through Your Personal Color Coding

This golden key came from an insight that my friend shared with me concerning what the masters referred to as the *etheric filter*. They said that every etheric body has a filter that works much like a lint filter in a clothes dryer. It was built to work automatically, but in most people it has become clogged over time. Thus light has not been able to pour through properly. Melchizedek said that it is of the highest importance to clear this filter. This is done through calling forth one's personal color-coding.

Each person has his or her unique color-coding. For example, Melchizedek told me that my personal color-coding is the platinum ray, the golden ray, the blue ray and the red ray. Melchizedek said that the platinum ray is the direct God-source energy; the golden ray is His ray from the Golden Chamber; the blue ray is the ray of Djwhal Khul's ashram; and the red ray is El Morya's first-ray ashram dealing with leadership. To clear your filter call forth from the masters your own personal color coding, which will help to clear your etheric filter. I would recommend doing this once a month as a tune-up.

Adjust the Etheric Web

This golden key is to ask Djwhal Khul and Lord Arcturus for an adjustment of the web of the etheric body. For those who are too empathic, a tightening of the etheric web may be in order. For those who are too closed down emotionally or psychically, a loosening of this web may be needed. Leave this up to your own Mighty I Am Presence and the wisdom of the Ascended Masters. Most people need a tightening of the etheric web, for it provides more protection.

Clearing Pets

This golden key has come from understanding the need to clear from pets all alien implants and negative elementals. This was brought home to me after I had had my implants cleared. I had forgotten to have my two cats, Patches and Rags, cleared in the process. Clearing pets is an easy procedure. Just call in the liquid-light technology and the golden cylinder form Lord Arcturus and the Arcturians and make a specific request that all negative alien implants and negative elementals be neutralized and removed from the animals you want worked on.

Clear Old Imprints from The Energy Field

The next golden key has been my request to Djwhal Khul and Vywamus for the removal of all negative imprints form my aura. Negative imprints usually are carried over from past lives. They include such things as a sword or knife wound in the energy field. Also request that all irritations and spots in the aura be healed and cleansed. All of these things are very easy to heal and remove if we just know what to ask for.

Request a Complete Genetic Clearing

The next golden key was a series of cosmic clearings that literally revolutionized and resurrected my entire four-body system. In the first part of this process I requested from Djwhal Khul, Lord Maitreya, Melchizedek and Lord Arcturus a complete genetic-line clearing of all sickness and weakness within the physical body in this life and all past lives.

As part of this, also request to the Arcturians the complete removal of all cancers and disease of all kinds that have formed within the etheric, mental and emotional bodies. Call for a complete removal from the physical and etheric vehicles of all that is not of perfect, radiant health. Request this for your entire bloodline: past, present and future.

Cosmic Cellular Cleansing

This golden key is to call forth to Melchizedek, Metatron and Vywamus for a cosmic cellular clearing. This will clear your entire cellular structure back through your first inception and incarnation on Earth.

*   *   *

I think you are beginning to see that by calling forth these different spiritual technologies, no matter how sick we are physically, emotionally, mentally or spiritually, we can be literally brought back to life. These are the advanced spiritual technologies of the future that are available now and the purpose of this book is *to make them available to you right now*. The most amazing thing is how simple they are to use and how effective. The spiritual path should be simple, I think you will agree.

I recommend that you go through this chapter key by key, in a systematic fashion, requesting and practicing each one of these procedures. In doing this your entire twelve-body system will be completely cleansed, purified and refined so that there will be no possibility of disease manifesting. This is because you are cleansing the subtler bodies where all disease begins.

These tools can be used for healing, health maintenance and prevention. I am showing you a way to heal and evolve on your own without having to pay money to other practitioners. Why should I give you a fish when I can teach you how to fish? All disease manifests in the etheric, emotional and mental bodies first. By keeping these bodies clear using these tools and in-sights, you can maintain health in your physical vehicle. Do you have any idea how much money I am saving you? Save your money and come to the next Wesak celebration!

16

The Psychological Causation of Disease by Djwhal Khul

To begin this chapter I thought the best way to start would be to quote Djwhal Khul's first law of healing as stated in the Alice Bailey book *Esoteric Healing*.

"All disease is the result of inhibited soul life, and that is true of all forms in all kingdoms. The art of the healer consists in releasing the soul, so that its life can flow through the aggregate of organisms which constitute any particular form."

All initiates of the Great White Brotherhood are healers. Not all initiates may work on healing the physical body, however all initiates are transmitters of spiritual energy. The four bodies that need healing are the physical, etheric, astral and mental.

Djwhal Khul says that 90% of the causes of physical disease occur within the etheric and astral body. This is because most people in the world are still emotionally polarized or identified. In a million years hence, when the human attention is more focused collectively in the mind, then the cause of disease will have to be sought in the mind realm.

The first work of any group of healers is to establish themselves in love and to work towards group unity and understanding. The two qualities of any true healer are "magnetism and radiation". The healer must be magnetic to his own soul, to those he would help, and to the energies needed to stimulate a transformation within the client. The healer must then understand how to radiate soul energy, which will stimulate into activity the soul of the one to be healed. The radiation of the mind of the healer will illumine the mind and will of the patient. The healthy radiation of the astral and etheric body of the healer will work in a likewise fashion upon the patient.

All disease is caused by a lack of harmony. Disease results as a lack of alignment between soul and form and/or subjective and objective reality. Lack of harmony, which we call disease, affects all four kingdoms of nature. The outer environmental causes of disease are four-fold, according to Djwhal. They are accidents, infections, disease due to malnutrition, and heredity.

The psychological causes of disease are also four-fold. These are:
1. Those coming from the emotional and feeling nature.
2. Those that have their origin in the etheric body.
3. Those based on wrong thought.
4. Those complaints unique to disciples and initiates.

Much of the failure of the healing methods people use come from the following reasons:
1. Inability to locate what body the trouble is stemming from.
2. Knowing where the patient stands upon the ladder of evolution.
3. Inability to differentiate whether the disease is from inner personal conditions, inherited tendencies, or group karma of some kind.
4. Inability on the healer's part to know if the problem should be dealt with allopathically, homeopathically, through right inner psychological adjustment, through soul power, or through occult methods invoking the help of a Master.

Djwhal says that healing is brought about basically through three ways:
1. Through methods of traditional medicine and/or surgery.
2. Through the use of psychology.
3. Through the activity of the soul.

It is the astral body for the majority of mankind that is the outstanding cause of ill health. The reason is that it has such a potent affect on the person's etheric body, which is the energy body and battery for the physical body.

Basically we are speaking here of uncontrolled and ill-regulated emotions such as fear, worry, irritation, anger, criticism, hatred, superiority and inferiority complex and so on. It is the corollary of the astral body, which is lower-self desire, which leads people to overeat and drink. Poor diet, hence, has its cause in the astral body. Other diseases caused by the desire body are the sexual diseases and over-indulgence in sexuality, which has a weakening effect on the etheric and physical vehicles.

The true healer needs to be trained not only in healing, but also in psychology, medical matters, and esoteric knowledge. Your average medical doctor has absolutely no understanding of the etheric body or the chakras, let alone the soul. The esoteric healer needs to be more aware of the physical earth plane knowledge that the doctor has.

Disease is most definitely a purification process when looked at esoterically. Traditional doctors must understand that disease may be a gradual and slow process of the soul withdrawing from the body to free it for other service. The overwhelming desire to keep the physical body alive, by most traditional medical doctors, is not always appropriate.

The astral body is the cause of most disease because it is the body the bulk of humanity are centering their consciousness in. It is also the most developed of the bodies being the latest to develop in collective mankind. It reached its high point of development in Atlantean days. This is also augmented by the energy coming from the animal kingdom which is entirely astral in its point of attainment. Even though we are in the Aryan root race, the mass of humanity has not achieved a mental polarization and identification yet.

The Three Major Diseases

The three major groups of diseases, according to Djwhal Khul, are tuberculosis, the sexually transmitted diseases (venereal, syphilis, AIDS) and cancer. Two other diseases which Djwhal says affects those who are a little above average are heart diseases and nervous diseases. These five groups, and there are various subdivisions, are responsible for most of the illness of humanity. The three most important aspects of diagnosis are the psychological, the work of the endocrinologist, and the physician.

Mankind also inherits disease from four basic sources:
1. From his own past in this life or previous lives.
2. From the general racial heritage of humanity.
3. From the condition of planetary life.
4. From parental inherited tendencies.

It is when the upper chakras above the diaphragm are awakened that a long series of lives with heart and nervous system lessons occur. These have been called diseases of the mystics.

The sexually transmitted diseases, except for AIDS (man made chemical warfare experiment gone awry), are remnants from over-indulgence in Lemurian times when man was totally polarized in the physical vehicle.

Cancer is from the Atlantean root race and is astrally and emotionally connected. Cancer is a disease of inhibition just as syphilitic diseases are overexpression and overuse.

Tuberculosis is a disease of the Aryan race, although it began in later Atlantean times. Tuberculosis is caused by the shift of polarization from the emotional body to the mental body, or from Atlantean consciousness to the Aryan consciousness. It is a disease of depletion of the emotional body.

Cancer came from the shift of life force from the physical polarization to the emotional polarization, or from the Lemurian consciousness to the Atlantean consciousness. As the race develops tighter emotional control, Djwhal says, cancer will begin to disappear.

Many of the problems of humanity are caused by the burial of sick, diseased bodies in the soil instead of cremating them. Djwhal has prophesied that in the New Age burial for bodies will be outlawed and cremation will become the norm.

Diseases of Worry and Irritation

Diseases of worry and irritation have the following affect on people:

The lower the vitality of the person, the more susceptible they are to disease.

The connection is poor in certain directions or aspects of the equipment.

The connection between the etheric and physical body is so loose that the soul has very little control over its vehicle.

The fourth reason is the opposite of the third. The etheric body is too closely knit with the personality and physical vehicle.

The third cause of disease in the etheric body is the over stimulation of the chakras. This, of course, has a very deleterious affect on the glands which affects the blood stream and all the organs.

Causes of Disease Arising Out of the Mental Body

The first cause of disease from the mental body is from "wrong mental attitudes." The second cause is mental fanaticism and dominance of thought forms. The third cause is frustrated idealism.

Diseases of Disciples

Most of these diseases arise from the transferring of the solar plexus energy into the heart. This transfer causes stomach, liver and respiratory problems. Djwhal says that all diseases and physical difficulties are caused by one of the following three conditions:

A developed soul contact which produces a vitalization of all the chakras. This necessarily produces stress and strain on the physical body.
- The attempt of the personality to negate soul control. The stress on the physical body here is obvious.
- A shift in the life force from personality to soul control, or from lower-self to higher-self, which causes re-adjustment problems within the physical vehicle.

Medicine in The Next Century

Medicine in the next century will focus on five basic premises:
1. Preventive medicine.
2. Sound sanitation.
3. The supply of right chemical properties to the physical body.
4. An emphasis on understanding the laws of vitality, vitamins and minerals, and sunshine.
5. The use of the mind in healing will be regarded above all else.

The Four Groups of Healers

In the future there will need to be much more synthesis and integration between the following four groups of healers. These four, as described by Djwhal Khul in the Alice Bailey book *Esoteric Healing* are:
1. Physicians and surgeons
2. Psychologists, neurologists, and psychiatrists
3. Mental healers, new thought workers, unity thinkers and Christian Science practitioners
4. Trained disciples and initiates who work with the souls of men

Liberation and Freedom

The ideals of liberation and freedom are integral to achieving perfect health for an individual and humanity as a whole. Djwhal says that there have been four great symbolic happenings in the past 2,000 years that have epitomized the theme of liberation. These are:
1. The life of Christ, Himself.
2. The signing of the Magna Carte.
3. The emancipation of the slaves.
4. The liberation of humanity by the United Nations.

Karma and Health

Djwhal has delineated nine types of karma. These are:
1. Elementary group karma of the primitive man.
2. Individual karma of the self-conscious developing man.
3. Karma related to the life of discipleship.
4. Hierarchical karma.
5. Karma of retribution.
6. Karma of reward.
7. National karma.
8. Racial karma.
9. Educational karma.

Karma is not an inevitable and inescapable happening. It can be offset where disease is concerned by four lines of activity.
These are:
1. Determining the nature of the cause and the area of consciousness where it originated.
2. Developing those qualities which are the polar opposite of the effective cause.
3. Practicing "harmlessness".

4. Mental acceptance, wise action along medical lines, the assistance of a healer or healing group, clear soul inspired visualization as to the outcome.

This could mean perfect health and the preparation for service on the inner plane.

How to Ascertain Location of Congestion

Traditional medical testing is extremely limited, expensive, and doesn't deal with the subtle bodies or psychological level, so it is not really useful in finding the location of congestion. The three methods Djwhal has recommended which will be much more in practice in the future are:
1. Clairvoyance
2. Clear knowing, which is a soul faculty.
3. Occult transference or occult empathy, where the healer registers the patient's difficulty in their own body.

Causes of certain types of diseases, arthritis, and diabetes, have their origin in the astral body. Diabetes is the result of wrong inner desires, according to Djwhal. This can originate in this life or a past life. Syphilis and arthritis are caused by overindulgence in "physical desire". Diseases such as measles, scarlet fever, smallpox, and cholera have their cause in the emotional body.

Fever is an indication of trouble and is a way of purifying and eliminating impurities. It is an indicator, not a disease in itself. This is why, if possible, it is best to let the fever have its way for a time. It has a definite therapeutic value as long as it is not too high temperature wise, nor lasts too long. Over-emotionalism is that astral correspondence to a fever. Over-mentalizing is the mental plane correspondence to a fever.

Germs

Where there is an inherent weakness in the physical body, there is a corresponding weakness in life-force in that area of the etheric body.

This congestion or area of arrested development leaves an opening for germs to grow. Where the vitality is strong and the soul and life force is flowing, germs cannot grow. I repeat, there is no such thing as contagious disease. There are only people with low resistance.

Humanity is one, and all people, whether they have Eastern or Western bodies, are prone to the same diseases and symptoms.

Mental Disease

The major causes of mental disease, according to Djwhal, are:
1. Disease of the brain
2. Disorders of the solar plexus
3. Astral domination
4. Premature clairvoyance and clairaudience
5. Obsession
6. Absence of mind
7. Soulessness

The Future Schools of Healing

The following list of the future schools of healing is from the Alice Bailey book on *Esoteric Healing*.
1. Psychological adjustments and healing
2. Magnetic healing
3. Allopathic healing
4. Homeopathic healing
5. Surgical healing in its modern forms
6. Electro-therapeutics
7. Water therapy
8. Healing by color, sound and radiation.
9. Preventative medicine
10. Osteopathy and chiropractic
11. Scientific neurology and psychiatry

12. The cure of obsessions and mental diseases
13. The care of the eyes and ears
14. Voice culture
15. Mental and faith healing
16. Soul alignment and contact.

The Rays and Disease

The syphilitic diseases are due to a misuse of the third ray energy. Tuberculosis is a result of the misuse of the second ray energy. Cancer is a misuse of the first ray energy.

The Basic Requirements of Healing

Djwhal Khul has enumerated ten basic prerequisites for healing. They are as follows:
1. The recognition of the great law of cause and effect.
2. Correct diagnosis of the disease by a competent doctor and spiritual clairvoyant.
3. A belief in the law of immediate karma. This means knowing whether it is one's destiny to be healed or make one's transition to the spiritual plane.
4. A recognition that healing of the physical body might be detrimental from the desire of the soul. In other words, the soul might want the physical body to die.
5. The active cooperation of the healer and the patient.
6. A complete acceptance by the patient of the dictates of the soul.
7. An effort on the part of the healer and patient to express harmlessness.
8. An effort by the patient to hold a spiritual attitude instead of a negative egotistical attitude.

9. The deliberate elimination of qualities, thoughts and desires that might be hindering the inflow of spiritual force.
10. The capacity of the healer and patient to integrate into the soul group.

It is of the highest importance for people and/or patients to remember that continuance of life in the physical body is not the highest possible goal.

Djwhal Khul, in the Alice Bailey book called *Esoteric Healing*, has listed fifteen qualities required by a healer. Do remember that all disciples on the path are healers, for all disciples channel spiritual energy.

15 Qualities Required by a Healer:

1. The power to contact and work as a soul. "The art of the healer consists of releasing the soul."
2. The power to command the spiritual will.
3. The power to establish telepathic rapport. This has to do with the healer knowing the inner thoughts and desires of the patient intuitively.
4. He must have exact knowledge. This quality has to do with understanding the knowledge of how to contact and invoke the soul and receive impressions. This is the exact science of knowledge the healer must have.
5. The power to reverse, reorient, and exalt the consciousness of the patient. The healer must become proficient as to "lifting the downward focused eyes unto the soul."
6. The power to direct soul energy to the necessary area.
7. The power to express magnetic purity and the needed radiance.
8. Power to control the activity of the mechanism of the head. This has to do with linking the minor chakra centers in the head.
9. Power of the chakras.

10. Power to utilize both exoteric and esoteric methods of healing.
11. Power to work magnetically. This means to be able to magnetically draw the power of the soul and spirit through oneself as a channel for the healing of the patient.
12. Power to work with radiation. This is the power to not only receive soul energy, but to send it.
13. Power to practice at all times complete harmlessness.
14. Power to control the will and work through love.
15. Power to eventually wield the law of life. This ability comes when one's merger with the spiritual triad (spiritual will, intuition,

Higher Mind is achieved. The spiritual triad merges with the threefold personality. Third Initiation is soul fusion. This would be monadic fusion at fifth and sixth initiations.

The Healer and His Attunement

The healer in the New Age will have the ability to make the following contacts with great ease:
- With his own soul.
- With the soul of his patient.
- With the particular type of energy in the soul or personality ray of the patient.

A person's disease is subject to three influences:
1. A person's past ancient errors.
2. A person's inheritance.
3. His sharing with all natural forms which the Lord of Life imposes on his body.

The Healer and His Ability to Diagnose

There are four aspects to a healer's ability to diagnose a proper treatment for his patient. These are:

1. The healer must train himself to know whether a patient is mentally or emotionally based.
2. He must be able to ascertain the psychological basis of the problem.
3. This will then lead to his ability to find the location of the disease.
4. This will allow him to know the area affected and the chakra in the etheric body that controls that area.

When a patient is a mental type, the approach must be through a higher center in the crown chakra. The healer must learn the following eight principles in relationship to himself:

1. Rapid alignment between the soul, mind, crown chakra and physical brain.
2. The use of the mind, illumined by the soul, in psychological diagnosis.
3. Methods for establishing a sympathetic rapport with the patient.
4. Methods of protecting himself during the transfer of energy brought about by this rapport.
5. The establishing of a right relationship with the patient.
6. Physical diagnosis and the locating of the area to which relief must come, via the controlling of the chakra.
7. The art of cooperation with the patient's soul so the etheric body focuses all its in-flowing energies in order to bring relief to the diseased area.
8. The technique of withdrawing his/her healing power when the patient is stabilized.

The Third Eye and The Perfected Man

In the perfected person the following relationships can be found, as described by Djwhal Khul in the Alice Bailey book *Esoteric Healing*.
- The eye of the soul, The agent of the spiritual triad, Will
- The third eye, Agent of the soul, Love
- The right eye, The distributor of Buddhic energy
- The left eye, Conveyor of pure manasic (mind) energy.
- The ajna center, Focusing and directing point for all these energies.

In the disciple who is beginning to function as a soul, it is interesting to see the differences.
- Third eye: Distributor of soul energy.
- The right eye: Agent for astral energy.
- The left eye: Agent for lower mental energy.
- The ajna center: Focusing point of these three energies.

The Laws and Rules of Healing

In this part I am just directly quoting with no explanation, the nine laws, and six rules of healing according to Djwhal Khul as transcribed by Alice Bailey in her book called *Esoteric Healing*. Some of the laws are a little esoteric and hard to understand at points, however some of the truths are so profound that I thought it would be worth the reader's time to place them in this chapter. For a greater explanation of these laws for those who want to learn more, do read Alice Bailey's book.

LAW I

All disease is the result of inhibited soul life. This is true of all forms in all kingdoms. The art of the healer consists in releasing the soul so that its life can flow through the aggregate of organisms which constitute any particular form.

LAW II

Disease is the product of and subject to three influences:

First, a man's past, wherein he pays the price of ancient error (reincarnational history);

Second, his inheritance, wherein he shares with all mankind those tainted streams of energy which are of group origin (racial-cultural history);

Third, he shares with all the natural forms that which the Lord of Life imposes on His body. These three influences are called the "Ancient Law of Evil Sharing". This must give place some day to that new "Law of

Ancient Dominating Good" which lies behind all that God has made. This law must be brought into activity by the spiritual will of Man.

Rule One

Let the healer train himself to know the inner stage of thought or of desire of the one who seeks his help. He can thereby know the source from whence the trouble comes. Let him relate the cause and the effect and know the exact point through which relief must come.

LAW III

Disease is an effect of the basic centralization of a Man's life energy. From the plane whereon those energies are focused proceed those determining conditions which produce ill health. These therefore work out as disease or as freedom from disease.

LAW IV

Disease both physical and psychological, has its roots in the good, the beautiful and the true. It is but a distorted reflection of divine possibilities. The thwarted soul, seeking full expression of some divine characteristic or inner spiritual reality, produces within the substance of its sheaths, a point of friction. Upon this point the eyes of the personality are focused and this leads to disease. The art of the healer is concerned with the lifting of the downward focused eyes into the soul, the Healer within the form. The spiritual or third eye then directs the healing force and all is well.

Rule Two

The healer must achieve magnetic purity, through purity of life. He must attain that dispelling radiance which shows itself in every man when he has linked the centers in the head. When this magnetic field is established, the radiation then goes forth.

LAW V

There is naught but energy, for God is Life. Two energies meet in man, but another five are present (seven rays/seven chakras). For each is to be found a central point of contact. The conflict of these energies with forces and of forces twixt themselves produce the bodily ills of men. The conflict of the first and second (the soul and personality) persists for ages until the mountaintop is reached. The first great mountain top. The fight between the forces produces all disease, all ills and bodily pain which seek release in death. The two, the five and thus the seven, plus that which they produce, possess the secret. This is the fifth Law of Healing within the world of form.

Rule Three

Let the healer concentrate the needed energy within the needed center. Let the center correspond to the center which has need. Let the two synchronize and together augment force. Thus shall the waiting form be balanced in its works. Thus shall the two and the one, under right direction, heal.

LAW VI

When life or energy flows unimpeded and through right direction to its precipitation (the related gland), then the form responds and ill health disappears.

Rule Four

A careful diagnosis of disease, based on the ascertained outer symptoms, will be simplified to this extent – that once the organ involved is known and thus isolated, the center in the etheric body which is in closest relation to it will be subjected to methods of occult healing though the ordinary, ameliorative, medical or surgical methods and will not be withheld.

LAW VII

Disease and death are the results of two active forces. One is the will of the soul, which says to its instrument, "I draw the essence back." The other is the magnetic power of the planetary life, which says to the life within the atomic structure, "The hour of reabsorption has arrived. Return to me." Thus, under cyclic law, do all forms act.

Rule Five

The healer must seek to link his soul, his heart, his brain and his hands. Thus can his presence feed the soul life of the patient. *This is the work of radiation.* The hands are not needed; the soul displays its power. The patient's soul responds through the response of his aura to the radiation of the healer's aura, flooded with soul energy.

LAW VIII

Perfection calls imperfection to the surface. Good drives evil from the form of Man in time and space. The method used by the Perfect One and that employed by Good is harmlessness. This is not lack of negativity but perfect poise, a completed point of view and divine understanding.

Rule Six

The healer or the healing group must keep the will in leash. It is not will that must be used, but love.

LAW IX

Harken, O Disciple, to the call which comes from the Son to the Mother (soul to body), and then obey. The Word goes forth that form has served its purpose. The principle of mind then organizes itself and then repeats that Word. The waiting form responds and drops away. The soul stands free.

Respond, O Rising One, to the call which comes within the sphere of obligation: recognize the call emerging for Ashram or the Council Chambers (heart center or head center) where waits the Lord of Life Himself. The Sound goes forth. Both soul and form together must renounce the principle of life and thus permit the Monad to stand free. The soul responds. The form then shatters the connection. Life is now liberated, owning the quality of conscious knowledge and the fruit of all experience. These are the gifts of soul and form combined. This last law is the enunciation of a new law which is substituted for the law of Death, and which has reference only to those upon the latter stages of the Path of Discipleship and the stages upon the Path of Initiation."

Summation

One more time I wish to acknowledge that the information for this chapter was garnished from the Alice Bailey book *Esoteric Healing* which I highly recommend for those who would like to take even a deeper look at this subject. We all owe a great debt to Alice Bailey for the wonderful telepathic information she was able to bring forth from Djwhal Khul on this subject!!!

17

Integrating Traditional and Non-Traditional Modalities

My readers, it is very important not to create a polarity between traditional and non-traditional healing modalities. There are some people involved in traditional medicine that reject holistic and New Age forms of healing. There are many in the New Age Movement that reject traditional medicine as barbaric and invasive. In my humble opinion, both of these views are not right.

There is enormous genius that comes from traditional medicine and incredible genius that comes from holistic and New Age healing modalities. It is time for all of us to have an open mind and not burn any bridges. There is much that both movements can learn from each other. A team approach is the best.

Western medicine is brilliant when it comes to emergency medicine, however, they have much to learn about the soul, the power of the mind, the power of emotions and the etheric body. Their brilliance in understanding the physical level is unmistakable.

Holistic health is becoming more and more acceptable as we move into the new millennium. The importance of positive thinking, a healthy emotional life, good diet, the power of prayer, vitamins, minerals and supplements, herbs, homeopathics, acupuncture and other such modalities are becoming more common place. Many traditional medical doctors are opening to these alternatives.

There is a third wave of non-traditional healing modalities which are beyond even the holistic, which I would call more spiritual healing modalities which traditional medicine needs to be more open to. By this I am talking about spiritual healing that can, for example, remove negative implants and negative elementals, repair the etheric body, repairing of tears and holes in the aura, and calling on the angels and inner plane Ascended Masters.

Traditional medicine, although fantastic, is too cut-off from spirit. The power of prayer in healing is unbelievable. Traditional medicine might say that this is unscientific. I would say that it is totally scientific and is governed by a similar set of laws that govern the physical.

The Masters are capable of helping to remove viruses, bacteria and even eradicating cancer. All disease begins first in the etheric, mental and/or astral body. This is what traditional medicine does not see. They are focusing too much on one fifth of every person's five bodies (physical, etheric, emotional, mental and spiritual).

Saving life is not the be all and end all. There is no such thing as death, for death is just a transition into another dimension where life continues. The physical body can die but the person inhabiting the physical body does not.

Euthanasia will be more accepted in the future. I do not support suicide, however, there are times when release of the physical body is the soul's wish.

In the future doctors will work with clairvoyants and even channels who will communicate with inner plane doctors and even the patients' own higher self and spirit. Such practices, as laying on of hands and energy balancing will be common place in hospitals.

When patients come to a hospital in the future all five bodies will be treated, not just the physical. The physical body cannot heal if the mental, emotional, psychological and etheric bodies are damaged.

In the future etheric healing teams will be called in this team approach. Not only traditional acupuncture will be used, but etheric acupuncture using etheric needles used by the Inner Plane acupuncturists.

Less invasive tests will be used that do not poison or damage the physical body. Experts in the use of a pendulum will be called in to help with dietary and medication needs.

There will be much more focus on herbs and homeopathics instead of drugs. Drugs will have their place and at certain times are very useful.

In the future hypnotists will be part of the healing team in hospitals. All doctors and nurses will be trained in hypnosis. As patients are under anesthesia in surgery and recovery, positive suggestions will be constantly given to the subconscious mind for more rapid healing. Patients will also be taught self-hypnosis to speed up the healing process.

Patients will be trained in prayer. Spiritual psychologists and counselors will be part of the team helping people resolve mental, emotional and psychological issues.

Science of mind practitioners will be part of the team doing treatments for people. Chiropractors will adjust people's spines. Muscle testing will be used for proper diagnosis and energy balancing.

Color therapy will be used, where patients are put in colored rooms with colored lights, for their particular healing needs.

Music and sound specialists will be called in to play scientifically designed music for each person's specific need. Toning and special healing chants will be utilized to maximize healing potentials.

Prayer specialists will be called in and the angels, the Inner Plane Ascended Masters and galactic healers will work in co-partnership with doctors. The Masters will be called in to remove all core fear programming. They will be called in to repair holes in the aura and remove gray fields. They will remove astral, mental and etheric dross. They will anchor the monadic blueprint body and remove all astral entities using advanced Inner Plane viruses and bacteria. Advanced technologies will be used to clear the meridians and balance the chakras.

Irritations, spots and leaks in the aura will be repaired.

Advanced computer technologies of the Arcturians will be called forth and work in conjunction with new energy computer technology that is now being created on Earth that can diagnose illnesses without having to pour dyes into the body for diagnostic purposes. There will be much less need to puncture holes in the body when diagnosis can be easily done through the science of energy.

In the future much diagnosis will be made by not only physical examination but also by spirit doctors who can speak through channels as well as clairvoyants who will be able to see the physical problems and blockages right off the bat.

Therapies such as Bach Flower Remedies and Aromatherapy will be common place.

Spiritual teachers will be part of the team, training patients to think properly and to release negative emotions. Patients will be taught in the use of affirmations, visualizations and prayer.

Marriage counselors will be part of the team helping people to deal with relationship and family issues that are contributing to stress.

In the future artisans will be part of the healing teams filling hospitals with beautiful paintings, statues and pictures that are healing and uplifting to the soul and spirit.

Hospice workers will be part of the team helping those patients who are ready to release the physical vehicle and transition into spiritual dimensions in the most divine way. These hospice workers will be trained in the science of the Bardo to help patients merge with the clear light of God at physical death. Ministers, Rabbis and Spiritual New Age Ministers of all faiths will be part of this process and all facets of the recovery process.

Every hospital will have a church or temple for prayer and meditation. Every hospital will have classrooms for educational training on all aspects of the healing recovery.

So, my friends, do you see how exciting this will be? In the future all these different practitioners will work as one cohesive, synergistic, cooperative team in conjunction with God, the Holy Spirit, each person's spirit and soul and the Archangels, Angels and Inner Plane Ascended Masters.

Hospitals will be spiritually and physically cleansed on a continual basis by spiritual practitioners to keep the psychic and spiritual atmosphere of the highest vibratory frequency. Do your see, my friends, that hospitals are now physically clean but they are not mentally, emotionally, etherically or spiritually clean. How is a person supposed to heal when the very atmosphere and physical walls are filled with spiritual disease and sickness?

This discussion is not a condemnation of traditional medicine. Traditional medicine is brilliant, however, it is only seeing through one fifth of a prism. In the future healing will be seen through a full spectrum prism.

In the future it will be a joy to go to the hospital for it will be like the most fantastic spiritual workshops you could possibly go to. It will be like going to a spa or health resort.

There will also be massage therapists, mineral baths, mud baths and beauty salons. All levels are a part of God and are important and will be honored and sanctified. When a person leaves a hospital in the future they will literally be reborn physically, emotionally, mentally, etherically and spiritually.

The true causation of disease will have been removed or at least be the process of complete removal.

There will be after case programs that will continue this process on an outpatient basis. This same concept will eventually be integrated into other spiritually bankrupt institutions such as our prison system, old age homes, day care centers, counseling centers and the like, however, this is material for future chapters in future books. This, my friends, is the vision of the soul and Mighty I Am Presence for healing in the New Age!

18

The Use of Color and Sound in Spiritual Healing

"Aum is the arrow, Brahman is the target."
Sathya Sai Baba

Everything in life is made up of energy. Becoming a Master has to do with one's ability to change and transform energy from one form to another. This can be done through prayer, affirmation, visualization, breathing, physical activity, and many other methods too numerous to mention.

Two of the most powerful methods of transforming energy is through the use of light and sound. This subject has been dealt with somewhat in the chapters from my first book, *The Science of the Twelve Rays* and the chapter on "Mantras and Words of Power."

In this chapter, I am going to expound on some of the other differing methods that can be used in this regard.

The following chart was given to me in a class I attended on this subject. I don't know where the teacher of this class extracted this from, however it serves as a helpful tool for understanding some of the basic colors and the effect they have on the human body.

Each color, of course, relates to one of the chakras. Each color in the chart also relates to a certain musical note. The chart delineates the color's effects and the problems that may be treated with that particular color.

The Spiritual Meaning of Color

The following information on the spiritual meaning of color, I have extracted from a book called *The Aha Realization Book* by Janet McClure, the founder of the Tibetan Foundation. This book is a channeled book by Vywamus, the higher aspect of our Planetary Logos.

There are many books on color, however, this information I am presenting here is from one of the highest Spiritual Beings that is currently working with this planet. He has brought through some added information that goes far beyond the standard information on color we are most aware of.

Red: The dynamic energy associated many times with thrusting into new/unknown areas. Your association with the male polarity, whether you are in a male or female body, your association with the evolutionary process and, for many of you, with the evolving Source.

Orange: The mental body, in both its logical and conceptual form, your association with structure or organization. Your ability to see the whole picture in any situation and in your life and in regard to the whole. Your ability to use the fifth dimension. For many of you, this color links you into a crystalline association with the mineral kingdom on the Earth. For about 50% of you there is a link here into the overall energy grid system associated with the Earth.

Yellow: This color is associated with clear thinking, intelligence and the means to freeing misperceptions through a magnification process, has third dimension transformational qualities. It has healing associations, especially when the healing moves through the Earth and back into the individual. Helps focus or gather energy together thus helps the mental qualities to be more focused, addresses scattering and the memory area, connects in directly with the physical aspects of Sanat Kumara and thus forms a chain or linkage system to the Solar Logos, Helios. In this connection, also see the color gold.

Green: Associated with healing, associated with growth and evolution, associated with harmony and tranquillity. Associated with a clear use of the emotional body, specific connection to the fourth dimension, has an artistic development connection including painting, music and dance. Is able to draw from the Source level itself, a perspective of wholeness thus addresses the area of allowing unlimitedness.

Blue: Blue helps balance the polarity area through the association of love and wisdom. Is an opener and a carrier of the electrical or silver energy. They blend together as the body becomes lighter. Is associated with purity of purpose and love. Helps to clarify purpose area through balancing and blending. Emphasis on service to the plan, keeps lighting up the plan.

Indigo: Identifies a deep source level connection and holds a focus on it. Helps to clear areas on separation, has often been associated with the Christ Consciousness energy, seeks to blend spiritual perspectives through a decrystallizing process. Decrystallizes in the surrender area, has seven levels which decrystallize as one "ascends" through them.

Violet: Transformation. Purification, transmutation, what has been called ceremonial "magic" or invoking through an integration of all of the other colors and what they represent, helps integrate all of what has been learned on Earth, helps heal "polarity splits," helps heal the emotional body through its association with the spiritual body, helps cleanse and purify the physical structure, helps align the mental and spiritual perspectives. Closely associated with St. Germain, closely associated with the New Age.

Pink: Associated with the heart energy and its characteristics, particularly love, compassion and gratitude. Helpful by softening any crystallization in the will area, helps the surrender process and reaches into and supports what is new, what has begun. Thus helpful in realizing divine support. Many times associated with the angelic kingdom.

Silver: Is a symbol for the electrical energy of the soul. Symbolizes the use of the soul's energy, works with being in the flow, will seek to break up or decrystallize blocks in the use of electricity, in all of its forms including all electrical and electronic devices used on the Earth. Many times associated with the angelic kingdom. Addresses the lightening perspective. Helps deal with blocks in the electrical flow of the physical structure through a penetrative process. Helps anchor more of the soul's energy in the cellular level.

Gold: The "perfect integrator." The accepting of the soul level is emphasized. The accepting of wholeness on every level is emphasized. Emphasizes linkage systems. Deals with full abundance. Helps to integrate the co-creator level, deals with putting together the pieces of any area that has seemed scattered. Connects through the Sanat Kumara or the planetary link directly to Helios or the Solar Logos consciousness level. Helps to develop through decrystallization more heart radiance. Seeks to help soften perspectives which need blending and thus they blend more easily. Deals with "kingship/queenship." Deals with assuming one's full power through the true identity level. Awakens within one the true reality level. Broadens the creative base through allowing it to flow. Accelerates blending levels of creativity together. Often acts as a "launching" into an integrated level of creativity.

Color Healing Using Candles

There are many ways that color can be utilized. The first that I would like to suggest is lighting colored candles. Light the colored candle that is appropriate for what you are attempting to manifest. If you want truth and purity, light a white candle.

If you want to gain knowledge, light a yellow candle. Light a pink candle to send love. Light a blue candle for the resolution of some spiritual problem. Green candles are good for all money and material concerns. Lavender candles are especially good for healing. Silver candles are good for protection.

As you light the candle say a little prayer and state what you need. It is important to be specific. Thank God for granting you what you need. The candle keeps your prayer and the color it is radiating continually manifesting that specific energy as long as it is lit.

Color Healing Using Lamp Radiation

This is a wonderful method that I have used myself very often. The idea is to get a small lamp and get different colored light bulbs. You can shine the type of light you need on to you in bed or while reading as you sit, sleep, or rest. Sometimes certain colored light bulbs are hard to find so at photography stores you can buy *"colored gel"* that can be taped over the lamp.

If you are reading and you want more energy use an orange colored light bulb or gel. If you need physical healing you might use a green light. If you want mental stimulation use a yellow light. If you want a more spiritual feeling use a blue or violet light. It is really fun to play with the colors and it is really easy to switch them around.

Colored Water Healing

This is a wonderful healing modality. The idea is to place the colored gels I spoke of, and wrap them around a clear glass water bottle. Place the closed glass water battle with the gel covering it outside in the sun. The sun will shine through the colored gel into the water and energize it with the sun's energy and with the color frequency of that particular gel.

You can, hence, drink the green healing vibration, or whatever color you desire. The water will not change color to the naked eye, however will most definitely contain that frequency of energy.

Color Breathing

Another method utilizing color is to breathe different colors into your body. Red, orange, and yellow are magnetic and should be visualized as flowing up from the earth toward the solar plexus. Blue, indigo and violet are electrical and are breathed in from the ether downward.

Green is the balancer of the spectrum and flows into the system horizontally. When breathing, breathe deeply and bring air into the lower abdomen. The best time to practice is before breakfast or dinner.

Color Visualization

Another way to utilize color is to just affirm and visualize yourself bathed in any given color you choose to resonate with. This can be seen as a ball of light or a tube of light in any creative way you can think of. You might just affirm to yourself that "I am now filled with emerald green." You are God, and anything you affirm or visualize takes place, for your word is law and you create with your mind.

Radiant Color Magnetism

This technique deals with channeling color through your hands for healing purposes. This can be done on yourself, or can be done on a friend, animal or plant you want to heal. It is just a matter of affirming and visualizing that you are doing this and it will be done.

Color Healing and the Rays

One of the most powerful ways of doing color healing is through calling forth from God, one of the twelve rays. This again can be done through calling forth the actual color of the ray, the number of the ray, or the spiritual quality of the ray.

I would refer you back to my first book on this subject, *The Complete Ascension Manual*, and the chapter on "Esoteric Psychology And The Science of the Twelve Rays." For your convenience, I will list the twelve rays and their corresponding colors.

First ray: Red
Second ray: Blue

Third ray: Yellow
Fourth ray: Green
Fifth ray: Orange
Sixth ray: Indigo
Seventh ray: Violet
Eighth ray: Green/Violet luminosity
Tenth ray: Pearlescent
Eleventh ray: Orange/Pink luminosity
Twelfth ray: Gold

Just call these rays in from Source, and see and feel yourself bathed inwardly and outwardly in their energy. They are always available, all you have to do is ask for them. Study the other chapter if you need a refresher course on the soul qualities that each of these colors embody. Calling forth the rays is a most powerful color healing technique.

Color Healing and The Twenty-Two Chakras

Another color healing process that in actuality is just as powerful as calling in the twelve rays and their colors is to call down your twenty-two chakras from higher dimensions into your physical and etheric body.

Each of your twenty-two chakras embody a certain color. As you spiritually evolve, your chakras descend downwards. Once you master your third dimensional chakras, the fourth dimensional chakras begin to descend into your body.

Once you master your fourth dimensional chakras, the fifth dimension chakra begin to descend. One of the fastest ways to accelerate your spiritual growth is to call these higher chakras down into your body to experience them and their corresponding vibration. They are happy to come down, however, they must be asked.

They look like bodies of light, and once anchored in your body will run their high level color frequency through your body to help you raise your vibration. They will not remain fully anchored until you are spiritually ready, for they don't want to burn your body out. They will only bring in as much high frequency color energy as you can handle.

Ask your monad and Mighty I Am Presence to guide the whole color chakra meditation process. In my book *Soul Psychology*, I have gone into much greater detail explaining all the twenty two chakras, however for your convenience I will list the twenty two chakras and their corresponding colors here.

The Twenty-Two Chakras and Their Corresponding Colors

Chakra 1: Red
Chakra 2: Orange
Chakra 3: Yellow
Chakra 4: Green or Pink
Chakra 5: Blue (Djwhal Khul recommended blue with an orange triangle in the center.)
Chakra 6: (third eye chakra): Indigo or Gold
Chakra 7: Violet or Rainbow White

These are the third dimensional chakras and the secondary colors I recommended. Here are, in a sense, the higher more evolved aspects of this third dimensional grid.

Chakra 8: Emerald Green and Purple
Chakra 9: Blue/Green
Chakra 10: Pearlescent
Chakra 11: Pink/Orange
Chakra 12: Gold
Chakra 13: Pale Violet/Pink
Chakra 14: Deep Blue/Violet
Chakra 15: Light Golden White

Chakra 16: Light Violet/White
Chakra 17: Multi-White
Chakra 18: Pink/Gold
Chakra 19: Magenta
Chakra 20: Violet/Gold
Chakra 21: Blue/Gold
Chakra 22: Platinum

Color Healing Through the Clothes You Wear

This is very straight forward. It might also suggest that you have your colors done to see if your physical body resonates best with Summer, Autumn, Winter or Spring colors. When you want to embody or cultivate a certain quality, consciously wear that color or wear jewelry or gemstones that carry that vibration.

The Planets and Color Healing

Sun: Gold or Bright Yellow
Moon: Silver
Mars: Red
Venus: Blue: Blue/Green
Mercury: Yellow or Orange
Jupiter: Purple or Violet
Saturn: Olive Green
Uranus: Electric Blue, Pale Green, or Citrine
Neptune: Dark Blue, Indigo, Grays, Green
Pluto: Yellow, Pale Green, Navy Blue
Earth: Lavender Blue

Astrology and Color Healing

Capricorn: Black and White
Aquarius: Blue with Silver Lights

Pisces: Soft Azure
Aires: Red
Taurus: Yellow
Gemini: Violet
Cancer: Green
Leo: Gold
Virgo: Purple
Libra: Yellow
Scorpio: Crimson Red
Sagittarius: Deep Clear Blue of a Morning Sea

Musical Notes and Their Correlating Colors

C: Red
C#: Violet
D: Yellow
D#: Glint of Steel
E: Pearly Blue
F: Dark Red
F#: Bright Blue
G: Rosy Orange
G#: Purple
A: Green
A#: Glint of Steel
B: Soft Blue

A Simplified Understanding of Colors

Violet: Spirituality
Indigo: Intuition
Blue: Religious Inspiration
Green: Harmony and Sympathy
Yellow: Intellect

Orange: Energy
Red: Life

Classical Music Compositions of Tremendous Healing Value

Schubert: *Ava Maria*
Mozart: *The Magic Flute*
Verdi: *Aida*
Beethoven: The Nine Symphonies
Tschaikowsky: *Swan Lake* and *Sleeping Beauty*
Wagner: *Parsifal, Lohengrin*
Handel: *Messiah*
Mendelssohn: *Midsummer Night's Dream*
Bach: *Passion of St. Matthew*
Wagner: *Tannhauser*
Pachobelle: *Cannon in D Major*

This music might be thought of as music of the spheres. A person cannot help but be healed and uplifted by listening to this type of music. Music was used in healing temples of Atlantis for just such a purpose. The science of sound and music in the future will allow doctors to heal cancer with just the power of sound.

I would recommend that every person get a set of tuning forks at your local music or metaphysical store. You can tune your chakras and clean out unwanted negative energies every day by using them.

Note: *C*; Color: *Red*; Kundalini Chakra: *Muladhara*
Note: *D*; Color: *Orange*; Kundalini Chakra: *Svadisthana*
Note: *E*; Color: *Yellow*; Kundalini Chakra: *Manipura*
Note: *F*; Color: *Green*; Kundalini Chakra: *Anahata*
Note: *G*; Color: *Blue*; Kundalini Chakra: *Visuddha*

Note: *A*; Color: *Indigo*; Kundalini Chakra: *Ajna*
Note: *B*; Color: *Violet*; Kundalini Chakra: *Sahasarara*

A friend of mine is going to a practitioner who, with the use of some kind of specialized computer, can listen to your voice and tell you what notes you are missing or over using. From this information he can do an entire personality work-up which is totally accurate. He then teaches you to reintegrate the missing tones and de-emphasizes the overused tones which totally change the personality.

Specific Music Associated with Specific Colors

In a wonderful little book called *Healing With Music and Color*, by Mary Bassano, she has done some interesting research as to correlating certain pieces of music to the basic specific color spectrum. This information will allow you to put on *red music* or *green music*, or whatever your mood is.

Blue Music

Classical:
Air on a G String by Bach
Ava Maria by Schubert
The Swan by Saint-Saens

New Age:
Divine Gypsy (Instrumental arrangement of Yogananda's Cosmic chants)
A Crystal Cave (back to Atlantis) by Upper Astral
Vocal Selection: *Be Still* by Rosemary Crow, United Research, Black Mt., NC

Indigo Music
Classical:
Traumerei by Schumann
Adagio Movement from Symphony no. 1 in C Minor by Brahms
Poeme for Violin and Orchestra by Chausson

New Age:
Angel Love by Aeoliah
Inside by Paul Horn
Venus Music from *The Planets* by Holst

Violet Music
Classical:
Piano Concerto in B Minor by Tschaikovsky
Liebestraume by Listz
Gregorian Chants

New Age:
The Great Pyramid by Paul Horn
Neptune Music from *The Planets* by Holst
Eventide by Steven Halpern

Red Music
Classical:
March Militaire by Schubert
Sousa Marches
The Sailor's Dance from *Red Poppy Ballet Suite* by Gliere

New Age:
Mars Music from *The Planets* by Holst
On the Edge by Mickey Hart
Diga Rhythm by Mickey Hart

Orange Music
Classical:
Hungarian Dance no. 5 by Brahms
Habanera from *Carmen* by Bizet
Cappricio Espagnole by Rimski-Korsakov

New Age:
Winterfall Music by Paul Warner
Jupiter Music from *The Planets* by Holst
Eagle's Call by Bruce Hurnow

Yellow Music
Classical:
Arabeske by Schumann
Fountains of Rome by Respighi
Piano Concerto no. 26 by Mozart

New Age:
Lemurian Sunrise by Warner
Dawn by Steven Halpern
Kitaro Ki by Kitaro

Green Music
Classical:
Melody in F by Rubenstein
Violin Concerto in E Minor by Mendelssohn
Clair de Lune by Debussy

New Age:
Pan Flute by Za Mir
Ocean by Larkin
Fairy Ring by Mike Rowland

19

The Issue of Spiritual Weariness and How to Overcome It

Many lightworkers on this Planet are feeling a little "Spiritually Weary or Fatigued"! This chapter is dedicated to discussing, understanding and trying to remedy this most interesting issue!

Let me begin first by saying this is a "multi-faceted" issue that must be approached from a "multi-faceted perspective!"

There is a small part of this understanding that is normal for everyone. I say this not in terms of feeling anything negative, but rather everyone knowing and understanding on some level we are visiting here. We have all come from GOD and Heavenly Realms in our Creation, so it is normal for everyone to have a Spiritual Desire to return home so to speak! This is not to say, however, that we cannot fully 100% enjoy Earth Life, for we can, and we need to fully Realize GOD on all levels!

It must be understood that Earth is a tough school, so this must be considered as well. It also must be considered that we happened to be incarnated in a tough universe (there are infinite numbers of them), for the "Theme" for our particular Melchizedek Universe is "Courage"! Other Universes have different themes! So to be successful in this Universe all Souls must have "Courage"!

Understanding these things, we now will examine some of the other less Cosmic Reasons that some Souls are feeling a little Spiritually Weary. In the original Divine Plan for this planet, our Physical bodies were never meant to densify to the degree that they have, so this also has added to the difficulty a great many souls have!

The things that I have mentioned so far are more Spiritual reasons. In listing these things I am not meaning to suggest in the slightest that we should feel Spiritually Weary, and if you don't this chapter is not meant to convince you that you should for many don't! This chapter is being written to try to explain why some or many do!

One other Spiritual Reason is that most Souls on this Planet have had an enormous number of Past Lives and this Soul Remembrance is in the deeper levels of the subconscious mind and some of those past lives have been difficult. This might be called past life "bleed through." We are also picking up on the past lives of all our 12 and/or 144 Soul extensions from our Monad who have usually had hundreds of past lives each as well!

Let us now look at the mental reasons why this is the case! On a mental level people feel fatigued because they have not been trained properly in Spiritual Psychology. This being the case they do not have full Self-Mastery of the mind. This can be very mentally exhausting and is the biggest reason for Spiritual Weariness. Many people also do not know how to quiet their minds, so the mind is always racing and in the western world people always tend to be doing and achieving rather than "being" which is also exhausting!

The more that you are in control of your mind the more energy you will have. The reason for this is that your thoughts create your reality, hence your thoughts create your energy! If you always think with your Spiritual/Christ/Buddha mind you will be filled with Personal Power, Unconditional Love, Active Intelligence, Harmony, Scientific Curiosity and a thirst for knowledge, Devotion, Thirst for Freedom, Enthusiasm, Happiness, Joy to name a few of the Spiritual/Christ/Buddha Qualities!

It also must be understood that you thoughts create your feelings and emotions so when you are in control of your mind your feelings and emotions are always positive, enthusiastic and energized!

Adding to this, when you are control of your mind and emotions you are in control of the negative ego/fear-based/separative mind, which is the number one cause of what drains your energy and makes you Spiritually fatigued!

I personally may be unusual but I don't feel Spiritually Weary. I am not saying this to toot my horn, I just don't! I attribute this to the Mastery I was just speaking of and also that my life is so filled with GOD, the Masters, Unconditional Love, Beauty, Unbounded Creativity, and Inspired Service work of many kinds, that I honestly can't wait to get up every morning! As *A Course In Miracles* says, "True Pleasure is Serving GOD!" When you integrate Spirit into every aspect of your Consciousness and Life everything becomes filled with Divine Enthusiasm and Energy! I am also so incredibly busy I don't have time! I am literally too busy! One of the keys is to make your Spiritual Service Work a way of making money! Many people have to work at jobs they don't like and I have great compassion for this. I also have great compassion for those who are feeling Spiritually Weary.

I will say, however, if you can learn to master your thoughts, feelings, subconscious mind, and transcend negative ego thinking and only think with your Spiritual/Christ/Buddha Mind this will go a long way toward getting rid of most of your Spiritual Weariness, if not all of it!

On a physical level, people get Spiritually Weary because they don't have enough physical energy, or they have chronic Health lessons and/or they are going through Spiritual Mutation! I also have enormous compassion for this. When the Physical Body is having lessons which you mentally and emotionally have to battle, this can become a little Spiritually weary! The key here, of course, is to take really good care of your physical body! Eat right, get lots of rest! Stay off of drugs, sugar, and artificial stimulants. Call on GOD and the Masters for help in healing your physical body and energizing it every day. Ask GOD and the Masters to help you partially live on Light. I am not suggesting that you stop eating, for the Masters do not recommend this. They do recommend, however, partially living on light, where the light sustains you as well as food! You might consider drinking some of the "Water of Life!" It is also important to understand in this regard that everyone has health lessons that go on with their bodies. It is very important to not give your Personal Power to your physical body! Mother Teresa had a heart condition most of her life but it did not stop her! The Dalai Lama had hepatitis and was on a Special diet. All lightworkers have aches and pains and different things and one must not coddle oneself. If we stopped our Spiritual progress over every ache and pain of the physical body the world would never change. To a great degree in lightworkers, Spiritual Mutation Symptoms and even sickness is most often a sign of your highly accelerated Ascension and Initiation process and that you keep purifying and cleansing!

Also, living in this polluted world we live in, in regard to our food, drinking water, air, electrical pollution, noise pollution, pesticides, fast foods, drugs instead of homeopathics and herbs, mercury fillings, ozone layer damage, Green house affect, Acid rain, smog, petrochemical pollution, metals, chemical pollution, and so on, is not the best for our immune system, liver or physical body, all this tends to weaken or de-energize it a bit. This again, is where a good diet, drinking lots of water, a good living space, homeopathics, herbs, and calling on GOD and the Masters and Angels to cleanse you of these things on a daily basis and help to rebuild and purify your immune system and body!

So basically the answer to remedying this feeling is by becoming an "Integrated Ascended Master!" The Higher you go in your Ascension and Initiation process, the more you will be filled with Light Quotient and Love Quotient! The more Integrated you become in this process, the more you will be filled with Radiant and Divine Light and Love on a Spiritual, Psychological and Physical/Earthly Level! When you learn to master all the levels in an integrated and balanced way you begin to really radiate this Light, Love and Power on all levels! You become totally infused by your Higher Self, The Mighty I Am Presence, the Masters, the Angels, the Elohim Councils, the Christed Extraterrestrials, Spiritual/Christ/Buddha Thoughts, Spiritual/Christ/Buddha Feelings and emotions, a Spiritual/Christ/Buddha Etheric and Physical body! Every action you take becomes God in action! Everything you think, say and do becomes filled with Unconditional Love, Joy and Godliness! Your life is filled with an absolute Divine Passion to Service and help your Brothers and Sisters. Your mind is Sparkling with Creative Potentialities! The Joy, Happiness and Bliss of GOD is constantly welling up within you. You are living a Melchizedek/Christ/Buddha/Spiritual life and everything you start doing begins turning to Gold for you Integrated Godly life is giving you the Midas Touch. You become so filled with the Love of GOD, the Love of your Brothers and Sisters, Love for your Family and Friends, Love of Service, so incredibly filled with the Creativity of GOD. So filled with Divine enthusiasm for life that even the "donkey work" begins to become enjoyable! For there is not separation seen in any part of your life. Whether you are doing errands, or cleaning the house, or taking out the trash, it GOD is in everything. Your attitude is so incredibly positive that you don't let anything bring you down. Everything that happens in life that does go according to your preferences is seen as a Spiritual Test and Spiritual lesson, and no matter how bad the situation, your attitude turns it into a positive. As I like to say, "turning lemons into lemonade"! This is the Consciousness of GOD! GOD turns everything into a positive no matter what! This is the Spiritual/Christ/Buddha Consciousness!

My Beloved Readers, are you beginning to feel how Spiritual Weariness can begin to disappear when "Integrated Ascension" is achieved?

Although this school can be difficult, we are so blessed to be here at this time in Earth's history where we are actually entering the Seventh Golden Age! Souls are lining up on the inner plane trying to find physical bodies to incarnate! I am not kidding! This is one of the hottest Planets in the Galaxy right now because of the enormous opportunity for accelerated Spiritual Growth and Service! Count your blessings!

The other key to relieving Spiritual Weariness is to be sure to balance your Three-Fold Flame! Nothing will make you exhausted quicker or will cause you untold problems in your life more than this. You must learn at all times to own your Personal Power at the 100% level unceasingly. If you do not own your Personal Power 100%, your psychological battery will go on energy drain. You will also become an immediate victim of your thoughts, feelings, nonreasoning subconscious, and negative ego lower-self mind. You must always manifest your energies only in Unconditional Love! You will be totally exhausted as well if you do not do this. Thirdly, develop Psychological and Spiritual Wisdom, the kind I am teaching in this book, and develop active intelligence. This means use your Power and Love to manifest your mission with Intelligence on the Earth!

My Beloved Readers, if you completely immerse yourself in your Spiritual Path and Service work in an integrated and balanced fashion your life will be so filled with Power/Love/and Wisdom that the cells in your physical Body and your entire being will become filled with Spiritual Current on a Spiritual, Psychological and Physical/Earthly Level! Your attitude will be so incredibly positive that you have inner peace, happiness and joy no matter what you are doing! You welcome adversity and thank GOD for it instead of letting it get you down! If everything is taken away you say, "Naked I come from my Mother's Womb and Naked shall I leave! The Lord giveth and the Lord taketh away, Blessed be the Name of the Lord"!

Are you getting a Spiritual, Feeling and Intuitive Sense of how if you become totally God Infused on every level of your being, that Spiritual Weariness can leave! It is now 2:00 in the morning that I am writing this and I have been typing for four hours and I have so much energy I do not know what to do with myself! This is the energy of GOD, I have taken the subject of Spiritual Weariness and energized myself to such a degree that I am not sure if I am going to be able to sleep tonight! I have just turned a Lemon into Lemonade!

The last two things I want to say here are regarding the issue of overcoming Spiritual Weariness and Fatigue. What I want to say is be sure to keep your Masculine and Feminine Balanced. If you allow yourself to be overly emotional this will drain your energy. If you allow yourself to become too mental or masculine this will drain your energy as well for there is enormous energy and enthusiasm in your feelings and emotions. To live in this world effectively you must be very strong and very tough. This is one of the secrets to not becoming completely Spiritual. You must have developed in your life the ability to be a Spiritual Warrior when you need to! You also must develop a good work ethic! I am not saying being a workaholic, for work must be balanced with Play and rest. Heaven must be balanced with Earth. The vertical must be balanced with the Horizontal. You must have, however, a very strong "Will to Live" and a "Will to Life!" This means an incredibly strong fighting Spirit! Never give up, Never give up, Never give up! To get to the place I am now in my life where life is not a struggle I had to first develop this ability to be a Spiritual Warrior and be very Tough. When I say Spiritual Warrior I do not mean life is a war! I mean no matter how many times you get knocked off the horse get back on! No matter how many times you fall back climbing the Spiritual Mountain you keep climbing! You never, ever give up, for if you give up you will get depressed!

As you learn to Master these lessons I am sharing with you in this book and my other books you will win this battle with your lower self and negative ego, and you will reprogram your subconscious mind with Spiritual/Christ/Buddha thinking and feeling! You will have fundamentally won the War of Armageddon within yourself. When this fundamental lesson of "Integrated Ascension" becomes achieved, Life no longer becomes a struggle. You have a "Spiritual Habit" of doing all these things. You may still slip occasionally, but that is not a big deal. Just another opportunity to forgive and learn another good lesson! I do not have to be a Spiritual Warrior anymore and have not for a very long time. It is just a habit now to own my Personal Power, to maintain my Self Mastery at all times, to be Vigilant at all times, to be the Cause of my reality, to keep my Three Fold Flame and 12 Rays in Balance! It is a habit to constantly call on Spirit and the Masters for help! It is a habit to remain in "Integrated Ascension"! By the Grace of GOD and the Masters, life is no longer a struggle! I love Earth life, I really do! I am so filled with Spiritual Current from all the different Spiritual things I am doing on some many different levels that Spiritual Weariness is completely gone! I did have to work to get to this place, and I share this with total humbleness and humility for it is by the Grace of GOD and the Masters go us all! However I share this with the utmost compassion for those who are feeling Spiritually Weary that the Spiritual Struggle is a phase that can and will be overcome as you fully realize your "Integrated Ascension!"

20

Practicing the Presence of GOD

The inspiration for this chapter came one day to me while sitting on my couch in our living room. It stems out of a Spiritual observation I have made on many occasions among many lightworkers and people on the Earth. It is such an important point I thought I would write a short chapter discussing this.

What I am speaking of here is the understanding that we all of course are very involved with our Earthly Life and Earthly missions. This is of course as it should be. For as we all know the purpose of life is to fully anchor and ground our Mighty I Am Presence fully into all our bodies which includes the physical, and help to manifest Heaven on Earth! So contrary to what a lot of lightworkers believe, the physical body and our Earthly Civilization is very important and is not just a means to graduate and achieve liberation and escape the wheel of rebirth. GOD's Divine Plan is to truly create a Fifth Dimensional Society and Utopian Society on Earth in a similar reflection as to how they operate in Heaven. So learning to love the Earth and Earth life is one of the most important lessons of the Spiritual Path!

A great many lightworkers do not like the Earth, and the truth is they will not truly Realize GOD in all his Glory unless they also learn to Love the Material Face of GOD as well!

Now people who are not on a Spiritual Path have the opposite problem, and that is they are so attached to the Earth and material life they see no other reality but this. This is not a healthy perspective either.

The interesting thing, however, is even lightworkers who are often very Heavenly and Celestial in focus and even do not necessarily like Earth or Earth Life are often still very attached to Earthly things. It sounds like a paradox, however, in truth it is not. Let me explain! What I am about to explain here is universally common on the Earth. It is also something that although almost all lightworkers know this, they continually forget this in the heat of Earth life so to speak. What I am speaking of here is that our lives on Earth are incredibly complex. We have romantic relationships, family, friends, service work, businesses, Spiritual Missions, students and all kinds of Earthly projects and involvements. It is the nature of Earthly life that no matter how Spiritual or together we are, things still do not always go according to our preferences or attachments. Even though we all know that everything in our life is a Spiritual Lesson, Teaching, Challenge, Opportunity to Grow, Stepping Stone for Soul Growth, and Spiritual Test, in the heat of Earth life and our involvement with it we tend to forget. For example, when someone judges or attacks, we sometimes forget that this is a Spiritual test to see if we can stay in our Personal Power, Bubble and respond back with Unconditional Love!

When someone steals from us we forget that it is not really about what has been stolen, as much as how we deal with the situation, that is really important. Do we stay Centered? Do we Forgive? Do we become angry and judgemental? How attached are we?

Let's say we are working on a very important project and it falls through. Is the most important thing the Spiritual Lesson GOD is teaching you or is the project the most important thing?

When something happens to a family member, is the first most important thing the Spiritual Lesson or the family member?

If someone cuts us off on the road, is the most important thing the Spiritual Test and lesson, or anger at the driver?

If a person is having problems with their car, and the car mechanic is overcharging you, is this really about your car, and being cheated, or how you are going to Spiritually deal with the lesson?

The phone company screws up your bill and phone service for the 50th time. Is this about the Spiritual Lesson and Test you are being given, or the incompetence of the phone company?

A friend or business partner makes a mistake and costs you $200,000 dollars. Is this really about the money and the mistake this person has made, or how you Spiritually and Psychologically deal with it?

What I am basically saying here is, that even though we all know that everything in life is a Spiritual lesson and Spiritual Test, most lightworkers in the heat of Earth Life and the often severity of the Lessons of Earth Life, forget that even though Earth Life is important, the real purpose and meaning of it all is that everything, and I mean everything, that is happening is really not about what is happening outside of self. It is about how you are responding to all the disasters, catastrophes, negative egos of other people, mistakes of other people, incompetence of other people, and unexpected as well as strange and unexpected things that happen in life. Everything that happens, bar none, is just to see if you will respond and demonstrate from your Spiritual, Christ, Buddha mind, or if you will react from your negative ego/fear-based/separative mind. No matter how severe, dangerous or unexpected the lesson, this is always the case. What happens is that most people and most Spiritual people of all kinds get so involved with Earth life that they forget really what the main purpose of everything is about. They may be involved with Channeling, Spiritual Teaching, Spiritual Study, or Healing, all day long, however, often when things happen during their daily lives, even in the Spiritual Projects they are working on, they forget the main purpose is not about what is happening physically, it is about maintaining one's Christ Consciousness. Even if it is a Spiritual Project or Spiritual Business and disaster has struck; it is not about the Spiritual Project or Spiritual Business. I am not saying it is not important to get these

Earthly matters straightened out, for they are extremely important. However, the first most important meaning of what has occurred, no matter how disastrous, how negative, how big a mistake someone made, how big a screw-up occurred, how negative a person has been, it is still most importantly about if you are able to remain in your Personal Power, Self-Mastery, Centeredness, Unconditionally Love, Forgiveness, Nonjudgmentalness, Evenmindedness, Happiness, Joy, Patience, Tolerance, Defenselessness, Harmlessness, Egolessness, God Consciousness, Christ Consciousness, Buddha Consciousness, Spiritual Consciousness. The key point, no matter what you are involved with and no matter how important it is in an Earthly, or Spiritual Sense, is did you Respond from your God/Christ/Buddha/Spiritual Consciousness, or did you react from your negative ego/fear-based/separative/selfish/self-centered/attacking/judgmental/impatient/depressed/upset/sad/irritated/annoyed/intolerant/consciousness? Now there is no judgement if you responded inappropriately, for this is just a lesson in which a golden nugget of wisdom needs to be learned, and forgiven. However, the key point is to not get so attached and even involved with the lessons of outer life and the Earthly world that you forget what the true meaning and purpose of what you have incarnated onto Earth for. It is not about all your Earthly involvement and projects as the number one priority. The number one priority is to "Practice the Presence of GOD"! Said in another way, to Practice being God in every situation of life! The more extreme the lesson the better the opportunity to practice!

My Beloved Readers, the reason I have written this chapter is that it is so incredibly easy to forget this!

Every single book, magazine, radio show, person, teacher in school, parent, family member, friend, counselor, psychologist, social worker, movie, television show and aspect of Earth life will be demonstrating the exact opposite of this.

To live life from this perspective means that you have to put GOD first in every situation. Even if the whole world is being destroyed your first responsibility is to deal with your Spiritual lessons properly. Many people in this world are much more interested in correcting the perceived wrongs in the world and in other people then truly learning their own lessons.

Animal Activists throw red paint on people wearing furs. Is that learning their lessons? A Spiritual teacher gets angry and attacks a student. Is that really the Spiritual Teacher learning their lesson? They may think it is but it is not! An AIDS activist interrupts a person giving a speech and won't allow anyone to hear what this person is saying. Is this AIDS activist learning their lesson? It is not from a Spiritual Perspective. These are extreme lessons, but the same thing applies to each and every one of the things that are happening in your life every moment of the day.

When your child is going through the terrible twos, and you become impatient and angry, is that your learning your lesson? How do you deal with people who are incredibly unclear and who are always making mistakes? How do you deal with people who make royal screw-ups in incredibly important situations? How do you deal with people who you find out lie, cheat and steal? Do you attack, judge, gossip, defend, engage in ego battles, compete, and/or try to punish? As the Master Jesus said, "Judge not that ye not be Judged! He that hath no sin, cast the first stone! Do not try and take the Speck out of the eye of your Brother when you have a Beam in your own eye!" I have said this before and I say it again!

It is of the highest importance to remember we are being "Spiritually Tested" every single moment of our lives. Although what happens in our Earthly lives is very important, it is not as important as Practicing Demonstration of GOD every moment of our lives first! This chapter is a gentle, loving reminder to put GOD first and respond in God/Christ/Buddha/Spiritual Consciousness and to then secondarily get your Earthly Life fully Mastered as well. Do this, however, only after you have made sure to master your Spiritual and Psychological lessons first, of learning to respond appropriately as GOD would have you respond.

One more last thought I would like to share on this subject is that in my experience when I chose to respond from God Consciousness and Spiritual/Christ/Buddha Consciousness first, not only do I have more inner peace and feel better about my self, I also very interestingly find that things on an Earthly Level are more likely to turn my way as well. For if you are not responding from your God Consciousness then by Cosmic law you are responding from your negative ego/fear based/separative consciousness and this will, in truth, only in the long run repel what you want. Any negative response is only going to cause a negative response from others. It is not about teaching other people lessons. It is about you learning your lessons, and demonstrating a better Christed Example for others. It is not about indulging our negative egos or indulging our negative emotions and punishing people who deserve it. It is about doing just the opposite. It is about learning our lessons, and reflecting the Self Mastery, Self Control, Evenmindedness, Pure Unconditional Love, Sweetness, Kindness, Gentleness, Harmlessness, Defenselessness, Forgiveness, Egolessness and Nonjudgmentalness of God to another. They will be so shocked at your response. For they have been trained to expect attack, criticism, judgmental-ness, punishment, that they will be deeply Spiritually moved by your example and they will work 1000 times harder to correct their inappropriate response because of your Spiritual Example. So you not only get the Spiritual Benefit of learning your Spiritual lessons as GOD would have it be, but you get the added benefit of the Earthly situation more likely to turn around in your favor. Realistically however, there are times this will not be the case. In those instances you will have the added benefit of living in God Consciousness, unconditional love, and inner peace even if the outer situation did not remedy itself in your favor. Plus you will have set a Christed example to another. They may not have learned their lessons but that is not important. All that is important is that you have learned your lessons. They will have to reincarnate again on Earth to learn their lessons. You will be freed from the wheel of rebirth for you have learned your lessons. In every situation of life you must choose: "Do you want GOD or do you want your negative ego? Do you want unconditional love, or do you want attack and fear? Do you want the permanent or the impermanent? Do you want truth or do you want illusion? Do you want liberation and graduation or do you want to reincarnate?

This chapter is a gentle, loving reminder from a fellow Spiritual Brother to remain joyously vigilant on this point and to keep Earthly life in proper perspective because the forces of indolence of the subconscious mind, physical body and mass consciousness will be constantly pulling you to react from the emotional body and negative ego, instead of your true God Consciousness! You are now being reminded by Spirit and the Masters of this most important Spiritual Practice and insight which is truly one of the true golden keys to achieving God Realization in this lifetime!

21

Turning Lemons into Lemonade: A Millennium Perspective

One of the absolute Spiritual keys to effective self-mastery and Self-Realization is the ability to turn lemons into lemonade. It must be understood that life will never always go according to our preferences. This is why the concept of having preferences rather than attachments is so important. If one is attached to having things go the way they want this person is going to have an enormous amount suffering of in their life. When we have only super strong preferences, we are happy no matter what happens. We still want our preferences met, but our happiness is not based on achieving them.

There is another "Noble Truth," however, which I am going to humorously add to Buddha's Four Noble Truths on the nature of truth and suffering, if he doesn't mind. I now humorously add, "The importance of turning Lemons into Lemonade." My Beloved Readers, let me now explain my meaning to begin to lay the foundation for this understanding. Besides the concept of preference, which is essential, we must also understand that from GOD's perspective everything that happens is positive and should be looked at as a gift. The proper attitude to everything in life is "Not my will but Thine; thank you for the lesson!" No matter what happens in life, no matter how horrific the example, this is the proper attitude. As His Holiness the Lord Sai Baba has said, "Welcome adversity." From GOD's perspective there are no accidents in the universe and everything happens for a reason. The reason is always to Spiritually teach a lesson that needs to be learned. Now sometimes the "negative" things that happen are caused from personal karma. Sometimes they are caused by planetary or group karma. Sometimes they are caused by past life karma. The truth is, it doesn't matter why it happened or where it came from, for if it happened, you can be assured that you needed that lesson for some reason and the proper attitude is to welcome it, accept it and look at it as a gift. From GOD's perspective everything that happens in life is a Spiritual test. In every situation in life we can respond from God consciousness or negative ego consciousness. We can respond from our lower self or our Higher Self. We can respond from unconditional love or from fear. We can respond from separation or from oneness. We can respond from our Melchizedek/Christ/Buddha consciousness or from personality level consciousness that is not connected to the Soul and Spirit. So Earth is a school to practice demonstrating GOD or to practice demonstrating being a Melchizedek, the Christ and/or the Buddha. The terms or names we use do not matter for they are interchangeable.

Now the truth of the matter is that life is constantly throwing us lemons. The key principle here is will you turn it into lemonade, or will you keep tasting the bitter taste of the lemon. This is all governed by your attitude and perspective. As His Holiness the Lord Sai Baba has said, "Your mind creates bondage or your mind creates liberation." So no matter what happens in life and no matter how catastrophic the occurrence, it is each person's responsibility to turn that experience into lemonade. We constantly see examples of people doing this. They do this as a means to heal one self and to create meaning. Victor Frankl in the concentration camps of Nazi Germany created a whole new form of therapy called Logo Therapy. The woman whose son was killed by a drunk driver creates an organization to prevent this from happening, so others do not have to suffer. The person with AIDS gives up everything and dedicates her life to travelling the world to raise consciousness about AIDS. The story of Job tells how a man loses everything, and I mean everything but ultimately turns it into a Spiritual test of his "Righteousness" in believing in GOD. Job's statement in the Bible is one of my favorite quotes where he says: "Naked I come from my mother's womb, and naked shall I leave. The Lord giveth, and the Lord taketh away, blessed be the name of the Lord."

In my own mind I have called this the Job initiation, and I have reminded myself of this on many occasions when I have been asked to give up certain things. No matter what happens in life the key is to "Focus on what you can do instead of what you can't do!"

If you lose your voice and can't speak any more, then become a writer. If you can't walk, then join the Olympics in a wheel chair event. Look at the inspiration Christopher Reeves has brought to himself and the world after becoming paralyzed. If you have an illness and can no longer go outside then dedicate your life to developing your inner life. If you are losing your sight and can no longer read, than listen to tapes. If you have digestive problems and can't eat without discomfort, then learn to live on light. No matter how much is taken away and no matter how many things you cannot do, there is always something you can do. Focus yourself and your consciousness on that which you can do! Your own Mighty I Am Presence and the Holy Spirit can always help you to find meaning, another purpose, and another direction to follow no matter what happens. A person who has an optimistic positive attitude will ultimately remain so, no matter what happens in their life. A person with a negative, pessimistic attitude will find a way to feel unhappy even if outwardly things are going well. The world is nothing more than a projection screen for our attitudes and interpretations. GOD would have us be 100% positive and optimistic no matter what happens in life, no matter how morbid the example. What ever happens in life is there to teach us certain Christed/Buddha qualities. The Master Jesus knew this, for that is why he said on the cross, "Forgive them Father, for they know not what they do." The Master Jesus saw this situation as a

Spiritual test and lesson in forgiveness, and demonstrated this understanding in a most extreme situation.

No matter what the situation of life, make lemonade out of the lemon you have been handed. If you lose a large sum of money and someone rips you off, you are being given the wonderful opportunity not only to practice forgiveness, but to not be attached to money. Whatever the situation of life, you are being given the wonderful opportunity to transcend negative ego thinking and feeling and to practice Christ/Buddha thinking and feeling.

Let's say you make a big mistake and the whole world finds out about it, like President Clinton did, for example. That can be transformed into lemonade by practicing true humbleness and humility. If you have to go to jail, look at it as a Spiritual retreat. Malcolm X, while in jail, basically educated himself. If one has to go to jail, use it as a time to totally focus on your Spiritual life and getting yourself psychologically and physically strong. Whatever goes wrong in your life, no matter how extreme, use that situation and become an expert in it. Dedicate your life to helping others, so they never have to go through what you just went through. There is no situation of life where GOD, your own Mighty I Am Presence, the Holy Spirit, the inner plane Ascended Masters and your own positive creative Spiritual consciousness cannot turn lemons into lemonade! We have all heard the expression that "This was a blessing in disguise." This understanding stems from what I am writing about in this chapter. The truth is everything, and I mean everything, that has ever happened in this world, is happening or ever will happen, is a blessing in disguise. If it happened, it means our Soul needed that lesson. There is no such thing as good luck or bad luck in this world; this is total illusion. Luck does not exist in GOD's reality. The concept of luck is an illusionary fabrication of the negative ego thought system. Everything in GOD's Universe operates out of laws on a Spiritual, mental, emotional, etheric and physical level, and if something happened then there is a cause. This is the immutable law of karma, or cause and effect. We cannot always control what comes into our life on an outer level, however, we can control 100% our attitude, interpretation and perspective of what happens to us. I remember Elizabeth Kubler Ross said that it was the atrocities of Nazi Germany that inspired her to dedicate her life to being a better person. It is not what happens to you, it is how you use what happens to you.

My beloved readers, in the ultimate sense there is no such thing as death for anyone, there is just translation from dimension to dimension, and the wearing of different bodies. So in truth as *A Course In Miracles* states, all perception is a dream. The purpose of Earth life is that it is an Earthly school to practice living and demonstrating GOD's dream rather than the negative ego's dream. It is to live the loving happy dream rather than the fearful, attacking, angry dream of the negative ego. If there is no such thing as death, then what is the worst that can happen? Is losing all material things that important? My beloved readers, it all comes back to Lord Buddha's Four Noble Truths dealing with attachment. If you are attached to people and things you will surely suffer. If everything in life is a super strong preference and you go after your preferences with all your heart and soul and mind and might, many of them will manifest. Those that don't, or go exactly the opposite, will not affect your happiness because they are preferences, which means you will be happy either way. Happiness and inner peace, hence, becomes a state of mind rather than anything outside of self. I like Paramahansa Yogananda's saying, "God is my stocks and bonds and financial security." So the key is to look at everything that happens in life no matter what it is as a Spiritual test. So no matter how bad the lemons are that you are given, you can thank GOD and bless this experience, for it has given you the opportunity to transcend your negative ego and practice Melchizedek/Christ/Buddha Consciousness. Even if everything is taken away on every level, then, my beloved readers, all that is left is GOD, and you can say: "Naked I come from my mother's womb, and naked shall I leave. The Lord giveth and the Lord taketh away. Blessed be the name of the Lord!"

You can bathe in passing the Job initiation and retaining your happiness and inner peace even though everything has been taken away. It is then you can rise again like the Phoenix and give birth to a new creation by focusing on what you can do instead of what you can't do. You find double meaning by then becoming an expert in the lemons you have been handed, and you dedicate your life and your Spiritual Path to helping other people not to experience the lemons that you had to go through. By selflessly giving in this manner you have practiced Spiritual and psychological alchemy and turned a negative experience into psychological and Spiritual Gold! You have healed your self and helped to heal the suffering of others through the wisdom you have gained, and your own positive, optimistic, creative Spiritual attitude. So let it be written.

22

How to Clear Specific Diseases: From the Perspective of the Masters

The idea for this chapter came to me one day while driving my car. The idea was to look through the DSM-III diagnostic handbook and list some of the common psychological and/or physical diseases and run them by the Masters in our meditations. Then get a short little synopsis as to their cause and cure from their perspective, rather than from the perspective of the field of traditional psychology, which to say the least is quite a limited perspective. I was really looking for short concise answers as to mental, emotional, physical or karmic causation. A person could write a book about each one of these diseases. Please don't take this as the "be all and end all" final statement. However, what is shared here can give one a handle and golden key to Self-mastery and healing in these areas. I began with asking about multiple personalities, which has always been something I have been curious about.

Multiple Personalities

Multiple personalities could be entities from a trauma caused hole in the auric field. It could also be separated subpersonalities that have fragmented out of fear. Or both. It could also be past life aspects that come through fragmented, unintegrated and unhealed. For example, a murder in a past life may bring up a trauma for that individual and cause them to fragment or split off into a personality that is constantly replaying the murder. This may draw in an entity, implants, parasites (negative elementals) which impinge upon the whole organism. This split can occur on a dual level or be multiple (three or more), which means a whole group of injurious parts have now fragmented off, as portrayed in such movies as "Sybil" and "The Three Faces of Eve", all breaking threads of connection, and all competing for the dominance of the personality or organism.

To heal, the person must create a stationary flow of the soul (Higher Self) to the personality, which functions as a witness or observer for the integration and balance of all parts, in the same way that we need to balance and integrate all our archetypes, rays and astrological aspects. In our case these parts have not split off or fragmented as in the case of a multiple personality. We are also hence not dealing with astral entities, implants, or parasites in this same kind of split-off manner.

The healing of a multiple personality comes in the removal of implants, parasites, astral entities, core fear, and the integration then of these personalities or archetypes into an integrated whole. The removal of the core fear, implants, parasites and astral entities along with proper philosophical understanding of the need for integration and the conscious mind being the unified director, will make healing a lot easier.

People who have had this dysfunction can become quite integrated and functional, with the help of a qualified therapist. It is usually very severe trauma, like extreme child abuse, that has triggered this whole process. However, just because a person has experienced extreme child abuse doesn't automatically mean that they will become a multiple personality. In truth this is quite rare.

Definitions of Common Negative Emotions

An old spiritual teacher of mine who has since passed on to the spiritual world, Paul Solomon, channeled this next section. Paul was and still is a wonderful spiritual teacher, and many called him the next Edgar Cayce. The following are definitions of some of the attitudes and belief systems that cause some of the well-known negative emotions. I think some of them are quite amazing, and extremely accurate.

Anger: loss of control over others and attempt to regain it.
(corollaries of anger: frustration, irritation, aggravation, indignation, impatience, annoyance, etc.)
Fear: entertaining a fantasy of a danger that has not occurred.
Hate: misplaced expression of love/protection of myself because of how much a person's opinion of me means to me when I don't feel safe with that person.
Worry and anxiety: incapacitating the self to keep from (or avoid) preparing for a situation.
Guilt: indulging in concern over a past situation in order to avoid taking action now.
Hurt: denial of responsibility for one's own feelings. Feeling another is not doing what I want him/her to do.
Confusion: laziness of mind to keep from dealing with a situation or making a decision.
Self-pity: indulging in helplessness as a luxury (substitute for self-love).
Grief: loss of control over a source of attention or love.
Resentment: anger and hurt.
Jealousy: misidentification and feeling of inadequacy and insecurity to a known or unknown competitor, or fear of loss.
Self-righteousness: Indignation, Contempt
Disdain: feeling superior in order to feel like a good person.

Boredom: not taking responsibility for your own happiness or own entertainment.
Loneliness: placing responsibility for your happiness on someone else.
Rejection: unsuccessful attempt to gain approval.
Shyness: waiting for someone else to tell me I'm okay.
Homesickness: loss of source of attention and source of self-identity.
Embarrassment: feeling that another will think I am a nincompoop.
Regret: Feeling inferior because I feel I've performed inadequately.

The following information came through in a Sunday morning meditation. This information comes from the combined intelligence of Djwhal Khul, Lord Maitreya, and Melchizedek with Djwhal Khul seeming to take the leadership role for this particular chapter.

Migraine Headaches

"Migraine headaches are unintegrated material coming up through the psyche where the person has not acknowledged their soul connection, is therefore unable to assimilate the pattern of behavior, and feels a pressure from this blocked flow of energy. Karmic themes from this lifetime and other lifetimes come into play here, having to do with pressures around the brain, temples, neck and shoulders. The proper integration of the soul allows one to not have to take on a burden they cannot carry or to avoid their own karma." Djwhal also said that there can be chemical or environmental causes. There can also be karmic causes from past lives.

Migraine headaches are always, however, connected with psychic pressure. He said that there can also be a pressure in the head that is created with the influx of high frequency spiritual energies. The high frequency energies cause the brain fluids to be detoxed of lower frequencies, imperfections and impediments, which causes an expansion of the energy field within the brain and an increase in the convolutions of the brain. This can sometimes cause quite a strong pressure, especially in the third eye and temples. Certain areas in the brain are often congealed or closed, especially around the sinus areas. The new energy field has to gradually penetrate the old field.

Djwhal Khul said this can be a process that is uncomfortable for some. It is a natural evolutionary process and not to be considered a separation from the soul, as was described in the aforementioned section. One can ask for energetic adjustment in the field around the head from the Arcturians, Masters, or inner plane Healing Masters to help in this regard.

Arthritis

Djwhal said it was "a withdrawing of the life energy psychically and spiritually. A withdrawing of love. An inability to channel out love and warmth." This causes a concentration and build-up in the joint area of a deposit of psychic material. When there is an outflow of love and acceptance there is not a rigidity.

Asthma

Djwhal said, "It is often a reaction to circumstances at birth or early childhood which have to do with suffocation." This can be psychic suffocation in which there is no freedom for the individual to exist. There may be a basic intolerance in the mother in being able to sustain motherhood. There is an unconscious attempt to stifle the child, to reduce the energies of the child, to control the child. The child hence has a reaction of feeling like it is being smothered. This can also be a reaction from actually being smothered or drowned in a past life. An inability to get the breath.

"Not enough life force is provided between the fetal environment and the early childhood. This creates an aura of sickness and/or of breath or energy. Asthma can be cured not only by physical methods, but also by doing a type of regression. One goes back to re-experience one's birth, asking to re-experience the relationship with the world through the relationship of the Spiritual Mother as opposed to suffocating by a personal earthly mother. Forgiveness is part of the process here also."

This also reminds me of one of the Edgar Cayce readings where a child had asthma and it was caused by a past life deep-seated guilt. Here the condition was caused by a lack of self-forgiveness for a past life mistake.

AIDS

Djwhal said here that all the viruses such as AIDS and others of similar genre are caused because of the imbalance that is occurring at the third dimensional level at this time. As the new energies are coming for evolution, there is a resultant struggle between the old and the new. This might be termed the Christ and antichrist energies. This also might be termed energies of love and hate or control. This struggle causes lower astral fourth dimensional entities to feed on this etheric conflict.

All disease begins in the invisible dimensions first, be it etheric, astral, or mental bodies. Along with the astral entities are negative elementals that feed upon this etheric struggle also. There is also much fear-based programming around viruses. This mass collective consciousness fear-based programming has a very negative effect on humanity's immune system. Viruses begin first as astral or etheric, or even mental viruses and then move into the physical.

The idea is to keep these other bodies clear and the physical will become invulnerable to disease. Diet and environment are important in the sense of keeping physical toxins out of the system. If the four-body system is kept fundamentally clear, viruses or bacteria cannot grow. The fact is there are viruses and bacteria everywhere and this is nothing we need to be afraid of. Viruses and bacteria have no possibility of manifesting in a person whose four-body system is balanced and who is soul and monadically infused.

From the perspective of the Masters, AIDS can also function as a catalyst for some to help them leave the planet when they need to be placed elsewhere, physical existence not being the "be all and end all" goal of existence. As I mentioned in my other books Hanna Kroeger has found a cure for AIDS with her herbs. Other more New Age doctors are having great results using energetic medicine and homepathics to build the overall immune system.

HIV and AIDS is not a guaranteed death certificate. Some of the symptoms many people experience have more to do with their beliefs about AIDS than the actual disease. Other symptoms have more to do with all the drugs they are being given, which is having a damaging effect on their immune system. AIDS like everything in life is not bad. It is a lesson no different then all lessons in life and must be used as a teacher and catalyst for spiritual growth.

Catatonic

In this case Djwhal Khul said that a person has created a wedge, or dark grey shelf between themselves and their God-Self, out of fear. The need here is to be completely unconscious of life, and to respond out of the most feeble life form. A person who is catatonic is barely conscious. Almost to the point of being brain dead. They have literally created a palpable substance of separation. To reach someone who is catatonic takes extreme patience, and unconditional love to break through that wedge. It is much like working with a person who has become possessed. It takes a person of great faith to ignite the Three-Fold Flame of Love, Wisdom and Power within an individual such as this, to help them accept themselves and their life.

The catatonic person is so afraid they are not even able to function. This could also be caused by a previous life thread coming up in the consciousness or from extreme abuse or experience in this lifetime. Djwhal said this may also happen when a person has been annihilated in a past life in a war, for example, the etheric body is in extremely bad shape, yet the person chooses to reincarnate immediately with no healing in between lifetimes.

It is very important for lightworkers to understand how damaged and tainted an etheric body can become. This is a very serious situation, for prior to ascension the physical body works off the etheric blueprint. If the etheric body is damaged there is very little possibility of true healing. We have all had very traumatic past lives. This is why it is a good idea for everyone to call in the inner plane Healing Masters and the Etheric Healing Team and the angels specializing in the etheric body to completely repair the etheric body to make it correspond with the true monadic blueprint.

This is another classic example of the shortcomings of traditional psychology and Western medicine that doesn't deal with this aspect. The catatonic is almost in the twilight zone. They are not physically dead and yet not psychologically alive. They are in "No Man's Land." The catatonic is not that different from a person who is having a life threatening illness and lapses into a coma. Djwhal Khul said in this case it is best for the healer in charge to call forth and help the person connect with their angels.

I saw an interesting TV show recently in which a very young body lapsed into a coma after being hit by a car. No matter what the doctors or family did the boy would not come out of it until they started to talk about his pet dog. The love the boy had for his dog began to cause a response. They were eventually able to bring his dog to the hospital and a full recovery occurred. The love for and from an animal, especially for children, can be an enormous healing influence.

Narcolepsy

A narcoleptic is someone who is constantly falling asleep. Djwhal Khul said that it is difficult for this person to stay firmly connected to third dimensional reality. This is a type of defense mechanism of an unconscious nature to escape the lessons of the third dimension. Djwhal said that the narcoleptic is often escaping to the fourth dimension in a type of dream state reality. Another possibility is someone who trances out very easily as in a case of someone who is very suggestible to hypnotic suggestion and is a classic somnambulist. This would be a deficiency in the psychic boundaries and ability to protect themselves psychically from suggestion. Another possibility is that the person is being exposed to certain environmental toxins and is having an allergic reaction to these toxins and is going unconscious again as a defense mechanism.

So we see here with the narcoleptic and, in truth, all forms of psychological or physical disease that there are mental, emotional, physical, environmental, and past life karmic reasons that can be a potential cause. There is not always just one quick pat answer or sole reason.

The narcoleptic actually has the potential to become a good meditator and have access to multi-dimentionality if this process can move to a psychic experience that is controlled rather than uncontrolled. The simplest answer here as to the cause of narcolepsy is the" unconscious avoidance response". Some people when they don't want to do or go someplace just get sick. The ideal here is to make the tough decisions in life and consistently use all your energies once a decision is made.

Insomnia

In the case of an insomniac, we have the opposite situation. Instead of falling asleep at inappropriate times as in the narcoleptic, here the person can't fall asleep at appropriate times. Djwhal said this is often connected to an inability to let go, a fear of resting, or a fear of surrendering. It can also be connected to a haunting memory in the conscious or subconscious. This memory could be from this life or a past life. It can also be a fear of being powerless in their life. A type of neurosis can also cause this where they have so much pressure and responsibility in their life they feel they cannot afford to take off the time to sleep. Fear is obviously connected here as with probably every single one of the symptoms mentioned in this chapter. It could be a fear, or fight or flight, where the person feels they must be on the alert, possibly from a past life trauma that the person is not even aware of consciously.

Endocrine Diseases

This has to do with the major glands: pineal, pituitary, thyroid, thymus, adrenals, kidneys and gonads. These diseases usually manifest as the glands being underactive or overactive. This is connected usually with one of the seven chakras being over or under active in function. This has a direct effect on the functioning of each gland. This over or under activity in the chakras can stem from an imbalanced philosophy, or psychoepistemology. It can develop from an imbalance in the functioning of the three minds or four bodies. It develops from a person's unconscious overidentification with one or more of their chakras, which is extremely common.

The reverse of this is, of course, an under identification with one of the chakras. An emotional person might, for example, overidentify with the solar plexus and heart and not use the third eye. This would tax the organs and glands connected with the solar plexus and cause an underdevelopment in the pituitary.

Hives

Animosities, grudges, or unkind thoughts are usually the psychological cause.

Polio

In one past life reading of Edgar Cayce's, a man had polio that was caused by jeering and mocking others in a past life. In a similar situation a child had infantile paralysis which was caused by a past life of using drugs and hypnosis to hurt others.

Constipation

Constipation can have a physical or dietary causation, but can also have a psychological component. The constipated person is often very fearful, and hence uptight, constricted and too controlled in their psychology. The person with chronic diarrhea is just the reverse. Their psychology is being too yin instead of too yang. We have all heard the expression of having diarrhea of the mouth. Without self-control, discernment and appropriate response present, our thoughts create our physical bodies. We are what we eat as well as what we think!!!

Manic Depressive

Manic-depressive behavior occurs when a person allows themselves to be run by the emotional body, negative ego, and subconscious mind in a victim psychology. The ideal here is to have personal power and self-mastery over the three-fold personality (physical, emotional, mental). When the emotional body and subconscious mind run the conscious mind, the negative ego becomes the programmer of your emotional reality and you are on an emotional roller coaster. The ideal is to develop self-mastery and see that your thoughts cause your reality and to develop evenmindedness, equanimity, unchanging joy and inner peace at all times regardless of what is going on outside of self.

Panic Attacks

Panic attacks, in its simplest understanding, are caused by the negative ego being in control. The essence of the negative ego is fear. The person who has panic attacks is constantly being victimized by the negative ego with this fear at inappropriate times or challenging times. There is a battle for the control of the personality going on. Personal power in service of love must take command here for this to be resolved. It does not matter if the fear is from a past life or this life.

Obsessive Compulsive

A person who is obsessive/compulsive is being run by a subpersonality in the subconscious mind that requires order and structure. The opposite of this would be the person who is, for a lack of a better word, a "slob." The slob lives a life of complete non-order and lack of cleanliness. Again too yang or too yin. The key here is to not be a victim of one's mind. In the obsessive/compulsive person the mind is running the person instead of the person running the mind. The lesson here is for the conscious mind to not necessarily get rid of this part but rather to make choices as to when to listen to it.

As soon as free choice comes into play the disturbed quality of this part becomes diffused. What we see here from this lesson, and all the symptoms described in this chapter, is that they all stem from "imbalances in the psyche". By this I mean either being too yin or too yang. Too heavenly or too earthly. Not balanced in the four-body system. Not balanced in the three minds. Not balanced in one's relationship of the inner parent to the inner child. Imbalanced in the understanding of the need to transcend and die to the negative ego and to only think with one's Christ Mind. Being a victim instead of a Master. Not recognizing that one's thoughts are causing their reality.

These basic and simple principles when not held as an ideal manifest as symptoms or psychological or physical disease. These symptoms, pathologies, psychological and psychic diseases are not bad, they are just lessons. They are actually gifts if looked at properly, teaching you obedience to God's laws. They are signposts that an adjustment needs to be made in your philosophy or psychoepistemology. They are teachers showing a need for greater balance within these principles. It is these symptoms that are the suffering and fire of life that are relentlessly pushing everyone to ascension and God-realization.

Senility

When an elderly person becomes senile, they are in a sense returning to a child-like state. This can be caused by both physical and psychological factors. A child is basically just run by the subconscious mind. As one moves into adulthood, the conscious mind takes charge and takes control. In senility due to the break down of the physical vehicle, due to old age, illness, environmental poisoning and/or psychological reasons such as giving up or loss of personal power and self-mastery, the person again becomes run by the subconscious mind. It is a return to a state of being victimized by the subconscious mind, emotional, mental and physical vehicles. This can stem from an improper philosophy, and often a lack of meaning and purpose.

Melancholia

Melancholia is an extreme state of prolonged sadness and depression. There is always victimization by the emotional body occurring here. An inability to let go of anger in one's life. Extreme attachment is always involved here. As Buddha said, "All suffering is caused by attachment." Victim consciousness, lack of purpose, and self-pity is very prevalent.

Possession

Where obsession is being victimized by a subpersonality, possession is being victimized by an astral entity. It is always the person's psychology and philosophy that allows this to occur and attracts this in. Victim consciousness is operating here. There is no judgment in this and it is extremely common. It is important to clear the unwanted entity out as soon as possible. Use the matrix removal program in combination with going to Djwhal Khul's inner plane ashram and have the Masters remove them.

The only entities you want hanging around you are Christed and Ascended Beings of the fifth dimension or higher. When a person is run by the negative ego they tend to attract these lower astral entities.

Almost all drug addicts and alcoholics attract them. The lesson here is to move from victim to Master, from effect to cause, and you will never be bothered again. We all have to occasionally deal with lower astral or dark force entities hanging around at times. Possession is a more extreme case of this.

Agoraphobia

Agoraphobia is when the negative ego, being fear, is projected onto the idea of it being dangerous to leave one's house. As with all phobias it is all within one's own mind. Your thoughts create your reality. Fear can be projected onto everything or love can be projected onto everything or everyone. There are only two ways of thinking. This fear can be built in this life or a past life. It can be helpful here to do regression and see where it came from. This is done in a hypnosis type situation, and often this can clear it up right away by just partially or completely experiencing the situation which catalyzed. I use the word catalyze here for the true cause was always your thinking, not any outside situation.

Fear projection or phobias will always be created and manifest until full personal power and self-mastery is claimed and full command of the negative ego, subconscious mind, mental body, emotional body, physical body and inner child are claimed. The fear and phobia is God's way of forcing you to either become dysfunctional or a God-realized Master. As *A Course In Miracles* says "There are no neutral thoughts." All thoughts are of the negative ego or are of the Christ Mind. One is being forced to learn to think with their Christ Mind and to extend only love and never attack fear/consciousness. The world is nothing more than a mirror of your own thinking. The idea here is to learn to stop "projecting fear" and to learn to only extend love!!!

Anemia

In the Edgar Cayce readings, a man in this lifetime had anemia and it was caused from a past life where he killed someone.

Leukemia

In another Edgar Cayce reading another man had leukemia this lifetime and this again came from a past life where he had knifed or shed someone else's blood with lower-self motivation. In this lifetime he was now shedding his own blood. As Edgar Cayce said, "Every jot and title of the law is fulfilled." These last two are not the only causes but they are certainly a great motivation to not create karma in this lifetime.

Liver Problems

Liver problems are often connected too much negative anger and/or overplanning or overthinking. On a physical level, drugs of any and all kinds are deposited in the liver.

Pancreas Problems

This can stem from a number of reasons. One is a lack of sweetness or joy in life. On the other side of the coin it can also be caused by too much focus on the sweetness or pleasures of life. One other interesting correlation of the pancreas is connected to the use of the will. Too much use of one's will or not enough use of the will can adversely affect the pancreas. As with the liver it is connected to the proper integration of the third chakra in balance with the other chakras. On a physical level; too much sugar, starch and even oil in one's diet can cause pancreas problems.

Heart Problems

This is obvious: inability to give love to self or others. The other side of the coin is an inability to receive love from self, others or God.

Homosexuality

I am listing this here but, in truth, this is not an imbalance at all from the perspective of the Spiritual Hierarchy. It is a normal part of God's creation for a certain percentage of the population and any attempt to change this and look for a psychological or spiritual or karmic cause is faulty thinking.

Sociopath

This is a very interesting psychopathology. A sociopath is someone who has no "conscience." They are completely run by the negative ego, and they will say and do anything with no consideration of others. They are often pathological liars. Their word means nothing. They are clearly disconnected from their Higher Self and oversoul. It also stems from a lack of education of the difference between negative ego thinking and Christ Thinking.

What is scary is that I know a number of people who are clearly on a spiritual path and have New Age type businesses that I would call sociopaths. It is mind boggling to me that they can believe in New Age stuff and even in the Masters and yet be so incredibly run by the negative ego. The sociopath usually also has enormous amounts of anger and is almost trying to punish the world. This can be karmic with the etheric body being extremely damaged in a past life and then quickly incarnating again before healing has taken place on the astral plane. Usually a lot of implants and psychic parasites are found.

Crib Deaths

Crib deaths have to do with the phenomena of a soul incarnating into a physical body at the time of birth and at the last second changing its mind. This can be a spontaneous occurrence or on occasion calculated for some karmic reason for the incarnating soul and for the parents. A physical body cannot live without a living soul to inhabit it.

Fear, Anxiety and Paranoia

These are all derivatives of negative ego, which can be most easily defined as fear-based thinking. There are only two emotions: fear and love. All other emotions stem from these two. Perfect love casts out fear.

There is fear-based thinking and love-based thinking. Fear is projected attack. If you believe in attacking others you will always live in fear. Edgar Cayce said, "Why worry when you can pray?" I would add, "Why worry when you can pray, do affirmations, visualizations and own your personal power?" Being loving at all times to self and others will remove fear. Giving up attack thoughts will remove fear. Praying, affirmations and personal power will remove fear. Denial of the negative ego and the embracing of the Christ Consciousness erases fear. Paranoia is fear taken to a more extreme and exaggerated condition. Fear here is being projected onto everything and everyone.

The world and people are nothing more than a mirror and projection screen for your own thinking. The single most important lesson of life is to learn to project onto this screen and mirror only Christ thoughts and not negative ego thoughts. There is about 1% of our thoughts that might be considered reality-based fears that can serve as a protective function for the physical vehicle. Ninety-nine percent of our fears, however, are illusionary and stem from faulty thinking.

Alcoholism or Drug Addiction

This is always an escape. It is using a drug to escape emotional and psychological problems. What the person really needs is a spiritual teacher to help educate them about the purpose of life and how to heal themselves through the kinds of things I speak of in my books. What exacerbates this problem is that what starts as a psychological and emotional dysfunction also moves into a physical addiction. This is why the person must often get physically detoxed before true psychological healing can really take place. Alcoholism and drug addiction attract astral entities, negative elementals and extraterrestrial implants, which also need to be cleared for a full recovery. Proper integration of all three minds needs to be achieved, owning one's full power in God, personal power and the power of the subconscious mind.

Narcissistic Personality Disorder

This is another character disorder I have often seen among lightworkers. Narcissism is an extreme case of self-centeredness. It seems also to be connected with being run by the inner child. A person who is narcissistic filters everything through a lens of how does this affect me. It is an over-preoccupation with the concerns of self. True God-realization is really just the opposite. It is to Self-actualize self so very little time needs to be focused upon self and one's life can be dedicated to the helping of others who are less fortunate then you.

I have seen a great many very high level initiates having very high levels of this type of character disorder which never ceases to amaze me given their initiation level. It just continues to point out the great discrepancy that can occur between one's spiritual development and psychological development. The narcissistic person processes everything in life as to how does this affect me and never asks the question how does this affect others. It is similar to how a five-year-old child behaves. The physical body has grown and become an adult but the mental and emotional consciousness is still stuck in this self-centered and often very self-indulgent stage.

Alzheimer's Disease and Amnesia

Alzheimer's disease is the person losing their memory and cognitive faculties over time. There has been some interesting studies done that one potential cause of this may be aluminum poisoning. Americans use aluminum foil and aluminum pots and pans all the time. I remember when I used to cook fish in aluminum foil two or three times a week, and one time I went to my homeopathic doctor who did bioenergetic testing and he said I had aluminum poisoning.

With many diseases we must keep the physical toxicity factors in mind. There can also be obvious psychological and spiritual diseases involved. A person with amnesia may just not want to remember as a type of defense mechanism. This could be a past life lesson or some kind of trauma to the brain. It is a fascinating phenomena how most people who have been sexually abused as children have no memory of it. It is usually in adulthood that these memories begin to arise again. This is a healthy defense mechanism of the human psyche that helps people to cope.

Sleep Walking

Djwhal Khul said that in the case of sleep walking the astral body and the physical body merge together and the person sleepwalking is actually walking around in their astral body. Because of this merger the physical body is carried along for the ride. Usually the astral body leaves at night and travels on its own plane of existence.

I will never forget the story of one of my clients that was a young adolescent and was doing a lot of acting out. He came in for a session one day and told me a story of how he was planning to steal his parent's car one night while they were sleeping and go visit his girlfriend. He was planning this out all night, however, at the last minute changed his mind before bed and decided not to do it. The only problem is that all his planning had programmed his subconscious mind. While sleep walking later that night he stole his parent's keys and opened the garage door and actually pushed the car out into the street without starting the ignition. He was afraid that starting the ignition would wake his parents up. He then pushed the car about two blocks down the street and got in it to start it up and "woke up". The person is actually doing this on the astral plane and doesn't realize that they are bringing their physical body along for the ride.

Epilepsy

Djwhal said that epilepsy is a short circuit within the body and within the nervous system that creates a short circuit within the brain pattern. It can often be connected to an overload of psychic and spiritual energies. What can happen here is that there can be a discrepancy between the readiness of the four-body system to receive these energies.

As a person becomes more soul and monadically attuned and infused and the etheric body more aligned with the Divine pattern and strengthened, it is possible for a healing to take place. Vywamus is a good Master to call on for the healing and repair of the electrical system along with the Lord of Arcturus and the Arcturians.

There also are certain karmic causes of epilepsy. In two different Edgar Cayce readings epilepsy was caused by overindulging in sexuality in a past life, and misusing psychic powers for an evil purpose in past lives.

Dyslexia

Dyslexia has to do with certain electrical wiring in the nervous system and etheric body being crossed. This condition is where people displace letters and numbers. I have personally noticed that these people are often very gifted individuals. Djwhal said that one possible cause was that in a past life the person was more right brained and in this lifetime they were using the left brain more. On a subconscious level they have not let go of the previous programming which at times overrides the existing program. It is connected with a third dimensional blockage. The right brain tends to block the use of the left side of the brain at times.

This may also explain my personal observation that these people are often very gifted because of this right brain development in past lives. The dyslexic often is connected to a whole other level of intelligence. Unfortunately in our society they are severely punished for not fitting into the classic left brain norm. The Masters said dyslexia is connected to the right brain being more predominate, with the left brain being more difficult to access.

The reverse of this of course would be the person who is more left brain predominate and has a difficult time accessing the right brain. This is less noticed in our society, and this person is considered normal and is your classic scientist who is Godless and is totally disconnected to the soul and Higher Mind. Here we would have the worship of the intellect and no connection to intuition, imagination and psychic senses.

The dyslexic doesn't operate the way they are expected to in school. They do operate how they are expected to operate in spiritual school. Now the ideal, of course, not that one side of the brain is better than another, is that they both must be integrated and balanced to their mutual full potential. Another way of saying this is the difficulty of left handed people to function in a right-handed world. Stress can also play a part as to the severity and occurrence of dyslexia. The Masters added here stress due to competitiveness and comparing.

Miscarriages

The Masters said that this is usually a lesson for the person who had the miscarriage. The cause can be physical, psychological, karmic, or energetic. The incoming new baby doesn't incarnate until right around the time of birth so that is why the lesson is more for the mother and husband then the new soul. As with crib deaths there is sometimes an antipathy or allergic reaction between the mother and soul on an emotional level that could be one cause.

There are obviously medical reasons why this can happen. In one case I heard about at a lecture, a woman and her family had an electrical fence around their house. She had over eleven miscarriages. As soon as they got rid of the electrical fence she was able to carry a baby to full term. A possible karmic reason would be a mother who had abandoned her child in a past life and now the child was abandoning her for spiritual growth reasons.

Very clearly a miscarriage is a catalyst for spiritual growth if it will be used by the consciousness for this purpose. Many people in the third dimensional world pin the whole purpose in life on family and kids and not on God and their spiritual path. A person like this might be a prime candidate for a miscarriage because of the attachment and overidentification with having a child. The basic law of life is that that which one is attached to is ultimately taken away. One must learn to be involved in life but not attached. One must learn to have strong preferences but not addictions.

Schizophrenia

The image I got when asking about this was a lightening bolt splitting the person and the consciousness. This split can be caused from a past life or present life trauma. It can be connected to an imbalance of the feminine and masculine sides. It can be a loading down of negative alien implants more on one side of the brain then another. This can also be similar with negative elementals.

The circuits are eroded due to these factors. This creates havoc in the nervous system, which leads to the nervous or psychotic breakdowns. This is in part due to gaps and holes in the circuitry of the etheric and nervous system field, thus leading to a very aberrant pattern. In the case of the schizophrenic, you have erosion of the psychic walls. In the case of the multiple personality you have the build up of the psychic walls.

Depression

Depression is a loss of personal power and in essence a subconscious and even conscious giving up and disconnection from the spiritual warrior archetype. The Masters said that depression can also be connected to a lack of understanding of the normal cycles of life and death within a given lifetime. Each initiation is a kind of death and rebirth process which people on the emotional level are often confused by. For example, at the fourth initiation the person disconnects from their Higher Self, who has been their teacher for eternity, only to be connected to a high level teacher which is the Spirit or monad. This is often disconcerting to the mental and emotional vehicles if not understood.

Some depressions are also brought in from other lifetimes that stemmed from decisions that were made in these past lives that were not correct. This created a deep-seated guilt that became so heavy it led to a depression of the whole system. This can be seen as dark cloudy areas within the aura where a lot of pain has built up from past lives or this life. This can also be seen as red areas in the aura where there is irritation and pressure because the person knows they have to do something to rectify some karmic lesson from their past.

This is often connected to the manic depressive roller coaster ride that stems from over-identification with the emotional body, subconscious mind, and negative ego, not yet having learned to heal their emotions through the science of attitudinal healing. The person in a depression may try a visualization of using a red ladder, which cultivates the first ray of power to climb out of the soup, so to speak. Often there is an etheric wound connected to the depression as well as a negative imprint (a sword in the heart for example).

Again implants and elementals and astral entities can be involved here. Again we say how traditional psychology is missing as much as three quarters of the pie in terms of what is often really going on. There is the saying that depression is anger turned inwards. Anger and depression always go together. Anyone who is chronically angry will also be chronically depressed during more receptive periods. The person who is depressed does not need negative anger but rather positive anger or personal power and spiritual warrior energy to pull themselves out of the pit. Anger and depression are two sides of the negative ego coin. Their true antidote is personal power and love.

The harder the blows of life, the stronger and more powerful you must become. Here we have the importance of the spiritual warrior archetype and the positive use of the destruction archetype. Cayce called it positive anger. It is the cultivation of first ray energy at times of crisis to not allow life to beat one down. Surrender is a Christ quality as long as it is combined with personal power and love simultaneously. The person who is manic-depressive must learn evenmindedness, equanimity and unchanging inner peace and joy regardless of outside circumstance. The person who is prone to depression finds happiness outside of self instead of in their "state of mind"!!!

Depression most definitely could be anger turned inward, or a negative anger turned outward. Anger should not be blocked but rather channeled as a source of power towards love and Christ ideals. The etheric wounds I spoke of earlier, such as a sword or other object still embedded in the etheric body, must be removed for it is creating an added pressure to the system. Eventually hospitals will have teams of people who can work medically, nutritionally, psychologically, psychically, spiritually, etherically, mentally and emotionally so a complete clearing and healing can occur.

In some ways it is amazing that people ever heal in hospitals adding to the fact that there is so much negative energy embedded in the walls and only the physical level is addressed. Even that level is not very effective given the rejection of such things as homeopathics, herbs, acupuncture, nutrition, radionics and so on. The drugs used poison the liver and body and create other problems, so really it is just for emergency functions that they have any real value. I personally never would go to a medical doctor except in this kind of situation.

Ronald Beasely, the great spiritual master from England who is no longer in embodiment, used to say that hospitals should be burned down every five years because of the build up of negative energy. It is hard for a person to heal in that kind of atmosphere. The level of healing they are working on is literally just a sliver of the whole pie. Can you imagine how great it will be in the future when a person goes to a hospital and has a medical doctor, spiritual counselor, psychic healer, nutritionist, massage therapist, wholistic practitioner, acupuncturist, hypnotherapist, radionics specialist, naturopath or homeopathist, social worker, family counselor, channel, astrologer, clairvoyant, and healer all consulting together and working together as a team for a complete healing?

Psychotic

A person who is psychotic is completely run by the subconscious mind and negative ego. There is no conscious control. There are always gaping holes in the aura, and usually they are possessed. This can manifest into a suicidal or homicidal form. The psychotic is filled with negative elementals and alien implants. The psychotic truly needs to be hospitalized to become stabilized for the long process of healing and recovery to occur. The psychotic's field may actually be black.

The Neurotic

The neurotic is not as bad off as the schizophrenic or psychotic. The neurotic is much more common, and their auric fields tend to be grey rather than black. The neurotic is still functional in the world where the psychotic and schizophrenic are clearly not. In the neurotic the circuits are often weak, mixed, confused, grey or cloudy, and often filled with etheric mucous. The neurotic often has different kinds of obsessive or compulsive behaviors which are all a product of allowing the subconscious mind to control the conscious mind too much. Not enough mastery has been achieved over the mental, emotional, physical bodies and negative ego.

This is also connected to improper inner parenting skills in regards to the inner child. The neurotic has not snapped or had a nervous breakdown or had a split in their personality. It is still in the realm of minor dysfunction not major dysfunction. Sometimes this can be connected to being unprepared for rising of the kundalini. This happens often among lightworkers where the spiritual bodies are more advanced then the psychological bodies. The energies rise and the Light comes in with greater intensity and the psychological self is not equipped to channel this energy properly through the mental and emotional vehicles. It thus may manifest as fear, negative emotions, uncontrolled sexuality and lower-self desire.

This is why it is very important to refine and develop all three levels equally (physical, psychological and spiritual). The rising of the kundalini can, in truth, manifest in all the symptomologies listed in this chapter if the person is not balanced in their overall understanding.

Contagious Diseases

One of the great illusions of western medicine is the concept of contagious disease. There is no such thing. There are only people with low resistance. This applies on the physical as well as the psychological level. The concept of contagious diseases was invented by a person with victim consciousness. We each are God and the cause not the effect of anything outside of ourselves. This applies to the negativity of others as well as the bacteria or virus infections of others. There is no disease that is contagious if you are in balance and hence have a strong immune system. Disease cannot grow in a healthy body environment. Even in regard to AIDS, not all people who are exposed to AIDS get it.

Cancer

Cancer basically has to do with a disintegration of certain cells in the body. This whole book is really dealing with the need for balance and integration of one's psychoepistemology, archetypes, rays, feminine and masculine energies and so on. When a person is not spiritually, psychologically and physically balanced and integrated this manifests within the cells because of the Hermetic Law, "As within so without, as above so below." Prolonged lack of integration and balance spiritually and psychologically will ultimately manifest physically. Now there are many reasons for cancer. Some forms can result from physical toxins such as prolonged exposure to pesticides or radiation. Some forms of cancer can come from energetic poisoning like electrical power lines or prolonged use of cellular phones or police officers using those radar guns. Other times it can come from the emotional body and prolonged running on negative emotions that eventually debilitate certain cellular structure.

It can result from the mental body and prolonged negative thinking. It can come from the spiritual body in the sense of prolonged lack of integration and fusion with the soul and Spirit. Being in a bad marriage or in a job you dislike can take a toll on the body. As can improper nutrition, or prolonged use of alcohol or drugs. Any one of these things or a mixture of these can be the cause. Sometimes cancer is a past life karmic lesson. The Masters said that sometimes the cancer is the body's reaction to prolonged affect from alien implants and negative elementals. Tumors are often formed around these areas. This again is an example of the shortcomings of Western medicine that may cut out the cancer, but since the implants and elementals are still there, it just grows back again.

The Masters basically said that all disease has to do with negative elementals or aberrant thoughtforms. Disease is the physical manifestation of negative ego thinking. Perfect health is the manifestation on the physical level of Christ thinking. The negative thoughts of the negative ego grow in the mental body, which creates a negative feeling in the emotional body, which builds negative energy in the etheric body, which eventually manifests into the physical structure.

This is really the "law of manifestation" working in the wrong direction. As sons and daughters of God we can't help but to manifest every moment of our lives. The question is not whether we can manifest, but rather what are we manifesting. It is just as easy to manifest health as sickness; it is just a matter of choice. As *A Course In Miracles* says, "Sickness is a defense against the truth." The truth is that each one of us is the Christ, Buddha, the Eternal Self and perfection is our divine birthright if we will just claim it.

Cancer can also be genetically predisposed. One way to remedy this is to ask the Masters to clear your entire genetic line, and to know that you do not have to be a victim of family genetics either. This is a choice also which most people aren't aware they have. One of the best cancer preventatives is to ask the Arcturians to clear all cancers in the entire body from the etheric, mental, emotional and physical fields.

Another cancer preventative from Edgar Cayce is to eat six almonds a day. Apparently almonds have some ingredient in them that repels cancer. Hanna Kroeger, the renowned herbalist, says that a fungus causes cancer, and that she has herbal remedies that will clear this up in a matter of weeks. The main thing is to work on all levels in a holistic and synergistic approach.

23

GOD, My Personal Power, The Power of My Subconscious Mind and My Physical Body are an Unbeatable Team!

One of the most important Spiritual practices of the Spiritual Path is prayer. I am actually amazed at how many lightworkers forget to do this! Not only do they forget to take advantage of the incredible love/wisdom/power of GOD, they also do not ask for help from Christ and the Holy Spirit! They don't ask for help from their own Mighty I Am Presence and their own Higher Self! They don't ask for help from the Archangels and Angels! They don't ask for help from the inner plane Ascended Masters and the Saints and Sages of all religions! They don't ask for help from the 14 Mighty Elohim and/or Elohim Councils, also known as the Creator Gods! They don't ask for help from the Christed Extraterrestrials such as the Arcturians and Ashtar Command, to name just a few!

It is also interesting how some lightworkers just limit themselves to GOD, or just the Angels, or just the Christed Extraterrestrials, yet do not partake of the help that is forthcoming not only from GOD, but also from the entire Godforce!

It was the Universal Mind through Edgar Cayce (the "Sleeping Prophet") that said, "Why worry when you can pray?" I never met anyone who did not wholeheartedly agree! It is such a simple understanding, but so easy to forget!

Why try and do everything on your own when you have the help of GOD, Christ, the Holy Spirit, your Mighty I Am Presence, your Higher Self and the entire Godforce to help? Whenever I need something really important I "address" the letter prayer to GOD, Christ, the Holy Spirit, and all the Masters and Angels of my choice, and help is always forthcoming! I honestly cannot remember one prayer I have ever made that did not come true! As long as it is a reasonable request that is not coming from your negative ego, or that would hurt someone, why wouldn't GOD and the Godforce help?

The reason that prayer is so important is that GOD and the Godforce are not allowed to help unless you ask! We have been given free choice, and GOD and the Godforce are not allowed to enter unless asked!

I personally ask for help with every aspect of my life! I am constantly praying! I ask for help in terms of my Spiritual life and accelerating my Ascension, Initiations, and path of God Realization. I ask for help for guidance and direction or mental clarity! I ask for help on feeling and emotional issues if need be! I ask for help constantly on an etheric or energetic level! I am always having them make energetic and electrical adjustments in my energy fields! Most people do not realize what fantastic healers they are and how much they do for you to clear your energy fields and even physical body of toxins! I also ask for help in every aspect of my business! You must realize that GOD, Christ, the Holy Spirit and the Godforce are Omnipotent, Omnipresent and Omniscient, so when you call them in you are literally calling in the infinite power of all creation to help! Any one of them you call in is powerful, let alone all of them! One of the biggest reasons I attribute to my humble success professionally is because of GOD and the Masters! I have a regular Huna Prayer in a long version form and short version form that I do every day for the entire year! When I really get going for the Wesak Celebrations I sometimes do it with my staff two or three times a day! I can instantly feel the energy pouring in! I also usually instantly see the results in increased phone calls, faxes, e-mails, e-mail orders, and opportunities! I invite Spirit and the Masters in, in organizing every aspect of the Wesak Celebrations and every aspect of my Earth life! Some lightworkers separate GOD and the Masters out from their Earthly life! Why do this when GOD is in all Four Faces! You will be absolutely amazed how much GOD and the Godforce can help you professionally and in every aspect of life! I even call them in when I have heavy things to lift! They send energy and come to help, and I swear to you, you will feel stronger if you do this! I pray in the morning for energy and it is amazing how I don't get tired and I can work all day at the computer! I pray before bed for healing and ask them sometimes to work on me all night and they do! I call on them for help in my relationship with Wistancia. If ever there is the slightest energy that is off between us, which honestly rarely happens, I call them in and have them clear our fields and help us to get reconnected! Sometimes I do it just as a maintenance or upgrade even when there is nothing overtly going on. I am always amazed, for if there is anything off it is immediately cleared! I ask for their help with all logistics at the Wesak Celebrations and have them help with every aspect of the Event. It is no small thing putting on an Event for 2000 people coming from all over the world! By the Grace of GOD and the Masters, we have had six literally perfect Wesak Celebrations in a row, which completely amazes me!

By the Grace of GOD and the Masters, I think that one of the biggest reasons for my success has been my belief in asking questions and asking for help! The infinite Power/Love/Wisdom of GOD and the Godforce is literally available for everyone, and they forget to ask, or no one specifically showed them how to ask, who to ask and what to ask for! By the Grace of GOD and the Godforce it is my great pleasure to do this service! God and the Godforce can remove your entire negative ego programming from your subconscious and energy fields if you will ask! What a revolutionary step in the field of psychology! Talk about revolutionary and cutting edge! My wife and I even call in GOD and the Masters sometimes when we make love! There is not one aspect of our lives where that we do not include them! I truly love GOD with all my heart and soul and mind and might, and I have absolute implicit faith and trust in not only GOD, Christ, and the Holy Spirit, but I also have absolutely implicit faith and trust in the inner plane Ascended Masters, Archangels and Angels, Elohim Councils and Christed Extraterrestrials! I can honestly say that they have never once failed me! I literally have absolute 100% faith and trust in them to supply for my every need! This GOD, Christ, the Holy Spirit, and the Masters will do for you as well; all you have to do is ask!

I ask for Platinum Nets constantly to clear my energy fields! I call for the Prana Wind Clearing Device, which I talk about in this book to clear my meridians and energy fields. I call for Axiatonal Alignments! If anyone is ever sick around me, I have them put up a wall of protection for them and for me and it really works! If I ever feel an energy virus or bacterial energy in my fields, I call Melchizedek, the Mahatma, and Archangel Metatron to run the viral vacuum program or the Bacterial Vacuum program! My Beloved Friends, they suck these energies right out of your field! If I need help financially they will help with that! There is literally nothing they cannot and will not help with! If I have some spot in my body that needs healing I will call in Dr. Lorphan and the Galactic Healers, who I wrote about in *The Golden Book of Melchizedek*! I also call in my Healing Angels! If I need more joy I call in the Lord of Arcturus and the Arcturian Joy machine! My Beloved Readers, it works every time! If I need more of a particular one of the Seven Rays, I ask them for that! If I need help developing myself in a certain area I ask for that! If I want to train at night in one of the inner plane Ashrams while I sleep I ask for that! If I want Ascension Activations I ask for that! In my book *The Golden Book of Melchizedek,* you will find, I humbly suggest, the greatest collection of the most profound Ascension Activations ever put together in one book! I also at times call in the inner plane Acupuncturist or Etheric Healers. I never go to the doctor anymore, for Spirit and the Masters take care of my every need! I even have them give me nourishment. They will give vitamins and minerals or any energetic substance you need in an etheric form! One of the most profound ways you can be helped is calling on the Holy Spirit for help! I have written a chapter on this in my book *How To Release Fear-Based Thinking and Feeling*, if you are interested! The Holy Spirit is the supreme master at "undoing" a mistake, karma, faulty program, faulty thinking, feeling, emotion, energy, health lesson, relationship lesson, life lesson. Just call on the Holy Spirit and the Holy Spirit will undo it for you in a mystical way that I do not claim to understand or be able to explain, for this lies within the realm of the unfathomableness of GOD! I cannot tell you how many times I have called on the Holy Spirit to get me out of certain lessons and I can honestly say it has worked every time!

It must also be understood that in the highest and most complete integrated understanding of Prayer it is not just enough to say the Prayer! To have its most beneficial effect, after you pray you first have to have "Total Faith" that it will be done! Many people pray, but then give in to self-doubt right afterwards, which does not completely sabotage the prayer, however, let's just say the results will be even quicker if Faith is maintained! Prayer in its fullest sense of the term is an "Integrated Process and a Co-Creative process" with every aspect of self doing its part. After Faith has been established, then one's attitude should go forward in life with 100% Personal Power and Positive attitude as if the Prayer were already accomplished! Now in truth, it is already accomplished, for GOD, the Masters and the Angels have received the prayer and they are now holding that vision and acting upon it as well! So, in truth, the prayer is a reality on the Plane of GOD, and we are now just waiting for it to manifest back down on Earth! GOD is the only True reality, so, in truth, the prayer request is already answered. So not only should you walk around with 100% Faith, Personal Power and a

Positive attitude after praying, you should also completely mentally, emotionally and physically "act as if it is already accomplished!" In truth, it already has been accomplished in GOD, and that is the only true "permanent' reality of life! Taking this one step further, you should even experience this truth with all five senses. See it being real, hear it, touch it, smell it and taste it! As far as you are concerned, for all intents and purposes, the prayer has already been completely answered and you should live your life on every level of your being as if this was the case! If ever you start to slip from this "immaculate conception" in your own mind, you should immediately do an affirmation and positive creative visualization to reaffirm the "Truth of GOD" back into your reality. The other way to reaffirm this truth back into your being is to repeat the prayer! Just the act of doing the Prayer is an affirmation in and of itself!

So, in other words, to pray properly, my Friends; the mental body, emotional body, energy body, physical body and five senses must all do their part! My Beloved Readers, when Prayer is done in this "Integrated Ascension" manner which causes there to be "consistency" on all levels of your being, this is when you will get the absolute quickest response to your prayer. Prayer will work even if you don't do this; however, if you pray in this "Integrated Prayer" manner this is what has been called "Miracle Mindedness"! It is this state of consciousness that causes Miracles to happen in your life!

Many lightworkers often pray, however it is not done from 100% Personal Power, owning the fact that you are a Son and Daughter of GOD! It is not done from the State of Consciousness that you are One with that which you are Praying for! It is done from lack of self-love and self-worth, so the negative ego is telling the person they are not deserving of the prayer! Or the person is holding some guilt and subconsciously believes they should not receive it. The person prays but does not have faith! Then they pray but do not keep a positive mental and emotional attitude and feeling! Then they do not act as if, they act as if it wasn't, not believing that which they have just prayed for! One must ask oneself if they believe in the love, wisdom and power of GOD or not! If you are going to Pray, then fully believe and know that what you are asking for is going to come about. Otherwise, why do it? The lesson is for you to be 100% decisive! If you are going to make the effort to do the prayer and call forth the Love, Wisdom and Power of GOD and the Godforce then stand behind that decision and believe in what you are doing. I say to even go one step beyond belief to "Knowingness!" I personally do not just believe GOD, the Masters and Angels exist, I know they exist! I do not just believe in their Love, I know their Love! I do not believe they will, I absolutely *know* 100% for sure they will help! I honestly have 100% faith in their love, wisdom and power! I have 100% Faith in GOD, Christ, and the Holy Spirit's Omnipotence, Omnipresence and Omniscience! I know you believe this too, my Beloved Readers, for we are all Sons and Daughters of GOD, so we are all, in essence, the same. in truth! So do not just believe in GOD, the Masters and the Angels ability to help, fully "know it!"

To continue this discussion, lightworkers often lack what I call faith, trust and patience! They do not only lack faith; they lack trust and patience! This has to do with trusting not only trusting GOD, but also trusting GOD's laws! The law is "Ask and you shall receive! Knock and the door shall be opened"! Trust in GOD and GOD's laws! Then one must also be patient, for we are living in a physical reality and matter vibrates at a much slower level then the mind, feelings, or energy! That must be taken into account! I am not saying that prayer cannot manifest instantly, however, I am saying that sometimes just a little bit of patience is needed as well! Many lightworkers lose their faith and trust because they become impatient!

So, lightworkers often pray but don't keep faith, trust, patience, don't own their personal power 100%, don't own their self-love 100%, and self-worth 100%, and don't keep negative ego thoughts out of their mind, which continues to erode the manifestation. They don't act as if, they act as if not! They do not affirm and visualize! They go back to worry, which are negative affirmations! They do not accept GOD's reality as the truth! They do not see it all coming to pass with all five inner and outer senses! They do not live their life like their prayer has already been accomplished! They do not pray again when their attitude and emotions start slipping back into lack of faith and knowingness on all levels! So what we have is not "integrated prayer," we have "fragmented prayer"! My Beloved Readers, do you see why prayer often is a little slow on this plane to come about? The person prays, but then does everything in their power to sabotage the prayer by not doing their part! Prayer is not just about GOD, the Masters and the Angels doing everything! True prayer is a co-creation between GOD and the Sons and Daughters of GOD who are Spiritual Masters and Co-Creators within themselves! This is the great misunderstanding and misconception of prayer! True prayer is "integrated prayer"!

My Beloved Readers, are you seeing now how important this concept of "Integration and Balance" really is! Integration and balance, and transcending negative ego thinking and feeling, and replacing it with Spiritual/Christ/Buddha thinking and feeling, are truly the keys to every aspect of your life!

My Beloved Readers, I am just touching the tip of the iceberg in terms of all they can do for you! The list is endless! I rely on them for everything! What is even more amazing than all of this, which is all available for your asking, is that the "Golden Key to Inner and Outer Success" is not just to rely on GOD and the Godforce, but to recognize that life is a co-creation and that you are God as well! So the real key to life is to realize the following affirmation, "GOD, the Godforce, my 100% personal power, my 100% unconditional love, my 100% wisdom, my 100% positive Spiritual thinking, the power of my subconscious mind, and the power of my physical body and right action is an unbeatable team!" For the key to successful living is to see that life is a balance and integration between all these levels! So I not only rely on GOD and the Godforce as I have stated, but I also strive on my own Divinity as

God being and utilize my own 100% personal power at all times! I also strive to own my 100% unconditional love at all times. I also strive to own my 100% wisdom at all times! I also use 100% positive and creative thinking, for God helps those who help themselves! My own Spiritual/Christ/Buddha thinking and feeling attracts only good karma to me. Then I supplement this with positive affirmations and visualizations, which additionally program the incredible powers of the subconscious mind! Then I don't stop there, but also utilize the incredible powers of the physical body to make right physical action wherever and whenever I need to! It is in utilizing all the levels of GOD that the true power of GOD is truly realized! These other levels of GOD are equally as powerful and important in the entire process, for only if these levels are equally balanced can God Realization be achieved! When all these levels are "cooking on all four burners" so to speak, then true "love/wisdom/and power" of God can be fully realized! If you rely on just one, it will not work effectively! If you rely on two, it will not work effectively! To truly be 100% successful inwardly and outwardly and manifest true God Realization and Integrated Ascension you must own to the best of your ability at the 100% level on all these levels!

When you own all these aspects of self at the 100% level, this is when the true co-creation of GOD can take place, and by the Grace of GOD and the Masters true miracles can take place!

So let it be Written! So let it be Done!

24

Physical Immortality

Most people involved with spiritual pursuits and/or religion believe in the immortality of the soul. In other words, we as soul extensions, or incarnated personalities, are eternal beings and our body dies, however, we don't. We just keep reincarnating over and over again until we achieve our liberation and ascension.

Many people don't realize, however, that the physical body is immortal also. It is not immortal for most people because humanity has a collective belief in the reality and need for death. Death is a belief, just as eternal life is a belief. Collective humanity, for most of its life, has been materialistically identified, hence it has listened to the voice of the negative ego on this matter instead of the voice of the soul and spirit.

The negative ego tells us we have to age and die. Spirit tells us that it is eternal and immortal. Spirit says that the physical body is the temple of the soul and ages because we program it to do so with our minds. One must remember that the subconscious mind runs the physical body. This can be clearly proven using hypnosis. The subconscious mind, given suggestions under hypnosis, can cause the physical body to do miraculous feats. We have all seen hypnosis stage shows where some of these feats have been demonstrated.

The subconscious mind, however, having no conscious reasoning, will be happy to create perfect health or illness and aging, depending on what you program it to do. This programming can come from yourself or what you allow other people to program into you.

What I am suggesting to you is that it *is* possible to program your body to "youth" instead of age. It is also possible to program your body to remain eternally the same. Many great Masters have done this. Babaji has remained the same for 1,800 years. Saint Germain lived for 350 years. Lord Maitreya resurrected Jesus' body and lived for another 31 years. Other Masters can materialize or dematerialize their body at will.

Thoth (Buddha), in Egypt, was said to have lived for 2,000 years. Jesus, in His last lifetime when He ascended, lived for 300 years. Did not Jesus say, "Everything that I can do, you can do and more." *A Course in Miracles*, which Jesus wrote, says, "Sickness is a defense against the truth." The truth is that we each are the Christ, or Eternal Self. God doesn't get sick and neither do we, because we are God.

So what causes sickness? It is the negative ego. Sai Baba says the definition of God is "God equals man minus ego." The ego doesn't exist in God's reality and ideally shouldn't exist in ours. When we get rid of the negative ego we recognize our perfection because we are "made in God's image."

The key to spiritual psychology is to get all levels aligned properly. We know that spirit and soul are eternal. The next lesson is to get only eternal thoughts, eternal feelings, and an eternal physical body. Does not the Hermetic Law state, "As within, so without. As above, so below"? If the spirit is eternal then, by definition, we can make the "without," or the body, eternal. Our true identity is the Christ, so by definition we should have only Christed thoughts, Christed emotions, and a Christed body. A Christed physical body is an immortal physical body.

The process begins on the thought level. It is our thoughts that create our reality and that includes our physical body. Any negative thought will manifest in our physical body. The same holds true for positive thoughts. Humanity is under a mass "negative hypnosis" in believing they have to age and die. Everyone believes it, so everyone does it.

Do you ever notice that people die where they have set their mental clock, so to speak? They think 75 years is old and they say to themselves,

"I want to make it to my granddaughter's 16th birthday and my 75th." They set it up in their mind to die at a certain time and sure enough that is exactly what happens.

The key to physical immortality on the mental level is to get rid of this "death urge" and replace it with a "life urge." The fact is, our body is already immortal. We just think it isn't, so it follows our command. The only thought we should allow in our minds concerning our physical body is that we are in perfect, radiant health. We are youthing every day and we can live eternally, or as long as we choose to.

The soul is eternal, so the physical body should be seen as eternal to keep proper alignment of the four-body system. This process begins with accepting this philosophy on the conscious mind level, and then programming it into the subconscious mind. This last point is important. Some people believe this consciously, but their subconscious doesn't. It will work only if all three minds believe it. The superconscious or soul does already.

To achieve physical immortality one must have absolute control over the subconscious mind. One also must maintain absolute vigilance over the thoughts you allow into your conscious mind, from self and other people. It is very easy to get negatively hypnotized on this subject because belief in death is so rampant.

It has been proven that there is a death hormone that the pituitary produces, as well as a life hormone. The pituitary is producing the death hormone in most people because we are unconsciously programming it to, because of all our death thoughts and emotions. By once and for all getting rid of all these death thoughts and emotions and replacing them with only life thoughts and emotions the pituitary will only produce the life hormone.

The use of positive affirmations constantly, in this regard, is essential. Constantly tell yourself that you are the eternal spirit and your thoughts, emotions, and physical body reflect this eternal and immortal nature. To achieve physical immortality one must have mastery over one's subconscious mind, three lower bodies (physical, emotional, mental), and mastery over one's negative ego. The negative ego's main belief is separation from God. If we believe we are one with God, and literally are sons and daughters of God, the next logical step, of course, is "we are immortal on all levels."

What we are demonstrating is that we have absolute self-mastery over all levels of our being in service of God when we believe in physical immortality. Physical immortality is not for weak-minded people, and neither is one's spiritual path. Physical immortality begins with the need to purify your four bodies of all negative energies.

On the emotional level the need is to get rid of all negative emotions. Again, remember your thoughts create your reality, and that includes your feelings and emotions. When you think only with your Christ mind, instead of the negative ego mind, then you live in joy, happiness, unconditional love, evenmindedness, and inner peace at all times. The world is a projection screen and you are seeing your own movie. The movie is the perception and interpretations you are making of life.

There is a way of thinking that will bring you this joy, peace and love all the time. This is the science of attitudinal healing. Negative emotions debilitate the physical body. Positive emotions energize the physical body. Living in unconditional love activates the thymus gland, which is your immune system. Physical immortality is just another by-product of being on one's spiritual path.

Purification on the physical level deals with eating a good physical diet, cutting down on the amount of meat you eat, stopping all drugs, alcohol, artificial stimulants, getting physical exercise every day, trying to get sunshine, fresh air, deep breathing every day. So we have physical toxins, emotional toxins, mental toxins, and energetic toxins in our etheric body. All these bodies must be cleansed.

In essence our goal to achieve physical immortality is to only have God thoughts, God emotions, God energy body, and God physical body. God is perfect and we are perfect. The microcosm is like the macrocosm. When all the bodies become purified and get into alignment with the soul and spirit, perfect, radiant health occurs.

As one moves spiritually through the seven levels of initiation, more and more light and energy are found running through the four-body system. At the third initiation, which is called soul merge, it causes a great increase in energy and physical health. At the fifth and sixth initiation, which are the ascension process, there is the complete merger with the monad, spirit, or I AM Presence, which guarantees physical immortality.

Ascension is where the I AM Presence, or monad, descends and turns all four bodies into light. The physical body is just densified spirit, and the spirit is just refined matter. We are here on earth to spiritualize matter. This begins with spiritualizing our physical bodies and raising it back to light.

Constantly hold in your mind that you are God and can't get sick, you can't age and you can't physically die. Hold the thought and feeling that you are in perfect health, you are getting younger every day, and you will live eternally. When any negative thought, any feeling, emotion or energy, tries to tell you anything to the contrary, get rid of it and immediately do a positive affirmation or positive visualization seeing yourself as the ascended master or eternal spiritual being you truly are.

Call to your Mighty I AM Presence to get rid of that negative egotistical belief and feeling and to consume it in the violet flame. Constantly call to your soul and monad and ask it to integrate and merge with you on earth. We are here to create heaven on earth. We are here to be God on earth on all levels. What I am sharing with you here is within every person's reach. Jesus said, however, "Be it done to you as you believe."

Your physical, emotional, and mental bodies are your servants, not your masters. Command them in the name of the Christ (which is who you are, in truth) and they will do as you order. Command your pituitary to stop creating the death hormone and only create the life hormone and it will do as you command.

The Bible says, "Ye are gods and know it not." The philosophy of physical immortality's time has come. It is time now to ground spirituality into the earth and into the physical body. For too long people have been into leaving their bodies to touch spirit, instead of touching spirit and bringing it back and grounding it into earth.

The entire universe responds to your every command because you are God!!! God doesn't determine when you die, you do. The key to physical immortality is to live as a soul and as spirit in your every thought, word and deed. In essence, become God, and sickness, death and aging will disappear. God does not get sick, age or die and neither do we.

Write down on a piece of paper all your thoughts and feelings about death and being physically immortal. Any thoughts that aren't of God rewrite in terms of positive affirmations that correct the faulty beliefs you are holding. Listen then for any faulty beliefs that arise again and write them down. Correct them on paper with new positive affirmations until you have cleared out your conscious and subconscious mind.

Also be open to cleansing any past life beliefs about death that are stored in your subconscious mind. Cleanse all fears of death. In truth there is nothing to fear because it does not exist, except in our own minds. Forgive yourself and always forgive all people, this is a prerequisite for physical immortality.

In more advanced stages begin to see yourself as "light" and every one else as "light." For, in truth, that is what we really are. What this really comes down to is where you put your attention. Do you put the attention of your mind on death, sickness, negativity and aging, or on perfect health, positivity, eternal life and youthing?

The problem with most people in the world is they live on automatic pilot and do not control where they keep their attention. Your attention, ideally, should be kept at all times on the soul, the spirit, the Mighty I

AM Presence, on Christ, and/or on God. Each person you meet on the street must be seen as God or you will not achieve God yourself.

One of the byproducts of holding this state of consciousness of physical immortality is that our physical bodies begin transforming from two strands of DNA to twelve strands of DNA. Twelve strands of DNA is the state of enlightenment. Affirm to yourself and pray to God that this transformation is occurring right now.

Hold the thought and image in your mind that you have been "reborn" in this moment and that you now have twelve strands of DNA. Did not Jesus say, "except that ye be born again you will not find the kingdom of God." Physical immortality is the consciousness of being born again into your true eternal Christ nature on all levels of your being. Realize in this "holy instant" the truth of this statement, and from this day and moment forward to not allow any thought or feeling to the contrary to enter your consciousness.

If something starts to interfere say, "get thee behind me, Satan" and replace it with a Christ-like affirmation. This is what Sai Baba calls "self-inquiry." It is the process of discriminating between what is truth and what is illusion, what is permanent and what is impermanent, what is negative ego and what is God. Sai Baba says that 75% of the spiritual path is nothing more than this practice.

This is the key practice towards physical immortality and towards your path of ascension which, in truth, are one and the same. Once physical immortality is achieved (which is any moment you choose it to be so), it doesn't mean you have to stay on earth for eternity. It just means you can stay as long as you "choose" to, instead of letting your physical body decide for you.

Physical immortality, hence, calls for remaining in your personal power and self-mastery at all times. Most people give away their power to their physical body, desires, emotions, feelings, mind, senses, and other people. To achieve physical immortality you must give your power to no one, because you are god. You do not have to be afraid of your power because you are using it only in service of God and your brothers and sisters, and in service of love.

Another key towards physical immortality is controlling your sexuality. You must learn to become the absolute master of this energy, so you choose when to identify with it, and when to raise it. The "overindulgence" in sexuality depletes the physical body and takes years off your life. Sexuality should be used only in service of love and intimacy, and in moderation. The kundalini will never rise if your energy is constantly moving out of your second chakra.

Self-control and the raising of this energy allows this energy to be used for healing of the organs and glands and overall physical body. Fundamental to physical immortality is a deep desire for physical immortality and God Realization. Most people allow themselves to be run by the desires of the lower-self or carnal-self, which weakens them physically, emotionally, mentally and spiritually.

Understand physical immortality is also a process as is the spiritual path. It is a process of moving from polarization or identification with the lower self, to polarization and identification with the Higher Self. In the beginning stages it is an all out spiritual war. In the later stages it becomes much easier as all one's habits get reprogrammed.

Another suggestion on the physical level is the use of water both inwardly and outwardly. Baths and showers can be seen as baptisms and cleansings of the entire four-body system every day. The drinking of large amounts of water purifies the kidneys and liver and entire system. Disease cannot grow in a purified body.

It can clearly be seen here that physical immortality and ascension will take a total commitment. Anything less won't get you to your goal. As Yogananda said, "If you want God (physical immortality) you must want Him as much as a drowning man wants air."

Physical immortality in the end is God Realization. Some people believe it can be achieved just with the power of the mind. I don't personally believe that. Holding only positive thoughts without a belief in

God will certainly greatly help your health, however, I don't believe that will get you physical immortality.

Physical immortality is the integration of all levels of our being. You can't skip any steps or levels. Just working on the mental or spiritual, and eating a terrible diet and getting no physical exercise is not going to do it unless you came in as a God-realized Master. For 99.9% of the rest of the world, all levels must be mastered and purified. Balance and moderation in all things is the ideal.

It is not disease and old age that kills most people. It is the belief in disease and old age and death that kills most people. Even cancer specialists agree that one of the keys to curing cancer is the "will to live". If a person doesn't have that, all other treatment is useless.

Every night as you are going to bed and falling asleep, or waking up in the morning, give yourself "autosuggestions" affirming your physical immortality. Your subconscious mind is more receptive at these times. Remember the body doesn't die, it is your mind and emotions and lack of spiritual integration that kill your body.

Other practices that will help in your achieving of physical immortality are meditation, prayer, chanting the name of God, singing devotional songs, fasting, growing your own food, eating organic food, reading uplifting spiritual books, cleanliness and orderliness in one's environment, not talking about one's age, and not going to funerals.

The idea is to keep your mind, consciousness, and feeling body in an elevated spiritual state at all times. If your mind is constantly attuned to God in your higher self, how can sickness, aging, and death enter into it? It can't. "If the mind and consciousness is constantly attuned to and affirming, praying, meditating, and chanting God's name and form, only perfection can exist. It gets easy after a while, becomes a way of living, becomes a habit.

The Fountain of Youth

The last section of this chapter on physical immortality deals with a book I was recently turned on to called *Ancient Secret of the Fountain of Youth* by Peter Kelder. In Peter's book, he tells of this amazing story of Colonel Bradford who had the opportunity to be stationed in India near the Himalayan mountains. While there, he constantly heard stories of a group of lamas or Tibetan priests who had discovered the Fountain of Youth.

To make a long story short, he eventually returned to India in search of these lamas and this fountain of youth and found it. In this monastery he was taught their secret. He was taught by the lamas that the secret to staying young was to keep the chakras revolving at a high rate of speed, and at a synchronous rate of speed with each other.

When one or more chakras begin to slow down, aging occurs. The slowing down of the chakras prevents the vital force (prana) or etheric energy, from flowing properly. The key to the fountain of youth was to get these chakras spinning normally again.

Colonel Bradford was taught by the Himalayan Masters five rites or five exercises. The exercises are easy to do and can all be done within 20 minutes once you learn how to do them. These exercises have the effect of speeding up all the chakras and causing them to revolve in harmony. The doing of these exercises causes the chakras to spin at a speed of that of a 25-year-old.

When Colonel Bradford returned to America he literally looked 30 years younger according to Peter. Peter didn't even recognize him when he saw him. With each exercise there is also a special way of breathing while doing the exercise. The exercises remind me a little bit of certain Hatha yoga postures, but are very specific in their purpose and effect.

These five rites must be practiced every day to get their full effect. A physically fit person can do them in ten minutes once you learn how. I, personally have an incredibly good feeling about them and have no doubt they do exactly what he says they do.

Colonel Bradford was given a sixth rite that was to be used only at those times when one wanted to raise one's sexual energy and use it for youthing the body.

I know I say this a lot in my books, however, I cannot recommend more highly that you get this small book. You can read it in 30 minutes, however it will take you a little while to learn how to do the exercises properly. Then all you need is literally ten minutes a day, a "small investment" for such a "large return." Djwhal Khul, Kuthumi, and El Morya were all Tibetan lamas. The Masters of the Himalayas truly knew what they were talking about.

25

A New Species of Light and Higher Light Body Integration

It is very important to understand that we are all in the process of becoming a New Species of Light! This is achieved through the help of Spirit, The Masters, the Angels, and the Christed Extraterrestrials. It is also achieved through our own positive thinking, speaking, feeling, actions and manifestation of our Spiritual mission and purpose on Earth!

One of the important things to understand, however, is that this transformation of our bodies into a new Species of Light is sometimes a Spiritual Mutation process that has a lot of physical symptoms. This is a normal part of the process! It has to do with really four things. Some of it is just the higher frequencies of light becoming integrated into the etheric and physical vehicle. Another part is caused by specific Ascension Activation Work that is being done by the inner plane Masters on large numbers of Initiates. Thirdly, it is also caused by, on some occasions but not always, certain blocks or genetic weaknesses in certain areas of the body! I want to make it clear however 99% of the time it has nothing to do with this. By this I mean, this will occur with a great many people even if they have no blockages or weaknesses. This is important to understand for many people think, or people lay trips on them, that they are doing something wrong because they have these symptoms and this is not the case. The symptoms are in truth just the opposite. It is a sign that just the opposite is true. The symptoms are a sign that you are in a highly accelerated Ascension Process. On the other side of the coin if you don't have these symptoms you can also be in just as accelerated ascension process, however because of your particular Spiritual Structure you do not need to go through these exact same symptoms. GOD creates each person uniquely and there are no generalized hard and fast rules for anyone!

Some of the symptoms that can occur from this Transformation into a new Species of Light and Higher Light Body Integration are: headaches, spinning, dizziness, nausea, heating up of the body, pain in certain areas of the body, pressure in different areas of the body, extreme fatigue, eye problems, inability to concentrate, short term memory loss, cramps, emotional imbalance, rashes, bumping into third dimensional objects. There are many more symptoms however I think you get the idea!

Part of the reason for this occurrence of symptoms is also how fast this Spiritual Mutation is occurring! There will be more Spiritual Growth on this Planet from approximately 1980 to 2025 than in the last 3.1 billion years on this planet! From the perspective of Spirit and the Masters this is a grand experiment. Even they are not used to this experiment of doing this so quickly! Even fifty years ago one initiation a lifetime was a lot. Now it is possible to go through all 12 in one lifetime! The Spiritual Body usually evolves much quicker than the mental, emotional, etheric and physical body. The physical body being of course the densest of all the bodies has the most physical resistance to overcome. The more blocks you have on all levels the more severe the symptoms, however it is essential to understand that even if you have no blocks or resistance it is very common for people to have many or all of these symptoms. Others may have none yet are going through the same or a similar process. I cannot emphasize the importance of not trying to make any hard and fast rules on this subject for the process is in truth very unique and specialized for each person given the unique complex make-up of each person's Spiritual, Psychological, Physical/Earthly, and 12-Body System Structure!

26

Eighteen Great Cosmic Clearings and Cleansings

The following eighteen areas of consciousness must all be cleared and purified to achieve Self-realization. This can be done by asking the Masters to help you. The Spiritual Path is amazingly simple because anything you want to achieve or attain is there for the asking.

In this book are the ultimate keys to accelerating your evolution. This has never been given forth to humanity is such an easy-to-understand, practical manner. These simple requests and invocations can literally save you many lifetimes and eons of spiritual work. The Masters are willing to do these things for you, but you must ask.

Go through each exercise one by one. The transformation you go through will be truly transfiguring, my Friends.

Humanity for many millions of years has not known what to ask for, or who to ask. This list tells you what clearings to ask for. Among the Masters to ask for assistance, I recommend Djwhal Khul, Lord Maitreya, Melchizedek, Lord Buddha, other Masters of your choice, and the Angels of Healing.

1. Genetic Line Clearing

Call to the Masters and request that they clear your entire genetic line. Your genetic line is connected to your genetics in this lifetime and all your previous lifetimes, tracing your physical body's heritage.

Just ask and the Masters will do this for you. How they do it is not completely clear, but that is not important. This is the first stage of planetary and cosmic purification and cleansing. It can be done in meditation, lying down, or at night while you sleep.

I asked Melchizedek where the core group and I were in this process. He said we had cleared 90% of our genetic line karma. I then asked if he would just clear the rest for us. He replied that he would be happy to oblige. I wondered if we should do a formal meditation or not. Melchizedek said he would do it while we slept.

As fully completed seventh degree initiates I think that the only reason this had not been completed before is that we had not asked. "Ask and you shall receive; knock and the door shall be opened."

2. Past Life Clearing

According to Djwhal Khul most people have had 200 to 250 past lives. Multiply this number by twelve if you want to include your eleven other soul extensions to get the total number of incarnations of the entire oversoul. If you want the total number of incarnations of your monad, multiply the number of past lives by 144.

This clearing process is specifically focused on your personal incarnational history. Call forth the Masters and request that all your past lives be cleared since your very first past life on Earth. This is one of the requirements for planetary ascension. I asked Melchizedek if we had cleared this level. He said we had, which I found interesting because I had never officially invoked this before. It was cleared as part of the initiation process!!!

If you want to get real fancy, you can also request to have your future and parallel lives cleared and cleansed!

3. Soul Extension Clearing

The next clearing process is the purification and integration first of your eleven other soul extensions of your oversoul, and then of your

144 soul extensions from your monad. This process then continues at the eighth level to the 12 oversoul leaders of the six monads or 72 soul extensions in your group soul. Next, at the ninth level, the monadic grouping of 864 soul extensions is cleared and integrated. At the tenth level the extensions at the solar, galactic, and then universal levels are cleared. At these levels the numbers are vast and near to impossible to figure out.

Do not ask for these higher levels of eighth, ninth, solar, galactic and universal levels until you first do your soul and then your monad. As an intuitive guess, you can figure on integrating and clearing one soul extension a week. The core group and I have nearly completed the cleansing and integrating of our 144 soul extensions. The higher levels can't be started until you finish this level first.

4. Archetypal Clearing

Next request from the Masters a clearing and cleansing of the twelve major archetypes and all minor archetypes. When this is complete request an imprinting into the core of your being of all Christ, Buddha and Melchizedek archetypes on a permanent basis. This clearing must be supplemented on a conscious level by intensively studying my book called *How to Clear the Negative Ego*, especially the chapter on how to clear the negative ego archetypes.

If the conscious mind does not completely understand this material there is the danger of building the negative ego archetypes back, even though the Masters have cleared them. The Masters will clear them energetically; you must clear them in your conscious and subconscious thinking process.

5. Cosmic Cellular Clearing

The cosmic cellular clearing combines the energies of Melchizedek, Metatron and Vywamus and is to clean out your cells or cellular structure, at the deepest possible level.

Again, it is interesting that many of these aspects are cleared in an overlapping manner. I had never spent much time focusing on this aspect in my meditations or invoking it specifically. Yet when I asked about this level Melchizedek said it was 98% clear for the three of us. It is good, however, to go through all the exercises at least once to make sure it has been cleared.

My motto is "better safe than sorry." I would rather overdo it a little bit than under do it. Some of the more advanced clearings on the cosmic level will take hundreds, if not thousands of meditations to fully clear.

6. Generalized Karma Clearing

The next great cleansing to invoke is for a massive generalized karma clearing. As you all know, you need to balance 51% of your karma to achieve ascension. Even after achieving your ascension the process continues and you want to strive towards balancing all your karma.

This begins with your personal karma from all your past lives, then karma from all your eleven soul extensions from your oversoul. After that the balancing of all the karma from your 144 monadic soul extensions occurs.

The Masters can help you in this process. It will take a whole lifetime of meditating to clear everything, however it is a noble goal to strive for. I think I mentioned before that just the process of integrating and cleansing our 144 soul extensions was clearing our core group of karma up to around 75%. Using the rest of these tools makes a goal of getting up into the high 90's a distinct possibility for all devoted and dedicated initiates.

7. Physical Body Clearing

This clearing is not for your genetic line, but rather just your present physical body. Call forth to the Masters and to the Lord of Arcturus and the Arcturians for the complete cleansing and purification of your physical vehicle. Request that all disease be completely removed including all negative bacteria, viruses, fungus, cancer, tumors, and genetic weakness. Request full permanent imprinting of the Divine monadic blueprint body and mayavarupa body to reign forever supreme.

8. Emotional Desire and Astral Body Clearing

This cleansing invocation is for your present astral body. Ask that all negative emotions, lower self desire, astral entities, and negative psychic energies of all forms and all kinds that are not of the Christ/Buddha archetype be removed. Immediately call for this in the name of the Christ, the Buddha, and Melchizedek. When your physical and astral body are clear, then move to the mental body.

9. Mental Body Clearing

Call forth to the Masters again and request a complete clearing of your mental body in this lifetime. Ask that all negative ego and imbalanced thoughtforms be removed and banished from your consciousness forever. Request that all remaining thoughtforms left in your conscious, subconscious, and superconscious minds be only of the Christ/Buddha/Melchizedek archetype.

10. Etheric Body Cleansing

Request of the Masters a complete clearing and repair of your etheric body. Ask that all etheric mucous be immediately removed and that your etheric body be restored to its original Divine blueprint.

11. Core Fear Clearing

This next clearing is connected to the astral body clearing. However, it is so important that I have given it a category of its own.

There are only two emotions in life. These are love and fear. This could also be termed Christ Consciousness and negative ego consciousness. Call forth to the Masters to anchor the Core Fear Removal Matrix

Program and request that you want all your core fear removed from this life, all your past lives, and from all your soul and monadic extensions.

During one weekend workshop focusing on this topic the Masters told us they removed 45% of our core fear from our entire lifetime. This clearing process may take a great many meditations. If you are aware of a specific fear, ask that it be pulled out as you become aware of it. After the clearing ask to be filled with Core Love.

12. Implants and Elementals

Call forth to the Masters that all negative Extraterrestrial implants and negative elementals be removed. Call forth the Golden Cylinder from Lord Arcturus and the Arcturians, and the Matrix Removal Program from Djwhal Khul and Vywamus to help in this process. When this is complete ask Archangel Lord Michael and Vywamus to place a golden dome of protection around you on a permanent basis.

13. Twelve-Body Clearing

This clearing process is an extension of the five-body clearing that has already been done. Request that all twelve bodies, which includes the bodies up through the solar, galactic and universal levels, be completely cleared by the Grace of Melchizedek, Metatron and Archangel Michael.

14. Fifty Chakras Clearing

First request of the Masters that your seven chakras be completely cleared of all energies that are not of the Christ. When this is complete then request that all 50 chakras leading up through the ninth dimension of reality be cleared and cleansed by the Grace of Melchizedek, Metatron and Michael.

15. Clearing Negative Ray Influences

Every person on this planet is under the influence of the Seven Great Rays. Each person's monad, soul, personality, mind, emotions, and body come under the influence of one of these rays. Each ray has a higher and lower expression, as does each astrological sign.

Call forth to the Masters and request a cleansing and purification of all lower uses and expressions of these ray influences. Call forth the Seven Ray Masters, El Morya, Kuthumi and Djwhal Khul, Paul the Venetian, Serapis Bey, Hilarion, Sananda, and St. Germain, to help in this work. These Masters are especially adept at this work for they are the Chohans or Lords of these rays. The Masters will clear you energetically in this regard.

However, your conscious and subconscious mind must understand this work also, for there is a danger of recontamination. Therefore, I recommend you study this more in-depth.

16. Clearing Negative Astrological Influences

Call forth to the Masters again and request a complete clearing and purification of all negative astrological influences. Each astrological sign, house, and planet has a higher and lower expression. Ask the Masters to cleanse all lower expressions of these signs. Then ask them to anchor and imprint upon the core of your being the higher Divine expression of these signs that God would have you manifest. At the end call forth an activation of the twelve heavenly houses for the highest possible ascension acceleration.

17. Monadic Clearing

For this next activation call forth Melchizedek, Metatron, Vywamus, Lord Buddha and Djwhal Khul. Call forth a cleansing of your entire monad. This invocation is much greater than just cleansing the 144 soul extensions. It is for the complete cleansing of all aspects of monadic existence.

I asked Melchizedek about this and he said that this is one of the more cosmic ascension clearings and will take a while to complete. Here you are taking on clearing your entire monad, not just your oversoul or just your self as one soul of twelve from your oversoul. The more you evolve, the greater responsibility you are taking for cosmic cleansing. This is a meditation you can do many times.

18. The Super Cosmic Clearing Invocation

This last Super Cosmic Clearing invocation was saved specifically until the end of this chapter. This activational clearing invokes a clearing of misaligned choices long before your first visitation on Earth. It goes all the way back to your original covenant with God at the beginning of your creation, at the highest cosmic planes.

Since your first creation you have had free choice. This cosmic cleansing clears all choices from the beginning of your existence. Melchizedek says it also clears your original Divine blueprint. This activation is really only appropriate when you are beginning your cosmic ascension process. You may invoke it before, however the real work won't begin until the planetary ascension prep work is done.

He also said that this is such a vast and immense clearing that it should only be done in a group. The core group and I were told that we were not to invoke this by ourselves individually. We were allowed to do it in our group meditations.

One of the benefits of coming to the Wesak Celebrations at Mt. Shasta each year for 1200 to 2500 people is that we have been given permission to do this activation and cleansing for the entire group. It is only because of the large group that this has been allowed.

For this activation call forth Melchizedek, Metatron, Archangel Michael, Buddha, Vywamus and Thoth/Hermes. The energies we are dealing with here are so vast and immense that it takes a group body vehicle of a very high level of magnitude and vibration to handle.

This clearing also clears our incarnations on other planets, in other solar systems, galaxies and universes. This is not something that can be cleared in one sitting. It would take a lifetime of meditating for we are speaking here of clearing all 352 levels back to the Godhead.

This might be called the Ultimate Cosmic Ascension Clearing Process (not planetary). Melchizedek said that this clearing also helps to clear the core field to allow the full impregnation of the mayavarupa or Divine blueprint body. It is not just for oneself, but is for the entire monadic group consciousness.

The monad, remember, is much larger than each one of us as individuals. We are, in truth, just facets of this greater being that is the monad or Mighty I Am Presence. This invocation is clearing the monad's or Mighty I Am Presence's existence back to its original creation as an individualized spark of God.

On an individual level it helps energetically to know and understand our place and mission on Earth from the highest cosmic understanding. Buddha, and his past life as Thoth/Hermes, is instrumental in orchestrating this clearing for the advanced initiates on this planet. Vywamus is also helping with this work as an essential key. He is the higher aspect of Sanat Kumara, who is currently overlighting the Buddha as Planetary Logos, as Sanat Kumara has taken his next step in his cosmic evolution.

This super cosmic clearing really involves all the other seventeen clearings already invoked and much more, to say the least! Melchizedek said that at Wesak we would literally be clearing hundreds and potentially thou-sands of monads. All other clearings have been focused more on planetary ascension levels and clearing from your first stepping onto the Earth's Planetary Mystery School, which may be as far back as 18.5 million years.

This clearing is from one's original conception and creation in spirit as a monadic consciousness. I think you can see then how profound this clearing actually is. The Super Cosmic Clearing Process is literally preparing and clearing the pathway back to one's original point of spiritual origin.

The Ultimate Divine Dispensation

Call forth to Melchizedek, Metatron, Archangel Michael, Lord Maitreya and Djwhal Khul for a divine dispensation to have the clearing work from the processes in this chapter occur every night while you sleep for the coming months leading up to the next Wesak on the full moon in Taurus, when all initiations are given.

By calling forth a Divine dispensation such as this, the work is done automatically without having to consciously ask for it. This saves an enormous amount of time and energy. Personally I am big on efficiency of energy and all short cuts to God-realization. What lightworkers must realize is that God has given us everything. As *A Course In Miracles* says in one of the lessons, "My salvation is up to me."

Your salvation is not up to God for He has already given you His kingdom. In truth, you are already the Christ. You already are and have everything. It is only our personal choice to identify with negative ego, separation and fear-based consciousness, rather than Christ Consciousness, that prevents salvation, bliss, inner peace, abundance and happiness.

God and the Masters are willing to answer any heartfelt request or Divine dispensation as long as your heart is pure and your motivations are sincere. The only requirement that God places upon you (which is the Golden Key to supreme ascension acceleration) is that **you must ask**. Ask and you shall receive; knock and the door shall be opened.

In this book and my other books I have laid out in a most practical easy-to-understand manner what to ask for. I have all but given you the Keys to the Kingdom. All you have to do to give salvation to yourself is really quite simple:

1. Take the time to meditate.
2. Ask for the help you need, and then receive it.
3. Practice the ascension techniques I have provided.

4. Practice the Presence of God and being an Ascended Master in your daily life.
5. Make the supreme commitment to be vigilant for God and His Kingdom, choosing Christ Consciousness rather than negative ego consciousness.
6. Dedicate your life completely to service of humanity in a balanced manner.

God and the Masters will deny nothing to a sincere heart.

Conclusion and Summation

I am here to tell you from personal experience that ascension and liberation is much easier to realize than any of us have previously imagined. By the Grace of the Ascended Masters they will do a lot of the work for you on the inner plane in meditation and while you sleep. They will do this if you will ask. They are prevented by Divine Law from helping without your simple requests. Request their help and they will give you the Kingdom.

Once you achieve your planetary ascension, which you all will, you can begin working on your cosmic ascension. That will be a much longer process. Knowing you have achieved liberation from the wheel of rebirth, and feeling your close connection with your soul and monad and the Ascended Masters will be a great comfort to you. Also having learned to think with your Christ Mind rather than your negative ego mind will free you from the bondage of your own creation. This will allow you to live in this world as an Ascended Being and a Bodhisattva, who is a liberated being that remains on Earth to be of service to their brothers and sisters. This is the destiny of us all.

Before too long we will return to the inner planes and continue our service work on more expanded levels of consciousness. We will have transcended the need to return to physical existence, and will continue evolving and serving until we ultimately achieve our cosmic ascension as well. Then we will become Cosmic Bodhisattvas whose work will not be complete until all our brothers and sisters have achieved cosmic ascension as well.

It is only then that God's Plan will be complete. Take comfort that the hardest part of our journey through our hundreds of incarnations is now over. The Light at the end of the tunnel is near. Victory is now inevitable. The Keys and the Map to the Kingdom are now ours. We are all blessed beyond our wildest imagination to be incarnated at this time in Earth's history.

What previously took four billion years is now being accomplished in forty years. All you have to do is, with full commitment and personal power, get onto this planetary rocketship. The Force is with us and all we have to do is choose to be with the Force. There is no faster spiritual path in this world than working with the Ascended Masters and the Ascension Movement.

As a fellow brother on the path I beseech you to take advantage of this golden opportunity that has been provided in this lifetime. Let us transform this world together and bring an end to suffering, glamour, maya and illusion. Let us all work together arm in arm, shoulder to shoulder, to transform the consciousness of humanity from a third and fourth dimensional consciousness to a fifth, sixth, and seventh dimensional consciousness.

Let us together make the Earth into a shining star and a truly heavenly planet to visit. There is much hard work to do to accomplish this; however, there is much love and joy in the fellowship. The goal we all seek for humanity and the Earth is inevitable. All people on Earth are God and nothing can stop the evolutionary process. The Dark Brotherhood can create minor problems; however, illusion cannot win over Truth. Ego cannot defeat God. We all have a most noble and sometimes difficult mission on Earth. But if God be with us, who or what can be against us?

We can do all things with Christ/Buddha/Melchizedek/God who strengthens us. God, the Ascended Masters, our personal power and the power of the subconscious mind are an unbeatable team. The complete transformation of planet Earth and humanity while being a not fully realized Ascended Planet is the thing legends are made of. Let us all work together to make this little speck of a planet in the outer reaches of the Milky Way galaxy a speck that all of Creation takes note of because of the courage, strength, love, devotion, and commitment to service of the great and noble beings who live here. Let us all take on now the mantle of leadership in this regard and be unceasing in our efforts until it is time to pass the baton on to the next generation ascension wave. Let us make our generation the pivotal turning point in this process and in this regard! Namaste!

27

How to Physically Ground Your Spirituality

This issue of grounding one's Ascension and/or process of Self-Realization is extremely important, not only to one's physical health, but also in regard to fully Realizing GOD and becoming a full-fledged Ascended Master on Earth. If we do not learn to love our physical bodies and love the material Universe, we are literally not loving a major part of GOD and ourselves. It is essential to learn to be happy on Earth. There is nothing wrong with understanding that we are visiting and that we come from Heavenly realms; however, the Material Universe is one of GOD's Seven Heavens.

It is very interesting that I am writing a chapter here called "How to Physically Ground Your Spirituality." There will be some that read this who are naturally good at this. However, I am here to tell you as a Spiritual teacher and a Spiritual psychologist, that most lightworkers are not. Most lightworkers are not only not well-grounded physically, but are also not well-grounded psychologically. I will say, however, that the number one cause of physical health problems is improper mastery and understanding of how to transcend negative ego thinking, and how to properly think with one's Christ/Buddha mind. If a person is not grounded in this understanding and in mastery over the mental body, emotional body, etheric body, physical body, subconscious mind, and inner child, they will have untold health challenges manifesting in their body. The physical body is a mirror of your consciousness and is completely controlled by how you think and feel. How you feel is governed by how you think because that is the cause of your feelings. So we see how it all stems back to whether you think with your Christ/Buddha mind or your negative ego/lower-self/fear-based/separative mind. Most people and most lightworkers have not been properly trained by parents, school, churches, counselors, and even Spiritual teachers, of the laws that govern Soul and Spiritual psychology and how to put them into practice. This is not a judgment of anyone, just merely an observation. Learning to transcend negative ego thinking and learning to think with your Christ/Buddha mind is the premier lesson of everyone's spiritual path. This is because it is our thoughts that create our reality. It is our thoughts that create our feelings, emotions, health or lack thereof, and what we magnetize and attract into our lives. If we, as sons and daughters of GOD, do not learn this lesson of transcending negative ego and separative thinking, it will not only create problems in ourselves, but will also misalign our relationship with GOD and our romantic relationships and all other relationships.

It will also completely foul-up and corrupt our channeling abilities and any clairvoyant abilities we might have. The negative ego will tell you, that this is not true; however, I assure you that it is. Never underestimate the negative ego's power of delusion. The second you think you have it mastered is the exact time you are headed for a fall. No matter what level of initiation you are at or how much work you think you have done on yourself, everyone needs to maintain constant vigilance.

I have seen ninth, tenth, and eleventh degree initiates with enormous numbers of followers, fame, channeling abilities, clairvoyant abilities, knowledge and wisdom, fall and become corrupted. The bizarre irony is that this has happened and they don't even realize it. If you ask them if they are run by their negative ego or if it has gained any control, they will adamantly say "no" and affirm that they are Masters when, in truth, nothing could be farther from the truth. I say this with no judgment, but rather just as a spiritual observation and spiritual discernment. No matter how many gifts they have and no matter how much spiritual and/or psychological training they have had, if they are not well-grounded in this one key understanding of the difference between negative ego and spiritual thinking, they will fall and become corrupted. If our thoughts create our reality and filter all our experience, how could it be otherwise?

The first lesson in learning to ground your Ascension, which means nothing more than fully merging with your Higher Self and Mighty I AM Presence or Spirit, on Earth; is grounding these aspects of Self into your psychological self. It is strange to think of grounding when talking about the psychological or mental or emotional level; however, this is exactly what it is. Most Spiritual mystery schools and Eastern paths focus more on the spiritual level rather than the psychological level. For example, you can chant, meditate, say mantras, repeat the names of GOD from here to kingdom come, however, this is not going to solve psychological and/or relationship issues.

There are three levels to the Spiritual path which must be mastered in order to fully Realize GOD. These are the spiritual, psychological, and physical. Each level must be mastered in its' own right. Spiritual practices will not resolve psychological problems, just as working psychologically or spiritually will not always resolve physical problems. For example, some people get sick because they eat terrible diets, consume too much sugar and/or drugs, and do not get enough physical exercise and/or sleep.

Many lightworkers are highly developed in one or two areas and a little weak in the third. There is no judgment in this, just the lesson that more focus needs to be put into that area. The most common theme in the New Age Movement is lightworkers being highly developed spiritually, but a little weaker psychologically. This can be checked by honestly examining your inner peace, joy, and happiness quotient. Also by examining if you are manifesting negative emotions, and the nature of your relationships and how harmonious they are. There is so much emphasis in the Spiritual Movement on achieving initiations, channeling, light bodies, building light quotient, meditation, prayer; however, I would suggest to you that developing a flawless character with the highest level of integrity in everything you think, say and do is of equal importance, if not more. Especially the practice of unconditional love toward self and others at all times.

This focus on developing flawless character and always thinking and interpreting life with your Christ/Buddha mind may not be as glamorous as some of the spiritual practices; however, I would ask you, so what if you are a seventh degree initiate, have lots of students and money and are world famous, yet are run by your negative ego? Again, we get back to Sai Baba's definition of GOD which is "GOD equals man minus ego."

The first step in grounding your ascension is grounding your Higher Self and Mighty I AM Presence and/or Monad properly into your psychological self and/or mental and emotional vehicle. This could also be stated as grounding your Higher Self and Monad properly into your conscious and subconscious mind. The next step is to ground your Higher Self and Mighty I AM Presence fully into your physical body and connecting it to the Earth.

Just as consciousness seekers and lightworkers have a difficult time grounding the Higher Self and Mighty I AM Presence into the psychological level, they also sometimes have an even more difficult time grounding themselves into the physical. Lightworkers, by definition, tend to be more focused on the Light and/or the Heavenly and/or Celestial Realms. This is understandable in that we all came from GOD and our true home is in Heaven. Earth is a school and service post we are all visiting. There are also many mystery schools and spiritual paths that are overfocused on the Heavenly Realms and higher chakras. Many of us live in cities that are not conducive to enjoying nature and the Material Universe. Also, in this modern technological civilization we have incredibly busy and complicated lives that do not give us as much time to commune with nature and the Nature Spirits.

For all these reasons and many more, learning to be physically grounded in our demonstration of God, Christ, Buddha and the Eternal Self on Earth is not always the easiest thing to do. Especially for lightworkers who tend to be more etheric by nature and very attuned to the Heavenly Realms. I have never seen any chapter in any book that has fully gone into this issue of how to physically ground one's ascension in great detail. Most of the time we are talking about all the Heavenly, Celestial and psychological things we must do. This chapter is dedicated to 100% honoring and sanctifying the physical body and the Material Face of GOD. This is not only extremely important to your physical health, but is also extremely important to fully Realizing GOD in all His Glory. On that note, we will now move into the fascinating subject of how to physically and completely ground our ascension into the sanctified Material Face of GOD.

How to Physically Ground Your Ascension

The whole understanding of Ascension is really a misunderstanding, because when you merge with your Soul and Monad or Mighty I AM Presence you are not actually ascending, you are descending, if you are doing it properly. The ideal is to merge with the Soul and Mighty I AM Presence on Earth. The idea is not to ascend and disappear and leave the Earth, but rather to descend and remain on Earth and serve as an Ascended Master and/or fully realized seventh degree initiate or above. It is possible to learn advanced Ascended Master abilities; however, these do not really even occur until after one completes their twelfth initiation. The focus of Ascension should not be on advanced Ascended Master abilities; it should be on unconditional love and service.

As I have already stated, physically grounding one's Ascension can be as difficult as grounding it into the mental body and the emotional body. For some lightworkers who are sensation-function types, or who have a lot of Earth in their astrological chart and psychological makeup, it is easy. For many other lightworkers who are mental types, emotional types, or Spiritual types; grounding one's Ascension or Self-Realization can be an enormously difficult process. It is an attunement that they are not used to practicing. This chapter is written for those individuals who make-up as much as three-quarters of all lightworkers.

To begin with, the grounding of one's Ascension starts with eating a good diet, getting physical exercise, and staying on top of one's earthly responsibilities. It includes being organized, taking care of business, running the errands you need to do, and basically meeting one's earthly responsibilities. Contrary to popular opinion, the mastery of this level, being a Face of GOD, is part of the Spiritual path. The new Seventh Ray energies coming into this planet deal a great deal with the grounding of the Divine Plan on Earth. In the Piscean Age of the last two thousand years, it remained a little bit in an ungrounded state.

Grounding one's Ascension deals with taking good care of the physical body, getting enough sleep at night, mastering money, and mastering material and professional success. It also deals with being connected to nature. Many people living busy lives and being raised in big cities have gotten cut off or disconnected from nature. In big cities there is almost no place to find it, for everything is paved over with cement. We live in such a technological world many have lost this form of attunement to GOD. When is the last time you communed with a tree or flower? Even many lightworkers spend most of their time attuned to the Heavenly and Celestial Realms and the inner plane Ascended Masters and hardly ever consider attuning to the Devas and Nature Spirits that live within the Plant and Mineral Kingdom. Our farms are filled with pesticides and our entire society has become cut off from the Plant Devas and Nature Spirits that are the foundation of all plant and mineral life on Earth. Our collective consciousness has pushed them away, as well as the chemicals and pesticides that we use. Even if we call on their help, we continue to worship science to a fault instead of the spirit that lives within all life.

When we think of the American Indians and how they relate to the Earth and revere the Earth we can see how disconnected that we have become as a society. I remember a channeling of the Universal Mind where it was asked what is the one thing that every person on the planet could do that would be most beneficial to the planet. To my great interest, the Universal Mind said that if every person would just plant one tree that was the Universal Mind's profound guidance.

There are many exercises, in addition to your meditations and spiritual work, that you can do for the purpose of grounding yourself to the Earth. Some of the most effective exercises are: feeling your feet on the Earth, walking on the beach barefoot so you can feel the sand, giving foot massages, and having foot baths, so as to not forget the feet. Another is planting your own garden and working in the soil, which is one of the best ways to re-attune to the Earth and the Earth Mother.

Next time you want to practice channeling, instead of channeling the inner plane Ascended Masters or Angels, try channeling a tree, flower or plant. You may be amazed what you learn from the incredible beings that live within the plant and mineral life around us.

Another aspect of grounding one's ascension is through cleaning the house or hiring someone to help you do it. We all know how good we feel when we get our car washed or have the house cleaned. We have all heard the expression that cleanliness is next to godliness. We want to make our earthly home be a place where Angels would choose to enter.

One aspect of physical grounding is being very considerate of other people's third dimensional needs and wants. Even though you may have transcended a great many third dimensional aspects of life, it is always important to be compassionate and allow for other people's consciousness and to go out of your way to meet those third dimensional desires, even if you do not have a preference for them yourself.

When preparing food do it with great love, almost like a Zen practice, for the food we eat will enter the temples in which you and your family live. When walking around the world realize that GOD lives as much in physical creation as in the heavenly realms. The Material Universe is the physical body of GOD. Take time to look at the stars at night and the incredible beauty of physical existence, always seeing the Material Universe as one of GOD's Heavens.

Have a ceremony in nature in front of a tree and bring with you five sticks of incense to offer to Mother Earth. Practice ecology and conservation as one of your spiritual practices to sanctify Mother Earth.

Also, pets are an excellent way to physically ground your ascension. For example, having a dog or cat roaming the house is a surefire way to keep you very grounded, plus they bring so much unconditional love into the household.

Practicing of massage with your partner or friends is another wonderful way to get yourself back into the body. Using hot baths before bed, with candles and a little incense, will physically ground your energies and help you to sleep better. One sign that you are getting too ungrounded in your life, either too heavenly or too mentally, is when you are getting foot or leg cramps, which is the body's way of telling you that it needs attention. The quickest remedy I have found is to take a hot footbath, a regular bath, or a hot shower. This will reconnect the flow of acupuncture meridians back into the physical.

Another excellent way to ground your energies is to, at the end of your meditations, call on Archangel Sandalphon, Pan, and the Earth Mother to help ground your energies to reestablish your connection to your physical body and the Earth. Also, in every ascension activation meditation ask that all the activations you are receiving also be given to the Earth Mother who has graciously and selflessly provided us a place to live. She and Her many kingdoms that serve us have been for the most part ignored and unappreciated by mass consciousness throughout the ages. It is time we honor and sanctify Her.

An excellent way to attune to what I call the Body Elemental, which is the innate Spiritual intelligence of the physical body, is to work with a pendulum. Ask the pendulum "yes" or "no" questions as to the physical body's needs. Once you become proficient at using a pendulum, the subconscious mind and body elemental can, for example, advise you as to what kinds of foods to eat and what supplements you should be taking. This is a way of communicating directly with the inherent intelligence of the body, rather than using just the mind or lower-self desire, which are both usually inaccurate in their assessments. The mind (lower-self) tells us that we need this kind of food or these supplements; however, if you really communicated with the body elemental you would be very surprised at what it really wanted. Nutritionists give you advice from book knowledge rather than really tuning into the energy of the body elemental of each person to see what it really needs. Supplements that may be good for one person may be poison to another, just as a food that is good for one person may cause an allergic reaction in someone else. Get to know your physical body and trust its inherent intelligence, even if it defies book knowledge.

A wonderful way to ground your spirituality is to create your physical home as a temple. Set up spiritual altars in different places around your house. Put up pictures of the Masters and Saints who you revere. Place spiritual statues of the different Saints and Masters around your home. These can be obtained from any metaphysical bookstore or garden store.

Yet another aspect of physically grounding yourself is to be open to expressing and exploring your sexuality in an unconditional, loving, mutually sharing manner. Some spiritual schools will tell you that sexuality should be avoided if you want to grow spiritually. This is illusion and spiritual teaching contaminated by negative ego programming. As Buddha said, "Follow the path of moderation." Either the extreme of overindulgence or needless asceticism are inappropriate. Sexuality was created by GOD and is a means of expressing love through physical communication. As long as this form of communication is channeled through the heart and is not selfish, it will accelerate your spiritual growth, not hinder it. The sharing of passion is 100% appropriate and acceptable, as long as it is spiritually physical passion and not lust (lower-self carnal passion). Those spiritual teachings that are saying that passion is bad have missed the mark. Lower-self passion is to be avoided not higher-self passion. The cutting off of passion would be the same as cutting off emotions and the Goddess energies Herself. I love Eastern religion; however, some of the Yoga teachings on this specific aspect are, in my humble opinion, inaccurate. How can that which brings greater unconditional love be wrong if it is done in a balanced and integrated way?

Ascension walks are a wonderful way to ground. You can do your ascension activation work while walking. It is like a walking meditation. This way you can be bi-located doing your physical work and your spiritual work simultaneously. The late Edgar Cayce said in his Universal Mind channelings that walking was the best exercise. This way you also can get fresh air and a little sunshine every day, which is very grounding. As you are walking, take time to explore your physical senses and/or sensation function. By this I mean your senses sight, hearing, taste, and touch. Sometimes we get so involved in our lives and spiritual work that we actually forget to use our five physical senses. This may sound strange but it is true. A great many lightworkers are not connected to their sensation function. They live more on the mental, emotional, and intuitive plane. This is not a judgment, just a simple spiritual observation that can be adjusted if you choose to set your intent with your conscious mind and will.

Another great way to physically ground your energies to light incense or have essential oils in your home. There is a whole science to aromatherapy which states that you can use different oils or incense to create a certain psychological and spiritual atmosphere. My favorite incense is the Sai Baba incense that is made in his ashram and is called "Nag Champa." Along with this I would highly recommend buying flowers at least once a week. This was something that Quan Yin asked us to do for the Academy. It is not that expensive. You can get an inexpensive bouquet of flowers for five or six dollars and then do what we do which is break up the bouquet into four parts and put them in different rooms. And, of course, you should put some of them on your altar. If you put a little sugar or a growth stimulator such as "Miracle Gro" in the water, the flowers will last for at least a week. Flowers create a wonderful atmosphere. I also recommend using lots of plants in your home and business as this helps the integration of Heavenly and Earthly energies as well as helping to purify the air. Call on the Devas and Nature Spirits to inhabit these plants in your little indoor garden. You might also want to get smaller statues of gnomes, elves, and fairies as an added honoring of the Nature Kingdom for your indoor and/or outdoor garden.

The kind of physical clothes you wear are an important aspect of physically grounding your spirituality. It is something you should pay close attention to since the first impression most people have of you is by your appearance. Masters on the inner plane wear beautiful clothes and jewelry, which are a natural byproduct of their spiritual radiance. Try to find clothes and colors that truly fit you and exemplify your true spiritual essence, and not something that speaks to ego or vanity. Clothes are important, as are the colors you choose to wear every day. They are statements about yourself. The colors you surround yourself with do have a very subtle effect on your vibration and feeling tone. In addition, as part of this understanding, pay close attention to your physical hygiene. Combing your hair, brushing your teeth, using mouthwash if necessary, properly washing your clothes, to name a few. To some people this may sound strange that I mention this; however, we all know people who neglect this aspect of self and how distasteful it is to be around them.

Strangely enough, another excellent way to physically ground your spirituality is to call on the Mahatma, who is the embodiment of all 352 levels of the Godhead. Most people think of the Mahatma in terms of the 352nd level or highest level. The truth is that the Mahatma embodies the first level up to the highest level and is therefore a very grounding consciousness to merge with. Asking to merge with the Mahatma can be invaluable in learning to integrate and synthesize Heaven on Earth. The Mahatma is the cosmic embodiment of synthesis itself.

Enjoying the highest physically creative aspects and talents of people is a great grounding technique. By this I mean going to museums (art, science, history, etc.), concerts, and even a zoo or a theme park once in awhile (especially with children) can be a lot of fun and extremely uplifting. Many of the art galleries also have beautiful gardens to walk in. Sometimes going to the theatre, or the opera, is a way of grounding one's energies and enjoying the beauty of this physical world. The Spiritual path is one of integration and balance. We are meant to enjoy the best of both worlds and to enjoy the physical material world, not reject it for the spiritual. Some call this the perfect integration of the vertical and horizontal aspects of life. Many spiritual people think that they must live in some vertical attunement and must reject the horizontal aspects of life. We are not meant to live in a cave or live as isolated islands unto ourselves. We are as the Master Jesus exemplified, to live in the marketplace. Anyone can be spiritually living in their room without ever living. The true test comes when you get involved with life and the relationships that are a part of it. Can you be spiritual and maintain Christ/Buddha consciousness while fully involved with Earth life? This is the true test of an Apprentice Ascended Master. Part of being involved with Earth life also means it's okay to have fun and take time for enjoyment and recreation. In fully embracing your Spiritual path you get the best of both worlds. You get the best of the Spiritual world and the Earthly world. A true, full-fledged Ascended Master is completely involved in this world but not attached to it. So the Realized Being lives fully in this world but is not of this world.

Another wonderful way to physically ground your energies while sharing love and enjoyment is to go dancing with your partner, a friend or even by yourself in the comfort of your home. There are numerous forms of dance to enjoy, plus it is a great way to get physical exercise while having a lot of fun. In addition, it gives the physical and emotional bodies a chance for self-expression.

Vacations are also a way to achieve this goal. So is physically visiting some of Earth's sacred sites such as the Great Pyramid, Stonehenge, Machu Picchu, and the Sedona Vortexes, the Taj Mahal. Other possibilities are Sai Baba's ashram in India or from any other ashrams of the great saints of India or around the world. There is also the Findhorn community in Scotland and the Buddhist temples that are located all around Asia. Perhaps visiting the Holy Land in Israel and/or Mecca, the holiest place of the Islamic religion, appeals to you. I would also like to extend an invitation to come to Mt. Shasta, California for the annual Wesak Celebration for 2000 consciousness seekers from around the globe. Visiting these places can be extremely grounding and yet incredibly spiritually uplifting.

Another great way to physically ground your energy while integrating your spirituality into the third dimension is to not ignore the political aspects of life. Many lightworkers and spiritual seekers reject politics and worldly news. This is not good. It is each of our responsibility to remain somewhat aware of what is going on in our world on a political and social level. This can be done by watching the news or reading a newspaper or magazine. I am not saying that everybody has to be a political activist; however, there are some lightworkers who hold this puzzle piece. Even for those who don't, have a responsibility to take physical action, it is each of our responsibility to pray, affirm, visualize and raise consciousness with our family, friends and students. Political life is not separate from spiritual life. One of the reasons spiritual people stay away from political life is that in our world politics is almost completely run by the negative ego. How is our worldly Earth going to change, if spiritual people do not get involved with politics and social activism? The inner plane Ascended Masters are asking that every person dedicated to the Light give ten minutes of their daily meditation to prayers for planetary world service. This way, even if you are not taking physical action you are taking inner plane action, which is of equal value. Many First, Second, Third and Seventh Ray souls and Monads are being asked by Spirit and the Masters to step into these arenas and puzzle pieces to make changes in order to make way for the Seventh Golden Age on this planet.

Attuning to the beauty of GOD in the material and physical form can also mean getting involved in some form of the martial arts. By this I don't necessarily mean karate or judo, but a form such as Tai Chi, Aikido, or Chi Gong. These are beautiful, non-competitive forms that flow with the natural rhythms of the physical universe, and in so doing, greatly increase the energy flow within the physical vehicle.

Feng Shui, the Chinese art of placement, aids in attuning yourself to the laws of physical harmony. GOD's universe is, of course, made up of laws: spiritual laws, mental laws, emotional laws, etheric laws, and physical laws. The science of Feng Shui helps one to become attuned to the physical laws of design in one's living space in order to remain attuned to the soul and spirit. A Feng Shui specialist is an indoor house designer who understands the psychological and spiritual aspects of this science. Certain rooms in your house deal with relationships, others economics, and others wisdom. The way in which rooms are arranged affects all aspects of life, beauty, harmony, and the psychological as well as the spiritual. There are books you can buy on this, but even more effective is to have a Feng Shui specialist come to your home. I had this done and the woman was fantastic! She analyzed my home and made numerous recommendations. For example, she highly recommended having a fountain in our living room. She said certain closet doors should be covered and aesthetic screens be set to close particular passage ways. The changes we made in our house were very simple, however, the effects were incredibly profound in terms of how we felt living in our house. So, for the small investment of an hour session it is well worth your time and money.

There is a similar practice that can be helpful in terms of grounding spirit into matter, and that is putting energy into what I call aesthetics. Aesthetics is the physical science of taking time to do normal physical functions in an artistic and pleasing way. For example, let's say you are going to bring your spouse some tea. You can bring him or her a cup of tea in a plain cup, or you can pick out a very pretty cup that would be more aesthetically pleasing. You can even go a bit further by putting it on a saucer or a little plate. Placing a small flower next to it with an aesthetically designed napkin and spoon is another possibility. You can place them all on a beautiful tray and maybe add an equally beautiful dish of cookies, crackers, or wafers. Do you see the difference, my friends? The same act can be done mechanically or it can be done with a great deal of love and artistic harmony. The same applies for how you set the table for dinner or breakfast, decorate your house, or wrap gifts. In truth, it applies to everything in life. This might be called the integration of the Second and Fourth Rays into everything you do. I guarantee you it will be very much appreciated by the loved ones around you.

Doing all the different things I have spoken of in this chapter has an incredibly uplifting effect on one's emotional, mental and Spiritual body, as well as the physical body. Seeing beautiful things in your home and observing the physical harmony uplifts your Spiritual life. You are literally grounding GOD into the physical and harmonizing yourself with GOD's laws on the physical plane. You are, in essence, creating Heaven on Earth. The Divine Plan is to create all homes on Earth and all of society on Earth honoring these principles. In truth, what you are doing is sanctifying and paying homage to the Material Face of GOD. You are becoming closer to GOD by embracing the physical, because as I have already stated, GOD lives in all four faces. Therefore, you are becoming more whole and more Self-Realized in your Realization of GOD by fully embracing the Earth and the material world.

The confusion of many Eastern and Western Spiritual paths who have rejected the world to a large extent, stems from a misunderstanding of the difference between lower-self and Higher Self thinking. When stated another way, they are confused about the difference between Christ/Buddha thinking and negative ego thinking. They are rejecting the world because they do not want to become tempted by the lower-self, lower desire, lower passions, lower temptations, and indulgences. In truth, they are on the right track, for these aspects, even in a full-fledged Ascended Master, are to be avoided. What these Eastern and Western paths have done, however, is to "throw the baby out with the bathwater." They have confused the world and matter with the lower-self and the negative ego and all lower-self desire. It is true that the lower-self and the negative ego and all lower-self desire is to be rejected if you want to Realize GOD. These Eastern and Western paths are partially blaming the world and matter as the problem, when, in truth, it is the negative ego and lower-self which is the problem. Matter and the world in and of itself is Divine. If used in the service of the Higher Self and Christ/Buddha thinking without negative ego and lower-self desire, then it is just an example of one of GOD's Heavens and Faces given perfect expression. GOD in His infinite wisdom and Divine Plan wants His idea perfectly expressed and demonstrated on all levels of Creation including the physical material universe. To reject the world and matter is to reject a large aspect of GOD and one of GOD's Heavens. This is the psychological reason this misunderstanding has taken place in some Eastern and Western paths. In essence, the confused negative ego does not see that GOD needs to be expressed and demonstrated on all levels including the physical.

Another very important aspect of your physical grounding is what city you choose to physically live in. Where we live physically has an enormous effect on us, much more than we realize. Many lightworkers are very sensitive in a positive sense, and others, who do a lot of channeling work or psychic work, are often very empathetic because of their particular puzzle piece. It is important for all Spiritual people to live in the right place; however, for these types of people it is essential.

When we are living in a big city, for example, we are bombarded with city noises, traffic, pollution, usually low quality drinking water, lack of nature, city smells, long lines, and unbelievable amounts of electrical pollution. All the power lines and electrical energy in a city are not good for the physical body. Every city also has a personality and soul ray. Many people live in cities that are not vibrationally right because of these ray frequencies. Each city also has a different level of soul evolution. Some cities are very young Spiritually, while others are more mature. This applies to the country you live in as well. Cities have a layer of physical, etheric, astral and mental pollution that surround them. The layers vary in the degree of pollution, as some have more than others, and the same holds true for their effects on people. There are lightworkers who are meant to live in these cities to bring in more light and to help clear this energy. This pollution I speak of is not just physical pollution. It is also the negative thoughts, emotions, and energy of all of the people living in that city. One thing you can do in your meditations is to say prayers to GOD and the inner plane Ascended Masters to help clear up this psychological and earthly smog, so to speak. There are, of course, certain physical areas that hold very high frequencies of energies, especially in or near vortexes and on mountains.

Living in a city with a higher frequency will not give you Self-Realization, for it is not where you live that determines this. It is your thoughts, words, and deeds that determine your evolution. If you are sensitive, however, your environment can affect all of your bodies unless you are really strong on all levels. So it is ultimately a good idea to consider living in your right geographical location. If you can't because of business, children, or your marriage, be not concerned, for again, your spiritual life is not created by where you live. If you do find yourself in that situation, at least create your home or one room in your home as a temple or sanctuary.

Another aspect of third dimensional grounding has to do with honoring the protocols of third dimensional living. Examples of this would be to pay attention to people's names, or remembering birthdays and anniversaries of family and friends. Also, writing thank you notes, and possibly sending out Christmas cards. Do you know how meaningful this can be to someone, and how touched people can be when you remember such things? One more example is to honor the bonds of your Earthly family and extended family. Some lightworkers become so identified with their heavenly heritage that they feel it is okay to reject any physical body blood relationships, so to speak. Spiritual people often do not feel connected to their Earthly families. Does this mean that we do not have a responsibility or an obligation to these physical body connections? From an integrated point of view and synthesis, meeting Earthly family obligations at times is appropriate, even if our emotional body may not always feel like doing so.

The same principle applies to the philosophical issue of GOD's law versus man's law. As the Bible says, "When in Rome do as the Romans do." In other words, from a Spiritual perspective it is still 100% appropriate to follow the Earthly laws of the country or society you live in. Remember GOD created the concept of civilization as well. Except in very extreme situations where your conscience can't really let you do something, it is more appropriate to abide by the Earthly laws of the civilization you live in. Now, for most people this is obvious and you do this; however, there are some Spiritual people who become very Heavenly oriented and feel that it is permissible as well as appropriate to reject third dimensional reality. Third dimensional reality is not a bad thing. It just needs to be guided by the Christed ideal rather than negative illusions, glamours, and maya!

In grounding your energies and integrating Heaven on Earth it is important to take on an important cause of our third dimensional world, such as saving the rainforest, saving the whales, and feeding the homeless, to name a few. I am always reminded by Sai Baba's famous quote, "Hands that help are holier than lips that pray." There are so many people in the world whose third dimensional survival needs are not being met. How is a person supposed to focus on Self-Realization when they do not have food to eat or a place to live? Many people in the Consciousness Movement would do well to focus their service energies on the physical needs of their brothers and sisters. There is no more noble service that can be provided. There are so many volunteer organizations where you can get involved in this type of work. I am reminded of Mother Teresa and the wonderful physical help she provided through her ministry. There are other causes such as helping our animal brothers and sisters who are so mistreated in our world. In addition, helping other people's third dimensional needs will aid in grounding your energies. Our Spiritual life isn't meant to be lived on only the inner dimensions, but also, and most importantly, to be demonstrated in third dimensional reality.

One of the most important ways to physically ground your energy is to do what I call "practicing the Presence." This means that as you physically walk through your daily life, practice being GOD or being the Christ/Buddha. Every person that you encounter as you walk down the street or do errands should ideally be seen as GOD meeting GOD or Christ/Buddha meeting Christ/Buddha. The Master Jesus has referred to this as the "Holy Encounter." Every tree and plant you meet is, in truth, a holy encounter, as well as every animal, insect, and even rock. The very ground we walk on is holy for all is GOD. We not only are GOD, we live and move and have our being in GOD. As you walk through your life see GOD in every thought, word, and deed. Sometimes we speak of traditional religion and the observation of how people often go to church but do not practice the church consciousness in their daily life. The same is often true at times with many New Age lightworkers. They often give wonderful channelings, healings, lectures, counseling sessions, or write beautiful articles or books; however, the true test is how do they treat their neighbors, employees, and strangers. How do they treat the checker at the market, the bank teller, the gardener, the cleaning lady, or people in general whom society normally considers beneath their professional or social status? In what way do they treat children, pets, and friends, especially when they do something they don't like? How do they treat their Earthly family members? This is one of the true tests of the Spiritual path. It is not so much the work you do but whether you are a demonstration of GOD and Christ/Buddha consciousness, moment by moment, in every thought, word, deed, and action. The most important aspect of the Spiritual path, believe it or not, is not the worldly recognition you receive from your professional work, but rather the moment by moment thinking, speaking, and actions you physically take with every aspect of GOD you come across in all GOD's Kingdoms, and especially with the people you are involved with every day.

Having a routine for your physical and Spiritual practices is also very helpful in grounding your spirituality. Many lightwokers have special needs that take organization, planning, and time management. Set up a time when you are going to physically exercise. It could be walking, stretching, yoga, aerobic work, and/or weight lifting. There are three aspects to physical fitness: flexibility, aerobics, and strength. Flexibility can be achieved through stretching or yoga. Aerobics through brisk walking, jogging, riding a stationary bicycle, using a rowing machine or stair climber, swimming, and aerobic dance, to name a few. Strength is achieved through weight lifting. The ideal weekly routine should include a little bit of all three aspects of physical fitness. Setting up a routine is a good way to build these habits into your daily life. Carl Jung, the famous Swiss psychologist, said, "Man's greatest sin is his indolence." Without some form of structure and discipline in our lives the subconscious mind and physical body usually follows the line of least resistance. Balance is ever the key, for too much discipline and structure is not good either.

There is a wonderful way to ground your energies and get physical exercise at the same time, which is to just do all of the physical work of maintaining a household. Mowing the lawn, weeding the garden, taking out the trash cans, doing all the shopping, and really cleaning the house. Cleaning the bathtub, floors, sinks, stove, vacuuming, sweeping and occasionally going through the closets. This maintenance includes washing the car, bringing order to the garage, sweeping the sidewalks, driveways, and washing the windows. All of these things take a lot of physical work. Now, if you want to hire someone that is fine. However, sometimes it is nice to get away from the spiritual and mental work of daily life and do physical work. So, your house gets clean and you get a good physical workout as well!

This brings me to the concept of practicing a Zen-type of philosophy in regard to such chores. Even the word "chore" is really the wrong word because it has a negative stigma. Cleaning can be a very sanctified Spiritual practice if done from the right state of consciousness and perspective. When you prepare food for your family or yourself it is a very holy act. When you wash the vegetables it can be done with great love and sanctity, or you can just rush through it with no love. When you clean your house you can do it with spiritual devotion as if you were cleaning the temple and/or church of the highest GOD, which, in truth, is exactly what all homes are. Sanctifying and honoring the Earth with devotion and reverence is a Spiritual practice of the Divine Mother and the Goddess energies. Imagine if you were cleaning GOD's Temple at the 352nd Level of Divinity, or cleaning the ashram of His Holiness, the Lord Sai Baba, the Masters, Jesus, or any great saint or teacher you revere. Would you do these things with love, joy, happiness, and sanctification? Is your home, family, and even your office, not worth the same reverence and Zen-like practice? Cleaning the house is just as spiritual a practice as doing affirmations, praying or meditating. If you clean the house the right way it is an affirmation, a prayer, a meditation. Do you see the split that many have created between Heaven and Earth?

Everything you do including sleeping is a Spiritual practice. Even when we sleep it is of the highest importance to control your thoughts, feelings, and energy, because where you go when you sleep and the kinds of dreams you have will be determined by this factor. The true ideal is to make earth life a walking meditation. I personally do not spend that much time meditating or doing ascension activation work. My life is my meditation and my time is consumed with planetary world service.

When you run errands, enjoy this time and make it a sanctified act. I do spiritual work even when I am standing in line at the bank, post office or market. There is never a time when we are not doing GOD's work. Our confused civilization has created a split between our Spiritual life and earthly life. Spirituality is legally not allowed in our educational, political, or prison system, and, in truth, all of our earthly systems. We have this crazy philosophy of separating church from state, which is in place to protect us from self-righteous zealots. This is good and appropriate; however, again we have "thrown the baby out with the bath water." Being protected from negative ego-oriented religious zealots is good; however, we must integrate true universally oriented soul and spiritual integration into all aspects of our civilization. How can you separate or remove GOD, Soul, Spirit, and Christ/Buddha consciousness out of earthly civilization and expect it to work properly? When you do separate or remove GOD, the Soul, Spirit, and Christ/Buddha consciousness out of earthly civilization what you have is the negative ego running civilization. This is what we see happening right now in our current society in our political, prison, educational, and economic systems, as well as in the media (television, movies, magazines, newspapers, etc.), how people do business, in psychology, traditional medicine, the entirety of science, the care of the elderly, the homeless, to name a few. It all comes back to negative ego as the cause of all problems. If religions were not so run by the negative ego we would not need to separate church from state. I am not putting down religion for I love all religions. The problem is, many people who practice these religions do not know how to control their own negative egos, so unconsciously they are self-righteous and very judgmental and try to impose their views on other people. Therefore, this is why separation of church and state has been partially needed to protect us from such negative ego run people. I think you can see the profound wisdom that is being imparted here. This insight is one of the key principles for healing our entire civilization.

Another very interesting way to ground your energy and to appreciate the inherent intelligence of the physical body is to dialogue with a part of your body when it is having problems. For example, if you have a backache, dialogue with your back in your journal and let your back speak to you. This may sound silly at first; however, I assure you it is not. Just as a flower, plant, or rock can be channeled, so can any body part. Have a conversation with your entire physical body or a part of it and you will be amazed at what it will tell you if you allow it free expression. The innate intelligence of GOD lives within every cell, organ, and gland of your body. They will tell you what they need if you allow them to speak in either writing, words, or the silence of your own heart.

Integrity is also an aspect of physical grounding. By this I mean, if you say you are going to call or see someone at a certain time and then don't, you are not being physically grounded. Many people give themselves permission to say things and then not follow through. This demonstrates a lack of integrity and consistency between your three minds and physical body. The ideal is for your entire being to function as a consistent, fully integrated unit.

There is an excellent way to achieve grounding which is by calling upon the Masters and Angels constantly for help for your physical and energy bodies. There are numerous areas that they can aid. For instance, if you have heavy lifting to do, call on the Masters and Angels and you will be amazed at how much stronger you will be with their energetic support. At the beginning of the day call on them to run their energies through you all day and see how much easier your work is, whether it is cleaning the house or doing your professional work. They are also helpful when doing your taxes, and in resolving mechanical problems. If someone is sick, whether in your family or at the office, call on them to put up a screen of protection around you and the person. When you want to have a deep night's sleep, the Masters can bring forth a special type of energy that will help you sleep better. Call on them as well when you are about to start any artistic endeavors. All you have to do is ask, inwardly or outwardly. Most people think of the Angels and Ascended Masters as only involved with spiritual or inner plane activities. The truth is they are happy and wanting to get involved with every aspect of Earth life. Their only limitation is that they are not allowed to enter in if they are not asked or invited to. So, do ask!

Grounding your mission is extremely important. Too often people have many ideas which they talk a lot about, but they do not physically ground all the creativity, Spiritual knowledge and wisdom within them. In this Aquarian Age, it is time to physically ground your Spiritual life here on Earth. Do not be afraid to take risks, and experiment in the different ways to ground you mission. Take advantage of the Computer Age. I highly recommend getting on the Internet and maybe even setting up your own Website. Learn how to use e-mail because it is a revolutionary new form of communication. If you don't have a fax machine, get one. All mailings can take place instantly now. Even if you are not good with mechanical things, these New Age tools have been brought in to speed up evolution and are not that hard to learn how to use. Again, get involved in life and make your ideas physically tangible upon this earthly plane!

Another aspect of physical grounding and physical programming is the concept of acting "as if". For example, if you want to learn public speaking join Toastmasters where you can practice giving speeches "as if" you are really good at it. When you act "as if," your emotional and mental bodies will follow suit in a short time. The same concept applies to Realizing GOD. If you want to be with GOD in Heaven then act like Him on Earth. In your daily life act like GOD, act like Christ, act like Buddha, act like a full-fledged Ascended Master, even if it is a little bit difficult for your subconscious mind and negative ego to accept. If you keep acting "as if," it will soon become more natural. This also applies to channeling. In the beginning you have to almost pretend that you are doing it, like a role play, however, over time your own Higher Self, Monad and the Masters can begin to intuitively glide through the role playing or acting "as if." This is one of the beginning steps in learning how to channel. Eventually there must be clear discernment as to what is role playing and acting and what is true channeling; however, for the very beginning student who is just starting this concept may be part of the initial or beginning practice. So, in many cases it is helpful to physically act "as if" as an excellent way to, at times, reprogram your subconscious mind as well as mental and emotional vehicles.

Another excellent way of grounding is to honor the sacred rituals of life. These can be the honoring and celebrating of holidays such as Christmas, Thanksgiving, Easter, and New Years, to name a few. Then there are also the sacred rituals and holidays honoring the full moons such as Wesak, which is the Festival of the Buddha in the full moon of Taurus. There is the Festival of the Christ, which usually falls in the full moon in April. Lastly, the full moon in June, which is the Festival of Humanity. These are three of the most sacred festivals of the inner plane Ascended Masters. Other sacred holidays could be celebrated, such as the birthdays of some of the great saints and religious leaders that have graced this planet. Eventually our planet will become more universally oriented where all religions and Spiritual paths will be honored, as they will all be seen as stemming from the same source and fundamentally teaching the same thing. It is also possible to create sacred rituals for yourself and your family, and/or the spiritual groups you work with. These can provide a physical structure and be very meaningful to a great many people.

One of the most important ways to physically ground your Spirituality is to take physical action in all areas of your life. Many people are libraries of ideas, but they don't physically act on them and physically manifest them. People are put off by the physical errands and responsibilities that are least enjoyable. This is okay to a certain extent; however, over the long term you will feel much better if you take care of business and get everything done that you have to do. With the Seventh Ray planetary energy coming into the world that is replacing the old Sixth Ray energy, grounding your physicality on Earth is one of the key points of the New Millennium.

Another key is to keep many physical lists and a physical journal, which is like a spiritual accounting and physical organization of the different aspects of your Spiritual/Earthly life. The act of physically writing things down can make a much greater impression on the subconscious mind than just thinking about them. When you have ideas write them down so you don't forget them. When you have dreams you want to remember, write them down. Keep files of all your different ideas and projects. Stay physically organized. I recommend keeping a little notebook in your pocket with a pen, so wherever you are, if inner guidance or ideas come to you you can jot them down. Just the act of physically writing them down is one of the keys to manifestation.

Yet another way to ground your energies is to keep physical objects that have great Spiritual power and energy around you. For some people this means wearing a crystal, while for others this means wearing jewelry with different kinds of gemstones. The wearing of a special watch or certain kinds of amulets can be an extremely Spiritual attunement. Others may want to carry certain gemstones, amulets, rosaries, and/or crystals in their pockets. Some people may want to carry a picture or pictures of some of the Masters in their wallet. Many practice this by even placing certain amulets or small pictures in their vehicle as well. For some, this practice is to choose to wear prayer beads. The main thing in doing it is to do this for a true spiritual purpose, and not for any type of negative ego, vain purpose. Do this because it brings greater Spiritual attunement in the highest and purest sense of the term.

When physically grounding your Spirituality you may want to consider changing your name to a Spiritual one. This can be done legally or to be used just with friends. The reason for this change is that a name has great Spiritual power and is like a mantra. For some it is helpful to have a name that one can grow into Spiritually as a type of ideal rather than one that may no longer fit you. Since your name is something you are constantly saying, writing and are identifying with, why not choose a name that truly fits your Spiritual essence?

Another aspect of grounding your Spiritual energies has to do with honoring earthly, physical laws. For example, when I established The Melchizedek Synthesis Light Academy, I asked the inner plane Ascended Masters if I should spend the money and time to get a federal and state patent on the name. They were very adamant in their opinion that this was well worth my energy and time. They said that it would have the effect of grounding the Academy on an etheric and third dimensional level. The lesson here is to take time to get legal name changes, or non-profit status for your church, and to follow all earthly protocols in setting up a center. This applies to setting up appropriate contracts with employees, even if they are friends and regardless of the fact that it is a totally spiritual business you are running. You never know what is going to happen in the future, so no matter how spiritual you are or how stable your business is, everything you do business wise should follow appropriate earthly protocol and third dimensional practices. Being spiritual does not mean that everything is based on the honor system and that you can let go of this aspect of life. Trust me on this point, for you never know where negative ego and issues of false pride, attachment to money, power, and fame are going to rear their ugly heads, even with people you would never expect it from. Following this good earthly advice will save you many future potential problems.

In Conclusion

In this chapter I have given you an overview of some of the basic principles and ways to physically ground your spirituality. This is essential for many reasons. One is to fully Realize GOD. Another is to become successful on the Earth and manifest your mission on Earth. A third reason is for your physical health.

There are a great many people on Earth who are either overidentified with matter; which manifests in a materialistic philosophy, a philosophy governed by negative ego thinking or underidentified with matter. The underidentification with matter, which is especially prevalent among religious and/or Spiritual people, creates lack of sanctification, love and integration of the Material Face of GOD and the GODDESS energies.

Eastern religions and philosophy tend to reject matter, while Western man tends to be too materialistic. Many in the New Age Movement and/or religion overidentify with Heavenly energies and/or the Celestial Realms, as well as not being fully grounded psychologically.

When looked at clairvoyantly, this can be seen as people walking around as just heads, or energetically cutoff at the waist or cutoff at the knees. In this new Aquarian Age it is time to balance and integrate the four Faces of GOD, the seven chakras, the 352 levels of the Mahatma, and all twelve of your bodies in a balanced manner.

It is time to honor and sanctify not only our own physical body, but also GOD's physical body, which is the infinite physical universe. By doing this we are also honoring and sanctifying the GODDESS energies, as well as the Divine Cosmic Mother and our Beloved Earth Mother. It is time that these beloved energies receive their due honor, sanctification and recognition which will only enhance and make more whole your own Realization of GOD and Divinity at all levels!

28

How to Develop an Integrated Christ/Buddha Living Space

An aspect of integrating the Goddess deals with the issue of developing a Christ/Buddha Living Space. To begin this discussion it must be understood that "beauty is in the eye of the beholder" and "in matters of taste, there is no dispute." So I am not going to write a chapter telling people how to decorate their home for that would be impossible. I would, however, like to share my own personal experience for this most important issue and share some underlying principals in regard to this issue that I think you, my Beloved Readers, might find of value.

There is an ancient Spiritual Science in China which I am sure you are all familiar with called "Feng Shui." This spiritual science deals with the art of physical placement of things in your home and environment for greatest spiritual benefit to all. I had a lady come to my home who was a Master of Feng Shui and she had some wonderful ideas. Certain rooms were for business, some for romantic relationship, one for prosperity. It was very important that certain closet doors be blocked. It was important that beds be pointed in a certain direction. She recommended that we get a fountain for our living room, which we did. I can't remember all the different ideas she had, but we implemented most of them and it really did add an enormous amount to the spiritual atmosphere and energetic radiation of our home.

In my other books, I have spoken about the importance of cleansing the etheric and/or energetic atmosphere of one's home by the practice of burning pots, sage, and incense. The walls become embedded with energy, thought forms, and feelings as well as the psycho/spiritual atmosphere of the house. Clairvoyantly this can sometimes be seen as gray or dark clouds in the house. Just as is it is extremely important to clean your house really well, it is also important to cleanse the psychic atmosphere on a regular basis. The best method I have found is the use of a burning pot, which is a pot with a hot plate under it where you add 1/4 of an inch of Epson salt with 1/2 an inch of rubbing alcohol. Light a match to it and it will cleanse the psychic atmosphere of that room in about 5 minutes. I recommend doing this once a week or once every other week in each room of your house. When people walk into your home, they can sense the psycho/spiritual atmosphere. In my experience, sage or incense alone is not enough. The other helpful method is to ask the inner plane Ascended Masters and Angels to help.

The next aspect of maintaining a Christ/Buddha Living Space is the importance of creating harmony, beauty and aesthetics. This again is individual to each person, however; here are some ideas from my own personal experience. The first idea that comes to mind is the creation of spiritual altars in your home and if possible one room dedicated to your spiritual life and spiritual attunement. This could be a place to meditate and pray. I highly recommend buying some spiritual statues and spiritual pictures as well as your favorite incense and maybe some crystals or gem stones. Each time you go to this altar or even this room, a habit of spiritual attunement is created. The physical beauty of your Spiritual Altar will be an immediate attunement itself. It also must be understood that these statues and pictures hold energy and form conduits and lines of spiritual force from the inner plane. It may be interesting for some of you to know that Spiritual Statues even have chakras and can be seen spinning and vibrating with energy.

I myself take the approach of my home and property being a Temple as well as home and business. My entire home is filled with beautiful

Spiritual Statues and pictures of the Masters and Saints of all religions. In a sense, every room is a Spiritual Sanctuary and Altar.

Quan Yin has advised me and my wife of the importance of having fresh flowers on our main Altars. This we do on a regular basis and it adds an enormous amount to the feeling in our home. We also have an enormous amount of plants, which we all know both Spiritually and Physically they cleanse the atmosphere.

I also recently have bought some beautiful silk flowers that are absolutely exquisite in color and beauty which have added another dimension to the overall aesthetic nature of our home.

Being very much attuned to the principle of Synthesis, Integration, and Balance, we have attempted to honor all kingdoms of GOD. For this reason, we also have a great many crystals and gemstones of a small and large nature all over our home. We also have a beautiful female Golden Retriever by the name of Brianna, and a wonderful male cat by the name of Mushroom, which adds to the family atmosphere. We also try to bring all the colors of the rainbow to our Spiritual Pictures, plants, silk plants, crystals, gem stones and spiritual accoutrements. I have these beautiful glass pyramids each of a different color of the different rays. We also have beautiful stained glass spiritual pictures adorning our windows. We also have our favorite photographs that have the most sentimental meaning.

The Art of Decorating is also very important in how one creates a Christ/Buddha living space. There is a whole art to the placement of pictures, furniture, plants, and objects to form Divine Order and symmetry. The importance of being surrounded by spiritual beauty, nature, beautiful colors, the smell of beautiful flowers and incense, beautiful sounds of nature, a fountain and/or beautiful music cannot be underestimated.

Also the importance of having nice beautiful furniture that is all so comfortable. All of these aspects when put together create an enormous radiation of Spiritual energy. These physical aspects uplift the Spirit and all 12 bodies. In one of the Universal Mind Channelings of Edgar Cayce, the Universal Mind said that one should make their Earthly home where Angels would choose to come. Creating a Spiritually beautiful home draws higher spiritual forces to you and to your home.

Part of the purpose of life is to create Heaven on Earth. Creating a beautiful spiritual home is physically grounding one's spiritual life and energy into the Earth. Ideally one should try to integrate all seven rays into one's home. Not only just in color but in principle. For example the fourth ray is the ray of beauty which we have been speaking of. The sixth ray deals with devotion and that could be grounded in your home by having spiritual altars. The seventh ray deals with ceremonial order and magic and this could be manifested by keeping your house and office very orderly and clean in the same way that you would keep a church or temple orderly or clean. Your home and environment is the physical body of GOD just as your physical body is the physical temple you live in. By creating our home also into a Temple or Spiritual Sanctuary, we are honoring and sanctifying the material face of GOD. When I look at our home and gardens, it honestly looks like an inner plane Ashram. Isn't that the purpose, however, to create Heaven on Earth? The Divine Plan is not to escape Earth or even leave Earth once Ascended, but rather be God and/or the Mighty I AM Presence on Earth and create a utopian civilization on Earth.

The fifth ray of New Age Science is integrated in the home by the Spiritually Scientific approach you bring to creating the Divine Order, Divine symmetry, and Divine Geometry to how you decorate it and create it. The second ray is integrated through the love and wisdom that is manifested in how you decorate, and the love and wisdom that emanates from the objects you choose to place in your home. The first ray is integrated through the Spiritual Power that emanates through the spiritual statues, spiritual picture, spiritual paintings, flowers, crystals, and gemstones as well as Divine Order. The third ray is integrating in the form of active intelligence by making your home not only spiritually beautiful, but also spiritually functional so enormous amounts of spiritual service work and personal, social and family activity can take place.

Another important aspect of maintaining a Christ/Buddha living space is the importance of putting things away after using them and not letting one's house become too cluttered. On the other side of the coin, one does not want to become neurotic or overly orderly to the point of losing one's inner peace if a physical object is out of place. A proper balance must be found in this regard that honors both the feminine and masculine.

This brings me to the first aspect of creating a Christ/Buddha living space which honors the Goddess as well, which is the outside environment and gar-dens of your apartment or home. My wife and I have spent an enormous amount of time creating a beautiful garden around the entire perimeter of our home. In this garden we have planted beautiful plants and flowers of all colors and varieties. We've also decorated our back yard with beautiful spiritual statues of Mother Mary, Quan Yin, Lord Buddha, Sananda, St. Francis and many different kinds of Angels. We also have little statues of Gnomes and Fairies. We also have beautiful little statues of all kinds of different animals honoring the animal kingdom. In our beautiful garden we have statues big and small of deer, swan, ducks, owls, pigs, frogs, raccoons, fox, birds, to name a few. Each Spiritual Statue and animal statue are spiritually, aesthetically and scientifically placed to create the perfect Feng Shui in the garden. In the flower beds there are even little statues of colorful butterflies, ladybugs, bumblebees and birds. Our garden is filled with the colors of all the seven rays and even the higher rays. It is a Synthesis Blending of all the Kingdoms. The Rocks on the property are spiritually and scientifically placed around the flowerbeds to honor the mineral kingdom. When we moved into this place there was a shed which we painted and turned into a Spiritual Chapel. The outside of this chapel is now violet and white, the inside is all white. We have carpeted it in a beautiful green carpet and placed some beautiful white flowers on the altar and a white chair for meditation.

We have also placed in our garden beautiful bird feeders, which have attracted an enormous number of birds. My office where I work all day long looks out to the entire garden and those bird feeders. As I sit in my office the garden is not only filled with birds but also many other kinds of wonderful animal life. There are chipmunks, butterflies, humming-birds, blue birds, bumblebees and squirrels to name a few. This does not even mention all the plant spirits and nature spirits that the garden is filled with and that we have invoked.

Now I must say that taking care of this property and garden and maintaining a Christ/Buddha Living Space takes a certain amount of work and time. The enjoyment that my wife and I, Academy, Ashram, friends, family and others experience being here is greatly worth the effort to maintain it. Besides the enjoyment factor, an even more important principle is that it is each of our spiritual responsibility as integrated Ascended Masters and as caretakers for the Goddess energy to take care of our homes, gardens and environment in a spiritually responsible manner. As I have mentioned many times in my writing, all four faces of GOD; spiritual, mental, emotional and physical, must be mastered and integrated to become a full-fledged Ascended Master and to fully integrate one's Goddess energies in the proper manner. I thank you for this opportunity to share some of my personal thoughts and feelings on this most important issue of creating a Divine Goddess/Christ/Buddha Living Space!

29

Honoring and Sanctifying the Material Face of GOD

In the study of esoteric thought it is understood that there are four Faces of GOD. There is the Spiritual Face, the Mental Face, the Emotional Face, and the Material or Physical Face. No one face is better than another; they are just each different aspects of the Creator. For our purposes, in our discussion of the Soul's perspective of physical health, this is a exceedingly important issue.

It is very common among people in the Consciousness Movement and lightworkers who are spiritually inclined, to gravitate more towards the Celestial and Heavenly realms in their attunement to the point of, on occasion, creating a little bit of an imbalance between Heaven and Earth. Earth is often seen as a place to escape from and lightworkers often are consumed with a desire to achieve liberation without what I would call the proper love for the Earth and the Material Face of GOD.

There is often a conscious or unconscious belief that the higher dimensions are more spiritual or sanctified than the third dimension of the Earth or the third dimension of the Universe. The Masters wish us to understand that there are many Heavens of GOD and the Material Universe is one of GOD's Heavens. One of the premier reasons of the Spiritual path is to love the Material Universe and one's physical body as the Temple of GOD and the Temple of our own Soul.

Lightworkers or consciousness seekers may be over identified with the Mental Face of GOD, being consumed in the intellect or sciences.

Other lightworkers may be primarily focused on the emotional aspect of GOD, being mostly focused on how they and others feel and, to a great extent on unconditional love, which is good, but not to the neglect of the other Faces of GOD. This is why I wrote *Integrated Ascension: Revelation for the Next Millennium*. The premise of that book being it is not just enough to ascend or to achieve one's seven levels of initiation; it is also important to do this in an integrated and balanced way.

The Divine Plan is not to escape the Material Universe and Earth, but rather, to bring Heaven to Earth. In other words, create a Christed/Buddha society on Earth. The work towards the achievement of such a society is based first on each individual attaining their own personal ascension. The term "ascension" is really a misnomer. When we ascend, we do not leave the Earth; we are grounding our higher self and spirit into our physical bodies on Earth. So ascension is really decension. The purpose of life is to become a walking embodiment of the Mighty I Am Presence or Christ/Buddha on Earth.

When we overidentify with the Heavenly realms or these other Faces of GOD to the neglect of the Material/Physical Face of GOD, this creates an imbalance in our chakras or spiritual energy centers. As we all know there are seven major chakras. When we overidentify with Heavenly energies to the neglect of the physical this causes all the energy we are running to be channeled through our higher chakras (maybe four through seven). This creates an energy weakness in our lower chakras (one through three). Each chakra is connected to a major gland and these glands secret hormones that enormously affect the organs and all aspects of physical health. Any chakra we under- or overidentify with will cause an imbalance in that corresponding gland.

Contrary to many spiritual teachings, each chakra could be looked at as a face of GOD as well. One of the premier causes of physical health problems among lightworkers is this imbalance in the chakra system. If we are too heavenly, all of our energies will be in the higher chakras (maybe five, six, or seven). If we are mentally identified, we will have more of our energy in chakras three, five, six, and seven. If we are emotionally identified most of our energy will be in chakras two, three, four, and five, most probably. If we are too materially focused, we will have most of our energy in chakras one, two and three. The ideal, of course, is to be balanced in all seven chakras, sanctifying all seven as windows and Faces of GOD.

The American Indians are a wonderful example of a culture that is very spiritual and greatly honors the Earth and the Material Face of GOD. Western civilization would do well to learn from their beautiful sanctification of the Earth Mother. The Essenes were also very attuned to the Material Face of GOD and integrated it into their practices. You can read more about this in my book *Hidden Mysteries*, if you like.

This understanding of the four Faces of GOD also relates to Carl Jung's well-known theory of types of people. Jung postulated that there were four types of people: the intuitive, thinking, feeling, and sensation/functioning. The intuitive would correlate with the Heavenly Face of GOD. The thinking would correlate with the Mental Face of GOD. The feeling type would correlate with the Emotional Face of GOD. The sensation/function type correlates with the Material Face of GOD. These types of people deal with how people are tuning into their world. The ideal is to be balanced in all four functions. Many people identify with one or more of these types to the slight neglect of another. For example, some people are constantly tuning into their intuition, maybe to the neglect of what their mind is telling them. Other people may focus on tuning in to how they feel as their most important way of accessing information. Others may be intuitive/feeling types, and others still intuitive/thinking types. Others still may be sensation/function types which means when they walk into a room, they are focusing their five physical senses: seeing, hearing, smelling, touching, and tasting. If you asked this person what color clothing every person in the room is wearing, if they had to close their eyes they could immediately do it. An intuitive/thinking type or intuitive/feeling type would not have the slightest idea because their consciousness is not focused on accessing that particular type of information. This all has to do with our belief systems and the over- or underidentification we maintain with the four Faces of GOD, the balance of our seven chakras, and the fundamental balance of our own four-body system (physical body, emotional body, mental body, and spiritual body).

30

The Dr. Joshua David Stone Suggested Program for Dealing with Cancer

Do not give your personal power to any mass consciousness stigma about Cancer for this is illusion. Do not give your personal power to your physical body, for you are not your physical body. You are God living in your physical body. Do not forget this!!!

First, I want you to get a session with my wife Wistancia (818-706-8533) to clear all negative implants and elementals. Secondly, I want you to focus your reading now on my books *Soul Psychology* and *How to Clear the Negative Ego*. Also read a book by Carl Simonton on cancer. I forget the title, but if you go to a metaphysical bookstore, they will be able to find it for you. Also get my book *Integrated Ascension* and read the chapter called "Dr. Lorphan's Healing Academy on Sirius." This will give you a great many tools to call on the Masters and Angels for help. We are putting you now on our Interdimensional Prayer Altar, which will allow the Masters to work on you immediately. I want you to say this affirmation 30 times a day: "I am in perfect radiant health!" Say it 10 times in the morning, 10 times in the afternoon, and 10 times in the evening, religiously, every day until the cancer is gone. Get my book *Beyond Ascension* and read the chapter on "How to do Huna Prayers" and create one for your health and say it twice a day; once in the morning and once before bed. There are lots of examples in my book. Next, get one of my Audio Ascension Activation Meditation Tapes called "The 18 Point Cosmic Cleansing Meditation." Listen to it once a day, every day for two straight months.

Until you create your Huna prayer I want you to Pray out loud every morning and every night to GOD, Christ, the Holy Spirit, Mother Mary, Quan Yin, Djwhal Khul, Sananda, the Lord of Arcturus, the Arcturians, your Healing Angels, and the Galactic Healers, to completely heal your physical body, tumor and all cancer! They will do it!

Next, make an appointment with Eileen Poole in Los Angeles, California. Her phone number is 310-440-9976. If you fly in for a day to do this it is worth it. She is a world famous Psychic Nutritionist and she will psychically tune into your body and tell you exactly what you should be eating. Follow her program exactly. Doing this one thing would probably heal you, let alone this comprehensive program. This way we are attacking the lesson on all fronts Spiritually, Psychologically and Physically.

Find a really good naturopathic doctor and homeopathic doctor and begin a program of Cleansing with Homeopathics and Herbs. Work with your traditional doctor as well.

Coming to Wesak will be an enormous cleansing and healing on all levels. You will be so infused with GOD and Cosmic Energies nothing will be able to live in that vibration but perfect Radiant Health. Remain happy and joyous.

I repeat again, do not give your power to your physical body. This is just a lesson and nothing more. Follow my guidance exactly as I have given it and you will be healed!

Also, whenever you start to worry, doubt, fall into fear, or if you start getting depressed, push those thoughts and feelings our of your mind and do your affirmation ten times and then pray to GOD, Christ and the Holy Spirit to undo the cause of your cancer. As Edgar Cayce said, "Why worry when you can pray!"

Also, once a day for while relaxing, maybe watching television or listening to music, call to the Lord of Arcturus and the Arcturians and ask to be taken to their Healing Chamber on their Starship and ask them to remove all cancer from you body! This is a Spiritual Test and nothing more. It is a means to accelerate your Spiritual Growth. This lesson will be a catalyst to accelerate your Spiritual Growth a thousand-fold! It has already begun. I think you can feel it. Cancer is totally curable.

Also, call a woman by the name of Sara. She is a friend of mine, a very good psychic. Tell her I recommended that you contact her. Tell her what the problem is and have a session with her in about eight weeks after following this Program. I will give you her number at that time.

Also, I would recommend getting the "Water of Life" as advertised in my information packet and on my Website. Just trust me, get it!

In about two months get all 11 of my Audio Ascension Activation Meditation Tapes and work with one tape every other day, and on the seventh day rest! This will Spiritually totally electrify your 12-Body system, fill you full of Spiritual Current, and totally raise your overall vibration and frequency.

If you do all these things you will be so clean and so pure nothing but GOD will be able to live within you and this whole lesson will be a blessing in disguise to accelerate your Spiritual Growth. Have Faith, Trust, and Patience.

Trust in GOD, the Masters, your own Personal Power, and your own ability to heal yourself. Trust as well in my guidance; you have just been put on the most profound Healing Program on planet Earth!

31

The Spiritual/Christ/Buddha Ideal and An Integrated and Balanced Approach to Physical Health, Prosperity and Life!

One of the basic core teachings of all religions and all Spiritual Paths is that our true identity is as Sons and Daughters of GOD! Said another way, each are the Christ, the Buddha, the Eternal Self, The Atma and/or God beings! This is why the Bible states, "Ye are God's and know it not"! The illusionary thought system of the negative ego really began when we as God or Spirit beings came into matter and began to think we were physical bodies instead of God beings living in Physical bodies! This, in truth, was the story in the Bible of the Tree of Good and Evil and the eating of the forbidden fruit! It was out of this faulty identification that the entire negative ego thought system began! So our true identity is the Christ, the Buddha or God! So, in truth, we all are perfect, for we have been created in the "image of GOD!" GOD cannot create anything but the likeness of GOD's Self! GOD is perfection and we are perfection! So, in truth, we already are God and we have always been and will be God! We have always been one with GOD, are right now, and always will be! The negative ego/fear-based/separative thought system tells us we are not Gods, but bodies! The negative ego/fear-based/separative thought system tells us we were not one with GOD in the past, are not one with

GOD in this moment, and will not be one with GOD in the future! This is of course, what is called illusion or faulty thinking! In truth, there is not any place to go on the Spiritual path but to own what you are already and to see this reality in your Brothers and Sisters as well! For to have it in your self you must all see it in your Brothers and Sisters! This has been called the Holy Encounter, in the sense that every encounter with a Brother or Sister is God meeting God, or Christ meeting Christ, or Buddha meeting Buddha. What religion or Spiritual Path you have been on, are on now, or will be on in the future does not matter; for we all are just Gods, which transcends all religions and all forms of Spiritual paths!

So the key question now is how does this apply to physical health? It applies in a very important way since our thoughts create our reality! One of the lessons of *A Course in Miracles,* which was written by the Master Jesus, states, "Sickness is a defense against the truth!" The teaching here is that if we each, in truth, are God or the Christ, then how can sickness be real? GOD did not create sickness. If GOD did not create sickness then where did it come from? It came from people who ate of the fruit of the Tree of Good and Evil! Said another way; sickness came from the misuse of free choice to think with our negative ego/fear-based/separative mind instead of thinking only with our God/Spiritual/Christ/Buddha mind! That first choice to think with the negative, ego/fear-based/separative mind caused a negative thought to enter the persons consciousness, which caused a negative feeling to grow, which caused negative energy to be created, which eventually manifested in the physical body as sickness!

This is the Hermetic Law: As within, so without! As above, so below! That state of consciousness we hold in our consciousness will be reflected in our physical body and outer world!

So the statement "Sickness is a defense against the truth" is teaching us that the true nature of GOD is perfection and this is our true nature! GOD can't be sick and we can't be sick in "truth" or in what I am calling here the "Spiritual Ideal!" If we each are the Christ, how can we be physically sick? The Christ or the Buddha is "perfection"! This is why Paramahansa Yogananda taught that you should be affirming that you are in perfect radiant health, even when you are 99 years old and on your death bed! You are affirming the "Truth of your Spiritual nature which is perfection and perfect radiant health! GOD is in perfect radiant health within His physical body, and we are in truth or in the "Spiritual Ideal," perfect within ours, for we are made in "His image and likeness!"

For those of you who have studied Science of Mind or the teachings of Christian Science, this is the basis of the treatments they do for themselves and others. All that is seen is the "Spiritual Ideal of Perfection" and everything that is thought and every treatment they do for themselves or others is based on seeing and affirming only this!

This is a very valid practice, for the two greatest things that affect your health more than anything else are the thoughts you think and the food you eat! It is your mental diet, which causes your emotional diet, which causes your energy diet, which causes your physical diet! In truth, it is even your thoughts that cause which foods you choose to put in your physical body!

Now I do want to say here that I do not agree with Christian Science in the sense that one should only stick to mental healing as the only form one should use. If one every does get sick they should work with all levels of GOD not just one. They should use prayer, positive mental attitude, affirmation, visualization, treatments, positive suggestions, diet, homeopathy, herbs, traditional doctors, holistic doctors, and all earthly help! As the saying goes, "whatever works!" However, I bring this up for most physical/earthly doctors and practitioners do not understand the incredible power of the mind! People use affirmations sometimes for health, which is good, however, it must be understood that every thought you think every moment of your life even when you sleep is an affirmation as well! This is why it has been said that 75% of the Spiritual Path is self-inquiry! Self-inquiry is the constant monitoring of your thoughts, feelings and energy, and keeping them in self-mastery and unconditional love every moment of your life! Part of this process is also keeping your thoughts in perfection! This means seeing yourself as God and seeing your Brothers and Sisters as incarnations of GOD as well! Given that we each are God/Christ/and the Buddha, then we cannot get sick! This is what we must affirm to ourselves for it is the truth of our being! GOD is perfect and has perfect radiant health and we are God, and are perfect and have perfect radiant health! All else is an illusion of the negative ego mind! Holding and maintaining this state of consciousness is one of the strongest ways to maintain perfect radiant health. This does not mean, however, that one should never go to the doctor and have a check-up. One must be balanced and integrated not a fanatic! Therefore, it is fine to go to the doctor for a yearly check up; however, when you go and while you're driving there, continue to affirm and visualize only perfect health and perfection. Even if the doctor says there is a slight imbalance in the blood! Take your medicine, change your diet, or do whatever you have to do, but affirm and see only perfect radiant health and perfection. If they diagnose you with some disease, take your medication, homeopathics, herbs, change your diet, pray, and work on all levels and accept only perfect radiant health and the perfection of GOD in your mind and image of self, for that is all that is real!

If a person is diagnosed with cancer, do whatever treatment is necessary on all levels, but think, affirm and visualize only perfect radiant health and perfection!

The truth is this philosophy should be applied to every aspect of life! For example, in regard to your finances! If your don't have any money in the bank don't believe it! GOD is rich so your are rich! Think, affirm, and visualize only abundance! Act as if you are a millionaire and see only this! This does not mean being irresponsible or spending more money then you have or getting into credit card debt. It just means maintaining "prosperity consciousness" even if you don't have any money! Don't let your outer circumstances determine what you are. Let your consciousness, which is attuned to GOD and your true identity as a Son or Daughter of GOD, determine who and what you are. That which you hold in consciousness will eventually manifest in your outer reality!

The same applies to success! GOD is 100% successful in everything GOD does! You are God so you have to be successful in everything you do! How can GOD, which is everything, not be successful? So hold this Spiritual Ideal of Perfection and know that you will be successful in everything you do and it is impossible for anything but this to happen! Yet be balanced and integrated in the process of how you do this! Work on all levels of GOD to achieve this as I have already talked about in this chapter and in this book! Yet hold this perfected ideal! What the outer physical body is saying, or the bank account is saying, or your outer life experience is saying in terms of success does is meaningless! It is impossible for GOD and God not to be in perfect radiant health, total wealth and money, and successful in every aspect of life!

This is what I call living as an "Integrated yet Christed or Ascended Master" in the way you should approach your health, prosperity and life! There are some that hold the ideal of perfection, but are not integrated and get all fouled up! Others strive for integration and balance, yet do not always hold the Christed or Perfected ideal! Hold the Perfected Ideal, but also have common sense and practicality while doing it!

In this book the Masters and I have approached integration and being the Christ/Buddha from all angles! We have spoken of Integrated Meditation, Integrated Prayer, Integrated Manifestion, to name just a few, and here in this chapter we speak of an Integrated Ascended Master and Christed approach to Health, Prosperity and Life itself! It is a common sense approach that approaches and honors the Spiritual Ideal of who and what we really are, but also honors the need to be integrated and balanced in everything we do, and recognizes the need to utilize all levels of GOD to truly be successful and not just get stuck on one! This chapter has been written to show how the Spiritual Ideal and Path of Integration and Balance can be reconciled, integrated and balanced in terms of how you live your daily life! This way you have the best of both worlds and do not become fanatical on any level, but instead live life like an "integrated and balanced God being"!

32

The Importance of Removing the "Earth Crystals" From Your Subtle Bodies

Another extremely important esoteric secret of GOD's infinite universe that very few lightworkers are aware of, is the understanding of the fact that when all souls incarnate onto this planet, there are certain Earth Crystals that are placed within the etheric body for the purpose of helping incarnated souls adjust to the physical incarnation process. These "Earth Crystals" are placed there by the inner plane Ascended Masters and the Angelic Hierarchy.

It must be understood that these Earth Crystals serve a positive purpose in the beginning and help to physically ground the individual in a mystical way that can not be described here. We must all realize that we are visiting the Earth and it is not our true home. Our true home is in heaven and/or Celestial Realms. To take a physical body and come under the limitations of third dimensional reality takes some adjusting for the incarnating soul. These Earth Crystals that are placed in the etheric body serve to help in this adjustment process to functioning effectively on Earth.

Those persons who are most etherically ungrounded, heavenly and sometimes Angelic in nature, tend to have more of these Earth Crystals. No matter how much Angelic clearing work you have done on yourself, these Earth Crystals will not basically be removed.

The problem is that once you move into adulthood and have embraced your spiritual path and initiation and ascension process, you do not need these Earth Crystals anymore. What was once a positive thing, now has become a "limitation" and a slight block in the full understanding and realization of becoming an "Integrated Christ"!

By the grace of GOD and the inner plane Ascended Masters and Archangels, I have received permission to share this information with you my beloved readers, and have secondly to share the good news that the Cosmic and Planetary Ascended Masters and Archangels will help you remove them!

Now I must say here that occasionally some of these Earth Crystals are very stuck or lodged in your four-body system and in some cases it may be necessary to get help from a trained initiate to remove them. The first step, however, is to ask the Masters and Angels to help remove them. If you still feel that there are some left, then give me a call and I will put you in touch with a trained member of the Academy who can remove them. I consider the removal of these Earth Crystals not as important as removing your negative implants and elementals, however, they would be second in the line to be removed!

Since I brought up the subject of negative implants and elementals, I would recommend all lightworkers to give me a call and set up a channeled phone session with the inner plane Ascended Masters for an "Ascension Clearing" and negative implant and elemental removal session. The meditation in this book called "The Mount Shasta 50 Point Cosmic Clearing Meditation," will clear an enormous amount of psychic debris and will probably clear a great deal of your negative implant and elementals. As was the case, however, with the Earth Crystals, there are certain negative implants in your subtle bodies that remain stuck and it really takes one channeled session with a trained initiate to remove them all for 100% sure. During this session you can also request that all your Earth Crystals be removed as well. This session will 100% for sure clean all your negative implants and elementals, however, in some cases the

Earth Crystals must be removed by a trained initiate healer in person. There are people I can recommend who will travel to your area to do this service for yourself and your friends. We'll be honest with you here, that most of my Earth Crystals that I came in with were removed by the Cosmic and Planetary Ascended Masters. The Masters have told me, however, that there are cases where a trained initiate may be needed to help remove some of them.

So, the process goes like this. First off, do the Mount Shasta 50 point Cleansing Meditation I have given you in this book. This will remove an astronomical amount of psychic debris from your auric field of an extreme subtle nature. We are polishing your diamond so to speak.

The second step is to ask in meditation, ideally right before bed, for the Ascended Masters and Archangels of your choice to remove your Earth Crystals. I would encourage you to include Melchizedek, The Mahatma and Archangel Metatron in this prayer invocation! Also call in the Ascended Master Djwhal Khul!

The third step is to set up an appointment with a trained initiate from the Melchizedek Synthesis Light Academy for an ascension clearing and negative implant and elemental removal, if you feel the need. I would highly recommend it; however, some of you may be able to do a complete clearing just using the first meditation.

The fourth step is, in this channeled session with the Ascended Masters, if you feel that some Earth Crystals still remain, ask the Masters to remove them in this channeled session if they can. You may not need this because the Masters may be able to remove them completely upon your own prayer request. This is a preventive measure to make 100% sure they were all cleared. Occasionally some are very stuck.

The fifth step is, if there are some Earth Crystals that are having a hard time coming out, it might be worth your while to set-up a session with a trained initiate healer who can remove them in person. The good news is that most of your Earth Crystals and all of your negative implants and elementals will be removed if you follow the aforementioned steps.

For those who have a few stuck ones you might want to consider this final step, however, it is not essential for the majority of them would have been removed. If you want this however, this service is available from the Melchizedek Synthesis Light Academy.

Be not concerned about having negative implants and elementals, for they are not something to be fearful about. They are not debilitating in any way. Everyone on Earth has them, and they are very subtle in nature. You could go through your whole life and not have them removed and function quite effectively. I only bring up this information for those who really want to advance on their spiritual path in a very quick and decisive manner. If you are very dedicated to the spiritual path and want to become a fully Integrated Christ at your highest potential, it is a good idea to have both of these aspects removed. On a subtle level, they do create energy blocks and some limitations in your spiritual energy field. These blocks and limitations are of a subtle nature, however, the entire spiritual path is one really dealing with subtle energies, and working with the information and tools in this book will basically allow you to do this on your own. If there are a few stuck ones left after following the guidance given here then I offer you these other services, as a service and courtesy to you, my beloved readers. However, they are not necessary or required and the majority of the clearing will take place from just reading this book and applying the instructions and tools given forth there within.

My beloved readers, I am happy to share this information and material with you for the purpose of accelerating your ascension and initiation process and helping you to become a fully Integrated Christ!

33

Learning to Co-Create with Nature

Another aspect of integrating the Goddess energies has to do with the whole understanding of Spiritual gardening rather than, what I call, materialistic gardening. Materialistic gardening approaches gardening only from the intellect and science and completely neglects the spiritual and Goddess aspects. Spiritual gardening on the other hand fully honors and recognizes the spiritual essence and life in all aspects of gardening and honors and sanctifies the Goddess in the process.

The first principle of Spiritual Gardening is "Love." Your plants and flowers as you know are incarnations of GOD and living beings. They have consciousness and feelings. Many gardeners and/or people have gardening knowledge, but no love and no understanding of the inherent nature of this kingdom. So, the first principle of spiritual gardening, whether indoor or outdoor, is "Love!" This can be done in just feeling or it can be done through talking to them and in your demonstration of care for them.

Principle number two is that our plants are like younger brothers and sisters and, hence, we have a responsibility to take care of them. This means providing them with water, proper fertilizer, plant food if necessary, and care on all levels.

Principle number three is don't try to garden only by science. When I say garden I am also speaking of taking care of your indoor plants. I am not saying one should reject science or book knowledge or advice from nurseries on how to care for plants. This is very important information to utilize and is one's spiritual responsibility to obtain, to properly care for trees, plants and flowers that surround you home or reside in you home. It is also our spiritual responsibility to intuitively tune into the heart of our younger brothers and sisters and to ask them what they want and need. To the surprise of many, they will talk back and answer your question. So, approach gardening in the larger sense of the term, from an intuitive and scientific point of view.

Principle number four: Each plant, flower or tree has different requirements just as people or animals do. It is important to tune into the heart of each specific tree, plant, flower, or vegetable to see what it wants and needs. One particular plant may need a lot of water and another very little. One plant may need to be planted in the ground and for another that may not be necessary. One plant may need extra plant food and for others that may not be necessary. Gather both scientific and intuitive knowledge about each plant, especially if they are not doing well.

Principle number five: Call on GOD, the Angels, the Ascended Masters, the Plant Devas, the Nature Spirits, Pan, the Elementals, the Earth Mother, Archangel Sandalphon, the Overlighting Deva of that type of part, and the Overlighting Deva of Your Property. Ask them all for help in taking care of your indoor and outdoor plants, trees, flowers, and shrubs. It must be fully understood that these beings will help your garden take care of, and nurture the plants. They can send light and love to your garden and do healing on them just as they do with people or animals. I recently asked these beings to connect the entire garden to a process of partially living on light. If people can partially do it, why shouldn't plants be able to do it as well. The Masters told me that this was a wonderful idea.

Principle number six is that it must be understood that every plant, vegetable, tree or shrub has a living spiritual being in it. Just as we are living in our physical bodies, they are incarnated in their physical bodies as well. Throughout Earth's history, this has been completely not understood and people have treated the nature kingdom like a machine rather than as the living spiritual/Earthly beings that they are. If you speak to them and treat them as the living beings they are, they will co-create with you and help your garden to flourish in a most profound and accelerated manner.

Principal number seven is that when trimming plants, speak to them and talk to them and tell them what you are about to do and why. Try to trim only what is absolutely necessary. The Plants are living beings and they do not like to be chopped up unless it is absolutely necessary. The main thing is to work with them, co-create your garden with them, and not do anything drastic without communing with them first.

Principle number eight is to try and maintain a harmonious ecological balance with all the living life in your garden. Do not kill insects for example, unless they are really hurting your garden. For example, in our garden there is an underground beehive next to our vegetable garden. Our back lawn is also filled with bees that are doing their thing, gathering nectar from the lawn. When we first moved in I was a little disconcerted by the number of bees. Now, however, we have an agreement, I don't bother them and they don't bother me and we have a great friendship and all is in harmony.

Principle number nine is that before you take any drastic action of killing insects or animals that might be attacking or disrupting your garden, speak to them on the spiritual plane first. I have a very excellent example and story to share with you on this. When we moved into our home and planted our vegetable garden the previous owner came by and told me that the vegetable garden would never last because the gofers that live in the field behind the garden would destroy it. He told me he planted one, the gofers would dig underground and would not only eat the vegetables and plants, but they would pull them right into the earth from underground. He lived here for over two years and was never able to have a vegetable garden. Upon hearing this I immediately consulted the Masters, Angels, Devas, Plant Spirits and the King of the

Gofers, and we had a big meeting. I asked for a Divine Dispensation of Protection for our vegetable garden and requested a deal be worked out where they could have the field behind our garden, which I like to call our UFO landing field, if they would respect the spiritual and physical sanctity of our vegetable garden. This seemed to be an agreeable situation to all concerned, and by the grace of GOD, the Masters, Archangels Michael and Faith, the 3 Ms, the Core Group, the Earth Mother, Pan, the plant spirits and nature spirits, our garden has not been touched and has been growing like crazy.

Principle ten is to try, if possible, not to use pesticides. Try to use all natural and spiritual means first. The plant and nature spirits do not like pesticides and neither do our physical bodies. As a last resort in an emergency a little can be used, however, avoid it if possible.

I don't claim to be all knowledgeable about gardening, however, the Masters have taught me that the above mentioned spiritual gardening principles will not only help your garden inside and out to flourish, but it will also greatly enhance your enjoyment and physical and spiritual experience of gardening. It will also bring you an attunement to the Earth Mother, nature and plant spirits, as well as the seasons of nature and to nature itself, which will greatly enhance your life. If you learn to listen to the still, small voice of plants, flowers, trees, shrubs and vegetables, you will be amazed at the knowledge and wisdom that can and will flow from them. I have actually received many great ideas for chapters in my books from being open to information and dialogue with these most beautiful and exquisite beings that embody all of nature. These beings are extremely loving and totally open to entering your garden and helping it to grow and flourish and creating a partnership with you of co-creation. There are a great many farms and gardens on Earth which these beings have left because of the mistreatment, pesticides, and lack of attunement to them. A big part of the reintegration of the Goddess into our world is the welcoming and sanctifying of their Beloved Beings in a process of full cooperation and co-creation.

Following these simple principles will not only help them, but will help yourself by helping you to fully master and integrate the Material Earthly Plane of GOD into your being. For as you all know, to become a fully integrated and full-fledged Ascended Master, one must master and integrate fully the Spiritual, Psychological and Earthly aspects of GOD. A great many souls on this planet are developed on one of these three levels and sometimes two. Very few souls have fully mastered and integrated all three levels. To fully become an integrated Goddess on Earth it is essential to fully master and integrate all three!

34

The Soul's Perspective on Transition, Death, Separation and Grief

My beloved readers, what I am about to share with you is a revolutionary new understanding of transition, death, separation and grief. It must be understood that there are two ways of looking at life and only two. You can see life from the perspective of the personality, or you can see life from the perspective of the Soul or Spirit. Said another way, you can see life through your lower-self or higher-self. You can see life from the negative ego's perspective, or you can see life from the Christ Consciousness or Buddha Consciousness perspective.

There are three levels of self-actualization. The first is personality self-actualization. The second is soul level self-actualization. The third is Spiritual level self-actualization or Ascended Master level Self-Actualization.

When this understanding is applied to transition, death, separation, and grief, what we find is quite interesting. Elizabeth Kubler Ross spoke of the four stages of dealing with death. These were denial, anger, depression, and acceptance. Everyone accepted this, and one could say from a personality level perspective, this is brilliant! It is not however, from the perspective of the soul. I do not say this as any criticism, but just as an insight into a revolutionary new way of seeing this process.

From the perspective of the Soul or Spirit, you do not have to go through these stages. These are all "negative ego" ways of interpreting reality. Traditional psychologists will tell you there is something wrong with you if you don't respond with anger, depression, or grief. This is illusion from the perspective of the Soul and Monad. There is no judgement if people respond this way, from the Soul or Spirit, however, they understand that it is your thoughts that create your reality and your perspective, not the outside situation.

As Lord Buddha so eloquently stated in his Four Noble Truths, "All suffering comes from attachment. All suffering comes from wrong points of view."

For example, in India when people die they "celebrate." They look at it as a positive thing, for the soul has been released from the confines of the physical vehicle. Everyone in India believes in reincarnation, hence, there is no such thing as death. There is only death of the physical body, but not of the person inhabiting it. In Western civilization, people tend to be more materialistic; hence, they interpret reality from their personality and negative ego rather than from the Soul and Christ/Buddha Mind. Death in and of itself is neutral. It is the mind or interpretation of death that causes it to bring grief or happiness. It is time for the western world to stop having funerals and start having celebrations of their loved ones lives. The more attached one is, the more suffering one will experience at the death of a loved one. The less spiritual one is in one's perspective, the more suffering they will experience. To love another is a beautiful thing! This must be done from having a right relationship to self and a right relationship to GOD first. This must be done with your loved ones being a super strong preference but not an addiction!

This understanding not only applies to the death of a person, but the death of a job, relationship, phase of your life, and material possession! As his Holiness the Lord Sai Baba said, "It is your mind that creates bondage and it is your mind that creates liberation." Your feelings about everything come from how you think! The world is nothing more than a projection screen of your own thinking! As the Bible says, "Let this mind be in you that was in Christ Jesus"! When you learn to interpret life from your Christ/Buddha mind, you will have only Christ/Buddha feelings and emotions. When transition, death, physical separation occur, it is your mind that will determine what you'll experience not the situation. I want to emphasize here very strongly that there is no judgement from the Soul, Spirit, or the Ascended Masters if you experience negative emotions, sadness, grief, or anything else. All that is being stated here is the importance of understanding that it is your thoughts that create your reality, and that the degree to which you are attached and the level of your Spiritual understanding and awareness, will greatly affect the kinds of feelings you will have during transitions, death and separation. To always know that you are causing your emotional reality by how you think, is a very comforting thought and understanding, for it places responsibility within you, instead of outside you.

Everything that happens in life is a Spiritual test to see if you can respond from your Godself rather than your personality and negative ego. As Lord Krishna in the Bhagavad-Gita said to Arjuna, "Whether you have profit or loss, pleasure or pain, sickness or health, whether people praise you or vilify you, remain the same." The GOD ideal is to remain in unconditional love, even-mindedness, joy, happiness, inner peace and equanimity at all times. Outer events do not control how you feel! It is your perspective on outer events. The world does not need an axis shift, pole shift, or Y2K problem to wake up. What the people of the world need is an axis shift from negative ego thinking to Christ/Buddha thinking. This, my beloved readers, is the Revelation for the Next Millennium!

35

Crosses to Bear

It is very important to understand that planet Earth is a school and a very tough school. As a matter of fact this is a tough universe. As you know there are infinite numbers of universes. The theme for our universe is "Courage." It is also a very important theme for living on this planet.

Every person who incarnates onto this planet and into this world has "Crosses to Bear"! Each person's cross, however, is different. Some people have weaknesses in certain bodies, which creates a type of cross to bear until that aspect is strengthened and developed. Some people's cross comes from a Spiritual weakness, some from a mental weakness, some from an emotional weakness, some from an etheric weakness, some from a physical body weak-ness.

There are a million and one things that can go wrong with the physical body over a life span that can be a type of cross to bear. Emotional weakness and lack of proper psychological training in life can be an enormous cross to bear. Mental weakness can also be an enormous cross to bear since it is our thoughts that create our reality. An etheric weakness often comes from early childhood trauma or past lives and can be a very difficult cross to bear because the etheric body is the energetic blueprint. If that is damaged and you do not know how to repair it, this can create a prolonged cross to bear. Then there is Spiritual weakness and lack of proper training, which can be one of the most difficult lessons of all. This is true because the Spiritual aspect effects all the other bodies.

Other people have other types of crosses to bear because in this world no one is spared. This is just the nature of living in this world. Some people have financial crosses to bear. Other people may have the cross to bear of losing a loved one. There are natural disasters such as earthquakes, fires, tornadoes, hurricanes, mud slides, floods, to name a few.

Some of the crosses we bear are not necessarily personal karma, as they are collective karma or planetary karma. The example of planetary disasters is a good example of this. Other examples might be World War I, or World War II. Look at how these wars affected people's lives. Look at how economic down turns can affect people's lives.

If there is one thing we can all be sure of, that is life does not always go according to our preferences. The key to proper living, as Lord Buddha said in His Four Noble Truths, is not to have attachments. It is very important to have super strong preferences, and to try to manifest your preferences with all your heart and soul and mind and might, but not be attached. If you do this, then you can be happy regardless of what cross it is you have to bear.

The other key to dealing with crosses to bear properly is to "Transcend duality." By this I mean learning to remain evenminded whether you have profit or lost, pleasure or pain, sickness or health, victory or defeat, whether people praise you or vilify you, remain the same! Happiness is a state of mind, an attitude and perspective, not anything outside of self.

One of the keys to successful living is to understand that everyone has crosses to bear. This does not mean we are victims. We are only victims if we let outside things and/or crosses take away our happiness and inner peace. I bring up this subject because many people have a very naive understanding about life. They float around in life living too much in their emotional body, and they end up getting beaten down by life. As Paramahansa Yogananda said, "Life is often a battlefield." In this world and Planetary Mystery School one must develop the attitude of being a Spiritual Warrior to be successful. This is especially true if you plan on moving into any type of Spiritual Leadership. It is also true, however, of life in general. It is true of living anywhere in this universe. To master the lessons of this universe one must have enormous courage.

There are an enormous number of obstacles and pitfalls of the Spiritual Path that each Disciple and Initiate must overcome and watch out for. One must also have enormous Spiritual vigilance to not allow the negative ego to contaminate one's consciousness. There is also an enormous amount of temptation in this world as well as glamour and mass consciousness that is easy to fall into. There is also an enormous amount of false prophets, false teachings, and fragmented disintegrated teachings. To become a Master in this world one must have enormous Spiritual Discernment and this quality is severely lacking in the New Age Movement. This is not a judgment, just a Spiritual observation.

The Masters have guided me to write this chapter to put incarnating into this Earthly world into the proper perspective. Lightworkers as a whole need to be a little tougher and a little more street smart as to the nature of this Planetary Mystery School.

Lightworkers also need to know that everyone has crosses to bear. There is not a single being on the Earth, and that includes Sai Baba, who does not have crosses to bear. Sai Baba being an Avatar and Universal Level Master even has crosses. His are a little different however. He does not have any personal karma, but His crosses come from taking on the personal karma from others. He has had in his physical body hundreds of heart attacks, strokes and all kinds of physical abnormalities, which he has taken on, over days or weeks, and which he transmuted to save his devotees from suffering and even dying. Still, he had to physically bear a cross of these illnesses through his physical vehicle.

One interesting cross that is very prevalent at this time in Earth's history is the process of Spiritual mutation lightworkers are going through. Those lightworkers who are physically suffering the most are the ones who are most often accelerating the fastest Spiritually. The enormous Spiritual acceleration of this Planet and the enormous amount of Light coming into the planet are causing enormous amounts of physical health lessons in lightworkers' physical bodies. A person of the Third Dimension might say, "This person is sick." The truth is just the opposite. Because this person is Spiritually advancing so quickly in their ascension process this is an unavoidable part of the process. The Masters want me to tell all of you, my Beloved Readers, that everyone on Planet Earth who is advancing Spiritually is going through this. This Spiritual acceleration on a personal and collective level is not only creating enormous numbers of physical health lessons; it is also bringing up tons of stuff for people emotionally, mentally, and Spiritually.

The Masters have guided me to bring up this issue, as well as this entire issue of how everyone has crosses to bear on multifaceted levels so that people have a more realistic attitude and perspective about the nature of Earth life. Some people have this Pollyanna attitude and perspective that life is a bowl of cherries and they can float around not owning their power, not having protection, not being vigilant, not being Spiritually discerning, and not having a fighting spirit and expecting life to go well.

Other people have the attitude and perspective that they are the only ones who have crosses to bear and the only ones going through massive Christ/Buddha mutations in their vehicles which is often uncomfortable. The Masters have guided me to write this chapter to let lightworkers know that both of these are not true.

Mother Teresa had severe heart problems in her adult life. Saint Francis had severe health problems. The Dalai Lama had a severe case of Hepatitis. There is not a single Spiritual Teacher or Leader on Earth who has not and will not continue to be tested. This, my beloved readers, is the nature of Earth life and the nature of living in this most accelerated time in Earth's history.

The purpose for writing this chapter is for you, my beloved readers, to know these things, and to have these things in the proper perspective, so you are more prepared to deal with the lessons and Spiritual testing of life and so you know that you are not alone and that all your Brothers and Sisters are sharing these same lessons with you. They may not share them in the exact same form or specific lesson, but they are sharing it.

Each person receives the tests and lessons that are perfect for them and there are no accidents or coincidences. Everything we receive is perfect for our soul growth and ideally should be welcomed as such. Everything that happens to us is a Spiritual lesson and a Spiritual test to see if we can maintain our mastery, centeredness, Christ/Buddha Consciousness and unconditional love.

Each person goes through their own Job Initiation at one time or another in life. This is true because everyone has to let go of all attachments to truly become a Spiritual Master. Knowing these things, have compassion for yourself and compassion for your Brothers and Sisters. For I say again, this is a tough school and things are moving very fast on all levels. Understanding these things and having them in proper perspective can make life a lot easier and more joyous knowing we are all in GOD's

36

A Battleplan as to How to Deal with Chronic Health Problems

This particular chapter is an extremely important chapter in this book. I would venture to guess that 50% of all lightworkers suffer from some kind of chronic health lesson. In a person's entire lifetime on Earth, probably 99% of all people will have chronic health lessons at some point. Every person on planet Earth, except maybe the descent of an Avatar such as Sai Baba and Lord Maitreya, has some weakness in the four-body system. I have never met a single person in my entire life that hasn't, including myself.

Some people have a weakness in their physical vehicle in some area. Others have a weakness in their emotional vehicle. Others in the mental vehicle and others in their spiritual vehicle. Others have a weakness in their bank account. If this weren't the case, you probably would not be incarnated on this planet.

Part of the reason for the physical health problems is also a spiritual one. Spiritual evolution is moving so quickly that certain health problems are unavoidable and are just a byproduct of growing spiritually so, in truth, maybe consider it a good sign. Other reasons for health problems are all the environmental pollution, pesticides, water pollution, metals poisoning, and the like. Another reason is that this is a very tough school and keeping the mental body, emotional body, physical body, and spiritual body all balanced all the time is no easy task.

Add to that the enormous amount of psychic negativity we all have to deal with living on this planet and which we see on television and the mass media. Then add to this all the past life karma that we are processing that can debilitate the body when wanting to move fast on the spiritual path. Add to this the genetic weaknesses we come in with from past lives and our genetic heritage. Add to this still the fact that we must process the karma from our twelve soul extensions from our oversoul and then must process the 144 soul extensions from our monad in terms of integrating and cleansing their karma. Then we have to deal with the collective consciousness karma.

We all live in a gray cloud of astral debris that surrounds this planet. The same is true of the etheric body, mental body and physical body of this planet. On the physical level this is called smog, pollution, gigantic holes in the ozone layer, and depletion of rain forests. The food we buy from the markets is dead and processed. The meat is filled with chemicals. The chickens have cancer and salmonella bacteria. Our food is being nuked by radiation and the FDA has approved this. There is a fast food restaurant on every corner. People eat way too much sugar. The produce is not energized because the nature spirits do not inhabit the farms because of the use of pesticides and man's inability to work with nature. Even the produce contains only 10% of the energy it should.

People then don't clear, pray and energize their food before they eat it with some kind of soma board, energy plate or formal prayer procedure. Even though it may look healthy, 90% of the time it will have a negative spin on it if you tested it with a pendulum. That is because of pesticides, the people who have touched it in the market or because of the red radar that is pumped through it at the grocery counter. Added to this is the fact that most people don't have good habits of food combining, or they overeat, or they're just lazy in regard to diet. In addition is the enormous amount of stress we are all under in our modern day society with workaholic tendencies. At times we also have to deal with alien implants and dark force attack.

The effects of occasional negative thinking, worrying, family responsibilities, money pressures, negative imprints, lack of self-love and relationship problems are more factors. All these things cause a weakening of the immune system over time. Then we have accidents of innumerable kinds that take a toll on the body, and other traumas such as divorces, deaths in the family and lost jobs. We have damage to the etheric body from past lives that has not been repaired which causes people to be working off an imperfect blueprint. Imbalanced psychoepistemologies, which are pretty much universal with everybody, also take a toll on the physical body.

We also have to fight off all the negative suggestions that get into the subconscious mind, such as in winter time the television ads that say flu season is here. One has to remain constantly vigilant to not let the subconscious mind be programmed by all these negative suggestions of people, friends, co-workers, family members and mass media. People are getting sick all the time around us with colds, flu, bacteria infections and viruses.

It is true that there is no such thing as a contagious disease only low resistance, however the problem is most people have a lowered immune system from all the above mentioned factors. If you live in a big city you can add the sound pollution which takes a toll much more then you realize. Take for example car alarms. If sound can heal, what does a car alarm do? Most spiritual people are very sensitive, much more than the average person, and it can be very difficult living in a world such as this. A lot of lightworkers are not used to doing such things as having to make money and being the Spiritual warrior they have to be to just make it.

People with kids have an even greater burden. Then we have modern day plagues such as AIDS and Epstein Bar. The problem is our environment doesn't really support us because so much of it is based on third dimensional not fifth dimensional consciousness. Given all these factors it is amazing and miraculous that our physical bodies hold us up as well as they do.

Another thing to factor in here is the higher one evolves the quicker your karma returns and the more sensitive you become. Where as a child or adolescent you could eat a bag of cookies and ice cream and feel fine. Now one cookie may foul you up or make you not feel right. Also the older one gets the more careful one must be. In our busy society most people don't exercise enough, get enough sunshine and fresh air, and don't eat as well as they should. I could go on and on and on.

You should congratulate your physical body and body elemental for holding up as well as it has. God forbid you do get sick and you have to stay in a hospital. With all the terrible energy, terrible food, and narrow-minded physicians it is amazing people ever recover.

Another factor here is that the higher one evolves in the initiation process the more planetary karma they begin processing through their system. This is part of the responsibility of becoming an Ascended Master and cannot be completely avoided. People in the healing professions often take on the karma of their students and patients not only during sessions but often at night while they sleep. There is so much that goes on at night on the inner plane that people don't recognize.

The most important thing is to not look at disease or ill health as a bad thing, for it is not. It is just a teaching lesson, challenge, and opportunity to grow. Earlier in my life I almost died from a very serious case of hepatitis. In the long run as I look back I would never be in the place I am now if I hadn't gotten so ill. Illness teaches us obedience to God's Laws. This experience completely changed my life forever.

One of the most difficult lessons in this world is dealing with chronic health lessons. I personally have great compassion for people who deal with this for I have dealt with it myself. It is hard for people who have never dealt with chronic health lessons to understand. As I said earlier, their lessons may be on emotional, mental, spiritual or financial levels which can be as great a hardship and sometimes even worse.

Lesson 1

The first most important lesson is that health problems are not bad. They are good, for they are teaching you something you need to learn. Djwhal Khul says disease is a purification process. If looked at properly it will help you to become stronger. If looked at properly it will accelerate your spiritual growth.

Lesson 2

When dealing with chronic health problems first look at it as a blessing in disguise and a teacher, secondly and most importantly do not give your power to your physical body. This is the great error of faulty thinking most people make. They see their personal power as being connected to their physical vitality and wakefulness. When they get tired and run down they connect their personal power to this. A most important thing in life is to maintain your personal power at all times regardless of what your physical, astral, mental or spiritual bodies are doing. As the Bhagavad-Gita says, "Remain in evenmindedness whether you have profit or loss, victory or defeat, sickness or health."

God-consciousness remains the same regardless of the state of health or lack there of. I cannot emphasize the importance of this more. If you do not do this every time your body goes out, your emotional and mental bodies will take a dive bomb with it.

Lesson 3

Just because you don't have, perfect health doesn't mean you can't have a life. There are many people who have cancer and live very full and effective lives. Many people have arthritis or chronic pain and still live full and active lives. Don't be a perfectionist. If you wait to have perfect health to live, you just may never live. Mother Teresa has serious heart problems and look at all she does. I have had digestive sensitivity most of my adult life. I have not let it stop me. I call this the Saint Francis Initiation. Saint Francis (Kuthumi in a past life) had enormous health lessons yet continued to serve. This is a concept and understanding that has been very meaningful to me. I recognized through this that God was testing me. If you have health lessons, be like Saint Francis and proudly and with great dignity live your life.

I remember a story Yogananda told of his great disciple Sri Gyanaata who had 20 years of chronic health problems. When she finally died and he gave his eulogy for her, God spoke to Yogananda and told him He was especially proud of Sri Gyanaata for she served him for the last twenty years with poor health.

Lesson 4

The next lesson for those with chronic health lessons of some kind is the Job initiation. I think you all know the story of Job, how he was tested by God and the devil to test his righteousness in the Lord. The story of Job is the story of each person on this planet who has at some point had everything stripped away. There is not a soul in incarnation that in one of their lives, if not most of them, has not gone through this initiation. In fact, it is actually part of passing the fourth initiation, which is the renunciation initiation, and the lesson of letting go of attachments. When the Job initiation hits, everything is lost. Health goes, often the marriage goes, the job goes, inner peace goes, and so on down the line in any combination. This is a spiritual test.

Every person can serve God when things are going well. How many people keep the faith and righteousness in the Lord when everything goes wrong. This is the true test. Money, fame, fortune, relationship, health, and power are idol worshipping if put before God. After suffering greatly Job finally realized this and said, "Naked I come from my mother's womb, and naked shall I go, The Lord giveth and the Lord taketh away, blessed be the name of the Lord."

If your health, relationship, fame, money, job, even life were taken away, could you make this statement? See the things that happen in life, even chronic illness, as spiritual tests given to you by God to test your faith. This will advance you spiritually like no other spiritual practice you can practice. Remember, to achieve ascension you do not have to have perfect health. I myself have had very serious chronic health problems for over twelve years in regard to my liver and pancreas. Yet in this time I have been able to achieve and complete my ascension and have been given a major position in the spiritual government. Never in a trillion years would I have ever dreamed this would be offered to me. But I have used my health lessons to forge me like cosmic fire into developing super-human mental, emotional and spiritual abilities to compensate for the digestive weakness.

Lesson 5

Focus on what you can do instead of what you can't do. Using myself as an example again, when I got so sick from hepatitis there were a great many things for a very long time I was not able to do. Instead of feeling sorry for myself and being depressed about my loss, I tried to turn a lemon into lemonade. I gave up my spiritual counseling practice, took a sabbatical, and focused on my spiritual growth.

Enormous growth occurred during this period of spiritual study and meditation. My chronic health lessons, although improved, still existed so I decided to write instead of focusing so much on individual counseling. You are now looking at a man who has written thirty books and has become a world famous author. I never planned to write books, I did it because physically it was not good for me to have an individual counseling practice.

The other adjustment I made was to only work with larger groups to conserve my energy. My health lessons forced me to leave my individual counseling and instead do larger group work, which was a blessing in disguise. After a while this started taking a toll on me also, so now I do groups for 1000 people maybe twice a year. I would never have done this in a million years on my own. I can thank my health lessons for this.

My health lessons have taught me tremendous self-discipline and self-mastery for if I got off my diet I would have instant karma. The health lessons have taught me to have absolute steel-like strength and willpower on mental, emotional and spiritual levels. I had to learn this or I would have physically died. I have allowed my physical health lessons to teach me to become very strong mentally, emotionally and spiritually.

On an earthly level a third dimensional person might look at my process the last ten years and say I didn't do very well physically. From a spiritual perspective I was making quantum leaps, which the Masters ultimately noticed to the point of offering me the job to take over Djwhal Khul's ashram and become the high priest spokesperson for the planet's ascension movement, and world famous through my books and Wesak workshops.

I know for a fact that 99% of the world that went through what I went through physically would have been long dead or had a nervous breakdown. Because of the spiritual training that I had previous to this lesson, I was able over time to turn this into an asset rather than a deficit. My health is much better and stronger now that I have completed my ascension but there are certain weaknesses that remain. I have learned to make adjustments and not feel sorry for myself or judge this. This brings me to the next key lesson in dealing with chronic health lessons.

Lesson 6

The next lesson is a super key and one in which many fall by the wayside. With anything that happens in life, including health lessons, you can either be angry, depressed or move into acceptance. This is usually a process for most people and was for myself. Anger and depression do nothing ultimately and the sooner you can move to acceptance the better.

The crazy thing about my life is that I have moved literally about ten million times farther getting so ill physically than I would have if I had never gotten sick. I know this for an absolute fact.

This lesson is connected with what the Masters call the "blessing system". Whatever happens in life no matter how negative, bless it. The negative ego will tell you to curse it. The Holy Spirit will tell you to bless it and look at it as a stepping stone to soul growth. Sai Baba says that whatever happens in life the idea is to "welcome adversity." Paul Solomon said that whatever happens in life say, "Not my will but thine, thank you for the lesson." We each have our cross to bear. Mine has been a physical weakness in my digestive system, other people have a million and one other physical health lessons. Others still have their weak spot in the emotional or psychological body. Others are weakest in spiritual development. Ill health does not cause depression or anger, it is your "attitude" that does.

Lesson 7

The next lesson has to do with the development of the spiritual warrior and the first ray archetype and energies. People who have chronic physical health lessons must be more mentally and emotionally powerful than the average person. When one of your bodies is weaker than another then one's personal power and fighting spirit must be developed to awesome proportions to be able to pull you up and keep up that persevering spirit.

I call this lesson the "Arjuna Initiation." Arjuna was the disciple of Krishna (Buddha was Arjuna in a past life and the Lord Maitreya was Krishna). The battle was about to begin and Arjuna fell into a depression losing his fighting spirit. This is what happens to many with chronic health lessons. Krishna then gave Arjuna a passionate speech about the nature of reality. At one point Krishna says: "Get up and give up your manliness and get up and fight. This self-pity is unbecoming of the great soul that you are." Arjuna did get up and fight and became

Krishna's greatest disciple. Krishna said fight for me with love in your heart and you will incur no sin.

Yogananda said that "Life is a battlefield." Christianity speaks of life in the time of the battle of Armageddon. Contrary to popular opinion, life is a battle. It is a battle between the lower-self and Higher Self, between illusion and Truth. Between fear and Love. Between the negative ego and the Christ Consciousness, between the Great White Brotherhood and Ascended Masters and the Dark Brotherhood.

The purpose of life is to win this war. So what that you gain the whole world but lose your own soul. The battle is to master Self. Health lessons will not stop you from achieving your graduation from the wheel of rebirth. I know this for a fact for I am a living example. The Masters have great compassion. They are concerned more with attitude and things of the spirit!

Lesson 8

The lesson dealing with chronic health lessons I call the "*Reader's Digest* Initiation." I don't know if you have ever read *Reader's Digest*, but they have great stories about people who have overcome unbelievable obstacles. The stories are quite inspiring. I always wanted to be like one of those people and make my life an inspiration to myself and others and God. This chapter is really my "*Reader's Digest* story."

Whatever lessons your are dealing with be it health problems, a divorce, a death, money problems, relationship problems, etc., make up your mind to pass the Reader's Digest Initiation which I have just invented. Make your life a living testimony of the triumph of the human spirit. We hear these types of stories all the time: about a man with no legs walking across the United States, or that Chinese student who stood in front of the tanks during the massacre in that famous square, armed with nothing more than his school books.

My life is a living testimony of the triumph of the human spirit and the power of the will under unbelievable adversity. I do not say this to be egotistical. I personally am more proud of what I have overcome to get to where I am than anything else. I do not want to bore you with the details of my life, but rather to just give you the intuition and feeling and sense of what I am talking about. We are all great souls, and destined for great things. Make your life a living testimony of the power of your spirit and your will. Let nothing stop you from achieving your spiritual and material goals.

Lesson 9

This next lesson for people dealing with chronic health problems is to always remember that health lessons are temporary in the sense that once you physically die you will have a perfect body again. This is a temporary situation that may be able to be healed in this lifetime or maybe not. This does not matter. It is okay to have a preference for this to be so, but not an attachment. Happiness is a state of mind not a state of physical health. Do everything you can to heal yourself on all levels but until you achieve this goal remain happy anyway.

Lesson 10

I call this next lesson the "Hanna Kroeger Initiation." Hanna Kroeger, if you have not heard of her, is a 90-year-old lady who is one of the finest herbalists on the planet. She does all her work with a pendulum, which allows her to energetically test everything. If you have not read her books, I highly recommend them. She has cures for AIDS, cancer, and every ailment known to man. She is a genius and totally of the Christ. One of her handbooks that is meant to be used in conjunction with a pendulum tests the seven kinds of illness that can manifest in the body. It is quite comprehensive and literally any physical health problem you have will fall under one of these seven levels which then has thousands of subsidiary divisions.

After ten years of purifying myself through every known remedy known to man and eating a perfect diet for seven straight years, I am in quite excellent health I never get sick anymore and the only health lessons I have left are a little weakness in the third chakra area and a little sensitivity in one lobe of my liver which can be irritated by being a workaholic (which I am) or improper diet (which I never indulge in). Other than this I consider myself in literally perfect health.

I found this pendulum handbook for diagnosis of one's health quite interesting. With a friend of mine, we both went through the whole procedure with our pendulums. It took about an hour. What was fascinating to me after ten years of digestive sensitivity from the hepatitis was that I came up absolutely perfectly clear on every level and was as clean as a whistle in terms of parasites, pesticides, metals, bacteria viruses and literally everything, except for one thing.

In one small subheading what came up was that I was completely physically clear and that any remaining health lessons or weakness "was for the glory of God." This was actually in her book. I was amazed that she actually even had this in her book. Now this story occurred about four years ago and my health has actually improved greatly because of the completion of my ascension and the light quotient and advanced light technologies I am always using. However I found this little statement to be quite meaningful and a confirmation of everything I believed in and had been working towards my whole life. I think this little section may apply to many lightworkers who may be reading this book. For this reason, I am officially calling it the "Hanna Kroeger Initiation." Whatever lessons you are dealing with dedicate them to the glory of God. So what that there are many things you may not be able do. The purpose of life is to achieve your ascension and liberation and to serve. Even if you are bedridden, these things can be achieved

Lesson 11

The next lesson is a super key to dealing with chronic health lessons. This is to call in the inner plane Healing Masters constantly. This will be like a meditation and you will feel the presence of the Masters with you and this will bring great comfort spiritually, emotionally, mentally and physically. The healing team is literally a Godsend and has rescued me before lectures and other major social events thousands of times when I have been feeling physically or emotionally off-balance.

The second part of this lesson is to call in the Lord of Arcturus and the Arcturians constantly if you have physical health problems. The Arcturians are the number one reason why my physical body has returned to its present state of health. I realize that this is a big statement, but it is true. I literally run their energies constantly.

I call for a 100% light quotient increase and then request that they heal and strengthen my pancreas and liver and whatever else needs healing. Literally, instantly I get relief. I have tried every being in the universe in regard to my health and by far the Arcturians are "the cat's meow." I ask to be connected to their computers and to be "put online." I constantly call on them to balance all my meridians after working or writing all day.

I am in love with the Arcturians. The reason that they are so effective is that they are using their advanced technologies and computers to do their work. They have said that there is no illness in the universe they have ever come across that they could not help with. Plus, the spiritual benefits are enormous.

The third aspect to this lesson would be to constantly go into Djwhal Khul's ashram and call in the matrix removal program as discussed in the chapter on alien implants, elementals, and astral entities. The matrix removal program will keep you clear and should be done every day if needed. It feels wonderful!

Also, call on the Prana Wind Clearing Device from the Arcturians to keep your meridians, veins and arteries clear which will keep your energy flowing properly. I am sharing with you here all the tricks I have come up with.

Lesson 12

Sit in the ascension seats I have listed in my *Beyond Ascension* book and *The Complete Ascension Manual* book as much as possible. The ascension seats and all the light invocations will have an enormous effect on the physical and etheric bodies. What I am suggesting is to be running the higher frequency energies all day and all night long. Ask before bed for the Arcturians to run the energies all night long. They have really helped me to resurrect my physical and etheric bodies which had taken quite a beating this lifetime. Their technology is incredible. Ask them to work with you on a full-time basis.

Lesson 13

Eat to live instead of live to eat. Good diet is important at all times but if you have chronic health lessons it is even more important. If you eat a good diet, disease will literally not be able to grow. Be very disciplined in this regard and cut out sugar if you can, or as much as possible, and of course all drugs. Get as much fresh air, exercise, and sunshine as you. The sunshine will energize the etheric body. Go for ascension walks every day if you can, either calling in light quotient building or one of the various ascension seats.

Realizing your tremendous connection to the Ascended Masters will lessen your feeling of missing things that health lessons might limit you from doing. All the things I am mentioning here should also be done by people who don't have chronic health lessons, as they are the ultimate in preventative medicine.

Lesson 14

Make sure to call in the etheric healing team to repair your etheric body completely and ask for the anchoring of your perfect monadic blueprint body, which can be done prior to your ascension.

Lesson 15

Seek balance and moderation in all things. As the Buddha said, the middle road is the path to Self-realization.

Lesson 16

In extreme cases of ill health, focus on salvaging the incarnation and making as much spiritual growth as possible. During the time I was the sickest and actually had hepatitis I was not trying to make a life, I was trying to just salvage my life. The hepatitis corresponded with my Job initiation, so I took this attitude which gave me a lot of comfort. I salvaged my life through focusing on spiritual studies and meditation and what at first was salvaging my life soon became probably far more advancement than most people in good health ever make.

If ever I would fall back in my health, I would call back this attitude which would make me feel better. This may sound strange to some who have not had chronic health lessons, however, each of these tools and principles are like little tricks to keep the emotional body and mental body on an even keel even though the physical body might be in pain or having problems. The real problem comes not when the physical body has problems, but when the emotional body takes a dive bomb also.

Physical health problems are actually not that bad if you have inner peace. This chapter contains some of the mental programming and positive self-talk you can give yourself to keep yourself in an enthusiastic and inspired state of consciousness.

It is important to understand that most illness can be healed especially with the advanced technologies I speak of in my books. There are some lessons that may not be destined to heal and that is okay. Whatever your lessons make your life an inspiration and an example for others, self and God. I can't help now but think of Christopher Reeve who played Superman in the movies, and had the horseback riding accident and broke his neck. Whenever you think that you have problems think of something like this and you should count your blessings.

Yet even Christopher Reeves has a wonderful fighting spirit that he has cultivated. Whatever lessons we have in life, no matter what they may be, are happening for a reason. It is not accident or fluke of nature. Everything in God's universe works in Divine order. Whatever lessons you have are perfect and need to be there or they wouldn't be there. Use whatever your lessons are on any level for spiritual growth, and to demonstrate Godliness. It is my hope and prayer that some of the ideas and tools I have presented here in times of physical, emotional, mental or spiritual testing will be found useful!

Lesson 17

Go and see a good homeopathic doctor that specializes in using bioenergetic types of testing using vega type medical technology to help cleanse all residual toxins from the body such as metals, chemicals, parasites, mercury fillings, radiation, bacteria, viruses, vaccines, fungus, environmental toxins, to name a few. Without homeopathics or herbs, these toxins deplete the immune system.

Lesson 18

Try and learn how to use a pendulum if you can. Some people have a knack for it more than others do. It would be of enormous benefit if you could learn how to use one, testing all the foods you eat as well as supplements. If not then see a good nutritionist and if possible one who is psychic in their abilities or uses a pendulum and does not give advice from just an intellectual point of view. Also drink lots of fresh pure water.

Lesson 19

Throughout the day call in light quotient building from Metatron, the Arcturians, Melchizedek and other Masters of your choice. This along with the ascension seats and Arcturian technology, inner plane Healing Masters and Djwhal's ashram will greatly energize your etheric and physical vehicle. I have never met anyone who after following this prescription did not feel a great increase in physical health after following this program. The higher you go in initiations the greater the stabilization of light quotient and the greater the realization of the mayavarupa body, so never give up hope. Physical immortality and complete resurrection of the physical vehicle is the light at the end of the tunnel if you stay unceasingly on the mark and on target.

Lesson 20

Call forth three times a day for a planetary and cosmic axiatonal alignment. This particular ascension technique is especially good for physical health for it balances all the meridians and aligns them with Spirit. This is something every person should do as a preventive health practice and it will also serve to accelerate your spiritual growth.

Lesson 21

"Sickness is a defense against the truth." This is a quote from *A Course In Miracles*. The truth is we all are the Christ. The Christ, being perfect, can only have perfect health and all else is illusion. The negative ego is in reality illusion so all sickness in the ultimate reality is an illusion. No matter what your physical health lessons are, many times a day affirm you are in perfect radiant health. Paramahansa Yogananda said that even if you are 99 years old and on your deathbed you should be affirming only perfect health. Affirm this, visualize this, and pray for this. Try not to talk about health problems with friends.

The subconscious mind will manifest into your physical body whatever image or thought you program into it good or bad. Ignore appearances and keep your mind on the Mighty I Am Presence and the perfected state at all times. In truth, all that exists is perfection. Convince your subconscious mind of this regardless of the appearance of your physical body. Eventually the physical body can't help but respond in kind. Be the computer programmer of your computer. Be God every moment of your life in every thought, word and deed. Think only positive thoughts. Spiritualize your emotions. Be vigilant over your mental, emotional, physical and etheric diet. Pray to God and the Masters constantly; do not let go of the Angel of Healing until it blesses you like Jacob of old.

If you practice all the things mentioned in this book and in this chapter then there is no way in this universe you are not going to get better. Be loving at all times and dedicate your life to service in whatever form is appropriate at this particular phase of your life. Let go of all self-pity, and thank God for all your blessings and all your lessons!

Lesson 22

Remain grounded, especially if you have chronic health lessons. Bring heaven to Earth. Some lightworkers are hovering above their physical bodies and not really in them, which makes it hard for the physical body to heal. Just as the feminine and masculine sides must be balanced, the heaven and earthly sides must be balanced and integrated also. Ascension is infusing the soul and monad into the physical body on Earth, not living in the spiritual world and celestial realms which a lot of lightworkers do.

There is nothing wrong with meditating there but the idea is then to come back and get grounded. Live in all parts of your body including hands, arms, feet and legs. It is helpful to keep a grounding cord connected to the center of the Earth. Run energies from the Earth up through your feet as well as heavenly energies downwards. Ask that your personal kundalini be connected to the planetary kundalini. Spend time in nature and with trees.

Spend more time being instead of doing, when going through a healing crisis. Be sure to sleep as much as the physical body needs. This may change at different ages and stages of your life. Find your perfect body rhythms. Mine for example is to sleep about five hours and take an hour nap in the late afternoon. This is the most energizing lifestyle for me, however each person is different. If you do have chronic health lessons, pray every night before bed for healing from all the Masters. Request that a healing platform be set up and that you be worked on 24 hours a day until full recovery is achieved. In cases of chronic illness, conserve your sexuality a little more than you normally would to use this energy for healing. An overuse of sexual energy can be depleting.

Lesson 23

Don't coddle yourself too much physically and become a hypochondriac, however on the other side of the coin don't be too much of a pusher and super trooper at the expense of the physical vehicle. Both extremes can be damaging to your physical and spiritual health.

Lesson 24

People with extreme sensitivities to pills, herbs and/or homeopathics may try radionics. I am one of these sensitive types, so I have two radionic machines that I use to send myself all the homeopathics, herbs, vitamins, and minerals energetically. I honestly don't understand how these simple machines work, but they do. I keep myself in perfect health using them and I never have to take a single pill or take any remedies orally. It is an absolutely mind boggling science and I have proven its effectiveness a million times over.

If you want more information on this call Susan and Sandy. They can do the radionics for you and/or might be able to show you how to set up a simplified system for yourself! The two radionics machines that I have are called a "black box" and the more modern machine is called an "SE-5." This is truly the technology of the future. One day everybody will have a radionics machine as they do a television. It is the ultimate self-healing machine. It can be programmed to send energy through words, through numerical codes or through energetically sending products. Instead of ingesting the physical substance, one's aura is bombarded with the energetic substance. If you are interested in this, there are many easy to read good books about this at your local metaphysical bookstore.

Lesson 25

Every night as you are falling asleep and as you are waking up in the morning give yourself a self-hypnotic suggestion or auto suggestion that you are in perfect radiant health. Take advantage of these hypnotic states where suggestions slip into the subconscious mind more easily. Also do this whenever you are meditating and a have achieved an altered state of consciousness. I would also recommend making a health focused sleep tape that you can play on an auto-reverse tape recorder all night long at a barely audible sound level.

Lesson 26

Contact a Science of Mind practitioner and have them help you write up a "health treatment" which you are to say every day religiously. Stay positive at all times and keep yourself focused at all times on spiritual pursuits for "an idle mind is the devil's workshop."

Lesson 27

Forgive yourself for all mistakes from this life and past lives in regard to your health. Forgive yourself and just start a completely brand new fresh cycle, like your life is completely starting over.

Lesson 28

Every night before bed pray to God directly in a most sincere, humble and non-attached manner for a miraculous healing, if it be God's Will.

Lesson 29

Every morning and every night pray for protection from Archangel Michael in the form of a golden dome that only the energies of the Christ frequency may touch you.

Lesson 30

Practice all the ascension techniques and meditations in *The Complete Ascension Manual,* the *Beyond Ascension* book and in the *Soul Psychology* book over a one year period. If you do this you will have so much light and advanced Christed technology in your field there is no way on earth you will not feel physically better. Be patient in your practice and don't do too much all at once. Pace yourself, in other words. Trust your intuition as what to practice when.

I have 15 ascension activation tapes that can be obtained directly from the Academy for $49.95 which I highly recommend getting. I have recorded these so you can just kick back and receive the activations with my voice. This is an incredibly comprehensive set. Call the phone number listed at the back of this book for further information and ordering.

Lesson 31

When you begin to explore homeopathy, radionics, naturopathic medicine, and bioenergetic medicine, health becomes a lot more than a positive report on a blood test. Western medicine, in truth, is still operating in the Dark Ages. To achieve good health and a healthy, functioning immune system all the physical toxins must be cleared. Most of these things Western medicine has absolutely no awareness of and couldn't cleanse if their life depended on it.

In dealing with chronic illness and/or the desire to really obtain good health, the following are some of the things I would recommend exploring to make sure you have cleared:

- Removal of mercury fillings and homeopathic cleansing of mercury from the body.
- Balancing of yeast and bacteria from use of antibiotics.
- Removal of all vaccines which are totally toxic to the immune system.
- Removal of all parasites.
- Removal of all viruses.
- Removal of all funguses.
- Removal of all improper bacteria.
- Removal of all radiation from color televisions.
- Removal of electromagnetic toxicity from powerlines and the like.
- Removal of all chemicals from body.
- Removal of all past drugs you have taken.
- Removal of all pesticides from vegetables, dairy products and other sources that are in the body.
- Balancing of the bioenergetic fields.
- Cleansing of the liver and kidneys.
- Upgrading of the glandular system.
- Removal of negative emotions through Bach Flower Remedies.
- Immune system building.
- Removal of environmental poisons.

- Proper balance of vitamins and minerals.
- Energetic check of physical diet.
- Blood cleansing.
- Cleansing of lymph system residual toxin.
- Clearing of tuberculosis.
- Clearing of all sexually transmitted diseases.

It must be understood that very often we carry these things subliminally in our system but this does not mean we will ever get these diseases. For example, tuberculosis toxin can be picked up by drinking milk or breathing the air in an airplane. I am speaking here of subclinical toxins that lodge in our system that deplete our immune systems. The medicine of the future works on a much more subtle level then Western medicine. The fact is a person can be dying of cancer and may still have normal blood. Western medicine worships science, which leaves out literally 90% of what is really going on within a person's reality.

Just as I have spoken in this book about the need to remove implants, elementals, negative imprints, astral entities, core fear, mental toxins and emotional toxins, there are also subtle physical toxins which Western medicine does not have a clue about. Just as traditional psychology is missing entirely the psychic and spiritual realm of what is going on, Western medicine is doing the same but even worse. It is only when you go to a New Age homeopathic, bioenergetic or naturopathic doctor that these residual toxins will be addressed. To be honest, even a lot of them don't address it so you must find someone good.

What I am speaking of here is the cutting-edge New Age work in the field of holistic medicine. In my books I have tried to bring forth the cutting edge work that is going on in the spiritual or ascension movement, the cutting edge work going on around the planet in the field of psychology. In this chapter, I am speaking very briefly on the cutting-edge work in the field of holistic health.

Other Things to Clear and Cleanse

All past medications. An interesting story on this point is that as an adolescent I took a great deal of antibiotics for some acne problems I had. Can you believe a doctor recommending antibiotics for acne? Is that barbaric or what? Anyway, over 25 years later I was seeing a psychic nutritionist by the name of Eileen Poole who told me that I was cleansing tetracycline from my field. I told her that was impossible for I had not had a single antibiotic in almost 15 years. It turned out that I was still cleansing the drugs from 25 years ago.

Now remember I am and have been a health food fanatic and exercise fanatic, as well as eating one of the purest diets on the planet. Yet 25 years later I was still cleansing. With a lot of these toxins, without homeopathics or herbs one may never be able to cleanse the system.

Make sure all Epstein-Barr virus is cleansed. Very often, we carry this on subclinical levels, which would never be detected on a blood test.

Make sure all staph and strep bacteria are cleared from the subclinical field. (What we are speaking of here is the whole field of "subclinical medicine.")

Stop using all drugs. Use homeopathics and herbs, which are not toxic for the body.

Never give your children or take yourself any vaccines, for they are absolutely poisonous to the body.

Clear all herpes virus on a subclinical level.

Clear all cold and flu medications, aspirins, and pain killers. All the medications you have ever taken are stored in the liver, poison the body and deplete the immune system.

Ask the bioenergetic specialist, or homeopathic doctor, or Susan and Sandy using a pendulum, or a naturopath, to do a complete work-up using energetic testing to check your entire program and to cleanse everything. The spiritual path is the path of purification. You want your physical, etheric, astral, mental and spiritual bodies cleared.

Cleanse all subclinical cancers, hepatitis and mononucleosis that might be present on subclinical levels.

Remember all disease begins in the astral and etheric bodies first, as well as in the mental body. Western medicine has no way of testing or recognizing the diseases that are manifest on these levels let alone on subclinical physical levels below the surface of a blood test. A blood test is an incredibly gross level. Many people are walking around with walking hepatitis, walking mononucleosis, Epstein-Barr or the like, and are being greatly debilitated.

Western medicine no matter how many tests they do will not be able to figure it out. The blood test is just the tip of the iceberg. The other 90% of the iceberg Western medicine has no way of scientifically detecting. The new technology that is now being invented and worked with is in the field of homeopathy and naturopathic medicine. Such machines as the vega machine and others like it, can scientifically detect the other 90% as accurately as a blood test on the gross level.

Of course, Western medicine rejects this as quackery when, in truth, the reverse is true. I would never go to a regular medical doctor unless it was for emergency procedures, which is the only thing they are good at. Western medicine with its focus on drugs and invasive testing is still in a very "barbaric stage." They reject homeopathic medicine, they never use herbs, they have no understanding of diet, and they reject acupuncture. They have no cure for viruses of any kind, when homeopathics and herbs can knock out any virus within a week to ten days and does not poison the body.

I can knock out any bacterial infection within a couple of days using homeopathics while the doctors prescribe antibiotics like candy for everything although it only works on bacteria. The doctors being so backwards and behind the times don't even tell the person to take extra acidophilus to replace the friendly bacteria. People really have no idea how barbaric Western medicine really is.

Once you have been exposed to the New Age holistic cutting-edge field of medicine and how everything can be tested through energy rather than invasive measures you will never consider going back except in emergency situations like a broken leg or car accident when immediate help is instantly needed. True preventive medicine and true healing is something that the traditional medical profession knows little about. Very often, they actually interfere in the process, for example, by giving a patient Valium for emotional distress. Antibiotics are given like candy for every known problem under the sun when homeopathics are just as effective and a thousand times better for the body.

Other things that need to be cleansed from the body are caffeine, drugs, alcohol, nicotine, metal poisoning (aluminum, lead), car exhaust, insect bites, malathion poisoning, coffee, and salmonella (According to the FDA, 75% of all chickens have salmonella poisoning). This again is what I am talking about when I say we all carry this stuff on subclinical levels. We all must clear all the preservatives we have eaten, pestacides, measles vaccine, chicken pox vaccine, past influenzas, mumps and polio vaccine.

All these things I have listed here get stored in the liver, kidneys, and in different areas of the body. Most of these residual toxins will never get removed from the physical body without homeopathics and specialized herbal remedies. All of these residual toxins and thousands of other ones I have not mentioned here deplete the functioning of your immune system. The biggest one probably being all the food poisons we have eaten in our life.

Going on prolonged and occasional fasts is an essential key to retaining good health. For people with chronic health lessons and for that matter really for every person who wants to become Self-realized I recommend that you get checked for all these things so you can become as purified in your energy fields as you possibly can on physical, etheric, astral, mental and spiritual levels. This book has been dedicated to help give you the tools and understanding to be able to do this to help you obtain perfect health on all levels and to help you realize God!

Lesson 32

This next lesson for people with chronic health lessons or occasional health lessons is to call in the "Acupuncture inner plane Healing Team." This is a phenomenal method, for the inner plane healing team will give you "etheric acupuncture" in the comfort of your own home any time you want. You have your own personal acupuncturist that costs you nothing out of your wallet. The only thing it costs you is your love and gratitude to the wonderful beings that perform these services on our behalf!

Lesson 33

The next method for people dealing with chronic health lessons is a new one which Djwhal Khul recently told me about. Call in the Inner Plane Healing Masters and your own Mighty I Am Presence. Then request that a radionics machine be set up on the inner plane to send you the energies you need on an ongoing basis 24 hours a day to correct whatever type of health lesson you are dealing with. This is a phenomenal method for I am basically giving you a radionics machine right now that costs you nothing, but, in truth, is maybe more effective then even a real physical/earthly radionics machine.

You can request at different times that it be programmed for different things. If you want energy and wakefulness request this. If you want immune system building request that. If you want to work on a long term basis on a specific problem request that. The other thing you request is that it send you whatever energies you need to keep you in balance with no specific focus.

The best method is probably a combination of all of these. The radionics machine can be used even to send you vitamins and minerals you need. The list is really endless. This machine can be used for anything a real radionics machine can be used with and more. Look at the amount of money I am saving you with these last two methods and tools! I do have one request for payment however. Tell your students, friends, family and local metaphysical bookstores about my books, if you like them. In doing this all can share in God's generosity and care for his beloved sons and daughters.

Lesson 34

One other healing tool for people with chronic health lessons or as a preventive tool which again will save you a ton of money in health care bills is to call the inner plane Healing Masters again and request to be given the vitamin and minerals you need as inner plane shots to remain in perfect physical health. Ask for all inner plane shots to be given to you over the next month that will keep your physical and etheric body in perfect energetic and chemical balance.

For example, let's say your family is sick and you want to build up your immune system, you might request an inner plane vitamin C shot every day to boost your immune system. You can also just request to the inner plane Healing Masters to give you any shot or substance that they feel you need to bring you back to balance.

With all the tools in this chapter there is no way that even people with chronic illness are not going to start feeling better. The most important thing in dealing with chronic illness is to have a fighting spirit and to not give up. As long as you are assertively attacking the problem with all these tools and methods the illness will not be attacking and depressing you. This chapter is your spiritual battleplan, so to speak, to win this war.

The using of these tools will not only help you to feel better physically, but will also serve to give you good practice working on the inner plane, and will accelerate your spiritual growth tremendously. It will also help you to develop more of a conscious relationship of working with the Ascended Masters. It will thin the veil, so to speak, and help you to recognize that you are never alone. It will also demonstrate to you in infinite ways how much God loves you, and the bountiful blessings He has bestowed upon you for the asking. Everything in God's infinite universe is literally available to you for the asking. My service is nothing more than sharing with you some of the incredible things that are available. It is up to you, however, to ask. Ask and you shall receive, knock, and the door shall be opened.

Lesson 35

This lesson contains four meditations involving your Solar Angels that were synthesized and condensed from a book called *Healing Yourself with Light*, by Launa Huffines. I have not read the book; however, someone I know thought they might be helpful to my readers, so I have added them here for your enjoyment, healing and light activation.

Meditation #1: Entering the Room of Inner Stillness

Relax, relax, relax, and breathe deeply and rhythmically. Allow yourself to get ready to enter into a room of utter stillness, tranquillity and harmony. Bathe in a cleansing shower of colors and then enter a room, your room of Peace.

Completely detach from the world, you are totally relaxed in your special place, your special room beyond the worries of the world, beyond the barriers of illness, for you are in a sanctuary of healing.

Find your position of comfort and let every cell float into relaxation. Think only of peace, serenity, harmony, wholeness and balance. Let everything become soft.

Invite your Solar Angel, for whom your Guardian Angel is but a mere reflection. Your Solar Angel is with you until you have completed your rounds of incarnation. It is itself, yet totally at one with our higher purpose. Solar Angels work for evolution, and when you invoke your own Solar Angel you will be bringing this Divine Presence into you, filling you with Light, healing and expansion.

In your private place, your quiet space, focus the eyes upward and invoke this Angel. Allow yourself to believe you can be healed. Invite your Solar Angel to come to you like a sphere of golden light. Allow this light to circle your head, your thought-field with its healing energy. This will form a subtle halo around your head.

Now ask the Solar Angel for help in the area that needs healing. Stay in silence and trust, enwrapped, enveloped by the healing, soothing energy of the Angel of the Presence. Feel the new sense of balance it brings, the optimism. Feel and take note of your inner sense of feeling that are beyond mind.

When you are through, give thanks and quietly leave, knowing that this room is ever available to you. Record each experience in your journal. You can now monitor your progress, what works best, how you come to a state of relaxation, as well as wisdom learned and your attitude towards your healing.

Remember, you create the room and the stillness. It is always there for you.

Meditation #2: Entering the Room of Light

Begin with your imagination. Get a sense of this room and the wisdom therein. Be sure to bathe in a shower of Light in the courtyard of the temple of healing. Bring the colors of light over you individually, drops of liquid light in orange, gold, yellow and rose. Then use shades of green, blue, and violet.

Cleansed, enter into your room to again meet your Solar Angel. Find a place to relax. Everything in the room glows, but the brightest point is where **you** are. You are surrounded by White Light and that White Light enters you. It is a living, intelligent Light, and makes offerings of wisdom. You sense the essence of Self and the essence of whatever else comes to mind. The mind calms, the emotions still and there is nothing but the radiance of your Solar Angel. Its essence of Love fills your heart and being.

The Solar Angel brings its light into the room from the heart of the sun. Its rays bring elements that are necessary for your life. To tap into these Solar Beings imagine the rays of Solar Light around your head. The more you allow the Solar Light to enter your mind and heart, the greater the illumination you bring. Think upon spiritual qualities and they are yours to experience.

Solar Light is also an agent of rejuvenation. Invite it into your body to heal and rejuvenate. The Light evolves your cells. It dissolves toxins as it filters into your cells and transmutes them. Through this connection, this column of Light, the Solar Light continues to restore your body cells. As you connect your inner sun with Solar Light, the two merge and distribute great Light throughout your body.

Use imagination to facilitate this reality. Picture your breath drawing healing light into every part of you. Look at the glorious morning sun. Think about the solar entities in these rays that can help you solve any health problems for that day. See in your mind's eye solar rays entering your body, healing each cell, vitalizing you with renewed life.

These are, in truth, living energies that heal, strengthen and evolves your body. Breathe into your heart with love and breathe out from your heart loving gratitude and feel renewed.

Meditation #3: Healing in the Room of Love

Bathe in a shower of liquid gold and rose. See each color rinse the dense frequencies from your energy field. Now enter the Room of Love and find your comfortable position in the room's center.

Breathe in the Healing Angelic Presence and the sweetness of the rose and white flowers about you. Through the open skylight above luminous particles of Love Essence flow down into the room. Open up any and all places in your four lower bodies that need more love.

Create a rose-colored triangle between your Solar Angel, your soul, and your four lower bodies. Through the energy of your rose triangle comes the Angels of Divine Love. This Love contains wondrously healing life energy. Ask that any emotion that has created a block or problem in your emotional/astral body be released. If your problem is specifically of a physical nature, call upon the Love of these Angels to intone their specific healing sound in that direction.

Chant "Ah" slowly and open your heart even more. Remember the rose filled triangle and connection with your Solar Angel.

Chant "El" (as in bell), calling to the One Creative Force. The note will travel up a column of Light to the top of the head. Visualize it. "E" is for serenity and "L" uplifts the soul. Peaceful concentration will lift you up to the angels of Love Divine.

"I" (pronounced "ee" as in see), takes you right into the center of healing. Place sound between and above your eyes as it vibrates between the eyebrows, feel the soul resonation.

As you say "O" (as in oh), bring a line of lighted energy from above into your head and down the spinal cord. Visualize the Angels of Divine Love bringing healing into every nerve in your body.

Chant or intone the full vibratory sound A-El-I-O seven times and imaging it ringing in your temple of healing. The response will resonate in your heart. Each syllable calls in more Angels of Divine Love.

Now bathe in the frequencies of their energies. It is love and joy that purify your heart and neutralize all past suffering. As they recharge you with Divine healing love so are you drawn even closer to the Healing Angels.

See this love flow through your four lower bodies, refining and purifying all density from the past. Tell your cells it is OK to accept this wonderful healing love. Fill up on it.

After this process and intoning the healing syllables your cells will vibrate with love from the Spiritual Dimension. Give your four lower bodies time to absorb this Divine Gift. Sit quietly, play beautiful or spiritual New Age music or look at beautiful art or nature. Stay within the serenity and peace of Love Divine.

Meditation #4: Color Baths

Healing Angels use specific colors in their healing. They weave the needed colors into your energy field to offer protection from disease. For vitality they use rose or orange hues. A clear hue of green is very helpful for general healing needs. It cools down the center of the atoms in order to bring them back into balance.

It is important to work within the triangles of your Solar Angel, your soul and your self (four lower bodies). Then you will receive the best healing colors for your purposes.

In general, for the physical body: for lung congestion an iridescent orange is called into the area. For infections, sapphire blue might help by acting as a disinfectant. Sapphire blue might be used for poison ivy or rashes as well. A rich green or a green tinged with yellow is often used for inflammation. For higher energy, they use stimulating color, such as a bright or golden orange or yellow.

For emotions: different hues of yellow, gold, orange, or rose are great for inducing cheerfulness, confidence, and optimism. Hues of rose from intense to pastel can create an inner feeling of Love. One needs to experiment for oneself to find just the right color to help generate the desired mood.

For thoughts: color is also invaluable to calm your mind. You can surround yourself with luminous green. For clear thinking and mental stimulation, you might try a shower of bright yellow over and around your head. A tint of yellow-orange may very well get you out of a mental fog. If your will to live is not very strong, try rose. Two or three shades of rose will build your will to live.

Color is already used to create healing and restful environments. Colors are energy and are used by the Angels and man. It is well to take note of and make use of color for health evolution and purification.

Final Summation

In concluding this chapter, I asked Djwhal Khul to eloquently give me a statement as to health and disease from the perspective of the Spiritual Hierarchy and Ascended Masters. The simplicity of what he said surprised me. Djwhal said, "Ill health is basically misdirected thinking."

Ill health then is the physicalization of negative ego thoughtforms. Health is the physicalization of Christ/Buddha Consciousness and thinking. Lack of health is not a bad thing, but a good thing, being nothing more than a neutral indicator of an imbalance or misdirected thought in the psyche. If we didn't have health lessons, we would never learn. It is our ultimate teacher to help us align our minds and emotions with God's Laws. Instead of cursing your body for getting sick, bless your body for being your neutral and objective guide that does nothing more than mirror your state of consciousness.

If our bodies never gave us these signals, we would never achieve liberation and true God Consciousness. Our bodies in essence force us to remain on our spiritual path. God is balance and it is our bodies that force us to hold to this ideal. God's sons and daughters can often be quite rebellious and disobedient, like little children. Health lessons are nothing more than the body communicating with us and they should not be judged or looked at as a bad thing. It is through our suffering and health lessons that most of us have found God and our spiritual paths. This is an extremely difficult school and it is amazing that people's bodies hold up as well as they do given all the abuse they take. When they do break down have great compassion and love and understanding for self and others. Let the physical body teach you to remain balanced, integrated and attuned to the Mighty I Am Presence at all times!

37

The Issue of Living on Light

There are a great number of people in the United States and around the world who are teaching the general public the benefits of living on Light rather than eating physical food. I am the first to say that this is possible, and I personally know many people who are very good friends of mine who are doing it. Although this is the case I have consulted in-depth with the Inner Plane Ascended Masters, and they have given me very clear, loving guidance that this is not something they like the general public to do. There are a small number of people on the planet that they said this is appropriate for. The people in the United States and around the world that are indeed doing this are very sincere, good people with a very high degree of integrity. They are practicing what they preach and should be commended for this.

The inner plane Ascended Masters, however, have asked me to write this chapter to correct a very slight misconception regarding this process. The misconception is that they do not want the masses trying to live on Light. They want the masses to live on a partial Light diet and not try to force themselves to live on a full Light diet. By this I mean the Masters want people to eat a good, healthy diet and to invoke and see GOD's Light and Love also sustaining them. People in general are too attached to food. Many people think they need seven course meals. They feel that if they miss a meal, they will get weak. They find it hard to conceive of fasting. Fasting is one of the most effective ways to heal the body when you are not feeling well. This, of course, can be done by just drinking water, vegetable juice, or vegetable broth for a day. Other types of fasting can be what I call a semi-fast of, let's say, just eating vegetables or fruit for one day or more. A wonderful fast is just eating apples for three days, for apples absorb the toxins in the body. Another wonderful fast, which I recommend even more, is fasting on Bieler Broth. Bieler Broth is green beans, zucchini, celery and parsley steamed in a large pot and then blended in a blender to create thick vegetable soup. This wonderful soup is an incredible liver cleanser and rebuilder. Fast on this for one or two days and it will do wonders for your physical health. I call it "Nectar of the GODs." While you are fasting call on GOD and the inner plane Ascended Masters, especially Melchizedek, The Mahatma, Archangel Metatron, and Dr. Lorphan to program your body with the Fire Letters, Key Codes, and Sacred Geometry to help you partially live on Light. This way you can occasionally fast without getting weak, and be sustained by the Bieler Broth and/or another form of fasting along with GOD and the Inner Plane Ascended Masters' Light and Love.

The Masters, however, only want people to fast occasionally; like once a week or once a month when you are not feeling well and need some rejuvenation and revitalization. The rest of the time they are recommending that you eat a healthy balanced diet high in vegetables, making sure you get enough protein in your diet. Many people eat too much starch and/or carbohydrates forgetting that protein is even more important. The Masters recommend drinking lots of pure water and getting a little fresh air, sunshine and physical exercise every day.

They also highly recommend learning to work with a pendulum to ask your subconscious mind and body elemental what kinds of foods it really wants, rather than the cravings of the lower self and the desire body. The Masters also highly recommend practicing the science of proper food combining. For example, fruits and vegetables should not be eaten at the same meal. When you eat fruit it should be eaten alone as a meal itself. This is because the sugar in the fruit causes fermentation in the digestive tract when combined with other foods. Fruit is also a cleanser where vegetables are builders. Another proper food combining is that proteins and starches should be mixed ideally. It is not that anything will happen if you do so or choose not to do it sometimes, but rather, as a general rule, your body will function much more effectively if you follow these simple food combining laws. If you would like to know more about food combining, any health food store will have inexpensive pamphlets explaining these principles. I personally highly recommend you explore this even if you do it just some of the time.

I would now like to get back to our discussion on why the Masters do not want most people to try to live on Light. The common teaching in the United States and around the world is that people can go on a 21-day program to transition to living on Light. Again, this is a wonderful process for those that have done it, and for a handful of people on Earth who have a specific mission/purpose for doing this. Again, these people should be commended for their example, and I emphasize that many of these people are dear friends of mine. The mistake that has been made, however, is that what is 100% right for some of these people has been marketed for the masses. The inner plane Ascended Masters do not support this. This process that has been taught does not take into consideration some extremely important factors:

1. A person's initiation level. Even if this was part of your true mission and purpose, the inner plane Ascended Masters do not recommend even considering it until you take your eleventh major initiation, and then most eleventh stage initiates are not supposed to do it.
2. The second point that has not been considered by these teachings is the person's physical health. Does the person have a health history that makes this unwise? Is the person too malnourished already from eating an improper diet?
3. The state of a person's psychological health has not been considered. As we all know the subconscious mind runs the body, and if a person is too run by the negative ego, lower self, astral body, inner child, and subconscious mind, such a practice can have disastrous consequences.

4. Is it the person's true spiritual mission and purpose to do this or is it glamour?
5. Often the inner plane Ascended Masters will recommend against it because the person it too ungrounded already. Living on Light would just exacerbate the problem.
6. Then there is the question, is the person doing this for ego or for the true demonstration of Godliness? Are they doing it to achieve fame or humility?
7. Not eating food also has a way of separating you from people since eating is such an integral part of the social fabric of our lives. The Masters prefer that people integrate with people, not separate.
8. These teachings recommend going on this program without any consultation from a medical doctor or qualified health practitioner.
9. Most people who try this program are unable to do it, not because there is anything wrong with them but, rather, because it is not the soul's or God's wish that they be on this program. They have mistakenly bought into a glamour of a teaching that is not right for them, and end up feeling bad and very confused about themselves emotionally and/or mentally for not being able to do what has been taught.
10. What is basically happening is most people are starving themselves and creating a malnourished condition. A program with an intent to help, in truth, could have the opposite effect if not guided properly.
11. A deep-seated guilt and/or lack of self-worth is often created at not being able to live on Light. Not enough psychological or spiritual support is given for those who don't and, in truth, should not do this program.

Conclusion

In conclusion, the Masters want me to say that 99.99% of the time they want lightworkers to not attempt to live on Light alone, but rather to strive to live on a partial Light diet that is balanced with a healthy physical diet. The people who are teaching the masses to live on Light are good and sincere people and are practicing what they preach. The only mistake they are making is trying to market it to the masses instead of just demonstrating this for themselves. The right path for one may not be the right path for everyone.

38

Dining with GOD

My Beloved Readers, this may be one of the most profound chapters I have ever written, so I humbly suggest you listen very closely to what I have to say here. We are all familiar with the importance of eating a good physical diet. Our physical bodies are chemically made up of the food we eat. Spiritual people are also familiar with the concept of eating a good mental diet, for in truth our thoughts create our reality and every person on Earth thinks with their fear-based mind or love based mind. Eating a good mental diet may be the single most important Spiritual practice on the Spiritual Path. It is only by doing this that we can learn to transcend negative ego thinking and learn to think with our Spiritual/Christ/Buddha Consciousness.

We also all recognize the importance of eating a good diet emotionally and energetically in terms of not seeing violent, low life, and horror movies that fill our minds and emotional bodies with negative thoughts, images, and feelings. We also recognize the importance of hanging out with positive uplifting people, and protecting ourselves where there is a lot of negative energy. These are all, in truth, aspects of eating a good diet Spiritually, Mentally, Emotionally, Energetically, Physically, Socially, and Environmentally.

A great many people in this world struggle with their weight, or just eat too much food they do not need or really want. This is not a judgement, just an insight into the fact that a great many people eat physical food for many reasons other than the physical body or the body elementals true needs. People eat out of boredom, habit, as a replacement for love, to stuff their feelings down, to ground themselves, to satisfy lower self desire, sweet tooth, from hypnotic programming on television, nervousness at parties. Other reasons are the mind tells them they should, they think they are supposed to, emotional satisfaction, just to name a few. Most people in this world live to eat, rather than eat to live. It is not just an issue of weight. It is also an issue of improper combining of foods, eating too much food, and eating the wrong foods, which causes a build up of toxicity in the body and causes the organs to become overwhelmed and sluggish. This often causes fatigue, and is in truth an inefficient use of our energies. There is an enormous preoccupation with food in our society. Most people eat for enjoyment and do not really eat what the body elemental really wants. Most people eat from their minds, or eat for emotional reasons and not from their essence. If people would test every food they ate with a pendulum to see if the body really wanted to eat that particular type of food, and the amount the body really wanted to eat, they would be shocked to find that maybe as much as ninety percent of what they are eating the body really doesn't want or need. They are eating the wrong foods, wrong amount of foods, at the wrong time, in the wrong combinations. This chapter is not about your physical diet, although it has been essential to lay this foundation for this discussion.

My Beloved Readers, what I am humbly suggesting here is that you may have been on the wrong diet, and you may have been going out to eat with the wrong companion. You have been going out to eat too much with your personality who by its very nature is too materialistically focused. My Beloved Readers, I am humbly suggesting that you leave this dining companion behind from now on, stop focusing so much on physical food, and instead start bringing with you a new dining companion. I am humbly suggesting that you begin "Dining with GOD"!

You have all been on diets, fasts and eating programs and have heard and seen it all. Well, my Beloved Readers, I am going to suggest a new Dining Program that I am sure you have never heard of or practiced, and that is "Dining with GOD". You have been satisfying yourself too much with the paltry satisfaction of physical food, when you could be eating what I like to call the "Smorgasbord of GOD." I am going to now offer you a diet from the "Restaurant of GOD". Once you taste this restaurant's food, and "GOD's Cuisine" you will never be interested in the meager diet of physical food you have focused upon most of your life. I am not saying here that you will stop eating physical food. What I am saying here is, that once you have tried the "GOD Diet," you will never be interested in doing any other diet ever again! Now I know you are all dying to hear what the "GOD Diet" is. Because you are my loyal and faithful readers, I am now going to share with you one of the "Secrets of the Ages." I am now going to share with you the "GOD Diet." This will eventually be the number one diet of the entire world, and will not be a fad like all the other diets. So listen very closely for here it comes.

The "GOD Diet" and "Dining with GOD" at GOD's Banquet is not focused on physical food, but is focused on "Spiritual Food." It is far more satisfying than physical food. Most people in this world focus most of their energy on physical food, and not on learning to be Spiritually, mentally, emotionally and energetically fed. "GOD's Diet" has all the vitamins, minerals, protein, carbohydrates, fats, and oils you will ever need. GOD's first main Course is "GOD's Light." This is absolutely scrumptious once you develop a taste for it. It builds your "Light Quotient" and fills your "Light Body."

The Second Main Course at "GOD's Banquet" is "GOD's Love." This is the perfect food to eat after eating and absorbing GOD's Light. This will totally fill your "Love Body," and will fill you with delight. The Third Course at "GOD's Banquet," is "GOD's Power." This fills all the Bodies with Divine Power and Energy. Believe it or not, this is only the First Course. At "GOD's Banquet" and Dining Out with GOD, every meal is a Seven Course Meal, and you will not gain too much weight, and you will not get tired. You are also guaranteed to get all the vitamins and minerals you need. It will not put any toxins in your physical body.

There is no problem with food combining. You will not get indigestion, and the organs will not get sluggish. They will actually work even better, and toxins will be removed in the process.

I forgot to mention that GOD also supplies all the Seasonings and Herbs you want, to make the Cuisine totally fit your palate. For Seasoning, GOD offers you one of the Twelve Rays. He will offer you a little extra (red power, blue love/wisdom, yellow active intelligence, green harmony, orange new age science, indigo devotion, violet freedom). For those of you with refined palates, he offers you the five Higher Rays, which are combinations of these Seven Rays with a little extra Luminescence. My Beloved Readers, I bet you have not had seasoning like this!

GOD, however, is not just satisfied with this type of Seasoning, for GOD is the "Master Chef" of the Infinite Universe. GOD also offers you other types of Seasoning. He also offers you all kinds of "Fire Letters, Key Codes and Sacred Geometries," to satisfy even the finest connoisseur of fine dining.

To drink He offers you the "Baptismal Waters of the Holy Spirit" and the "Waterfall of GOD." As an Appetizer, He offers you a taste of the Many Ascension Seats of GOD.

For the Second Course, GOD offers you the Anchoring of your Higher Chakras into your Twelve Body System of which there are actually 330, which he is happy to anchor and activate upon request. GOD provides you with a "Menu" which I am listing and it is your free choice and pleasure to order whatever suits your palate. With the Higher Chakras also comes the Anchoring of your Higher Bodies of which there are too many to list here. Some of these are: "Your Anointed Christ Overself Body, Your Zohar Body of Light, Your Higher Adam Kadmon Body, The Lords Mystical Body, Your Monadic body, Your Soul Body, Your Solar, Galactic and Universal Bodies, Your Higher Light Body" just to name a few. My Beloved Readers, I ask you, is this not more satisfying than just always eating the same physical foods over and over again?

GOD will also provide you at this meal with the full Anchoring and Activation of your Higher Self and Mighty I Am Presence. Now if this isn't "Good Dining" I don't know what is?

For your Third Course of the Meal, GOD offers you the "Music of the Spheres" in each Dimension and Level of Creation. He also offers you the Most Beautiful Celestial Sounds and Angelic Choirs. He also offers you at this Course, the most beautiful Scents and Smells of GOD like Beautiful Roses, Jasmine, and the Most Divine Incense. He also offers you a continuing downpouring of Light in all the Colors of the Rainbow and more. He also brings forth at this most important meal the Cosmic Rays of White Light, Copper Gold, Refined Gold, and Platinum Light. He also brings forth the Entire Color Spectrum of the Ten Lost Cosmic Rays and the Yod Spectrum. My Beloved Readers, can you ever be satisfied with just eating the same old boring physical food to satisfy your personality and lower self cravings ever again?

GOD also brings forth a "Light Shower, Love Shower and Power Shower" for those who would like to feel and sense the "Touch of GOD." For a Dessert at this Third Course, GOD offers you the "Divine Nectar and Amrita," for those with a little "Sweet Tooth." Is not this better than a store bought cookie?

The Fourth Course of Dining out with GOD is a most satisfying meal that includes the "Breath and Prana of GOD". Feel the Holy Breath Of GOD fill your being with help from the Holy Spirit. I forgot to mention that GOD even provides you with Special Clothing for this meal at this most Elegant Restaurant. He provides you with Robes and Dresses of Pure White Light, ordained with Diamonds, Jewels, and Crystals of GOD.

At this Course for those with a more Grounded Appetite, GOD supplies you with a direct flow of energies from the Earth Mother, Pan and the Nature Kingdom through your Feet Chakras and Grounding Cord that is connected to the very center and Core of the Earth Mother. Is not this better than Meat and Mashed Potatoes?

GOD also Spices up this Meal with a direct feeding from the Many Ashrams of GOD. Some of the choices you have on your Menu are El Morya, Kuthumi, Serapis Bey, Paul The Venetian, Hilarion, Sananda, Saint Germain, Lord Maitreya, Lord Buddha, Helios And Vesta, Melchior, Melchizedek, and as a final "Piece de Resistance," The Ashram of GOD. These Divine Feedings you drink with a straw and are available to all for the ordering and asking. My Beloved Readers, is not this the most amazing Restauran and Menu of Foods you have ever seen? Did I not tell you that you have never been to a Restaurant or been on a Diet such as this? But wait, we are only at the Fourth Course and we are not even done yet. I forgot to mention one more important thing about this diet. That is, you never get over full. Occasionally there are extreme cases of "Bliss," or extreme cases of "GOD Intoxication." This Bliss only lasts for a few hours or few days, however, and never causes a hangover or headache.

For some added Condiments here, GOD adds his "72 names of GOD" and "72 Divine Attributes". This is sure to bring your food to the most Divine and Perfect Taste, just how you like it. To finish this Fourth Course, GOD adds just for flavoring a Balancing of your Chakras and an Axiatonal Alignment. My Beloved Readers, was this Fourth Course not one of the Most Scrumptious Courses you have ever tasted? Isn't it wonderful how well all your Spiritual Foods are combining! Are you even thinking about eating junk food at this moment, when GOD has offered you this? What is amazing is this has always been available to you, and this Restaurant has been right around the corner, and you have never even gone inside. You have instead, out of habit, kept visiting the personality's restaurant, which of course is a "fast food restaurant" filled with just physical food. Now that you have found this new restaurant, do you really want to spend as much time there?

Anyway it is now time for GOD's Fifth Course. This is one of my favorite Courses. GOD has prepared for us The Light, Love and Power Packets of GOD, made directly from the "Treasury of Light, Love and

Power" at the 352nd Level of Divinity. Here all of GOD's "Waiters and Waitresses" are in the form of the Archangels, Inner Plane Ascended Masters, and Elohim Masters, bringing forth the Light, Love and Power Packets of GOD from the Tablets of Creation, The Cosmic Book of Life, The Elohim Scriptures, The Archangelic Scriptures, the Cosmic Ten Commandments, the Torah Or. Absorb these through your Crown Chakra and let them blend into your entire being. Is not this not one of the most Delicious meals you have ever tasted?

For our Sixth Course, GOD has prepared a most Divine Dish. He has prepared a direct Divine Feeding from the Archangels and Angels of the Light of GOD. For those who like a little more Yang in their diet, GOD has also provided a direct feeding from the Elohim Masters. For those who would like a little taste of the Goddess, The Divine Mother and all the Lady Masters have also stepped forth to bring forth a "Goddess Feeding" as well. My Beloved Readers, I have not met anyone who has not been most satisfied with this Sixth Course. As an added dessert at this meal to clean the Palate, The Lord of Arcturus, the Lady of Arcturus, The Arcturians, and Commander Ashtar and the Ashtar Command, have stepped forward with an Ascension Activation from the Christed Extraterrestrials. A most sublime finishing taste and touch to this most delectable Sixth Course.

For the Seventh and Final Course, GOD, "The Master Chef of the Infinite Universe," has something very special planned. GOD feels it is especially important here that this Banquet He has created be sure to feed all your bodies, including your physical body. So for this Meal, in conjunction with the Earth Mother, Pan and the Nature Kingdom, He has a very special Recipe planned. First off, He has called upon Dr. Lorphan and the Galactic Healers along with your Healing Angels, to step forward and fill your Etheric and physical body with Universal and Galactic energies for physically healing the body. Melchizedek brings forth a Platinum Net to cleanse all your bodies of imbalanced energies and toxins on every level. GOD anchors a "Pillar of Light" and an "Ascension Column of Light" around you directly from Source. Dr. Lorphan, the Galactic Healers and your Healing Angels feed your physical body, your DNA, your blood stream, your organs and glands, your bones, and entire physical body with Light, Love, and Healing Energies. They also fill you with the extra vitamins and minerals, protein, carbohydrates, fats and oils, all in the proper balance. They fill you full of extra Vitamin C, and activate your immune system to its highest potential. They give your aura, electrical fields, 12-body system and meridians, an activation and balancing. They bring forth the bacterial and virus vacuum with the help of Melchizedek, the Mahatma and Archangel Metatron to vacuum up any viruses and bacteria that should not be there. The inner plane Ascended Masters step forth and bring forth the "Core Fear Matrix Removal Program" and pull out, like weeding a garden, all fear based negative ego programming. GOD for this final meal is giving you a complete clearing and cleaning to allow you to fully absorb all the wonderful foods he has provided. The Masters are also removing all negative extraterrestrial implants and negative elementals. GOD now gives you a Complete Ascension Clearing. With the first part of this Course now being complete, GOD brings forth an Anchoring of GOD's Core Love to fill all that has been cleaned and removed. GOD now asks Archangel Michael to step forward and cut any cords that are connecting you to people and things that are not 100% of GOD, if you give GOD Permission to do this in this moment. GOD now sends in his Healing Teams, to fully repair your etheric body, mental body, and emotional body from any tears, holes, spots and leaks.

GOD now sends in The Mahatma, also known as the "Avatar of Synthesis," to perfectly Integrate and Balance your 12-Body System in all ways and all things. As a Special Final Gift, the Mahatma anchors into each person's Highest Potential an aspect of all 352 levels of His being as a Special Dessert for this Meal.

As this aspect of this Seven Course Meal is complete, GOD now wants to make sure you are completely satisfied, so he has called forth the Entire Cosmic and Planetary Hierarchy to fully anchor and activate their combined Light, Love and Power Bodies into us to insure that we feel full and satisfied and do not leave hungry. GOD of course being the Perfect Host, is not satisfied yet. GOD wants this to be a meal you will never forget, so he anchors your "Cosmic Antakarana or Tube of Light," and a direct flow of GOD Spiritual Current directly from Source. Take a moment now to absorb this into your being, like a sponge that is absorbing Divine Energy from GOD.

Feel the Earth Mother, Pan, and the Nature Kingdoms filling you full of Earthly Spiritual Current from the Material Face of GOD as well. Feel your auric field and all your bodies expand and become completely filled with the Light, Love, and Power of GOD.

As a final Dessert from GOD to complete this Banquet, GOD calls forth the Entire Cosmic and Planetary Hierarchy, and all the Archangels, Angels and Elohim Masters of the Light of GOD, as well as all the Christed Extraterrestrial Races. He requests with His help and the help of Christ and the Holy Spirit, a "Combined Light and Love Shower," the likes that has never been given forth at one of GOD's Restaurants before! Receive this "Combined Light and Love Shower" now if you would like to order this Course! Feel yourself being filled with the Combined energy of GOD, Christ, The Holy Spirit and The Godforce, as you have never been filled before. As GOD's Final Dish this Evening, GOD serves a Dish that has never been served at this Restaurant before. However, in honor of you, His Sons and Daughters of GOD, He now Anchors and Activates His Own Light, Love and Power Body of GOD and Three-Fold Flame fully into your Heart. My Beloved Readers, is this not the most Tasty Dish you have ever eaten?

My Beloved Readers, GOD now thanks us for coming, and humbly requests that we come again whenever we want. He most graciously tells us that this Restaurant is open for Breakfast, Lunch, and Dinner, and is open 24 hours a day and never closes. GOD also tells me that He never runs out of food, and that every dish on the menu is always available. GOD says he specializes in Planetary, Solar, Galactic, Universal, Multi-Universal, and Cosmic Dining. He says He never met a customer He didn't love, and He never met a customer who didn't like His cooking once they truly tasted it. His Final Suggestion is to consider changing dining mates since you have been out to eat so many times with the Personality, and to broaden your Social Calendar and "Sup" with Him more often. For He has most enjoyed Dining with You, His Beloved Son and Daughter, and would like to do so more often. He even suggests coming two or three times a week, or even more if you like. He has an unlimited amount of food and Loves the Company. He tells me He loves cooking, and the more the Merrier. His Final Words of Wisdom are that if you give his cooking a chance you will find the eating of just physical food or just eating for the wrong reasons will never be of interest again when you know that His Restaurant and Banquet is always open for Business! One last thing GOD asks me to tell you, and that is, "All Meals do not cost any money, for they are always on the House!" Bon Appetite!

39

The Incredible Importance of Mastering, Loving and Taking Responsibility for the Earth and Earth Energies

It is very interesting to me that there is so much focus on loving GOD and our Brothers and Sisters, which, of course, is the most wonderful thing in the whole world. However, there is not as much talk about loving the Earth and Earth life! In my humble opinion, if Jesus was on the Earth again in this New Millennium 2000 years later I think he would add a "New Commandment"! I think he would say, "Love the Lord thy GOD with all your heart and Soul and Mind and Might; love your neighbor as you love yourself; love all the Kingdoms of GOD and love Earth life!" For as I have said in this book many times, there are *four* Faces of GOD! All four need to be loved: Spiritual, Mental, Emotional, and Material! One will not realize God fully without mastering, integrating and fully loving Earth life!

Now it is a common belief among many people and may lightworkers on Earth to not like the Earth. Some look at it as a prison. Others look at it as being not important and only the Heavenly Worlds and Celestial Dimensions as being important! Others still do not see the Material Universe as one of the Seven Heavens of GOD that it truly is! Others still think that matter is lower and unimportant, and all that matter is good for is that we use this world to free us from the wheel of rebirth! Others still do not recognize that GOD exists as much in the Material Universe as he does in the Mental, Emotional, or Spiritual dimensions of GOD! Others still do not recognize that if they do not learn to master, integrate, and fully love the Earth, Earth Energies, and Life, they will literally be missing one quarter of God Realization! A lot of lightworkers also do not realize that part of God Realization is integrating and balancing the God/Goddess within. One can never fully integrate the Divine Mother and the Goddess energies if you do not fully love and integrate the Material Face of GOD!

Now, my Beloved Readers, I am not just talking here about just loving the Earth Mother and loving the Animal Kingdom, the Plant Kingdom, and the Mineral Kingdom. I am also not just talking about loving Pan, the Nature Spirits, the Plant Devas and Elemental Spirits. I am not just talking about mastering, integrating and loving the Earth and Earth energies! I am also not just talking about loving Nature, which is one of the easier aspects of Earth life to love. I am also not just talking about loving even Earth life! I am not saying there are not negative things that go on and a lot of negative people! I am not saying that it does not take a lot of courage! I am not saying it is not a difficult school! Maybe one of the most difficult! However, I am saying that if you do not learn to master, integrate and fully love the Earth and Earth life you have not fully learned your lessons in regard to the Earth in terms of your reason for coming!

I have always been a very Spiritual person. This was always my greatest passion. I also incarnated into a family of psychologists so I had a very strong connection to understanding working with psychology as well. Over the years, however, I have come to also have an unbelievably strong mastery, love, and connection to the Earth, Earth energies and Earth life! I really have come to more fully understand the Material Face of GOD! My single greatest passion in life deals with the understanding and recognition that to fully Realize God, it must be done so on three distinct levels. It must be done on the Spiritual Level, the Psychological Level, and the Physical/Earthly Level! Each level is equally important! One is not better than another. Each level is a doorway to God Realization! I have always appreciated the Spiritual and the Psychological levels of GOD! I have always functioned well on the Earth and have had great mastery over Earth energies. However, it has just been in the last 10 years that my full appreciation of how God may be realized through the Earth has been fully appreciated and realized within me! It has opened a whole new window to GOD and appreciation of GOD! The profundity of GOD on the Spiritual Level goes without saying! The profundity of GOD on the Psychological Level, as you can see from reading this book and my other books on the subject, is equally as profound! Both of these levels of God Realization are so profound that they defy description! This book gives you a real appreciation of the Psychological and Spiritual profundity of GOD! What I want to share with you, my Beloved Readers, is that GOD is equally profound on a Physical/Earthly Level! I really have come to fully know and understand this! I incredibly appreciate the concept of mastering Earth energies as I do mastering the mind, emotions, and/or things of the Spirit! I also incredibly the love and appreciate the concept and experience of grounding Spiritual energies, ascension, and the Mighty I Am Presence into my physical body and fully onto the Earth! As I have said many times: Ascension is *descension*. The purpose of life is not to leave the Earth, but to ground one's Mighty I Am Presence, Higher Self, and Soul fully into one's physical body and fully into the Earth and Earth Life!

The purpose of this chapter is to convey the importance of seeing the Material Face of GOD as an integral part of God Realization. In truth, literally one-third of God Realization would be missed. We would never even consider not loving the Spiritual dimensions of Reality. We would also not consider not loving the mental and emotional aspects of life. Yet, a great many people and lightworkers do not love the Earth and Earth life for many of the reasons I mentioned earlier in this chapter!

This, my Beloved Readers, with no judgment intended, is faulty thinking! The Material Universe and the Earth is "GOD"! Earth life is GOD! To not fully love the Material Universe and the Earth and Earth Life is to not Love GOD! To not learn to enjoy Earth life and be happy on Earth and to love Earth life, is to not fully learn your Spiritual Lessons! Many lightworkers do not want to hear this, however it is the truth! There is a classic saying in Spiritual thought that says you never leave a situation until you have become happy in that situation, for if you haven't, you have not learned the lessons of that situation and are likely to repeat them. This applies to the Earth as well! As I said at the beginning of this chapter, to fully learn our lessons we must Love GOD, our Brothers and Sisters, and All Kingdoms of GOD (Animal, Plant and Mineral, Nature, Etheric Nature Spirits and Devas, Mother Earth, God/Goddess, and last but not least the Earth and Earth life!) All of it must be loved! We must love and care for Earth life! Many Spiritual people are not political, or don't care about social issues or changing our society, for they believe it is not important. They believe only the Heavenly world is important, not what is going on in the Earthly world. This, of course, is faulty thinking! It is our purpose to love this world and turn it into a fifth dimensional society, a utopian society. This is why Sai Baba has said, "Hands that help are holier than lips that pray"! Cleaning up the pollution is important. Politics is important. Saving the whales is important. Saving the rain forest is important. Repairing the ozone layer is important. Picking up trash off the ground is important. Beautifying your home is important. Having a garden and taking care of it is important. Planting trees is important. Spiritually educating our world is important. Manifesting Spirituality on Earth is just as important as any Spiritual pursuit. Even more important, in truth, for that is why we have come; not to Ascend and leave, but to descend and build a new Spiritual Civilization on Earth. Creating beauty in this world in architecture and in all ways through the Arts is important. Helping to bring through new scientific discoveries on Earth is important. Revamping the religions of our world so they are free from negative ego contamination is important. Creating new structures on the Earth to make society run better is important. Being a gardener is important! Picking up trashcans is important! Cleaning toxic waste dumps is important. Every profession on Earth is important! Changing out society is incredibly important. Grounding your Spiritual mission on the Earth is incredibly important! Many lightworkers never ever ground their Spiritual Mission. Why have a physical body if you are not going to Spiritually Ground your mission. You could have done Spiritual and Psychological work without a physical body! You have come here to transform Earthly civilization. You did not come here to ascend and turn into light and leave this world. This is illusion. You have come here to become an Integrated Ascended Master and remain on Earth and transform this Earthly world! To think that you just came here to achieve your own personal ascension and leave is actually selfish, in an egotistical sense of the term. You are here to become an integrated Ascended Master and be of Service on the Earth. You are here to fulfill your Spiritual puzzle piece on Earth, not in Heaven! It is time for lightworkers to get out of the clouds, come back to Earth, and fulfill their Spiritual mission; which is to bring their unique abilities and talents to change this world! We are here to create a God civilization on Earth as it is in Heaven. We are here to create Heaven on Earth! I am not saying it is an easy job! I am the first to admit all the corruption and all the negative ego-run institutions in our world. Almost every institution on this planet is run backwards and is corrupt! Look at our prison systems. Is this how GOD would have us run them? Look at our educational system, is this how GOD would have us run them? Look at our political system and the partisan politicians and corruption, and negative ego spinning. Is this how GOD would have us run things! Almost every institution on the planet is run from the personality and negative ego, and not from the soul and Spirits perspective! We are here to fix all this! An enormous number of lightworkers are not fulfilling their responsibilities and are not focusing on what they need to be focused upon. Massive numbers of lightworkers are focused on their own Spiritual growth and are not focused on the service work that they Spiritually contracted to do! Massive numbers of lightworkers have their head in the clouds and are too ungrounded! Massive numbers of lightworkers are too much in their mental bodies and focusing too much on esoteric knowledge, and are not fulfilling their Earthly/Spiritual responsibilities of Service work. A great many lightworkers are too much in their emotional body and not focusing on the Earth and loving the Earth and Earthly civilization! If we do not Master the Earth, Love the Earth and Earth life, be happy living on the Earth, and take responsibility for the Earth, we will not achieve full God Realization. If we do not fulfill our Spiritual mission, purpose and puzzle piece "on the Earth," we will not achieve God Realization! Framing it in this way is what lightworkers need to hear and understand because it is the truth, and something not that many Spiritual Leaders and Teachers are talking about!

So, the first step is that we master the Earth and Earth energies within our own being. Then we must always love the Earth, Earth energies, and Earthly Life! Then we must take responsibility, fulfill our Spiritual mission, purpose, and puzzle piece on Earth! This is an indisputable Spiritual Lesson every lightworker must fulfill if they wish to achieve God Realization! The time of living in a Spiritual world and not being part of Earth and the Material Universe is over. The time of being ungrounded and not fully loving and appreciating the Earth and Earth life is over! The return of the Goddess has finally come! It is time for lightworkers now to get their acts together. Lightworkers are the caretakers for Mother Earth and Earthly Civilization. Our civilization is still backwards in a great many ways! If lightworkers do not fix it, who is going to fix it? It is our responsibility! To just focus on one's own Spiritual Growth is selfish! It is time to call a spade a spade! We each have a Spiritual responsibility of making changes in this world and making changes in this society. For some it will be through Politics, others through Spiritual Education, others through Active Service in the world, others through the Arts, others through the Sciences, others through Religion, and others through Business, Economics and changing the institutions of our civilization! It does not matter what you chose to do or how you do it, what is important is you are doing something!

I am not saying there is not a phase where it is important to work on oneself for there is. This is a crucial phase. However, at some point it is necessary to be of service. At some point it is necessary to do service work and make some contribution and give back to the people of the Earth, the Earth herself and the Civilization we were brought up in. At some point, it is necessary to help others! If we truly have unconditional love and compassion how can we sit around and focus only on our own Spiritual Growth when people all over the world are suffering Spiritually, mentally, emotionally and in an Earthly sense! The Mother Earth has been enormously abused! If we are truly God's and everything is all part of us, how can we not want to get our hands dirty and help! How can we not dedicate our lives to service!

How can you love the Divine Mother and Goddess energies without loving Mother Earth, the people of the Earth, and the Civilization of the Earth and want to help contribute to heal it!

So, it is essential to master all aspects of Earthly life. It is as important to learn to master all aspects of Earthly life as it is to master all aspects of one's Spiritual Life, Mental Life and Emotional Life! All Four Faces of GOD must be mastered! Then we must fully unconditionally Love the Material Universe, the Mother Earth and Earthly civilization! The Mastery is the First Ray influence in relationship to the Material universe! The Second Ray influence is the need to Unconditionally Love every aspect of Earth life! Out of these first two Rays then comes the Third which is Active Intelligence, which takes the Power and unconditional love, and grounds the power and love into the Earth in the form of active physical service. One of the reasons that a great many lightworkers are not mastering Earth energies and are not taking responsibility for the Earth, is they are not balanced in the Seven Rays. They are weak in Third Ray energy. For example a lot of Second Ray souls or Monads have all this Love and Wisdom, but it never makes it to the Third Ray where it is grounded into the Earth in the form of active physical service! This is what the Third Ray is about, grounding Spiritual Energy physically into the world in the form of active physical service! In a lightworker who is primarily Second Ray, the Spiritual energy floats above the Earthly Plane but never gets grounded! It is time for lightworkers to really wake up on this point. Another reason such an unbelievable number of lightworkers have difficulty grounding their Spiritual missions is that they are not only weak in the Third Ray of Active Intelligence, they are weak in their First Ray as well! They have not been trained how to fully own their 100% Personal Power at all times! This inability to own your Personal Power will, of course, make you completely unable to master Earth Energies or any other type of energies for that matter. It will make you a victim of your mind, feelings, emotions, physical body and Earth life, while it will also cause you to be ungrounded and floating all the time! Life will push the person around instead the person mastering life and they will of course be unsuccessful! Many who are strong in the Fourth Ray have a physical connection though the Arts and usually appreciate the Beauty of the Earth, but most souls usually incarnate with a ray configuration of 2/4/6 or 1/3/5. The 2/4/6 pattern makes one more emotional and if the person is heavy in the Fourth Ray we have the classic starving artist type; who has enormous creative energies but cannot fully master Earth life. If they don't have third ray, which most don't, then the business side of life will be very weak. This is very common in artist types. So, we have the inability to master Earth energies. If a person has too much First Ray, they may be able to master Earth energies but not enough 2/4/6 to fully love the Earth! The predominately Second Ray type may have the ability to love the Earth, but can't master it from lack of Personal Power and Mastery of the First Ray, and can't ground their Spiritual Energy because of lack of Third Ray! The emphasis upon the Fifth Ray has the scientific mind to master

Earth life and maybe take some responsibility for it; however, may not have enough 2/4/6 to fully love it and appreciates its beauty! Six Ray is very devotional and idealistic. When this predominates and continues in the 2/4/6 pattern, mastery of Earth Energies will be extremely weak. Business and grounding of Earth Energies will be very weak, and grounding of one's Spiritual mission may be very weak because of lack of first ray, third ray, and fifth ray! When Seventh Ray predominates, it could bring mastery and responsibility for Earth; however, danger of lack of love from the strong influence of Divine structure and order!

I would subtitle this last section as "The Lack of Integration of the Seven Rays and its Effect on One's Relationship to the Earth and Earth Life!" The Rays are not the only thing that is causing lightworkers to not Master, Love, and take Responsibility for the Earth. It is also their Psychologies and Philosophies. It is their Spiritual Training as well!

My Beloved Readers, you will not become a full Melchizedek, Christ, or Buddha if you do not Master, Love, and take responsibility for the Earth and Earth life! It is as important to take care of a person's physical needs as it is to take care of their Spiritual needs, mental needs, and emotional needs! In truth, even more important. If a person is physically ill, it is hard to focus on Spiritual growth! If a child or person is starving and malnourished, it is hard to focus on Spiritual concerns. If a person is homeless, it is hard to focus on Spiritual Concerns. If a person is living on survival mode, it is hard to focus on Spiritual Concerns. If a person has no money, it is hard to focus on Spiritual concerns when they can't pay their rent, buy food, take care of their family, and get medication if they need it! My Beloved Friends, how is this world ever going to change if we each don't master Earth Energies, totally and completely love every aspect of the Earth, and physically take action to heal it! GOD and the Masters aren't going to do it. They can't, they don't have physical bodies! Don't you see, that is why we are here! We are instruments and channels of GOD and the Masters to make changes in this Earthly world. GOD's Divine Plan is to make this world function here, as does civilization in the higher worlds! This world is not just here as a Spiritual School to achieve Ascension and then we leave! GOD wants this world to have a fifth dimensional civilization! This is what creating Heaven on Earth really means! The Purpose of Life is to achieve Integrated Ascension and then remain on Earth and turn this world and its Civilization into the Seventh Golden Age on Earth! It is not the easiest job; however, it is what we have volunteered to come to do. So this chapter is a clarion call from Spirit and the Masters to achieve Integrated Ascension; and in the process of doing so to begin focusing more on service work and on fully grounding your Spiritual Mission and puzzle piece, and doing your part to bring the Seventh Golden Age onto this physical/Earthly Plane! This chapter is a clarion call for lightworkers to now get their priorities in order, and to fully master the Earth and Earth energies, to fully unconditionally love the Earth and Earth life on every level, and to take responsibility for doing your part to heal Mother Earth and help build the New Jerusalem on Earth!

So let it be Written! So let it be Done!

40

What Does Spiritually Mastering the Earth and Earth Energies Really Mean?

Again, it must be remembered that to achieve God Realization you must become a Spiritual Master on all three levels. These three levels are the Spiritual Level, the Psychological Level, and the Physical/Earthly Level! These are the three levels of God Realization that must be mastered, integrated, and balanced to achieve full God Realization. I have spoken extensively in this book and my others books about Spiritual, mental, emotional, and energetic mastery.

Spiritually mastering the Earth and Earth energies is just like Spiritual mastery, mental mastery, emotional mastery, and energy mastery; however, this is mastery in regard to the mastery of the Physical Body, Earthly Energies, and Earthly Life! The best way to describe this to give examples! To begin with, this deals with mastering the physical body: learning to physically eat right, taking care of physical fitness, developing good sleep habits, mastering the understanding of your body rhythms and learning to work with them. Mastering you sexuality and not being run by lower-self desire, yet integrating your sexuality in a Spiritually balanced way! Mastery of Earth energies deals with mastering money and developing prosperity consciousness and not poverty consciousness. Spiritual Mastery of Earth energies deals with staying organized in your Earthly life and having proper time management, Spiritual, and Earthly structure, and prioritizing your goals and projects.

Mastering Earth Energies deals with getting all the work done you need to do, getting your errands done, taxes done, accounting, bookkeeping, banking, grocery shopping and so on! Keeping up with returning phone calls, letters, e-mail, and correspondence! Being successful in your business! It has to do with keeping your house and office clean and organized! Taking care of your home and garden! Taking proper care of your animals! It means beautifying your home and environment. Paying attention to aesthetics. It means proper grooming, and paying attention to the clothes and colors of the clothing that you wear! It means pursuing excellence in every aspect of Earth life just as you pursue excellence in your Spiritual life and Psychological life! You want to strive to be Spiritually immaculate on all levels!

Earthly mastery means learning to be grounded. I have dedicated an entire chapter to this in this book; for it is a Spiritual Practice that many lightworkers have lost sight of, or have forgotten how to do and what the mechanics of staying grounded really are! Earthly mastery means flossing your teeth and taking care of your gums and all aspects of your physical body that need maintenance. It means going to the dentist or to doctors when needed, and not looking at the care of the body as being of lesser importance than that of your Spiritual, mental, emotional, or etheric bodies! It also means taking your car in for maintenance, doing maintenance on your computer, printer, and any other machines you have! It means taking proper care and sanctifying Matter as an aspect of GOD! It means doing the dishes as a Spiritual devotional practice instead of seeing it as drudgery. Since the Material Universe is a Face of GOD, it means all dealings with matter are a Holy Encounter as well! To beautify and clean matter is to polish the Diamond that is GOD! It is to look at your physical body as a temple of God! It is to look at your home as a temple of God as well! It is to create shrines and altars in your home. It is possibly the practice of feng shui, or the art of Spiritual design and balance in your home! In our home we have Spiritual Statues, Pictures, Gemstones, and Spiritual objects adorning the grounds both outside and inside!

Physical/Earthly Mastery means taking care of one's Physical/Earthly needs, not just Spiritual, mental, emotional and energy needs! When you have guests, making sure they are comfortable and have something to drink and eat is an example of taking care of Physical/Earthly needs! Making sure the inside temperature is pleasing is another example! It is possibly giving money to charities, or tithing. It is paying attention to politics and all the social issues concerning the Earth, and raising consciousness and contributing to their healing through physical actions or inner plane Spiritual work such as prayer! It means voting in your elections! A great many lightworkers' information banks are filled with Spiritual knowledge and some with Psychological knowledge; however, some are very weak in Earthly knowledge! Earthly knowledge is important as well. What if a person did not know how to read, write, speak or spell, or know any arithmetic? This would be a great disadvantage in your Spiritual mission. There are a lot of other forms of Earthly knowledge that are similar. Watching the news and/or reading the newspaper and keeping up with Earthly current events! You want to be Spiritually knowledgeable, psychologically knowledgeable, knowledgeable of your physical body, and knowledgeable of Earthly life!

Other aspects of Earthly mastery are: remembering birthdays and anniversaries, meeting family obligations, keeping up with friendships, paying your bills, making sure your car has gasoline and oil, vacuuming the house, watering the plants, dusting, sweeping, putting food in the bird feeder, etc! My Beloved Readers, these are all Spiritual practices to the sanctification and Glory of GOD! They are just as important as meditating, praying, saying affirmations, visualizations, or any other Spiritual and Psychological practice! Do you see the attitudinal shift Spirit and the Masters are asking you to make! See all these things as "holy acts of God and Spiritual practices"! Whether you choose to look at them this way or not, this is what they are! They are literally Spiritual practices! By doing so your are honoring and sanctifying the Material Face of GOD! What can be more holy or more beautiful? When life is looked at from this manner then everything you do is a "holy act and Spiritual Practice and exercise"! Lightworkers have commonly spoken of this as being Zen-like. I do not practice Zen; however, the idea is to live in the now and give your full attention to whatever you are doing! So if you are washing the dishes then stay in the now! Spirit and the Masters are adding to this concept to do all physical acts on Earth as a Spiritual Practice and as a Devotion or Sanctification to GOD! When you are Mastering and taking care of the Physical/Earthly things you are mastering and taking care of literally one-third of what GOD really is! The Spiritual aspect is one-third, the Psychological is one-third, and the Physical/Earthly is one-third of GOD! Living life in such a manner makes every Earthly thing you do become a Spiritual practice and form of Sanctification, honoring, and caring for the Material Face of GOD!

When you live this way, everything you do then Spiritually, Mentally, Emotionally, Energetically, and in a Physical/Earthly sense becomes a Spiritual practice and form of Spiritual Service! Seeing the Material Face of GOD and mastering it will give you a much greater sense of self and being a Spiritual Master! To be a Spiritual Master on all three levels; Spiritually, Psychologically and Physical/Earthly, in a balanced and integrated manner, will give you a tremendous sense of love and appreciation for GOD! You will literally see GOD in everything you do! There will no separation between levels! Literally every action you take in life will be a Spiritual Practice, a Sanctification and Act of Service! Is this not a most wonderful way to live? No level will be seen as better then any other. All four Faces of GOD: Spiritual, Mental, Emotional, and Material, will be honored. All you will see is GOD in everything you do. You will be paying your rent to GOD on all levels. Spiritual practices will not be seen as better then Psychological practices or Physical/Earthly practices. Don't you see, my Beloved Readers, that they are all the same! They all are equally important! They are all GOD! People and lightworkers have fallen into the trap of thinking that one level is better or more important than another! Some think Spiritual energies are better. Some favor Psychological energies over Spiritual energies. Some are too Materialistic! Some are more Spiritual and Psychologically focused! Some are more Psychologically and Materially focused! Some are more Spiritually and Materially focused and disown the Psychological! Don't you see, my Beloved Readers, this is all faulty thinking and fragmentation! How can one Face of GOD be better than another? Do not let the negative ego mind confuse you or fragment you in such a way. It is all one, and each Face of GOD must be honored equally! To not do so would be as absurd as saying one of our bodies is better than another. All four bodies must be balanced! We have a Spiritual body, mental body, emotional body, and physical body! If you do not integrate, balance, and honor all four bodies equally you will have disease and discomfort, for you will be defying the Laws of GOD. You will get an immediate lesson pointing this out to you! The same is true of the Four Faces of GOD. If you do not honor all Four levels equally the level you disown will hound you! You will be given intuitions, signs, signals, dreams, and clues. If you don't pay attention, you will start being given karmic lessons! Spirit and the Masters are giving you the opportunity here in reading this chapter to learn by grace and not karma! Honor and Sanctify all Four Faces of GOD, and this includes, of course, the Physical/Earthly level! The negative ego tells you that focusing on the Physical/Earthly level will take you away from GOD! This is only true if you overidentify with it and let it become a form of "Materialism"! Lightworkers have gone to the other extreme and have "thrown the baby out with the bath water"! They have rejected and disowned the Material Face of GOD, and then abused Mother Earth and defiled the Goddess energies! It is now time for the Divine Mother, the Goddess energies, and Mother Earth to be properly honored and cared for as well! I am sure all of you, my Beloved Readers, agree!

Part of Mastering the Earth and Earth Energies means anchoring your Spiritual Mission on the Earth and not just talking about it, not just thinking about it, not just visualizing it, not just getting excited about it, and not just meditating and praying about it! "Hands that help are holier than lips that pray"! As of the year 2000, it is time to manifest on the physical. All this other stuff is fine, but it is time to deliver on the physical! Just manifesting on the Spiritual Plane and the Mental and Emotional Plane does not cut it any more! It is time to integrate all Seven Rays, not stay stuck in just a few of them. It is time to master money, master business, and master Spiritual leadership! It is time to fully own your First Ray and Personal Power 100% so you can do what you need to do on the Physical/Earthly Plane! It is time to master the Third Ray so you can take physical action in the physical world. It is time to own your Fourth Ray so you can beautify the physical world in Honor and Sanctification of GOD! It is time to integrate your Fifth Ray so you can make all these changes in your Physical world, scientifically and logically! It is time to own and fully integrate the Seventh Ray so you can put the Spiritual, Psychological, and Physical/Earthly structures into place in the Physical/Earthly world. It is time to make the changes that need to take place in our Earthly Civilization to create the Spiritual, Psychological, and Earthly Freedom that we are all striving for as a society!

Part of Mastering Earth Energies is embracing your Puzzle Piece in GOD's Divine Plane and manifesting it on the Earth. It is now time to do your Service work. It does not matter what it is, but it is time to do it. Do not wait for GOD to conk you over your head with a hammer and tell you what it is. Start doing something! Life is a co-creation and it is not just Spirit and the Masters' job to tell you what to do. It is also your job to tell yourself what to do with the incredibly creative God mind you have been given! GOD helps those who help themselves! It is time to fully anchor and integrate your Seven Levels of Initiation into all your bodies including your physical body! It is now time to physically ground your Ascension! It is now time to fully Ground your Mighty I

Am Presence on Earth! It is now time to become an Integrated Ascended Master on Earth! It is time to pay attention to physical details and not let them slip by so easily as if they are not so important!

It is time to express your love physically, not just mentally, emotionally or Spiritually! This may mean buying flowers or sweet gifts for your Spouse or friends! This may mean expressing love through hugs and physical touch! This means loving your physical body in all ways and caring for it properly. It may mean not throwing trash on the ground, and picking up trash to keep GOD's body clean! It means giving love to animals, plants, and the mineral kingdom, and caring for our younger animal, plant and mineral Brothers and Sisters! It means honoring, respecting, loving, and integrating Pan, the nature spirits, and the plant devas, and inviting them back into our gardens, farms, forests and the Earth!

Mastering the Earth and Earth Energies means conservation and ecology practices! It means being aware of not ingesting into the physical, chemicals, pollution, heavy metals, and toxic substances. It means not using recreational drugs! It means cutting back on medical drugs and using more homeopathics and herbs. It means learning more about holistic health, naturopathy, homeopathy, herbal medicine, and the many forms of health and healing practices.

Earthly mastery means becoming aware of all the political and social causes, and helping to raise consciousness, send money, or physically help. It means possibly writing letters to your congressman, participating in marches, political and social action, or inner plane Spiritual Activism! It means doing everything you can, every moment of your life, that is within your power to make this world a better place for our children. It means praying not just for yourself, but for all the Political and Social Causes! This means educating yourself on all these issues. I would humbly suggest reading my book *Manual for Planetary Leadership*, which gives the Spiritual Hierarchy's views on a great many of the political and social issues of our time. It is fascinating reading and totally debunks this myth that Spirit and the Masters are not 100% involved with every aspect of Earth Life! The main purpose of the inner plane Spiritual Government and inner plane Ascended Masters is to create Heaven on Earth! We are GOD's mouth, hands, and feet to make this happen. Always recognize, however, that Life is a co-creation and that it is not just GOD and the Masters working through us, but it is also us with our own personal power, will and creativity with our free choice doing our part as well! It is the sparking of our full 100% personal power, unconditional love, and active intelligence; grounding our personal power and love on Earth in conjunction with GOD, Christ, the Holy Spirit, our Mighty I Am Presence, the Higher Self, and the inner plane Ascended Masters, Angels, Elohim and Christed Extraterrestrials overlighting and guiding us in this process; and using all the love, wisdom and power at their disposal as well that really makes things happen! It is the full co-creation of both. Enormous numbers of lightworkers are waiting for GOD, Spirit, the Masters, or Angels to do it for them! This will never happen! You must help yourself! The responsibility is yours. As you own your full 100% personal power, unconditional love, active intelligence, and the rest of your Seven Rays at the 100% level; and move into Earth life as best you know how, GOD and the Masters will overlight the process and help to guide you! When you run into roadblocks or obstacles, immediately pray for GOD and the Masters help and it will be forthcoming! As the Universal Mind through Edgar Cayce said, "Why worry when you can pray"! Therefore, it is now time, my Beloved Brothers and Sisters, to "Be about the Fathers business on Earth"! My Beloved Brothers and Sisters, it is also time to "Be about the Divine Mother's and Goddess' business on Earth"! No more procrastinating, no more being lazy, no more not owning your full 100% personal power, no more not 100% loving the Earth and Earthly life and honoring and sanctifying the Earth Face of GOD! No more disowning the Third Ray of Active Physical Action and Service on Earth! No more waiting for God to tell you what to do! Think of something and just start doing it! If you need to change forms of service then do so! No more living in a cave! No more living in a monastery! No more living on a mountaintop! Those phases of your life were 100% appropriate and honorable! It is now time to physically ground your Ascension and your Spirituality! It is now time to integrate the horizontal plane of life, not just the vertical plane of life! It is now time to become balanced in the God/Goddess energies! It is now time to give back to the Mother Earth as she has so graciously given to you! It is now time to give the Divine Mother the honor, respect and love she so richly deserves! It is now time to live in the marketplace as the Master Jesus did! It is now time to enter Earth life fully! It is now time to Demonstrate your Divinity, not just on the Spiritual Plane, or the Mental Plane, or the Emotional Plane, but on the Physical/Earthly Plane! It is now time to fully Practice the Presence of God on Earth! It is now time to Be God on Earth! It is now time to Be Melchizedek on the Earth! It is now time to Be Christ on Earth! It is now time to Be the Buddha on Earth! It is now time to Be the Eternal Self on Earth! It is now time to cure AIDS, cure cancer, save the whales, save the rain forest, repair the ozone layer, stop all polluting and abusing of the Earth, return the Earth back to its Edenic State, stop all war on Earth, create a lasting peace in the Middle East, stop all partisan politics, unify all religions, revamp and Spiritualize the prison system, bring the Soul and Spirit in a universal way back into the educational system, have food for everyone, stop homelessness, provide proper health care for everyone, stop gang violence, provide better care for the aged, stop child abuse, stop abuse of animals, stop spousal abuse, stop all crime, stop all disease, help and honor the veterans, properly dispose of nuclear waste, end terrorism, bring the knowledge of the Extraterrestrials to the Earth, stop all drug abuse and alcoholism, clean up all pollution and develop new non-polluting energy sources, to name a few!

My Beloved Readers, this is just the tip of the iceberg of some of the changes that need to be made in our world! It is now time we each take on the "Earthly Mantle of Christ" that we Spiritually contracted to do before we came; and work arm and arm, shoulder to shoulder, and Heart to Heart, to turn our civilization into the Seventh Golden Age, the New Jerusalem, the thriving City and World of GOD that is its destiny to become! It is time for the cities and countries of Light to be anchored and physically manifested and demonstrated on Earth and around the world. It is now time to fully understand and welcome the Christed Extraterrestrials to the Earth, for they will be of invaluable help in making a lot of these changes. No need to reinvent the wheel when other Christed Races have solved a great many of these issues thousands of years ago. This has already begun to happen and will happen openly very soon. So, my Beloved Readers, do not feel burdened by the job at hand!

GOD, Christ, the Holy Spirit, our Mighty I Am Presence, our Higher Self, the inner plane Ascended Masters, the Archangels and Angels, Elohim Councils, and the Christed Extraterrestrials will help every step of the way. Allah Gobi and El Morya are helping on the Political Front from the First Ray Ashram of the Christ. Melchizedek, the Lord of Sirius, Lord Maitreya, Master Kuthumi, and the Ascended Master Djwhal Khul are helping with Spiritual Education for the planet from their inner plane Planetary and Cosmic Second Ray Ashrams! Master Serapis Bey is helping in the area of active physical service and business issues on Earth from his Third Ray inner plane ashram! Master Paul the Venetian is helping with Spiritualizing the Arts on Earth through his Fourth Ray inner plane ashram! Master Hilarion is helping with bringing forth all the New Age Sciences to the Earth from his Fifth Ray inner plane ashram! Sananda is helping integrate and reform the world's religions from his Sixth Ray inner plane ashram! Saint Germain and Lady Portia are spearheading the reform of our civilization and all its institutions from the inner plane Seventh Ray ashram! Lord Buddha, as our Planetary Logos, is holding the Divine Blueprint Vision in his mind's eye for all the changes that are to come on the Earth as the

Spiritual President of this Planet at this time, while simultaneously being overlighted by Sanat Kumara!

The Archangels and Angels are working overtime to now restore the Divine Plan on Earth in every aspect of Earth life! By the Grace of GOD, the Archangels and Angels are here in force!

The Christed Extraterrestrials, such as the Arcturians and the Ashtar Command, are also here in force protecting this planet, and help to bring new light technologies to the Earth. There are many other Christed Extraterrestrial Races who are circling our planet and who will soon be more fully revealing themselves to the Earth! The Love, Information, and Knowledge they will bring will accelerate our world at an unimaginable speed. Our civilization will advance more from the years 1980 to the year 2025 then it did in the last 3.1 billion years!

So my Beloved Readers, do not feel burdened, for the amount of Spiritual, Psychological, and Physical/Earthly/Technological/Scientific help in every aspect of Earth life will be absolutely staggering! This planet, however, is *our* home! We are its Spiritual Leaders! We are its caretakers! We are the light bearers for the New Age to bring in this New Heaven and New Earth. We are, my Beloved Readers, the Externalization of the Hierarchy!

It is time for all Earthlings to step forward in Spiritual Leadership and Planetary World Service! It is time to now 100% fully claim your love, wisdom, power, Spiritual leadership, Planetary World Service, and physically master, unconditionally love, anchor, and ground your Spiritual mission and puzzle piece on Earth! It is now time to fully become a Spiritual Master, a Psychological Master, and Physical/Earthly Master in an integrated and balanced manner! It is now time to 100% Demonstrate GOD on Earth and 100% rebuild the civilization of GOD on Earth, and fully own our reason and destiny for physically incarnating into physical bodies and into this world! The clarion call now goes forth from Spirit and the Cosmic and Planetary Hierarchy to mobilize their energies, and fully now manifest and demonstrate the Spiritual service mission and purpose for coming on Earth now at this momentous time in Earth's history! GOD, the Masters, the Archangels and Angels, the Elohim Councils and Christed Extraterrestrials are now gathering the Sons and Daughters of GOD on Earth to make the final big push to transform this Earthly World and Civilization into the "Shining diamond and clear bright star" it is meant to become!

So let it be Written! So let it be Done!

41

The Importance of Loving and Enjoying the Earth and Earth Life!

My Beloved Readers, one of the most important lessons of the Spiritual path is learning to love the Earth and Earth life! As we have already talked about in this book, Matter is one of the Four Faces of GOD! Matter is literally the Temple of GOD! The Earth is part of GOD's material Universe! The Earth is like a molecule in the Physical Body of GOD! To not love the Earth is to not love GOD, for the Earth is part of GOD! The Earth as you all know is a living being! This is "Mother Earth"! Mother Earth has been greatly unloved and abused in the history of this planet! Her essence or Spirit has been abused and her physical body has been abused! This has been part of the defilement of the Divine Mother and the Goddess energies on Earth by a patriarchal negative ego-run history! This is now changing! We have finally reached a point in history where is it is time for the return of the Divine Mother and the Goddess energies to their rightful place! This balance is imperative for the Seventh Golden Age to be realized! So when I say love the Earth and Earth life, I am not just talking about Mother Earth, nature, Pan, the Nature Spirits, Plant Devas, Mineral Kingdom, Plant Kingdom, Animal Kingdom and so on. Yes, this is all part of loving the material Face of GOD and loving the Earth! These are, in truth, our Brothers and Sisters. Jesus said the whole law could be summed up as "Love the Lord thy

GOD with all your heart and soul and mind and might and love your neighbor as you love yourself"! Your neighbor is also your animal, plant, mineral, nature spirits, plant devas, trees, rocks, elements of nature, elementals, and so on. These are our younger brothers and sisters who are in our care, who we have not always cared for as we should in our planet's history! These beings are incarnations of GOD! This is a fact! To not 100% love all of them in physical and etheric form is to not love GOD, for they are God!

Now we need to take this issue of loving the Earth and Earth Life one step further! This means loving Earth life itself! Now lightworkers, of course, commonly think of Earth as unimportant, a prison, just a means to achieve liberation. They think only Heaven and the Celestial realms are important. This is completely untrue. The Earth is one of the Seven Heavens of GOD as I have already said in this book! The Material Universe is literally a heaven. Everyone wants to get to heaven, and I tell you we are already in one of GOD's Heavens! The outer world is really just a reflection of the inner world. The inner worlds actually look a lot like the outer world except more refined! There are a great many things on Earth which one cannot experience in Heaven. Eating food is quite an interesting experience. Making love is quite an interesting experience! The five physical senses are quite an interesting experience! Nature is quite an amazing experience! The experience of living in a physical body and experiencing Earth life is quite an interesting experience! Enjoy it while you can for once you achieve liberation you may never ever experience this again! There are enormous numbers of souls on the inner plane who are quite fascinated with the Material Universe and the opportunity to experience GOD through a physical body! This is also a most amazing time to be incarnated! Maybe one of the most amazing times in the history of the Earth! Souls are literally lining up trying to get into a body for the potential for Spiritual growth and evolution is greater at this time than maybe ever in the history of the Earth!

This issue of loving Earth, I would now like to take one step deeper, which is the importance of loving your physical body! You physical body is part of GOD as well! It is your temple! It is made of the substance of GOD! It is Divine! Honor it and sanctify it! There is an intelligence within the physical body called the body elemental! Honor and try to communicate with it. Many do this using a pendulum! To not love your physical body is to not love GOD, for all matter is made up of GOD!

Now let's take this discussion one step deeper. It is not enough to just love all that I have said so far to achieve God Realization, you must also love Earth life itself. Again, a great many people do not think that Earth life is important. They think it is a lower level, or just again a means to achieve liberation. They see no value in trying to reorganize, restructure and rebuild our earthly society and world! This, my Beloved Readers, is "Faulty thinking"! This is the negative ego sabotaging that person. GOD's Divine plan is to create "Heaven on Earth!" GOD wants this Earthly Civilization to become a utopian society! He wants it to become a fifth dimensional society! The purpose of life is not, I repeat, is *not* to just achieve liberation and ascension and leave and say, "who cares about the Earth and Earth life, good riddance!" This is not loving GOD! Earth Life is a part of GOD, my Beloved Readers! You will not achieve God Realization in the fullest sense of the term if you do not learn to enjoy life on Earth and fully take responsibility for and love Earth life! GOD's Divine Plan is not that we just love the heavenly realms and look at the Earth and Earth life as some lower class citizen! It is all one! GOD wants all Seven Heavens to fully reflect His Glory! Remember what I have said about the importance of "consistency and integration"? GOD wants His Glory to reflect on all seven levels, not just the first six heavens and leave the bottom one as a garbage dump! The Divine Plan is to reflect GOD's full glory on the earthly plane! Are not the pyramids on Earth a glorious thing? Is not the Taj Mahal a glorious building that truly reflects the profundity that is GOD? Are not the Sacred Sites of the world glorious places? GOD wishes every aspect of Earth life to fully reflect His Glory! So GOD does not want people to just ascend and see Earth as just a lower class world to be used as a means to an end and then discarded like a piece of trash! This is GOD's Body we are talking about! Is not the Sistine Chapel a fitting Tabernacle of GOD? GOD wishes the entire world to be a Sistine Chapel! GOD wants all his Glory to be outpictured in and on the Earth in every aspect and in all rays and ray functions! GOD wants a God Civilization on the Earth!

Mother Earth, who is a living being, is taking her initiations as well! Her mission and purpose will not be complete unless this takes place! The Planetary Logos or President of this Planet is now Lord Buddha! His aura literally embodies this planet! His Spiritual mission will not be complete until this takes place. What are we wanting to take place, you ask? What we want to take place is the Seventh Golden Age on this planet! What we want to take place is the return of this world to the "Edenic State" that it was in the time of Lemuria before separation occurred!

We all know that when we go camping it is always important to make our campsite more beautiful when we leave than when we arrived! My Beloved Readers, it is time the six billion souls on Earth return the Earth back to its pristine state! It is time to rid the Earth of all pollution! It is time to give back to Mother Earth who has cared for and nurtured us! The whole purpose of the Spiritual Government on this planet and all the Ascended Masters and Planetary Hierarchy and Seven Ashrams of the Christ is to bring the Earth back to this Edenic State on all levels in terms of how our society operates. The First Ray Department is in charge of getting the governments and politics of the world back to operating on a Spiritual wavelength! The Second Ray Department is in charge of getting all the people of the Earth spiritually educated, psychologically and Physical/Earthly educated, integrated and balanced and to have right relationships with each and all aspects of Earth life. The Third Ray Department is in charge of getting all the business and economics of the world operating from a God Perspective. The Fourth

Ray Department is getting all the arts, music, architecture, plays, and dance to attune and reflect the profundity and beauty of GOD! The Fourth Ray Department is also for beautifying the Earth! The Fifth Ray Department is to bring all the New Age Sciences to the Earth to solve all the Earth's problems. The Sixth Ray Department is to unify all religions and cleanse them from the contamination of negative ego thinking! The Seventh Ray Department is in charge of completely reorganizing and restructuring civilization from a personality based negative ego-run society to a society based on Soul and Spiritual principles in every aspect of civilization!

My Beloved Readers, the purpose of life is not just to achieve Spiritual Growth! It is to achieve Spiritual Growth and fulfill your Spiritual Mission and Purpose. Every person on Earth, every single one, works out of one of these seven ray departments! Every person has a Spiritual Assignment and a puzzle piece to fulfill in GOD's Plan to create Heaven on Earth! I think you all can see this quite clearly now! Taking care of the rainforest, planting trees, helping the homeless, stopping drug addiction, stopping child abuse, cleaning the environment, stopping animal cruelty, repairing the ozone layer, stopping the greenhouse effect saving the whales, restructuring and reordering society, are as important Spiritual practices as meditation, prayer, channeling, and chanting the names of GOD! In fact, they are even more important for this is why you have come! You are not here to be obsessed with your initiation level! You are here to unconditionally love and serve all Kingdoms of GOD! People and lightworkers thought it was enough just to be loving to their Brothers and Sisters! This is the wake-up call of the Divine Mother and the Goddess energies and the Material Face of GOD! It is not enough! To achieve full God Realization you must serve all of GOD, not just part of GOD! GOD is in all Kingdoms and in the Material Universe and in earthly life, society, and civilization. It is time to see and serve all of GOD, not just a part of GOD! I have it on good authority that Jesus' New Commandment is "Love the Lord thy GOD with all your heart and soul and mind and might and love your neighbor as you love yourself, and love the Material Face of GOD, all your younger brothers and sisters, love Mother Earth, Pan and all the nature spirits and plant devas, love your physical body, love nature, unconditionally love Earth life and fulfill your Spiritual mission, purpose and Divine puzzle piece and create Heaven on Earth in every aspect of earthly civilization and society! My Beloved Readers, I have it on good authority that this is Master Jesus' new commandment for the Aquarian Age and this next 2000 year cycle! This is also the new commandment of the Divine Mother and the Goddess energies to bring balance and harmony back to the Earth and to bring in the proper God/Goddess balance back to the Earth and the Seventh Golden Age!

People think they have been realizing GOD just focusing on the heavenly realms! With no judgment intended, they have blind spots to GOD! If you think GOD is glorious in the heavenly realms, wait until you see the glory of GOD in the psychological realms and in the physical/earthly realms! To be perfectly honest, most lightworkers only know a third of GOD! They are highly developed on the Spiritual level but they are not fully trained in Spiritual psychology and do not fully appreciate the absolute profundity of GOD on the physical/earthly/material level! If you think you have known the ecstasy of GOD on the Spiritual level, wait until your experience the ecstasy of GOD on the psychological and physical/earthly/material plane as well! These make up the Four Faces of GOD! The Spiritual, mental, emotional and material. The mental and emotional making up the psychological aspect of GOD! For those who want to realize the psychological level of GOD in all its Glory, read my books *Soul Psychology* and *How To Release Fear-Based Thinking and Feeling: An In-depth Study of Spiritual Psychology*! This chapter is another key to help you adjust your consciousness and perspective to fully love the material, earthly, physical and earthly life aspect of GOD!

Getting back to earthly life and society for a moment. This is why Sai Baba has said, "Hands that help are holier then lips that pray!" This is a very profound statement! Is God Realization only demonstrating God on the Spiritual plane? Is this consistency and integration of all levels of God and your own four-body system Spiritual, mental, emotional and physical? Is this paying your rent to GOD on all levels? Your physical body is as Divine as is your mental body, emotional body and Spiritual body! Until you see this you are blinded to understanding the full Glory of GOD! Do you know who fully taught me this? This is going to surprise my readers! The Mahatma! The Mahatma helped me to fully understand and appreciate the full Glory of GOD on the physical/earthly level! The Mahatma is a group consciousness being of all 352 levels of GOD! There is no higher Cosmic Energy coming to the Earth than the Mahatma!

Beloved Readers, it is just as important that when you have company that your company's physical needs are met, as well as their Spiritual, mental or emotional needs! Maybe even more important! If people on the Earth are starving or homeless and on survival how are they supposed to focus on GOD! The Masters have told me that no person on Earth will achieve full God Realization and Integrated Ascension unless they fully enjoy Earth life and fully love the Earth and Earth life! When you do physical things, do it as a sanctification of GOD! If you wash the floors, you are washing GOD's body! How would you treat your Spiritual Teacher or Guru if they came to visit? What if they were dirty from a long trip and big storm. How would you care for their physical needs? Do the same for GOD! For the Material Universe is GOD's Body! When you honor, sanctify and love the Material Universe, you honor, love and sanctify GOD! If you go to church or temple would you want to go to a church or temple that is filthy dirty? Do you want a physical body filled with toxins that is sick all the time? How about Mother Earth's Body or GOD's Material Body! When we dump toxic wastes and pollute the Earth, air, and water we are polluting GOD's Body! We are polluting Mother Earth's Body! The same is true in regard to civilization! Civilization is a part of GOD! Everything is a part of GOD! When we don't care for our earthly civilization and let it be run by the personality and negative ego, it is like the surface life of GOD's body has skin cancer! Is this the proper way to honor and sanctify GOD!

We have incarnated into the world not only to achieve liberation and ascension but also to be and demonstrate God on Earth! GOD does not want us to ascend and leave, it wants us to ascend and remain on Earth and demonstrate God on Earth! As I said in a previous chapter, to just ascend and not give anything back to GOD on all levels is selfish! It is not fulfilling the Spiritual Mission, Purpose, and Puzzle Piece you came to fulfill! You came to create Heaven on Earth! You came to be God on Earth! You came to reorder and restructure Earthly life, civilization, and society in the area of expertise you have in one of the seven Ashrams of the Christ! I myself have a Second Ray Monad, and my Spiritual mission is to Spiritually educate lightworkers as to how to achieve God Realization, integrated ascension, psychological and physical/earthly mastery and to fulfill their Spiritual contracts regarding their Spiritual mission and puzzle piece in a grounded way on Earth! For too long, lightworkers have not been able to ground very well! They can't even ground themselves, let alone their Spiritual Missions! This is not meant as a judgment, just a Spiritual observation and statement of fact! During the 2000 year Piscean Age much growth occurred, but it did not make it very much to the physical/earthly plane. It remained on the Spiritual plane, or on the mental or emotional plane! As the political speeches on the Earth often say, "It is time for this to end!" It is time for lightworkers to "Ground" their Higher Selves and Mighty I Am Presence fully into their physical body and fully into Earth life! It is time for lightworkers to master Prosperity consciousness, and to master Earth life and Earth energies in service of GOD! It is time now for lightworkers to fully "Demonstrate God" on Earth, fully in Earth life! It is now time that we as the collective lightworkers on Earth stand together, arm in arm and heart to heart, to do the Spiritual mission we have come to do! This is to recreate our society and civilization according to GOD's design. All the plans on how to do this have already been set up! Lord Buddha our Planetary Logos has all this knowledge! The blueprints for every aspect of our new God Society have been figured out in every detail. GOD gives the Divine Plan to Metatron, who gives it to Melchizedek our Universal Logos, who gives it to Melchior, who gives it to Helios and Vesta, who gives it to Lord Buddha, who gives it to Lord Maitreya the Head of the Spiritual Hierarchy, who gives it to Allah Gobi and Saint German the "Manu" and the "Mahachohan," who all give it to the seven Chohans or Lords of the Rays: El Morya, Kuthumi, Serapis Bey, Paul the Venetian, Sananda, and Lady Portia and Djwhal Khul! Djwhal Khul runs the eighth Ashram of the Christ, called the "Synthesis Ashram" under the Second Ray, because Spiritual education is so important an extra ashram was created under Kuthumi's Second Ray Ashram, and holds the focus of "Spiritual education" and also synthesis of all the rays! This focus on Synthesis of all Seven Rays is also why it was created as well! This is the Ashram I work out of and Djwhal Khul has asked me to take over this inner plane Ashram when he moves on to take his next Cosmic position. Melchizedek, the Mahatma, Archangel Metatron, and Djwhal Khul have also asked me to anchor this Ashram and Academy on Earth! This was why I created the Melchizedek Synthesis Light Academy! It is a real life inner plane Ashram and Teaching Academy that has been manifested on this earthly plane to extend the Divine Plan of the Second Ray ashram! This is why I speak so Spiritually passionately on these things, and why I am so well-versed in the importance of integration and synthesis on all levels!

The Mahatma is the Avatar of Synthesis on the Cosmic level for all Creation! The Mahatma embodies all 352 levels of GOD! The Mahatma knows and understands that the first level of GOD is just as Holy, Sanctified, and Divine as the 352nd! To ignore one is like saying "I only love my head but I am going to dislike and hate my legs or feet"! It is like saying "the 7th Chakra is good but the first chakra is bad, no good, unimportant and not holy"! All chakras, all bodies, all Faces of GOD, all

352 levels of GOD are, in truth, equally Divine! One cannot realize God unless all levels are equally honored, loved, and sanctified!

Anyone who has had a garden understands the Glory of GOD on the physical/earthly level! To see each morning how flowers, plants, buds, and leaves grow is absolutely unbelievable! Anyone who has gotten very attuned to nature knows the Glory of GOD! However, the Glory of GOD can be experienced everywhere on the Earthly Plane! I remember when I went to see the *Phantom of the Opera* in Los Angeles, I thought it was one of the most profound Spiritual experiences of my life! I felt like I was lifted up into the fifth dimension for three hours! Traveling in Europe to visit the Sistine Chapel, Louvre Museum, the Acropolis, the Holy Land, and other sacred sites! Watching the birds, rabbits, butterflies, chipmunks from my window where I work! Watering the garden and tuning into the plant spirits and devas! Communing with nature! GOD is everywhere! Looking into the sky and clouds and blue sky! Wistancia and I sometimes sit out at night in our country home and just look at the stars in the vast open piece of land behind our home! Our dog Brianna is literally an angel from heaven in a dog's body! She is the embodiment of love. God is everywhere!

All the colors in the garden! All the incredible smells of nature! Seeing the roses bloom! Feeling the wind and the sun! Watching the birds eat from our bird feeders and listening to them chirp! All the little bees and insects flying around doing their thing and all working in harmony! Having a vegetable garden and seeing overnight how a zucchini plant pops out these gigantic zucchinis in a matter of days! It is really incredible to watch and witness.

I can honestly say I really love and enjoy Earth life! I recognize I am visiting here and that my ultimate destiny is to return to the seventh Heaven; however, I really do see this Material Universe as the first heaven it is! It really is incredibly beautiful. We have decorated our home and the Academy with hundreds of Spiritual statues of Masters, Angels and Saints! We have hundreds and hundreds of pictures of the

Masters and crystals, gemstones, and Spiritual objects! We even have all these things in the garden as well! We have all kinds of ascension columns and pillars of light and Ascension Technologies that also blend with all the beautiful earthly things and nature things! Our garden may be the center of our home and what draws us the most!

In writing this chapter on loving the Earth and Earthly life I was tuning into Spirit to see the best way to convey this message of Spirit and the Masters on the importance of loving the Earth and Earth life! The guidance I received was that the most effective way to help people appreciate this process of God Realization and love of the Material Face of GOD and the earthly/physical level was to share from my personal experience! I have been hesitant to do this too much for this can be misinterpreted, so although my books are very personal and I write like I am speaking to each one of you in my living room, I am always very careful to not get too carried away. In the rest of this chapter, however, I am consciously choosing to share my personal experience on this matter rather than theoretical knowledge, to try and give you my experience of loving earthly life! This is the most effective way I feel to help people feel and experience the profundity and love of the material/physical/earthly Face of GOD! When you open to God's Vision on this level as well, then everything in life on a Spiritual, mental, emotional and physical/earthly level becomes a sanctification, love, enjoyment, and communing with GOD! GOD can be communed with, loved, and enjoyed on all faces! This chapter is dedicated to the Material Face of GOD communion, love, and enjoyment!

So to share my experience on a personal level of loving and enjoying the Earth and Earth life, I would like to speak from a spontaneous flow that comes to mind! I love eating! Although, in truth, I do not eat very much and I mostly live on Light I do eat some food! When I do, I really enjoy it! I eat very pure food when I do because it gives me enormous pleasure and joy! This is something I might miss at times when I no longer have a physical body! Very often when I eat I like to watch the news! I love watching the news! I love being kept up to date on everything that is going on in the world. I do not see earthly affairs being separate from my Spiritual path! It is all one! When I hear of some injustice on the news I pray about it and ask GOD and the Masters to enter that situation. In the Academy, we have an Interdimensional Prayer Altar. I often will write down prayers for worldly events, people, and situations! Just as I enjoy gaining Spiritual knowledge and psychological knowledge, I also very much enjoy gaining earthly knowledge! Much of what I write about I get from watching the news or from educational television programs. Everything is grist for the mill, so to speak! I keep a list of ideas and I am constantly writing little notes to myself when I get ways to serve, pray or ideas for chapters! So eating in combination with the news is something I greatly enjoy! CNN was made for me!

I love hot showers. This is something I will miss if I don't have a physical body! I do some of my best channeling work in the shower! I love the computer! What an incredible invention. I get up every morning at around 4:00, take a hot shower and then begin my processing and channeling work! Then I go to my computer and start working! I love the early mornings when no one is around and it is totally quiet! I have about five hours to myself before my employees arrive! This is my favorite time every day. I get some of my best writing done! I love starting these days getting organized! The great thing about a computer is I have my entire life and all my books organized in it! I work at lightening speed whipping around the computer, with all my ideas and inspiration pouring in a mile a minute! I absolutely love e-mail! What an incredible invention! It goes instantly, no postage stamps. I thought faxes were great until I got into the computer world!

Then there is the Internet and Websites! I adore the Internet and my Website. I see the Academy Website as my Sistine Chapel. It is the never-ending book and architectural Taj Mahal in cyberspace! I think computers and the Internet are one of the greatest inventions in the history of man! For almost no money I have a store that people from all over the world can visit. I don't even have to hire employees! It is incredible!

Three quarters of my business comes through the Internet! I could literally stay home and never leave if I wanted to! What a freedom this can provide people!

I love being married and spending time with my wife Wistancia! I love going to the movies with her on our date night! Movies are really something I will miss when I no longer have a physical body! We get special videos as well and there is nothing like getting into the comfort of one's own bed or a comfortable couch and watching a good video! We also have a few favorite TV shows. We watch "Touched By An Angel," the "X files" if it isn't a violent one, and "Roswell." I also occasionally watch some of the news magazine shows like "60 Minutes." I use a lot of the things I hear about to raise consciousness in my books, articles and teaching! I love learning on all levels.

One of my favorite things is working in the garden! I love watering the garden! It is like the most glorious meditation. Sometimes I can get so tuned in I can just feel the pulsation of GOD running through everything! I love communing with the plants themselves and the Nature Spirits and Plant Devas!

I even enjoy doing errands. I don't do a lot of them for I send my employees to do most of them, so when I do do them, I really enjoy them. I do a lot of writing and working at my desk so getting out sometimes is really a nice break! I love buying flowers and little gifts and snacks for Wistancia at my favorite stores.

I love communicating and talking to people! Every person is such a precious incarnation of GOD and we are all so similar, in truth! I love answering e-mails, letters, and faxes from people. I love to help people and I find it quite enjoyable to commune with fellow Brothers and Sisters around the world! It is always so interesting what the e-mails, fax machine and post office bring in each day!

I even enjoy doing chores. I am blessed to be able to afford to have employees that help me do almost everything; however, I do not see anything as separate from GOD. Whatever needs doing, if they are not around I am happy to do. I look at it like an opportunity to get some physical exercise. I call the Angels and Masters in to help me! They run Spiritual current through my body!

I love writing books! This is one of my great joys! I usually try and spend at least five hours a day writing chapters. Some days even more. Writing books is such a high! It is really an art form to me! I always use the metaphor of being an artist or a musician, for every word is like a brushstroke or musical note. A great chapter is a like an exquisite painting, fresco, or musical concert!

I love counseling, teaching, chanting the names of GOD, and meditating! I love talking and communicating with my friends. I love Spiritual leadership and planetary world service. It is a big responsibility, however, I love all the work!

I love sleeping after a long day of work! Usually my head hits the pillow and I am out in two seconds! I really love to sleep! However, I love Earth life so much and I love all the projects and everything I am doing so much I literally can't wait to get up in the morning! I honestly can't wait! I find working energizing! It is almost like the more I work the more energized I feel, for everything I do, I do with 100% personal power, 100% unconditional love and 100% active intelligence! I love experiencing life through all seven Rays! I even enjoy the business end of life! I love doing Huna prayers every day and calling in GOD and the Godforce for help! I love making my lists of everything I have to do and everything my employees need to do. I love the feeling of crossing things off my lists and getting things done. I love to accomplish things and create! I love to bring things into form. There is such a feeling of accomplishment when a new book is published. I love to receive letters from people to see how they have been helped. This is the greatest feeling of all! Helping people in a truly selfless and egoless manner to the best of my ability! To truly see everything as GOD! There is no better feeling than to turn people onto GOD, the Masters, on how to achieve inner peace, prosperity, and God Realization!

The other thing I love is the enormous creativity that pulses through me. I know this is the creative energy of God that is in everyone! I have so many incredible ideas! Spirit and the Masters give me so many ideas! I love the third Ray action of actively taking my full 100% personal power and love and putting this into action and physical form! I am not a procrastinator and I am not lazy! I know how to take care of business and get things accomplished!

I also love a good sports event! I love, for example, watching the Olympics. I love watching the track and field. I love watching the gymnastics. I love the swimming. I love seeing incarnations of GOD manifest their highest potentials. I even wrote a chapter in my book *How To Release Fear-Based Thinking and Feeling*, on "Spirituality and Sports"! I love watching a championship basketball game, the Super Bowl, the Rose Bowl, the World Series, or Pete Sampras playing tennis. It is truly an art form and can be quite inspiring! To watch Magic Johnson or Michael Jordan play basketball! To watch Michael Johnson run! To watch Mark McGuire hit 70 home runs in a season. I really appreciate what professional athletes must go through to achieve success at that level for I used to play sports! I truly see it as a "Spiritual Art Form"!

I love to listen to music. I often listen to Sai Baba Bhajans, or Santana's "Supernatural" album when I drive. Music is truly a doorway to GOD! I love burning Sai Baba incense, the Nag Champa!

I love talking to Wistancia at the end of the day and just catching up on things! I love having the car washed and watching it go through the car wash and get cleaned. I love the feeling of getting a haircut! It is like after I take a shower every morning! I love wearing my beautiful, colorful clothes! I love wearing my tuxedos at Wesak. I now have seven different kinds of tuxedos. My newest one is all white and floor length. I like to dress as the Masters dress on the inner plane!

What I love most is practicing the Presence of GOD on Earth! I love to Be God on Earth in Action! I am very much into grounding GOD! This is why I wrote this chapter showing lightworkers and people how to ground into Earth life! The whole purpose of life is to Be God and Demonstrate God on the physical/earthly plane!

I love the feeling of feeling like I am actually doing something to help people and to help change this physical world! I love the feeling of fulfilling my Spiritual mission and fulfilling my puzzle piece on Earth! I love taking on Spiritual assignments and perfectly fulfilling them on Earth! I love the feeling of really making a Spiritual impact in this earthly world! I love the feeling of seeing myself as a light bearer for the New Age and being one of the Spiritual leaders that is really able to make a difference in this earthly world. Someone has to do this! GOD in Heaven is not going to do this. The Masters and Angels are not going to do this, for they don't have physical bodies! I love being the hands and feet for GOD, Christ, the Holy Spirit, and the Masters! The Masters told me once that I was like their point man on Earth! I like being a point man! It is a tough job, for a point man can take a lot of fire on the front lines, however, it is quite fulfilling to be relied upon by Spirit and the Masters to demonstrate mastery and competence and love in doing such assignments! I humbly suggest that not everyone has what it takes to do this and I am trying to suggest to each one of you reading this book to take on the "Mantle of the Christ" and step forward in Spiritual leadership and planetary world service. If you step forward from the consciousness I am describing in this book you will succeed and you will experience great love and joy in doing so! My books will provide you with all the "Psychic Self-Defense" tools you need to deal with being on the front lines! I love Spiritual leadership! I love planetary world service! I also have learned how to take care of myself, protect myself, and set boundaries. This is part of self-love!

I love to work hard but I also love to laugh and have fun when I work! I love to put all my 100% Spiritual passion into everything I do! My main goal is to be consistent and integrated on all levels! I am not just satisfied to realize God on the Spiritual plane, or the mental plane, or the emotional plane, or energetically and etherically. I want to demonstrate

God on the earthly plane as well. I want to be the Mighty I Am Presence on Earth! I want to be God on Earth! I want to be a fully realized God on Earth! I am not just satisfied with ascension. I want to also fully realize my physical ascension and turn my physical body into light! Once I do this, I am not going to leave! I am going to remain on Earth and continue serving! Someone has to turn this world around "And for me and my house I will serve the Lord!" I ask you, my Brothers and Sisters, to stand with me! GOD is not going to change the Earth and neither are the Masters. GOD and the Masters are counting on us! I ask you now to stand with me and all the other courageous souls around the planet who are doing the same, and let's change this world. We will change it with our 100% power, love, and wisdom! We will change it with the power of our Three-Fold Flame and all our other God qualities! When all you see is GOD, and all you see is love, it is not hard! It is really pleasure! The Power of GOD and the entire Godforce will come to your aid for they know what a difficult assignment it is to be a lightbearer for the New Age! I personally have great confidence in my fellow Earthlings! We are made of the substance of GOD and I will proudly stand with any Brother and Sister Earthling who will stand with me to completely reorganize and restructure our society! With our 100% personal power, unconditional love, and wisdom and the 100% personal power, unconditional love and wisdom of GOD and the Godforce, we cannot be stopped! Let us show the Infinite Universe the "Strong, Loving and Wise Spiritual Stock" us Earthlings are made of! It is time to change this earthly world and the time is now! Let us roll up our sleeves and be about the Father's business! Let us roll up our sleeves and be about the Divine Mother's business as well! Let us roll up our sleeves and be about the Earth Mother's business as well! Let us roll up our sleeves and completely transform and change our earthly civilization and society into the utopian fifth dimensional civilization it is meant to become!

I always try and get the most difficult jobs done first so then everything else is easy! I love manifesting all my incredible ideas into Earthly existence. This is why I have written 27 books! I really would humbly and Spiritually like to leave a legacy in this world that can continue to help people. Books are a great way of doing this. I have also set up almost 15 branches of the Academy around the world as of the year 2000 and I am sure that within the next five years we will have over 200 branches. I just started opening them and I have been opening almost two a week! I receive almost 400,000 hits a month on my Website and many people have read the flyer I have posted there!

I love working on the Wesak celebrations at Mt. Shasta for 2000 people. The experience each year of starting from scratch and being in charge of every aspect of the event on a Spiritual, psychological and physical/earthly level, and see it grow over a year's time and then to pull off a successful event is one of the most amazing experiences I have ever felt. To manifest something that size that is so incredibly complex, with the help of Spirit and the Masters and others in the Academy, is incredible! By the grace of GOD and the Masters we have as of the year 2000 had six perfect Wesaks! By the grace of GOD and the Masters all six events have worked out perfectly! It is such a high Spiritual experience to have put so much work into a project each year and to see it come into manifestation on the Earth and help so many people! I am a firm believer in grounding everything I do! This is the energy of the Third Ray. I also incredibly enjoy making everything I do beautiful and harmonious; this is Fourth Ray energy! I love, for example, always decorating our home, bringing new little statues of angels for our home and the garden. We do the same thing for the Wesaks!

I love to understand the science of all things and to explain to people how the science of all things works. I love the feeling of making an impact and Spiritual contribution in the world. This is a tough school and a lot of people have a hard time on many levels. By the grace of GOD and the Masters, I am in a position to help people and I feel a little bit like I have taken kind of a partial vow of the Bodhisattva to be of service any way I can! Something that Jesus said in *A Course in*

Miracles always touched me and corresponded to how I feel and I have stated this many times in my books! Jesus said, "True pleasure is serving GOD"! This is truly how I feel! I can honestly say I never ever feel like I am working! From other people's lenses and eyes they would say I am a very hard worker. That is not the way I experience it! I really don't! I absolutely love what I am doing! Working energizes me! I feel electrified with energy most of the time for everything that I am doing is done in the context of serving GOD! If I am washing the dishes, I am washing GOD. If I am watering the garden, I am watering GOD! If I am typing, I am typing the ideas of GOD and expressing the feelings of GOD. If I am meditating or praying, I am tuning into the essence of GOD! When I meet people on the street, all I see are incarnations of GOD and/or Christs or Buddhas! Every specific thought I think, feeling I feel, word I speak, action I take, is in the context of serving my Spiritual path and GOD! I see and sanctify GOD in all Four Faces! I love GOD equally on all four levels. I have worked out my book series so I basically have 10 books written on the Spiritual level, 10 books on the psychological level, and 10 books on the physical/earthly level! This, my Beloved Readers, is the kind of thing that excites me the most! I love mastering GOD on all three levels! I love experiencing GOD on all three levels. I love sanctifying GOD on all three levels! I love loving GOD on all three levels!

I think one of the things I enjoy and love most about earthly life is co-creating with GOD and the Masters on Earth! I love the sparking of ideas! I love how GOD and the Masters really rely on us to fulfill our Spiritual missions on Earth! They cannot complete their Spiritual assignments unless we complete ours! We are their channels! God is using God to manifest a God world and New Jerusalem on Earth! I don't think Earthlings have fully realized how much Spirit and the Masters rely on us to fulfill the Divine Plan on Earth! Spirit and the Masters don't want us to just be their channels. They want us to be God Realized beings and Masters in our own right as well! That is when they can really rely on us! I love co-creating with the Masters! This is why my enthusiasm and passion is so strong! It is a combination of my 100% personal power, unconditional love and wisdom, in combination with absolute total faith, trust and patience that GOD, Christ, the Holy Spirit, and the Masters, Angels, Elohim and Christed Extraterrestrials will help me with my every need if I pray and ask! I pray and ask constantly! The reason I enjoy and love Earth life so much is I know how to be a Master on a Spiritual level, a psychological level and a physical/earthly level. Once you learn how to do this life is not nearly as hard! The hard part of life is not really Earth life! It is not having mastery over your thoughts, feelings, emotions, energy, negative ego mind, lower-self desire, inner child, and subconscious mind. One you learn to master these things then life is really a piece of cake! Our thoughts create our reality; our thoughts create our feelings and emotions! Life is not that hard once you learn to truly cause your own reality! When you learn to transcend negative ego thinking and feeling and only see life from your Spiritual/Christ/Buddha thought and feeling system all you see is God and unconditional love in everything! You are no longer a victim, and you become emotionally invulnerable for you cause your own reality by how you think! Then when you learn to live life as a co-creator with GOD, Christ, the Holy Spirit and all the Masters you have the full love, wisdom and power of God utilizing the full love, wisdom and power of GOD and the entire Godforce. So how can you not succeed in everything you do? Can GOD not succeed! It is almost comical! Can GOD not win this Spiritual battle against nothing more than illusion! Do you realize that is all you are battling! In truth, there is nothing but GOD, and separation does not exist! Once you get all your energies aligned, Earth life really becomes extremely enjoyable even if you really do have a big Spiritual assignment! The key is to practice God Realization on all levels. Whatever you do, do it 100% decisively and do it Spiritually, mentally, emotionally, energetically, physically and in an earthly sense! This is the great problem with lightworkers. Very few are doing it on all levels. Some do it Spiritually. Some do it mentally. Some do it emotionally. Some are doing it on the Earth but don't have the full Spiritually. Some do it Psychologically and in the Earth but don't have the full Spiritual. Some do it Spiritually and Psychologically but not Physically and in the Earth! The great lesson of the New Millennium and Seventh Golden Age is that lightworkers must "Be God" on all levels at all times! I have used the term "fragmented ascension." This is where lightworkers are ascended in a Spiritual sense but not on other levels. This is "rampant" in the Spiritual Movement! This book and my book *How To Release Fear-Based Thinking and Feeling: An In-depth Study of Spiritual Psychology* have been written to heal and correct this, and if you will read these books I humbly suggest you'll see that it does just that! Please turn all your friends, family, and students onto them, for there is no message lightworkers need to hear more!

So, in conclusion, my Beloved Readers, I have shared with you the full Spiritual passion of my heart and soul; the wondrous nature of the material/physical/earthly face of GOD! It is my sincere hope and prayer that my sharing has opened your consciousness and eyes to the wondrous nature of GOD on this level! I can honestly say I really totally love and enjoy Earth life! This is not an affirmation or positive thinking, I really mean it! I go from one thing to another all day long, from my shower to my computer, to having something to eat and watching the news, back to writing, and e-mails, and having fun with my employees, and visiting with Wistancia, and having millions of creative ideas, to talking to people, to co-creating with the Masters, to praying, meditating, being in the garden, making money, watching the birds, playing "bally" with our dog Brianna, watching favorite TV shows with my wife, talking with friends, being with family, running errands, practicing being and demonstrating God, seeing God in everything, making love, being of service all day wherever I can, counseling, teaching, doing workshops, sharing, growing, and evolving into greater and greater God Realization! What is not to love! Sure there are challenges. However, I see them as Spiritual tests and as ways to be even more God-like! Each time I overcome a challenge I am even more God-like, because of what I have learned and what I have mastered. Each lesson makes me stronger as I overcome it and learn from it! When you co-create with GOD, Christ, the Holy Spirit and the Masters, and constantly pray for their help, you will become absolutely filled with Spiritual current. I am running so much Spiritual current through my 12-body system, I do not know what to do with myself! I constantly feel filled with God Energy for I am always claiming it, affirming it, seeing it, praying for it and demonstrating it! Everything in life becomes one continual flow of God! With so much Spiritual current, Spiritual power, Spiritual love, Spiritual wisdom, Spiritual beauty and harmony, Spiritual science, Spiritual devotion, Spiritual freedom, order, structure and magic running through me and living a consciousness and life as I describe, what is not to love? I literally love everything about Earth life! I am sure I will love Heavenly life just as much! However, as long as I am here I will love and enjoy it completely and fulfill my Spiritual mission with 100% self-mastery and personal power as well! Don't you see, my Beloved Readers, you can have it all! You can have your cake and eat it too! You can have the best of the Spiritual world, the best of the psychological world and the best of the earthly world! You can have total 100% self-mastery and get all your work done! You can have total 100% unconditional love of everything including Earth life in every facet! You can have 100% total wisdom on a Spiritual, psychological and earthly/physical level! You can have totally 100% Spiritual ecstasy, bliss, and joy, on a Spiritual, psychological and physical/earthly level. You can have total 100% self-discipline, emotional invulnerability, and protection and be a total cause of your reality! You can have total 100% God and Goddess energies! You can have the best of your own co-creator consciousness and the best of GOD, Christ the Holy Spirit and the Masters! In truth, my Beloved Readers, you are God! You have and are everything! All that exists is God! So whatever happens in life just say, "Not my will but thine oh Lord, thank you for the lesson and Spiritual test!" Welcome adversity! It is all just stepping stones for Soul Growth! The key, my Beloved Readers, is to just approach life from the proper perspective! As Sai Baba has said, "Your mind creates bondage or your mind creates liberation!" Once you learn to see life from your Spiritual/Christ/Buddha Consciousness and not from your negative ego/fear-based/separative mind, life becomes a trillion times easier! All you see is God and unconditional love in whatever place you look!

My Beloved Readers, it is my sincere hope and prayer that this chapter has helped you to open your eyes a little more to the importance and profundity of fully "unconditionally loving and enjoying the Earth and Earth life!"

So let it be Written! So let it be Done!

42

The Soul and Mighty I Am Presence 21 Day Program for Mastering Bad Habits and Addictions

The whole subject of addictions is a most interesting subject! It is actually a subject I have not written about as a chapter! After writing 27 books it is always fun to come up with new subjects for chapters which I have not specifically written about, in a totally focused manner where this was the only subject I was covering! I have referenced the subject in a general sense but not in a focused sense like I am planning to do in this chapter! So on this note I will begin!

To understand addictions it is first essential to understand that the subconscious mind can also be referred to as the habitual mind. The subconscious is where habits are stored. Now some may think that habits are a negative thing, however, this is not true! One can have the habit of eating right, exercising, meditating, thinking with one's Spiritual mind rather than with one's negative ego mind! So, in truth, one of the main Spiritual practices of the Spiritual path is to fill one's subconscious mind with good Spiritual habits!

The problem is that in past lives we have had bad habits, and we bring these negative programs and bad habits with us when we incarnate into a baby's body. Second, when we incarnate into children's bodies we pick up both good and bad habits from our parents, family, school, television, peers, and mass consciousness!

An addiction is an "attachment" or "bad habit" on a thought, feeling or physical level. Now, most of the time we think of addictions as being focused on a physical or outer thing! For example, being addicted to cigarettes, alcohol, food, sex, drugs, painkillers, shopping, gambling, sugar, or even to a person. The truth is, although all these things are physical in nature it is the "feeling" that is often addicted to! Let me give some examples of what I mean. The person who drinks too much alcohol to escape the pain or anguish they feel. They are trying to get a different kind of a feeling! Food, for example, may be used as a replacement for love, for greater protection, or to stuff feelings! Drugs may be used to get a certain kind of a feeling that the user is looking for. Shopping, because of the feeling it gives one in the moment. Gambling, because of the high of winning. So we see that addictions are often to escape a negative feeling or to try and create a new one!

A person can actually be addicted to feeling! We have all heard the title of the book, *Women Who Love Too Much*. I have not read the book; however, the truth of the title is obvious in some cases. A person can be addicted to love or addicted to power, or addicted to activity and cannot be still and meditate! This is kind of interesting for these are the first three Rays of God (Power, Love, and Active Intelligence)! So we see people can be addicted to a Ray in its lower aspect! Each of the Seven Rays has a higher and lower aspect! So we are beginning to see here that a person can be addicted to an idea that goes along with a feeling as well. A person may be addicted to a group of ideas and feelings such as power, fame, material things, sex, or money!

Addictions can also be connected with energy. One example is people who are addicted to doing dangerous things like bungie jumping, sky diving, or hang gliding! They go from one dangerous activity to the next because they love the "energy rush"! They love the adrenaline and the fear and excitement!

So, we see that addictions can occur on a mental, emotional, energetic and physical level. Most often, in truth, all these aspects of self are interconnected to addictions.

The next interesting thing to understand is that some addictions can have a physical component. For example, cigarette smoking serves an emotional and mental need, but also is addictive on a physical level because of the nicotine. I think it is common knowledge the cigarette companies look at cigarettes as nothing more than "nicotine delivery devices"! So, the addiction takes on a mental aspect because of the mental habit of doing it. It takes on an emotional addiction because of the feeling it gives the person when they are feeling nervous, uptight, or anxious. It also satisfies the physical addiction. The more you do it, the more it becomes engrained like a tape recording in the subconscious mind, and the more the nicotine gets into the cells. The same is true of heroin, alcohol, sugar, drugs, and so on! So what happens over time is the constant doing of these activities forms deeper and deeper grooves in the subconscious mind and a habit is formed and over time it becomes a very ingrained habit on a mental, emotional, energetic, and physical level. Although it is totally poisonous to the soul, every part of these three lower bodies craves this poison! The mind, emotions, and body actually crave toxicity because of the improper mental, emotional, energetic and physical programming!

So, the next key question we must ask ourselves is "What is the cause of addictions?" The original cause is always the same thing! It always begins with a negative/fear-based/separative thought instead of a Spiritual/Christ/Buddha thought! This leads to a negative/fear-based/separative feeling! The person in a past life, or as a child, adolescent or adult, does not know how to escape this negative thought, negative feeling, and suffering, and begins to try and use an "outside source" to solve the problem instead of Spiritual mastery and being trained in Spiritual psychology! If they were trained in how to master their thoughts, feelings, emotions, energy, physical body, negative ego, desire body, inner child and subconscious mind in service of GOD and Spiritual/Christ/Buddha consciousness, there would be no need to have to form addictions!

So addictions can be caused as way to escape pain and suffering or they can be caused by not having a healthy psychology, philosophy, and mindset! Let me explain this second cause of addiction. Because people are not trained in Spiritual psychology by their parents, or in school, or at church or temple, or by psychologists and counselors, or even in the New Age Movement, they are off-center in this area. The person may be highly Spiritual, and even highly successful in an earthly sense, however, without proper training in Spiritual psychology, their psychologies and/or philosophies are off-center and off-kilter. For example, most people are not in control of their minds. Their mind or subconscious mind runs them; they do not run their mind. Another reason is that most people are run by their emotional body. They are not masters and causes of their feelings and emotions. Third, most people are run by their desire body. This is an interesting one, for the desire body is always connected with addiction. When you are run too much by your emotional body, you are also going to be to run by your desire body, for the desire body is connected to the emotional or astral body! When a person allows themselves to be too run by their mental and emotional body, they end up being run by their desires. When the mind and emotional body run you too much, the negative ego mind becomes the director and programmer by psychological law. If people allow themselves to become a victim rather than a master and cause, then the negative ego will program their emotional life. This causes negative feelings and emotions such as fear, worry, sadness, depression, hurt, abandonment, loneliness, anger, judgement, impatience, irritation, frustration, lack of love and lack of inner peace. These feelings of course can lead to addiction. Then what happens is because the emotional body is too much in control, the desire body automatically becomes too much in control. This is why in Buddhism and Hinduism they teach to abolish all desire as one of their main teachings! In truth, however, you don't want to abolish all desire, just all "lower-self" or negative ego desire! You want to channel all your desire into "Higher Self" desire which is desire only for Self-Realization, God Realization, Ascension, completion of your Twelve Levels of Initiation, Integrated Ascension, and so on! So what happens is people are not properly trained in how to do this, so the fact that they are too run by the feelings, emotions and negative ego also causes lower-self desire to be in control, which leads to overindulgence and getting involved with lower-self types of habits such as cigarettes, too much alcohol, drugs, overindulgence in sex, pornography, gluttony, sugar, junk food, drug addiction, recreational drugs, and an overly outer focus!

The lack of training in the difference between negative ego/fear-based/separative thinking and feeling and Spiritual/Christ/Buddha thinking and feeling, and not being able to demonstrate this self-mastery in their daily lives, is the biggest cause of addictions. Our thoughts cause our reality. If we don't think right, then we will not be in control of our emotional bodies and desire body and we will have too many negative feelings and emotions and too much lower-self desire. This all leads to addictions and bad habits!

Then because people do not know how to master and control the subconscious mind, this causes all those aforementioned things to take place as well. The subconscious mind has no reasoning whatsoever. So, if you let the subconscious mind run you in the slightest, the negative ego mind becomes your director, which leads to addiction. Then if you have not been trained in Spiritual psychology you have not been trained in how to properly parent your inner child. Most people either repress their inner child or are run by it. This causes the emotional body to run the person and causes the negative ego to become the programmer, and the desire body to take over which leads to addictive behavior and bad habits!

Then because of all these things going on, because of lack of training in Spiritual psychology, which is no real fault of the person, the negative ego causes people to have "attachments rather than preferences"! This is because people are not trained in how to think properly! As Buddha said in his Four Noble Truths, "All suffering comes from attachments"! All suffering comes from wrong points of view. Attachments and addictions are very interrelated. People get attached to alcohol, for example, instead of it being an occasional preference. People get attached to having to eat and have sugar, instead of it being an occasional preference. The negative ego mind causes the person to latch on and become attached or addicted to certain types of behavior which then form habits in the subconscious mind on a mental, emotional, energetic and physical level! A preference is an attitude that goes for what it wants, but if it doesn't get it, the person remains happy!

So my Beloved Readers, in truth, it is all these factors combined that form the root cause of all addictions! Addictions are deeply ingrained mental and emotional negative habits of faulty thinking and emotional patterns, which have moved from the mental and emotional plane into the physical body and material plane! An addiction in essence is a mental, emotional, energetic and physical bad habit! An addiction is often a physicalized negative ego thought and emotional process that has formed a bad habit and is usually focused on trying to seek happiness and inner peace through an outside source instead of through inner means. It is the direct result of lack of Spiritual mastery, victim consciousness, and lack of Spiritual and/or psychological understanding and demonstration. It is not a judgment to have addictions. Everyone has had them in past lives and this life. They are just signposts that more Spiritual and psychological mastery are needed! It is not the fault of people for having them, for, in truth, they are just caused by a lack of proper training in Spiritual psychology as I have said. There are not that many people on the planet that, in truth, truly understand Spiritual psychology. Our parents did not understand it, schools don't, extended family doesn't, churches and temples don't, counselors don't, psychologists don't, social workers don't, psychiatrists don't, and most Spiritual teachers are just that, Spiritual teachers, not psychological teachers. Spiritual psychology is a tremendously in-depth science as you can see from reading this book and my other books. For the most part, it is the weakest area in most lightworkers, Spiritual teachers, channels, and healers. I do not mean this as a judgment; it is just a loving statement of fact. Lightworkers overall have very highly developed Spiritual bodies and even physical/earthly selves, however not as developed psychological selves. This is because there are not as many good Spiritual psychology books, classes, workshops, and seminars as there are Spiritual ones. Spiritual psychology, in truth, is the foundation of your Spiritual life! All Spiritual life will ultimately be corrupted if this level of God Realization is not addressed properly.

Addictions are very deeply ingrained mentally, emotionally, energetically and physically, however with the proper training can "easily" be overcome.

The other thing that can cause addictions is not being on a Spiritual path and not being connected to one's Higher Self and Mighty I Am Presence! The key question here is if your Higher Self, Mighty I Am Presence, and the Holy Spirit (Still, Small Voice Within) are not your guides, then who is? The answer is the negative ego, lower-self, emotional body and desire body! This will lead the person into negative thoughts, negative feelings, bad habits, and addictions!

The proper way to live life is with "involvement, but to also be detached simultaneously!" The idea is to live in this world but not of this world! The ideal is to live in Heaven and Earth simultaneously. It's kind of like straddling two dimensions simultaneously. The ideal is to bring your Heavenly consciousness to Earth in an integrated and balanced way. If one is not on a Spiritual path, which is a "higher life," then what is the other alternative? The other alternative is a "low life"! We all know what that is. It is a life filled with low life or lower-self habits and addictions. Because people in this world have not been properly trained in Spiritual psychology, they do not realize that one of the premiere purposes of life is to master and get rid of the lower-self thoughts, feelings, emotions, desires, habits, attachments and addictions and completely reprogram their being into having only Higher Self or Spiritual thoughts, feelings, emotions, desires, habits and preferences! If you do not live to realize the soul and Spirit within you, then you live out of your "personality" instead of realizing you are a God incarnating into a body. You think you are just a person or physical body totally separate from GOD, if you even believe in one, and separate from your Brothers and Sisters and life! When you live out of your personality you can still strive for success and a type of self-actualization, however, it is a worldly success, not what is called "Soul Self-Actualization" or "Monadic (Spiritual) Self-Actualization"! Personality level self-actualization is good, but is only one third up the "Spiritual Mountain" or ladder you are here to climb. Most of the world is still either living out of their personality or a mixture of personality and soul! This is only because they have not been trained in Spiritual psychology! Can you imagine, my Beloved Readers, if the kinds of things I write about in this book and my other books were taught in school from the first grade onwards? Children and adolescents would be absolutely on fire for GOD! They would love to come to school! If people knew what they were supposed to do and understood clearly in very simple and easy to understand charts, books and explanations, who in their right mind would not choose a Spiritual path. I guarantee you almost no one. The reason being is "we each are God!" That is who we are! The only person who would not choose this is someone who still has too much disturbed programming in their subconscious and energy fields from past lives or this life, and this could be cured and healed in every case over time, with the proper unconditional love, nurturing and care!

So, my Beloved Readers, when a person lives out of their personality and not totally out of guidance and merger with the Soul, Spirit, Higher Self, Monad, Mighty I Am Presence, Holy Spirit and your Spiritual/Christ/Buddha consciousness, then they may have some degree of personality level self-actualization such as a movie star, successful businessman, lawyer, professional person, or professional trade person for example. However, they are still going to have some negative thoughts, feelings, emotions, lower-self desires, bad habits, and addictions. Maybe not as many as the person who is totally run by the lower-self and negative ego, however some will still be there. The reason is that they have not totally switched over to "100% living out of the Soul, Spirit, and Spiritual/Christ/Buddha consciousness!" The only way Self-Realization, full Self-Actualization, Enlightenment, full Liberation, Resurrection, God Realization, Ascension, your Twelve Levels of Initiation, and Integrated Ascension will be achieved is if you live 100% fully out of the Spiritual! Most people on Earth and even lightworkers, my friends, are still split because of improper training in Spiritual psychology. They live half out the Spiritual/Christ/Buddha consciousness and half out of negative ego/fear-based/separative thinking! They live half out of personality level self-actualization and half out of Soul and Spiritual self-actualization! They live half out of the personality and half out of the Soul and Spirit! Now the key thing to understand is that this is not because they are not totally sincere in their Spiritual path, and it is not because they are not good people and totally dedicated to GOD and Spiritual growth or living a good life. It is because of this lack of proper training and understanding of what exactly they need to do. It is kind of like they have not been given the "Spiritual map, workbook, and directions." So, they are working to the best of their understanding and ability and are totally sincere in their efforts, however without the "Training Manual" I think you would agree progress is going to be slow and there is going to be much confusion! Lightworkers like to think they fully understand, but with no judgement intended, they don't. Spiritual psychology is an incredibly in-depth and complicated Spiritual science. Reading one book on the subject or taking one course does not make one a master. In truth, it is a lifelong study, and no matter how advanced you are, it is possible to lose it and become unclear in the a "twinkling of an eye"! The negative ego mind and the psychodynamics of thinking, feeling, desire, the subconscious mind, the inner child, inner parenting, the physical body, Spiritual development, Spiritual/Christ/Buddha Consciousness, and integrating and balancing all one's Seven Rays, Twelve Archetypes, Twelve Signs of the Zodiac, Twelve Sephiroth on the Tree of Life, all the cards in the Tarot Deck, three minds, four bodies, Four Faces of GOD, God/Goddess, feminine and masculine, Heaven and Earth, can be very complicated and a very intricate process. People and lightworkers have a lot of really crazy ideas that they think are true, but are not. There are also, as the Bible states, an enormous number of false prophets, cults, twilight masters, disintegrated Spiritual teachers, fragmented Spiritual teachers, personality level psychologists and counselors, channels that are not clear, people who claim to be God Realized and are not, and Spiritual and psychological teachers and counselors, who are very highly developed Spiritually or psychically, but not necessarily psychologically. There are enormous numbers of teachers, channels and healers who are extraordinarily gifted in one area, or even two, but very few are total Spiritual masters on a Spiritual, psychological and physical/earthly level, and very few are totally clear of all negative ego/fear-based/separative thinking, feeling, bad habits and addictions! Most are extremely highly developed in one area or maybe two, but weaker in the second or third! Lightworkers see these Spiritual teachers, channelers, psychics, or healers and think that because they are so extraordinarily gifted in one area that they must be total Spiritual masters! They are Spiritual masters in one aspect or area of God, which is great! However, God Realization is much more complicated than that! You must be a master of all three levels (Spiritual, psychological and physical/earthly) and you must be the absolute master of all negative ego thinking, feeling, bad habits, and addictions to truly be a God Realized being. You must be able to totally ground your Spirituality on Earth and fulfill your Spiritual mission and puzzle piece on Earth! You must be able to do this in a totally balanced and integrated manner! You must be able to develop all your talents on a Spiritual, psychological and physical/earthly level. This is where the confusion lies. Lightworkers develop their Spiritual talents and gifts in one area like channeling, Spiritual teaching, healing, science, psychic work, clairvoyant work or psychology, for example, and this again is wonderful. The problem is if they don't do it on all three levels (Spiritual, psychological and physical/earthly) with no negative ego/fear-based/separative influence, and if they don't do it in a totally integrated and balanced manner, integrating the Seven Rays, twelve archetypes, balancing the vertical and horizontal planes of life, integrating and sanctifying the Four Faces of GOD (Spiritual, mental, emotional and material), God/Goddess, feminine and masculine, Heaven and Earth, balancing four bodies, three minds, properly parenting the inner child, mastering the subconscious mind, mastering lower-self desire, mastering the mind, mastering the feelings and emotions, totally mastering the physical body, mastering one's energy, just to name a few, then disintegration and fragmentation can and will take place! Limited lens seeing will take place. Faulty thinking and negative feelings and emotions will slip in. Wrong motives will be prevalent. Some bad habits will be prevalent. Health lessons will present themselves other than for reasons of just Spiritual mutation! Addictions will be prevalent as well! All these things will occur at times in even the most gifted Spiritual teachers, channels, healers, psychics, clairvoyants, Spiritual scientists, counselors, and lightworkers! This occurs because most on Earth are developed in one area or at most two, but very, very rarely are they developed in all three in all the ways I am talking about in this chapter! So, the key question now is what does this have to do with bad habits and addictions? What I have written here is absolutely essential to understand. For it is not just people who are totally run by the negative ego and lower-self who have bad habits and addictions. It is also Spiritual leaders, teachers, channels, psychics, healers, counselors, scientists, metaphysicians, and lightworkers! This stems from either lack of full training in the area of Spiritual Psychology and/or because of this aspect of being extraordinarily highly developed in one area, or maybe at most two, but not in all three and not in a way that is totally free of all negative ego/fear-based/separative/lower-self influence. It also occurs because of lack of integration and balance of all the aspects I mentioned previously! Also, because they have developed their talents or came in with them in one area or level of God, however, they have not learned to develop their talents on all levels of God!

This lack of total self-mastery and integration on all levels of God in all the things I have mentioned here causes there to be imbalances, weak spots, blind spots, and limited lens seeing in some areas, even though the person is so incredibly talented and gifted in one area or level of Self-Realization! Because of this, bad habits and addictions in some areas set in.

What I have shared here is incredibly important for Spiritual leaders and lightworkers to understand about themselves so they don't get overly comfortable in just being gifted and talented on this one level. Strive to develop yourself on all three levels in the way and manner I have described in this chapter. This is the key to getting rid of all negative thoughts, feelings, emotions, energy, health problems, bad habits, and addictions!

Second, this understanding is incredibly important to Spiritual leaders and lightworkers to be much more Spiritually discerning when dealing with other lightworkers, and to see that just because someone is extremely highly developed in one area, it doesn't mean they have achieved full God Realization, and this doesn't mean they do not have negative thoughts, feelings, emotions, health lessons, bad habits and addictions of some kind! This is why many Spiritual leaders and lightworkers who are quite highly evolved in a Spiritual sense still have bad habits and addictions!

Now, my Beloved Readers, I contemplated about going over each addiction in infinite detail, however upon further attunement and contemplation I really find that this is unnecessary, for, in truth, all bad habits and addictions result from the dynamics I have talked about in this chapter. So instead, what I have been guided to do here is give you a program for mastering all bad habits and addictions, for, in truth, they all come from the same set of causes! So whatever bad habit or addiction you have; Spirit, the Masters and I have designed a 21 day program that is personally guaranteed to help you to master whatever bad habit or addiction you are trying to master and reprogram! I have been guided to set this program up for 21 days because it takes 21 days to fully cement any new habit into the subconscious mind. Even though I am setting this for 21 days, it is recommended that you continue the program for two months just to make sure that the bad habit and or addiction is 100% cleared and reprogrammed. The mastery of the bad habit and/or addiction will take place, however, within 21 days if you follow my guidance, directions, and instructions exactly!

It is now my great joy, with the help of Spirit and the Masters, this day to show you how to get rid of all your addictions quite simply and easily! It is for all the aforementioned, reasons and more that Spirit, the Masters and I now bring up the Soul and Mighty I Am Presence 21 Day Program for mastering your Bad Habits and Addictions!

The Soul and Mighty I Am Presence 21-Day Program for Mastering Your Bad Habits and Addictions

- 100% fully claim your personal power and self mastery over your every thought, feeling, word, deed, subconscious mind, desire body, physical body, inner child, and every aspect of self and earthly life!
- Write a Spiritual Vow out on a piece of paper that as of this moment, as GOD, the Masters, and the Angels are your witness, that you are going to officially stop this or these habits!

- Monitor and remain Spiritually vigilant over your every thought and feeling, and push out of your consciousness, in thought or feeling, that which is not of GOD and replace it with a thought and feeling of GOD!
- Deny entrance into your consciousness of any negative ego/fear-based/separative thought and feeling and replace it with the opposite Spiritual/Christ/Buddha thought or feeling!
- Do the affirmations in this book for personal power, self-love, Bubble of Protection, and Spiritual attunement for 15 minutes every morning and 15 minutes every night! Also do them any time you feel your energy attunement sinking or if you are being tempted!
- Write out a Huna Prayer, which is a letter to GOD, Christ, the Holy Spirit, The Mighty I Am Presence, your Higher Self, the Masters and the Healing Angels, for help in helping you to stop this bad habit and/or addiction! Say this prayer two times every morning and two times at night, out loud! If you feel so guided, at the top of the prayer the Masters or Saints you feel attuned to. For example: Jesus, Buddha, Moses, Mohammed, Mother Mary, Djwhal Khul, the Mahatma, Archangel Metatron, Archangel Raphael, Galactic healers, to name just a few.
- Call forth every morning and evening for fifteen minutes for 21 days, a short meditation where you call to God and all the aforementioned God Force and ask for them to officially anchor the Core Fear Matrix Removal Program! Ask Spirit, the Masters, and the Angels to officially remove the bad habit and addiction from your energy field and subconscious mind. Spirit and the Masters will literally pull the bad habit out of your energy field like a gardener pulls a weed out of a garden. Spirit and the Masters will pull them right out of your Crown Chakra. Ask for this also every night before you go to bed and request that Spirit and the Masters pull this programming, all core fear programming and negative ego programming out of you all night long! Do this for 21 straight days!

- Every morning when you first awaken, pray to GOD, Christ, the Holy Spirit, your Mighty I Am Presence and your Higher Self, with all your heart and soul and mind and night, for their help in not indulging in that bad habit and addiction that day!
- Then make a second prayer directly to the Holy Spirit and ask the Holy Spirit to "undo" the original cause of this bad habit and addiction and to completely remove it from your energy field and subconscious mind! Do this every morning when you first get up and when you got to bed at night!
- If you are ever tempted, immediately pray to God, Christ, the Holy Spirit, your Mighty I Am Presence and your Higher Self to remove this temptation from your consciousness! Then visualize yourself taking the Blue Flaming Sword of Archangel Michael and slicing the cord to that temptation and say "Be still, and know I Am God!"
- Say a special prayer to Archangel Michael every morning when you wake up and before you go to bed every night, and ask him to cut all energetic cords within your being to this bad habit and addiction!
- Every morning when you first get out of bed, do a one-minute meditation where you put on your "Spiritual Armor of Protection"! Visualize that you are claiming your blue sword or Archangel Michael as your symbol of claiming your personal power, and see it in your right hand! Then place a pink or red rose in your heart for unconditional self-love and unconditional love for others. Then place around yourself a "Golden Bubble of Protection" that will keep all negativity of others out of your consciousness and energy fields all day long! Then visualize a tube of light going all the way up to your Higher Self, Mighty I Am Presence and then all the way back to GOD! Then pray to GOD, Christ, the Holy Spirit, your Mighty I Am Presence and your Higher Self for a "Tube of Light and Pillar of Light" of protection

to be placed around you all day long! Reinforce this every afternoon and before bed for one minute for 21 days!
- Do a one-minute meditation every day for 21 days where you visualize and see your inner child and give it a big hug, lots of love, and tell it that you need to be very firm in regard to stopping this bad habit and addiction. Then ask you inner child for its cooperation for this is something you must do and are going to do no matter what, and it would be easier if you had the inner child's cooperation. Ask the inner child if there is anything it wants or needs! Tell the inner child you are going to raise it from now on with firmness and unconditional love and you are not going to spoil it or be too critical anymore!
- Call forth a "Golden Net" three times a day from your own Mighty I Am Presence and Higher Self to cleanse your energy fields!
- Go on a physical fast for two days on Bieler Broth and a little bit of protein. Steam a big pot of zucchini, green beans, with a little bit of celery and parsley. Put it in the blender with just a little bit of hot water from cooking and blend it up so it is like thick soup. Eat this for two days straight, if you feel a little weak add a little bit of protein. This will clean out your liver of any toxicity!
- Send a prayer request to the Academy for help for stopping the addiction and I will place it on our Interdimensional Prayer Altar!
- If you are so guided, order my Ascension Activation Meditation tape called the "18 Point Cosmic Cleansing Meditation" and listen to it once a day for 21 straight days! This will totally cleanse your energy fields! Not required in this program, but can be a helpful tool!
- Call to Spirit, the Ascended Masters, and Healing Angels before bed every night for 21 days to remove all your negative implants and negative elementals from your energy field!
- Call to Spirit, the Masters, and Angels, to repair all your bodies and balance your chakras every night before bed for 21 days!

- Call to Spirit and the Masters to anchor into your field once a day for 21 days the "Prana Wind Clearing Device" which serves like an etheric fan which will blow all the negative or stuck energy in your meridians and acupuncture points right out so your energy will run smoothly! Do this for five minutes! It is quite enjoyable and you will definitely feel it!
- Once a day call forth from Spirit and the Masters for a "Light and Love Shower" for one minute! Ask for this as well if you are ever tempted!
- If you are ever tempted, say this mantra:

> I am the Monad!
> I am the Soul!
> I am Light Divine!
> I am Love!
> I am Will!
> I am Fixed Design!

- This will immediately reconnect you to your Higher Self and break any lower-self or lower-self desire connection!
- Once a week put burning pots in all the rooms of your house to cleanse it. This is done using a metal pot with rubbing alcohol and Epsom salt. Put a plate under it so nothing catches fire. Put it in the middle of the room and light it with a match. It will burn for about five minutes. This will cleanse all the negative energy in the room so you are living in a clean Spiritual atmosphere!
- If you are ever tempted by the bad habit or addiction, immediately start chanting the name of "GOD" or any of your other favorite names of GOD or Mantra of GOD! No habit or addiction in this infinite universe can withstand the Name of GOD!
- Another good tool to battle any temptation is to say the "Lord's Prayer"!

- Upon getting up every morning for 21 days, call forth from Spirit and the Masters for an "Axiatonal Alignment"! This will balance your energy fields!
- Eat a good diet!
- Try to get a little physical exercise, fresh air and sunshine; even if it is just a little bit of walking every other day!
- Call to Spirit and the Masters before bed each night for 21 days, for the anchoring and activation of your "Anointed Christ Overself Body, your Zohar Body of Light, your Higher Adam Kadmon Body, and your Monadic Blueprint Body"!
- Ask that your entire house be also placed in a Pillar of Light and Ascension Column of Light!
- Call to Dr. Lorphan and the Galactic Healers and Angels to repair any physical or etheric damage that was done to these bodies from the past bad habit or addiction!
- While on this program and over the next two months read my books: *How To Release Fear-Based Thinking and Feeling: An In-depth Study of Spiritual Psychology, Soul Psychology, The Golden Book of Melchizedek: How To Be An Integrated Christ/Buddha In This Lifetime,* and *The Complete Ascension Manual*! All these book are available from the Academy!
- An idle mind is the devil's workshop, so keep your mind and actions totally focused on activities of GOD, your Spiritual path, and positivity!
- Keep a positive mental attitude and feeling at all times!
- Keep your attention only focused on GOD and your Spiritual path at all times!
- Why worry when you can pray?!
- Remain Spiritually vigilant for GOD and His Kingdom!

My Beloved Readers, if you follow this basic program set forth by Spirit, the Masters and I, I personally guarantee you that there is no bad habit or addiction in this infinite universe that can withstand your full personal power, the power of your mind as a Son or Daughter of God, and the love, wisdom and power of GOD, Christ, the Holy Spirit, your Mighty I Am Presence, your Higher Self, the inner plane Ascended Masters, the Archangels, and the Angels of the Light of GOD!

So let it be Written! So Let it be Done!

43

The Eight Point 21 Day Program for Creating Unconditional Self-love and Self-worth

One of the single most important Spiritual qualities to develop in life is unconditional self-love and self-worth! This chapter is dedicated to simply and easily explaining this process and sharing with you a very practical program to achieving this and/or increasing your present unconditional self-love and self-worth to the highest and most Spiritual/Christ/Buddha level you can achieve! It is actually a very simple process to achieve this once you understand it, how-ever it is one of those things that is sometimes like not being able to see the "forest for the trees"!

There are eight basic things one must understand to master, achieve, and then practice this program! The first key to developing unconditional self-love and self-worth is that you must own your 100% personal power, unconditional love and wisdom in life at all times! This, of course, is your own personal Three-Fold Flame! You can't achieve true lasting unconditional self-love and self-worth if you don't fully 100% claim your personal power and self-mastery at all times! If you don't own it, then you give it away to other people and/or your own subconscious mind, negative ego, and emotional body, which will "run you into the ground." This is not because they are inherently bad; it is just because they have no reasoning. They were never created to cause and create your life. You were! You cannot do this if you do not fully 100% claim your personal power, self-mastery and be the captain of your ship! You cause your own reality by how you think. To remain the cause and creator of your reality you must remain in your personal power and Spiritual vigilance at all times, in regard to keeping out negative ego/fear-based/separative thinking and feeling and always maintaining Spiritual/Christ/Buddha thinking! Secondly, you must claim your 100% unconditional love towards self and others at all times. To maintain unconditional self-love and self-worth you must maintain the attitude of unconditional love at all times, not only to yourself but others! You cannot maintain unconditional love towards self if you do not give it to others as well. Thirdly, you must 100% claim your wisdom at all times! For unconditional self-love and self-worth cannot be maintained if you do not do this as well! It takes great wisdom to properly parent your inner child and yourself, and maintain the perfect balance of this Three-Fold Flame in your daily life! So part of this first lesson again is keeping the negative ego/fear-based/separative thoughts and feelings out of your consciousness and mind, and constantly affirming the Spiritual/Christ/Buddha thoughts and feelings instead. The constant process of doing this will reprogram your subconscious mind and lay the foundation for creating unconditional self-love and self-worth within yourself!

The second key point is that you do have an inner child! The first key to developing unconditional self-love and self-worth is learning to parent your inner child properly. The key here is to parent your inner child with "firmness and unconditional love!" Just like in real life, some parents are too firm, critical, and judgmental! On the other side of the coin, some parents are too spoiling and permissive! The ideal is the proper balancing of masculine and feminine energy here! Either extreme of either criticalness or spoiling will cause the development of lack of self-love and self-worth in the inner child and in your self! If you are too critical, the inner child will feel beaten down, rejected, and psychologically abused! If you are too permissive, your inner child will act out, become spoiled, rebellious, and overindulgent. It is your job to always be unconditionally loving, but very firm and disciplined with the inner child and self! This is the ticket to create a balanced, healthy inner child and personality!

Now, the third key point to developing unconditional self-love and self-worth has to do with the understanding that there are two levels or two kinds of unconditional self-love and self-worth! There is the "form" level and the "essence" or Spiritual level! You cannot develop true unconditional self-love and self-worth unless you work on both levels! Let me begin with the "essence" or Spiritual level! The essence of the Spiritual level of unconditional self-love and self-worth is that you have are unconditionally loveable and have worth because GOD created you! You are a Son and Daughter of GOD. You are the Christ, in truth! You are the Buddha, in truth! You are God, in truth! You are made in the "image and likeness of GOD!" The microcosm is like the macrocosm. "As within, so without. As above, so below"!

My Beloved Brothers and Sisters, of course we have unconditional self-love and self-worth because GOD created us and we literally are incarnations of God! We could have a choice in the matter as to our self-love and self-worth if we created ourselves, however we did not, although the negative ego mind would like to think so. We did not create ourselves, GOD created us! Of course we have unconditional self-love and self-worth. When we raise a child, we make a distinction between the child and their behavior. We sometimes do not like their behavior, but we always unconditionally love the child. The same applies towards the inner child. The inner child or self may do things we don't like, and there may be lessons to learn and/or mistakes to adjust or correct; however, we always unconditionally love our self, we may just not like our behavior. This is a very important distinction here. The inner child and inner self is always worthy and lovable, for we are, in truth, incarnations of God in the process of fully Realizing GOD! We are incarnations of God, this is a fact, however we have not yet fully Realized GOD consciously on all 352 levels of integrated initiation, which is what the process of evolution is all about! At the end of this chapter, I will be providing you with specific affirmations for developing this "essence" level of unconditional self-love and self-worth to practice for 21 days!

The fourth key point to developing unconditional self-love and self-worth is to understand that there is not just an "essence" level to life where we are unconditionally loveable and worthy, there is also a "form" level of life that must be addressed as well. We must feel good about ourselves on this level as well. If all we did all day long was take drugs and drink alcohol, watch television, indulge our lower-self and sleep, and did not even try to be Spiritual in our daily lives and try to accomplish anything, we would still have "essence" level unconditional self-love and self-worth; however, we would not have a "form" level of self-love and self-worth! Now it is important to understand here that "Righteousness in the eyes of GOD is trying!" GOD expects us to make an effort in life to try and live a Spiritual life with honesty and integrity! GOD is less concerned with the outcome as He is the effort! Even if you are making mistakes, this is fine with GOD as long as you are trying to practice the Presence of GOD in your daily life. Said another way, trying to be of a Spiritual/Christ/Buddha consciousness in your thoughts, words, and deeds!

Now most people in life do "try," yet many do not have unconditional self-love and self-worth! Why is this? This is because they are not affirming the lovableness and worthiness on the "essence" level. They are not recognizing that "Righteous in the eyes of GOD is trying!" Thirdly, on the "form" level they are not recognizing in their own consciousness the successes and progress they are making! They are instead listening to the negative ego/fear-based/separative mind that is being critical, or having them compare and compete with others. We all know how the negative ego mind can turn gold into garbage. It turns diamonds into mud! Even though, in truth, from GOD's objective perspective you are doing wonderfully and GOD and your own Mighty I Am Presence and Higher Self are totally pleased with your progress and efforts, your own negative ego mind is having you "forget" all of your successes and efforts on a "form" level. There is a very easy remedy for this called a "Victory Log" and a "Gratitude Log"! The Victory Log is the key to developing unconditional self-love and self-worth on the "form" level. What you do is just make a list for your entire life of all the reasons you feel good about yourself. You list everything you can possibly think of. List Spiritual things, mental things, emotional things, energetic things, physical things, actions you have taken, Spiritual achievements, earthly achievements, social achievements, books you have read, every possible thing you have accomplished that you feel good about. This first Victory Log is one for your whole life.

Then make a second Victory Log for everything you have been doing recently in the past year, past six months, past month and past week. Remember your thoughts create your reality! Is the glass of water half empty or half full? We often, because of the negative ego mind, look at ourselves as half empty instead of half full! The Victory Log is one of the most profound Spiritual tools ever invented that hardly anyone knows about on Earth! It will immediately bring you back to a "half full" perspective! You will see the donut instead of the hole! You will be taking the optimistic view of self rather than the pessimistic view of self. You will be taking GOD's view of self rather than the negative ego's view of self!

Then after doing the first two Victory Logs do one more which is a future Victory Log, and list all the things you are planning to accomplish and achieve that you really feel good about! Then do one last log or list, which really is a gratitude list! Make a list of everything in your life you have to be grateful for! We often do this at Thanksgiving time, and we always feel wonderful doing it, however we should be doing it everyday, or at least until it is a habit in our subconscious minds to think this way!

My Beloved Readers, if you will do these four types of Victory Logs and/or lists, I personally 100% guarantee you that you will feel like a million dollars! Be sure to be humble at the end and thank GOD and the Masters for all their blessings for as the saying goes, "But for the grace of GOD go I!" So feel like a million dollars as you should, and be grateful to GOD and the Masters for all the bountiful blessings they have bestowed upon you, including your health! There are plenty of people in this world who have it a lot worse off than you. Look at the freedoms you have living in the country you do. How about your physical health? There are people with missing arms or limbs, or are paralyzed, have AIDS, dying of cancer, and the list could go on and on! Thank GOD for your blessings and all you have going for you! I am sure you feel even better about yourself after just reading this chapter and you haven't even started your Victory Log yet! Do you see the power of the mind? The truth is, you never had to feel bad about yourself, and you could have done this process at anytime in your entire life and you would have felt a million times better. This is the kind of thing that should be taught in schools from first grade onward! Kids would do much better in school if they had more unconditional self-love and self-worth!

Do you see, my Beloved Readers, after doing this process with the "essence" level affirmations and visualizations I am going to give you, and the "form" level affirmations and visualizations I am going to give you, you are going to feel like a million bucks for the rest of your life, and if you ever start to slip you just go back to doing these practices and you will immediately get pumped back up again! The great secret of the universe is that your thoughts create your reality and that we as children, adolescents, and adults are not given all the proper insights and Spiritual and psychological tools we need to easily do these things. People are suffering all over the world for no reason, when it is completely unnecessary and could be remedied in moments! It is your job once you master this 21 day program within self, to share it with family, friends and students, and spread it around the world, for lack of self-love and self-worth is one of the single most important psychological problems on this Earth and is the core cause of most problems along with not owning your personal power!

The fifth key point to developing unconditional self-love and self-worth is to recognize that everything that happens in life is just a lesson and not a sin. Mistakes occur in everyone and this is normal and unavoidable. You do not go out of your way to make them, but when they happen the key is to just learn from them, gain the golden nugget of wisdom, and then "forgive yourself!" You cannot develop unconditional self-love and self-worth without self-forgiveness, and forgiveness for others! I emphasize the point of "for others" as well, for the outside world is really a projection screen for your own thoughts. To insure that you are able to maintain unconditional self-love and worth over the long term you must forgive self and others for all of it is God, and you are God! So in forgiving others you are really forgiving yourself as well! This last thought is not something you will find in any "personality" level understanding book on understanding self-love! Yet it is an essential key ingredient to maintaining self-love, otherwise the law of karma will bring those unforgiving thoughts towards others back to self, which will affect the personal level of self-love! In truth, you forgive others as well not as a charity to them, but as a charity to yourself! Your forgiving them has nothing to do with them, it has to do with correcting faulty thinking within yourself!

Many, however, on this earthly plane forgive others but do not forgive self. This is faulty thinking for everything is forgivable! This world is but a dream of GOD! There is no such thing as death! Earth is just a Spiritual school to see if you can forgive self and others in all circumstances. If Jesus can do it on the cross while being crucified and physically killed, then you can forgive yourself and others for all your lessons! That is why he demonstrated this example! So your negative ego could not say my lessons are worse!

By forgiving self for all mistakes, all guilt is relieved as well as regret! By learning from the experience and making a specific Spiritual vow to never let that mistake happen again, you can let go of all guilt and all regret! To not forgive self is to just make another mistake that you will need to forgive your-self for! As *A Course in Miracles* says, "Forgiveness is the key to happiness"! There is no mistake in the history of the Earth and of the history of this infinite universe that is not 100% forgivable by GOD, and this is a fact! It is only the negative ego mind that holds grudges. The Spiritual/Christ/Buddha conscious-ness sees nothing in life to even forgive for mistakes are positive not negative. Perfection is not, not making mistakes. Perfection is trying to not make conscious mistakes! Even the Ascended Masters make mistakes! This is how we learn! It is true. However, the more of a Spiritual Master you become, the less mistakes you will make! As Paramahansa Yogananda said, "A Saint is a sinner that never gave up"!

The sixth key point to developing unconditional self-love and self-worth is the process of Spiritual Alchemy or turning negatives into positives. In GOD's eyes there is nothing that you have ever done in this life or a past live that cannot be turned into a positive, no matter how bad the mistake! The gaining of the golden nuggets of wisdom is of course a big part of this process. Also using that mistake and lesson to help others. Use any big mistakes you have made to become an expert in that area and then dedicate a part of your life to helping others not to make that same mistake. This is how lemons are turned into lemonade! If a person kills someone in a car crash because of drinking alcohol, they could, for example, then dedicate their life to educating people to not drink alcohol and drive. If you took drugs and lost all your money, destroyed your marriage and alienated your kids, you could then dedicate your life to remaining drug-free and educate others about the danger of drugs, using yourself as an example. If you have been in prison, then educate adolescents about crime and prison so you may help another not suffer as you have! My Beloved Readers, "Grace erases karma!" Even King David in the Bible, who was "Beloved of GOD," lusted over another man's wife and had her husband sent to the front lines of the war so he would more likely be killed and David could have her. David repented for his sins, and became one of the greatest kings of Israel! GOD always welcomes his prodigal Sons and Daughters home no matter what they have done! It is true that all karma must be balanced! Karma can be balanced by grace, by learning and by service! Even Hitler is forgiven and, in truth, is an incarnation of God! He will have to achieve Spiritual/Christ/Buddha consciousness first and balance all his karma though before he will be allowed to return to his Spiritual home. This will happen, for the Divine Plan will not be complete until all souls return home! Again I repeat, there is absolutely nothing in the history of the infinite universe that is not 100% forgivable! It is only the negative ego that thinks not. However, the definition of GOD is "GOD equals man minus ego"!

The seventh and final key point to achieving unconditional self-love and self-worth is the recognition that just as we are a Spiritual parent for our inner child and/or inner self, GOD and our Mighty I Am Presence and Higher Selves are our Spiritual parents! In the Huna teachings of Hawaii, the Higher Self is called the "Aumakua" or "utterly trustworthy parental self"! Just as our Higher Self is the "utterly trustworthy parental self for us," we must learn to be the "utterly trustworthy parental selves" for our inner child and/or inner self! So part of the process of achieving self-love is allowing yourself to receive unconditional love from GOD, Christ, the Holy Spirit, your Mighty I Am Presence, and your Higher Self! So you not only receive unconditional worth from GOD because GOD created you and you are an incarnation of God, but you also allow yourself to "feel" the flow of GOD's love for you! This way you as a Spiritual parent unconditionally love your inner child and self, and GOD, Christ, the Holy Spirit, your Mighty I Am Presence and Higher Self unconditionally love you! Through this process you also give unconditional worth to your inner child and self.

Plus, you receive the same unconditional worth from GOD! Plus, you are being firm and loving with your inner child and self, just as GOD is firm and unconditionally loving with us as a parent. For just as GOD is, of course, unconditional, He is firm in the sense that he does have universal laws He expects us to learn and to follow, and if we don't follow them and become obedient to them, we cause suffering upon our self. The suffering is not a punishment, it is just a reminder or a signal to seek truth and understand GOD's universal laws on a Spiritual, mental, emotional, etheric, physical, and earthly level!

So by applying all the aforementioned things, you become right with self and right with GOD before entering into any other relationship! You are fully unconditionally loved and worthy before entering any other relationship! You are fully balanced within the masculine and feminine of firmness and love before entering any other relationship! In doing this you will not need to seek love outside of self or from other people, for you will be giving it to self and allowing yourself to receive it from GOD first! Hence, you go into life fully empowered because as we already spoke of you are going to be fully claiming your 100% personal power, unconditional love, and wisdom! So you go into life fully empowered, fully loved, fully balanced, and fully whole and complete within self! This way you will not need to seek power, love, worth, approval, acceptance, or wholeness outside of self, for you will have found it within your relationship to self and relationship to GOD! Plus, you are fully owning that, in truth, "you are God!" So you will not seek false gods outside of self, or put things before GOD and your Spiritual path, for you fully know that you are God, you are the Christ, you are the Buddha, you are the Eternal Self as are your Brothers and Sisters! You will hence not only see this within self, you will also see this in your Brothers and Sisters who are part of GOD with you! By seeing this in your Brother and Sister, it insures that you maintain this in yourself, for, in truth, they are part of your self in a Spiritual sense! You will have achieved unconditional self-love and self-worth within yourself and will be giving unconditional self-love and self-worth outside of self to others and to your greater and larger Spiritual self as the infinite God-being you truly are. So the circle will be complete, so to speak! Most important you will be right with self and right with GOD, which will allow you to be right with all other relationships in your life! For you cannot be right with others if you are not first right with self and right with GOD!

As the saying also goes, you cannot love others if you do not love yourself. If you do not love yourself you can still love others in a romantic relationship, however the type of love relationships you form will be an addictive love, a dependent or co-dependent love. It will be a complementary love of a mother/son or father/daughter psychological love, rather than a mutually independent or adult/adult love in regard to a romantic relationship!

So my Beloved Readers, you see how incredibly important developing this unconditional self-love and self-worth is, otherwise you will look outside of self for it rather than find it within your relationship to self and relationship to GOD!

The last key to this process of maintaining unconditional self-love and self-worth is maintaining your Spiritual vigilance and Golden Bubble of Protection at all times around yourself! This is important because there is a lot of negative energy in the world and a lot of people who are run by the negative ego! So it is not only important to be Spiritually vigilant against allowing your own negative ego to try to enter your consciousness and mind; it is also essential to put your Golden Bubble of Protection up every day almost like a piece of clothing you put on every morning to keep out other people's negative energy! Because most people have no training in Spiritual psychology, even lightworkers are extremely run by the negative ego! They are very Spiritually advanced in their Spiritual bodies or "light bodies," but they have a lot of rough edges around their psychological selves and bodies from lack of proper Spiritual training which is not really their fault! This is something our society should provide in schools, but it does not. Because of this there are constant attacks, criticisms, judgements, put downs, self-righteousness, competitiveness, anger, intolerance, impatience, irritableness, and frustration, which of course are all negative ego qualities. If you do not keep your Golden Bubble of Protection up, these outside negative ego thought forms and energy can act as negative programming to try and counteract the Spiritual work you are doing. The key is to put this Golden Bubble of Protection on every morning from your "energetic or etheric wardrobe," and place it around yourself so that when other people are manifesting this type of negative energy it just slides of your bubble like "water off a duck's back"! Or it just bounces of your Golden Bubble like a "rubber pillow"! This, my Beloved Readers, is the final eighth point to insure that you will always have unconditional self-love and self-worth! You can see from my explanation that it is something that is really so very simple to understand once you "get it." However, it is one of these things if you try to figure it out yourself you can search for lifetimes and not be able to figure it out and get all the puzzle pieces to fit together. Well I am happy to say there is no reason to have to reinvent the wheel, for Spirit, the Masters, and I have been very happy to have the time to explain this most wondrous process to you!

Now since this "Eight Point Plan to Achieving Unconditional Self-love and Self-worth" has now been explained we will now move to the final aspect of this chapter, which is the 21 Day Program that Spirit, the Masters, and I have put together to implement and cement in this program! As you all know it takes 21 days to cement any new habit into the subconscious mind. So practice everything I have said in this chapter and follow the program I am about to lay out for you, and within 21 days you will have developed a habit of having 100% unconditional self-love and self-worth! It will actually be a habit where it will actually be hard not to have! You will always have to be Spiritually vigilant against negative ego thinking from within and without, however as long as you do this you will be set for life on this most important Spiritual issue!

The 21 Day Program for Developing Unconditional Self-love and Self-worth

The first part of this 21 day program is to work with the personal power, self-love, invulnerability and Spiritual affirmations (also called my favorite affirmations) in the chapter in this book called "affirmations." These affirmations will help keep your Three-Fold Flame of power, love, wisdom and Spiritual attunement and protection working at 100%! Say these affirmations three times a day for about ten minutes each time, out loud, and anytime you feel yourself sinking mentally and emotionally and you need to get pumped up! Do this for 21 days, and longer if you like!

Secondly, work with the following "essence" affirmations I spoke about earlier in the chapter, for five minutes, twice a day, for 21 days!

I have unconditional self-love and self-worth because GOD created me!

I am blessed as a Son or Daughter of GOD!

Be still and know I Am God!

I am made in the image of God, so of course I am worthy and loveable!

I am God and fully know it, and am fully deserving of unconditional self-love and worth!

I am, in truth, the Christ, the Buddha, the Eternal Self, so of course I have unconditional self-love and self-worth!

I am literally an incarnation of GOD, and although I make occasional mistakes, that does not affect my inherent unconditional self-love and worth!

The next Spiritual practice to develop unconditional self-love and self-worth is to do your four types of Victory Logs as described in the beginning of this chapter. The Victory Log or list for your entire life. The Victory Log or list of all your recent victories in the last month or week, no matter how small. Then the future victories you are planning on achieving. Then the Gratitude List for the entire past and recent past! Doing this will revolutionize your consciousness and completely reprogram your subconscious mind. Then every day, once a day, read this list over, out loud, for 21 days. Keep adding to the list each day as new things keep coming to mind! If ever you feel yourself sinking, either read the list or type it over! It is guaranteed to pump you back up mentally every time without fail!

The next Spiritual practice is to start your day by calling for a Golden Net from your Mighty I Am Presence to clear your energy fields. Then say the following mantra:

I am the Monad!
I am the Soul!
I am the Light Divine!
I am Love!
I am Will!
I am Fixed Design!

Call to Archangel Michael and your own Mighty I Am Presence for a Golden Dome of Protection to be placed around you!

Then call forth to GOD, Christ, the Holy Spirit, your Mighty I Am Presence, and your Higher Self, for help this day in developing unconditional self-love and self-worth!

Then make a specific prayer to the Holy Spirit to "undo" all conditional self-love and self-worth programming and to remove the cause 100%!

Then call forth your Mighty I Am Presence, your Higher Self, the Ascended Master Djwhal Khul, Sananda, your Spirit Guides, your Guardian Angels, Healing Angels, and call forth the "Core Fear Matrix Removal Program"! Then ask them to remove all core fear programming in your subconscious mind, conscious mind, and energy fields! Then ask them to remove all conditional love programming. Do this for 20 minutes every morning and 20 minutes before bed every night! As you go to bed at night ask them to continue working on you all night until all conditional love and fear-based programming is removed!

Then ask them before bed to imprint into your subconscious mind unconditional self-love and unconditional self-worth programming, however, make a statement that you will only accept this from your own Mighty I Am Presence and from the Ascended Masters of the Light of GOD and from no one else!

Continue these practices every day religiously for 21 straight days! If you do this, you will be completely transformed after three weeks!

The next Spiritual practice is to on the first day you begin this program write out or type out on a piece of paper a specific Spiritual vow you make to yourself, GOD, and your inner child that "From this moment forward you will 100% give yourself unconditional self-love and self-worth every moment of your life to the very best of your ability!" Then say, "So let it be written! So let it be done!"

Call to the Divine Mother, Mother Mary, Quan Yin, Isis and the Lady Masters before bed and ask them for help as well in developing unconditional self-love and self-worth! Ask them for help in training you at night while you sleep, and helping you in any way they can during the day!

Then for one minute, twice a day, call forth to GOD, Christ, the Holy Spirit, your Mighty I Am Presence, your Higher Self, the inner plane Ascended Masters and Angels for a "Love Shower"! Bathe in this Love Shower for one minute and then go about your business! Do this for 21 days!

Put your affirmations on an audiotape and listen to it as background music while working around the house. Also play it very softly as you go to bed at night so the affirmations go into your subconscious mind as an autosuggestion or self-hypnosis type of method, taking advantage of your greater suggestibility as you fall asleep at night! You do not have to do this method, however, if you want to try it it is effective and quite comforting. It's kind of like a lullaby of self-love and self-worth affirmations very softly putting you to bed for 21 days after your nightly prayers!

Then every other day, have a dialogue in your journal with your inner child. Talk to your inner child and ask it how it is doing! Then in your journal become the inner child and let it talk back! This is kind of like role-playing or a type of voice dialogue in your journal! Ask your inner child if there is anything it wants. Ask it how it feels about this new program you are doing. Ask it if it feels if you're striking a good balance of firmness and love in how you are parenting it. Ask it if there are any adjustments it would like to make. Ask it how it feels about your current life plan!

Then do the same thing with your own Higher Self and/or Mighty I Am Presence! Ask it if it has any further guidance for you on this 21 day program that you are doing! Does it have any other suggestions or adjustments it would have you make? Ask it how it feels about your current overall life plan and the direction you are going! Do any changes or adjustments need to be made? Then become your Higher Self or Mighty I Am Presence and talk back to your self! This is good channeling practice as well! You will be surprised what comes through. Just do the process and do not filter it. It does not matter if you think you are not doing it right! Let go of all that! Just do the process and see what comes through! We are just trying to open the lines of communication a little more clearly and consciously between you, your Mighty I Am Presence and inner child! This process helps these three levels become more integrated and cohesive!

The next Spiritual practice to do for 21 days is to write out on a piece of paper the words, "personal love, unconditional love, wisdom, firmness with inner child, unconditional self-love to your inner child, spoiling your inner child, too self-critical to your inner child."

Then everyday, every morning and before bed give yourself a percentage score from one to one hundred on how you have been doing that last 12 hour period manifesting the qualities I have listed! The ideal, of course, would be to have 100% on everything except for "spoiling" and being "too self-critical." Those ideally would be zero! We, of course, are not expecting perfection but improvement! This is a psychological logging tool. Its purpose is to make you more conscious of what you are doing every moment. By keeping a log, it is kind of a little game you are playing with yourself to see if you can raise the percentage of your scores! By doing this every day for 21 days you can raise your scores and see your progress! If your scores are ever too low then just write out a new specific Spiritual Vow on paper or just say it out loud that you will improve in that area! Work more closely with the affirmations that I have given you that apply to the quality you want to improve, or make up some additional ones that specifically fit the quality you need to develop!

Every morning when you get up and when you go to bed, put on your Spiritual, mental and emotional clothing.

First put on your personal power, which might be visualized as holding a blue flame sword of Archangel Michael.

Then place a red or pink rose in your heart from the Divine Mother symbolizing unconditional self-love and unconditional love for others as well!

Then place your Golden Bubble of Protection around you as mentioned earlier in this chapter!

Then call forth a Tube of Light and Pillar of Light of Protection from GOD and your own Mighty I Am Presence! See and visualize a Tube and Pillar of White Light surrounding you from GOD and your own Mighty I Am Presence! Then place around yourself the Mantle of Spiritual consciousness, Christ consciousness, and/or Buddha consciousness! This can be visualized as some kind of Golden White Mantle that you take out of your closet! It can be visualized as a Golden White Robe. It can be visualized as a beautiful Golden White Dress. It can be visualized as a garment of Christ/Buddha light!

Just as they get dressed every morning with physical clothes, most people don't realize they need to dress themselves with Spiritual, mental, emotional, and energetic clothes! They will absolutely be amazed what a powerful and profound effect this simple exercise will have on you. Do this as you get physically dressed every day. When you finish dressing physically, then take one minute to dress yourself Spiritually, mentally, emotionally, and energetically as well!

The last of the Spiritual practices in this 21-day program are creative visualization practices. In the first one, see and visualize yourself in the morning and before bed for one or two minutes as the true God-being, Christed-being and Buddha-being you are. See yourself in your mind's eye as GOD created you! You might see yourself in our Ascended Garment of Light! In a golden white robe! Again, in a beautiful Christed dress! Imagine how you would look, and, in truth, as you really are as an Ascended Master! Imagine how you looked upon your creation by GOD! Recognize fully that you are still that being! You are just that being living in a physical body! Visualize this! Then say to yourself again "I am an incarnation of God and so, of course, I am 100% deserving of unconditional self-love and self-worth!"

Then visualize your inner child playing in a grassy field! See yourself as the adult you currently are, walking towards your inner child! See the inner child seeing and recognizing you, of course, and running towards you and leaping into your arms. See and visualize yourself giving it a gigantic hug and your inner child hugging and loving you! Tell the inner child in your mind's eye how much you love it! How you will always take care of it, protect it, be firm and disciplined with it, but always give it 100% unconditional love and forgiveness at all times! Tell the inner child that you and it will begin a new start of this day and this three-week period!

Then see GOD, Christ, the Holy Spirit, your own Mighty I Am Presence and your Higher Self appear above you as a gigantic golden white light! See them wanting to join in this hug, and see them pouring love down from Heaven upon the both of you! Totally receive this! Then both you and the inner child send love back up to GOD, Christ, the Holy Spirit, your Mighty I Am Presence, and your Higher Self!

Then see the love flowing back and forth up a Tube of Light and Pillar of Light! Then see the Light of GOD descend and anchor itself on Earth, in you and the inner child, forming a perfect integration and harmony!

Conclusion

My Beloved Readers, I humbly suggest that this is one of the most profound Spiritually integrated programs ever put together to create "unconditional self-love and self-worth!" It is 100% guaranteed to work, for it is based not on whimsical things, but on GOD's laws on Spiritual, mental, emotional, energetic and physical levels! Integrate this within yourself and then share this information and book with your family, friends and students! The majority of the world is suffering from some form of lack of self-love and self-worth! There is absolutely no reason for this to be, for it can be easily remedied! Just the reading of this chapter without even starting the program has almost done it already! Once these principles are understood, and you see how easy they are to understand and how much sense they make, everything just starts to fit and come together! Share this information and book with as many people as you can, for these are, in truth, the nuts and bolts of the Spiritual path that our fellow Brothers and Sisters are crying out for the most! Working all together as fellow Sons and Daughters of GOD we shall transform this world and help to bring all Sons and Daughters of GOD "to the peace and love that passeth understanding"!

So let it be Written! So let it be Done!

44

The Negative Ego and the Return of the Divine Mother and the Goddess Energies to Earth

My Beloved Readers, I consider the following chapter to be one of the most important chapters in this entire book! I have really been looking forward to writing this chapter since it is so incredibly important at this time! I have much I want to say and as the ancient Chinese proverb says, "The thousand mile journey begins with the first step"! It is and will be a most enjoyable thousand-mile journey indeed! On this note, I will humbly begin!

There was a time on Earth during the time of the ancient civilization of Lemuria (which predated Atlantis) when the God/Goddess energies were in perfect balance! In the Bible, this could be referred to as the time of the Garden of Eden, or first Golden Age on this planet! However, when there was the first eating of the fruit from the "Tree of Good and Evil," this Biblical story speaks to that time when man, for the first time on Earth misused his free choice and thought out of harmony with GOD! This, of course, was the beginning of negative ego/fear-based/separative thinking and feeling! This was the first time mankind thought out of harmony with GOD and out of harmony with the Spiritual/Christ/Buddha consciousness!

It was this choice of fear, separation, selfishness, lower-self desire, conditional love, judgement, anger, grudges, guilt, hurt, depression, sadness that also began the process of rejection and abuse of the Divine Mother and Goddess energies on Earth!

This misuse of free choice also began a process of mass consciousness on the Earth to identify with masculine energies over feminine energies! The mind over the heart! Thinking over intuition! Thinking over feeling! Thinking over psychic perceptions! Thinking and science over Spirituality! Thinking, selfish-ness and technology over anything in regard to Mother Earth and Nature!

My Beloved Readers, this caused an overidentification with the Patriarchy over the Matriarchy! Left brain became more important than right brain! Men began to control society and women were not seen as equals! This overidentification with masculine energy caused there to be too much aggressiveness, willfulness, loss of sensitivity, psychological and physical violence, inability to nurture, pridefulness, loss of compassion, jealousy, competition, loss of unconditional love, and a focus on war as a means to get what one wanted!

There became a focus on science and technology over Spirituality and Mother Earth. Nothing was real except if you could experience it with your five physical senses! Logic was favored over intuition, channeling, or psychic perception! There was the rejection and disowning of the 22 Supersenses of GOD that go beyond the five physical senses!

Women were forced to become more subservient and lesser class citizens. Just think about it, my Beloved Readers, people have been on the Earth for 18.5 million years and jsut 20 years ago we were voting in the United States for an equal rights amendment for women! What have we been doing for 18.5 million years?

Descartes, the famous philosopher, said, "I think, therefore I am"! I ask you, my Beloved Readers, how come he didn't say, "I feel, therefore I am," or "I intuit, therefore I am"! Women were burned at the stake in the Middle Ages for just being mystics and channels! Women in the Orient are still brought up to be subservient!

In our modern day society, women are often portrayed as sex objects! They do not get the same pay as men! There has never been a woman President of the United States, and very few women leaders in this world! There are still very few women members of the Senate and House of Representatives as compared to men!

It was only 150 years ago that women were even allowed to vote! Only men could vote up until that time! Again, I ask, what has been going on for 18.5 million years? The cutting off of the Feminine also cut off Spirituality to a great degree. It caused a total disconnection from Mother Earth and the living Being that she is. There was the total disconnection from the Animal Kingdom, Plant Kingdom, and Mineral Kingdom. Animals were seen as objects or just pets, not as younger brothers and sisters. They were and still are greatly abused by our society! They are used in the most abhorrent scientific experiments with no regard for the God Beings that they are! They trap and kill animals for furs in the most inhumane ways you don't even want to know about! I heard a report recently from China where they put bears in small little boxes for their entire life, unable to move so they can extract bile from their gall bladder for the bear's entire life! This is one of the most abhorrent things I have ever heard of! We all know about the experiments scientists do on animals.

We have the same disregard for plants! Plants are incarnations of GOD as well. They have consciousness and feelings! Maybe not in the same way we do, but they still have a form of consciousness! Yet we rip things out of the ground and just use this Kingdom for our purposes with total disregard! We have all heard about the book *The Secret Life of Plants*! Plants are living Beings and must be worked with, not just used. We also tear down the rain forests and foul up the oxygen level on the planet all in the name of greed and technology!

My Beloved Readers, it was this same greed and technology which destroyed Atlantis! This disownment of the Goddess and focus on the mind, science and technology, caused the civilization which followed Lemuria on the other side of the globe to eventually be destroyed in a series of massive catastrophic Earth changes which were basically caused by mankind's abuse of the Divine Mother, Mother Earth and their own Goddess energies!

Even the word mankind! How come we don't call mankind "womankind"? Even our Spiritual books are all written in patriarchal language! Part of this is the problem of our language, however part of this is because it became the accepted norm of our society, so of course the inner plane Ascended Masters just had to follow the norms of our society to get their point across. Have you noticed how a great many of even our favorite Spiritual books have been written in patriarchal language? This is not a judgment upon these books, as much as a product of our society!

My Beloved Readers, the supreme example of this is that even GOD was seen as being masculine! When we referred to GOD, we were taught to call "Him" the Heavenly "Father." The feminine aspect was seen as Mother Earth! The Divine Mother was completely rejected from Spirituality!

The Heavenly Father and the Earth Mother form the two sides of GOD's nature! Kind of like sitting on GOD's left and right side! The whole study of the Divine Mother is left out of most Spiritual training and schools of thought for it is not understood!

How come GOD was not portrayed as a woman in all the ancient artwork and in our books? Of course we are not looking to do a pendulum swing and overidentify with the Matriarchy, for that would be just as bad as overidentifying with the Patriarchy. It is balance we seek!

Here is another very interesting one, my Beloved Readers! Have you ever wondered why there is a negative stigma about a woman being a "feminist," however there is not a similar stigma of a man being a "masculinist"?

Women who don't have a husband are "old maids"! Men who don't have wives are eligible bachelors and "studs"! In Hollywood, men get more of the key roles! Our heroes are portrayed as these violent, egotistical protagonists on the side of good, having sex with beautiful woman after beautiful woman! There is the incredible focus on a woman's physical looks and not as much as on her Christed nature!

Even the Masters who formed our religions have all been men! This is not the Masters fault for they are not patriarchal, they just had to incarnate in male bodies otherwise they would not have been listened to by the unconscious mass consciousness! Even the Spiritual Hierarchy that governs our planet seems to be mostly men. This is not really true; this is just what mass consciousness through the lens of Patriarchy has allowed us to see! The Divine Mother and the Lady Masters basically had to back away!

My Beloved Readers, in a great many of our modern day religions women are not allowed to be priests or priestesses! In ancient times the priestesses were revered. With the eating of the fruit from the "Tree of Good and Evil," over time the priestesses had to go into hiding! This not allowing women to be priests occurs in Fundamentalist Christianity, Catholicism, and the Mormon faith! In the Jewish religion there is the Kabbalah of Jewish mysticism. Women, up until recently, were not allowed to even study the Kabbalah, only men were!

Then we see in our society all the spousal abuse, usually its' women! We also see this towards children as well! We also see how women have to put up with all the sexual comments and if they report it they lose their jobs because of a men's club who are in control! There are very few women corporate leaders or who really have the power in our world.

Have you ever asked yourself what our world would be like if women were in charge from the beginning? Would there be as much war? Would there be as much violence? Would Mother Earth be as abused? Would technology be put before Spirituality? Would the mind be made as more important than the heart? I think we all know the answer to these questions!

Getting back now to the Mineral Kingdom! Mankind has had no regard for the Mineral Kingdom. Minerals, gemstones, crystals, and even rocks have a form of consciousness as well! All mankind has done is strip the Earth for greed and its energy concerns. Showing no appreciation or love for this kingdom! We strip mine and rape the Earth and leave it polluted, basically for money! We dump toxic waste into the Earth. We don't remediate our trash sites properly. We dump nuclear waste into the Earth! We pollute our oceans and rivers, air, and earth! We put gigantic gaping holes in the ozone layer. We create the "greenhouse effect"! We kill off animals to the point where they are extinct! We have as a species, greatly abused the Earth Mother. We have not cleaned up our "campsites" after we have left, so to speak. We have not given back to Mother Earth. We have not planted trees! We have gotten so disconnected from Goddess energies that we have lost all contact with Pan, the Nature Spirits, Plant Devas, Gnomes, Elves, Sylphs, Salamanders, Undines, Nature Elementals and all the Etheric Beings that overlight and live inside the flowers, plants, vegetables, shrubs and trees! It is these beings that create nature, and most of mankind has no idea they even exist. Instead of working in cooperation with these beings and nature, the rejection of the Goddess has caused us to use pesticides, chemicals, and treat nature as some kind of mechanical mechanism instead of the Divine process of GOD it is! We as a species, as part of this rejection of the Goddess, have driven the Nature Spirits, Devas, Elves, and Elemental beings from our farms and nature spots! Yet they have forgiven and waited patiently, as has the Divine Mother and Goddess energies, for the time of their return to Earth, to be honored and sanctified in their rightful place! My Beloved Readers, this time has come!

My Beloved Readers, you have all heard of the movie the *Return of the Jedi*! Well, I tell you, as we now enter this New Millennium, Aquarian

Age and Seventh Golden Age, I say unto you that we have now entered the time of the "Return of the Divine Mother and the Goddess Energies to Earth," after 18.5 million years! Enough is enough!

There have been times in Earth's history where the Goddess energies made a slight comeback, however the negative ego minds overidentification with God energies over Goddess energies has always abused them in the end and driven them back out! As they say in the political speeches at the conventions, "It is time for this to end!" It is not only time for this to end, it *is* going to end, and we as the Spiritual leaders and lightworkers of this planet are going to make it end!

I just had another insight while writing this. Have you ever noticed how we make a special consideration to integrate the Goddess energy, but do not have to use the same special consideration for the God energies. Even the term is a foreign term! In truth, God energies should be both God and Goddess energies however, in our world it is not!

The word feminism exists, but there is no such word as "masculinism"! Our world is unbelievable. We as species have not fully recognized the degree to which we are seeing through a masculine lens.

My Beloved Readers, listen very closely to what I am about to say! God Realization, the Divine Plan and Integrated Ascension will not be achieved if the Divine Mother, the Goddess energies, the Lady Masters and Mother Earth, Pan, the Nature Spirits, Plant Devas and Elementals, are not brought back into their rightful Divine place within yourself and our society as a whole!

Even in the way Earthly and Spiritual history is recorded, women are not given their proper respect! We have all heard the saying, "behind every great man there is a great woman"! This is true, but those great women have not been honored and recognized enough! Even in the way we describe Spiritual history, even as Spiritual leaders and lightworkers! Mother Mary for example, I don't believe she was given enough credit in the whole story of Jesus for the incredible demonstration of Godliness she lived out. What Jesus demonstrated was incredible, however, what

Mother Mary demonstrated was also incredible and I don't think this is talked about enough.

Another interesting point is that one of Jesus' teachers, according to the Universal Mind channelings of Edgar Cayce ("the Sleeping Prophet"), was a woman by the name of Judy! This, of course, is not talked about!

My Beloved Readers, have you ever noticed that women usually make up 90% of every Spiritual workshop, seminar, and lecture? I have been doing this work for almost 30 years and this never fails to be the case! Thank GOD for women who have" held up the flame' for Spirituality on this planet for 18.5 million years!

Have you also noticed in the New Age Movement that there is a great focus on Spirituality but there is an overidentification with Heavenly energies and a lack of appreciation for the Material Face of GOD? The masculine path of GOD has stressed the Occult knowledge and understanding the Laws of GOD. It has also focused on the Heavenly and Celestial realms, the Ascended Masters, Archangels and Angels, Elohim, Christed Extraterrestrials, dimensions of reality, and the study of psychology! This is certainly all wonderful! However, the feminine path of GOD honors all this but also seeks to "feel life and fully embody life!" It seeks, of course, to always live in the Heart! It seeks not just deductive thinking, but also inductive knowledge and wisdom. This means asking Spirit and listening! The feminine path of GOD fully recognizes the Earth and the Material Universe as much a part of GOD as the psychological level and Heavenly or Spiritual level! The feminine path of GOD recognizes the need to master the Earth, totally love the Earth, and take responsibility for the Earth, in the form of honoring and sanctifying the Earth Mother and the Nature, Devic and Elemental Kingdoms and the Animal, Plant and Mineral Kingdoms, but also our Earthly civilization itself! The masculine path of GOD just seeks to use the Earth as a means to achieve liberation. It is the feminine path of GOD that teaches the purpose of life is not to "Ascend and leave the Earth" but rather

"Descend and anchor God onto and into the Earth and Earth life!" The Four Faces of GOD are equally revered, "Spiritual, Mental, Emotional, and Material!" The feminine path of GOD wants to bring Heaven to Earth! It loves our civilization as much as it loves Mother Earth and nature. The feminine path of GOD recognizes that your Spiritual path is not really complete unless you physically ground it into the Earth and Earth life. Your Spiritual path is not complete unless you demonstrate GOD on Earth! Your Spiritual path is not complete unless you complete your Earthly/Spiritual mission and purpose on Earth! Your Spiritual path is not complete unless you totally sanctify, revere, honor, and appreciate the Material Face of GOD! The feminine path to GOD realizes we have contracts and Spiritual commitments to fulfill, which we made on the inner plane before we came. The feminine path of GOD wants to fully embody God on Earth! It wants to feel life to its fullest without getting into negative ego forms of feeling! The feminine path of GOD often experiences "Goddess Tears," which are not the negative ego's forms of tears, but more occasional "Spiritual tears" of unconditional love and Divine compassion! Men on a masculine path of GOD often do not understand this and judge this as just women being taken over by their emotional body and negative ego again! This is, of course, not true, and is even Spiritual men's limited lens patriarchal seeing!

Women, of course, have to be careful not to overidentify with the Goddess path and not become matriarchal in nature, feminist in the sense of anti-masculine, overemotional where they are victims of the emotional body, and negative ego mind. Women have to be careful to avoid being too right brain where they lose common sense or logic, and become too empathic. The true Goddess path does not try to oppose the masculine path of GOD, but to just properly integrate it. The same is true of the masculine path of GOD! In its truest form, it fully integrates the feminine path of GOD! So as to avoid confusion here, sometimes men and/or women in the past and very much presently as well, embrace a masculine path of GOD that is rejecting the feminine path to

GOD. Sometimes as a counter balance or pendulum swing women, and sometimes men as well, have taken on a feminine path of GOD that has rejected the masculine path of GOD! Each side has thought their path to GOD was better! Both of these states of consciousness are illusion. The only true path to GOD is one of integration and balance! Please listen very carefully, my Beloved Readers, to what I am about to say. "No one on Earth will achieve true God Realization in the fullest sense of the term, which integrates all Four Faces of GOD (Spiritual, Mental, Emotional and Material), if they don't fully embrace the masculine path of GOD and the feminine path of GOD! It is only then that you will know the "Wholeness of GOD"! The problem is that in our Spiritual history and in our present day society, it is the masculine path of GOD that is being focused on and the feminine path of GOD that is being rejected to a great extent!

Now again, to avoid confusion and to explain my terms here clearly. In the true Goddess path there is no over- or underidentification with the God/Goddess energies! Equally as true, in the true God path there is no favoritism to God over Goddess energies. I am, for the sake of clarification of Spiritual principles, pointing out here how a masculine path of GOD can and is being overidentified in our past history and in our current civilization. I am also pointing out how the feminine path to GOD needs to be much more developed in people and lightworkers around the globe to hence then find the proper God/Goddess balance that true Gods and Goddesses both want! The feminine path to GOD has been disowned! Lightworkers on Earth and in the New Age Movement are extremely imbalanced! Their Spiritual bodies are highly developed, but their bank accounts are not! Their light bodies are highly developed but their love bodies may not be equally as balance! They may be communicating with the inner plane Ascended Masters, but they are not communicating enough with Mother Earth, Pan, the Nature Spirits, Elementals, and Plant Devas! Lightworkers may be achieving their higher levels of initiation but they are not grounding their Spiritual missions on Earth! They are also not loving the Mother Earth and earthly civilization enough! They are also not taking enough responsibility for healing Mother Earth and healing our society! Lightworkers are taking Spiritual action, but not political and social action. Remember the Material Universe is one of the seven Heavens of GOD! The Divine plan is to bring Heaven to Earth! To create cities and countries of GOD on Earth! Lightworkers are enjoying their Spiritual life but not enjoying their Earthly life with the same fervor! Lightworkers are embodying Spirit, but they are not embodying Spirit on Earth! Lightworkers are becoming filled with love, wisdom and power, however are not demonstrating this enough on Earth! They are not living in the marketplace! Lightworkers are loving God and the Masters, but not loving their physical bodies enough!

My Beloved Readers, look at the reverence the American Indians have for the Earth and the Material Face of GOD! The Essenes at the time of Jesus had a similar type of reverence for the Earth and the Material Face of GOD and this was why Jesus was raised in an Essene community! My Beloved Readers, the Divine Mother and Goddess energy brings us not only a reconnection to our feeling nature but also the ability to "Ground our Spirituality!" The Divine Mother and Goddess energies help us also to fully Realize GOD through embodying God on the Earth! Lightworkers largely have no idea of the profundity of God Realization, they are actually "missing" by not fully embracing the Earth and material life! Fully embracing the Material and Earthly Face of GOD will add to your Spiritual path infinitely! Without doing this you will not really fully understand and appreciate the full profundity of GOD and the entire process of GOD's Divine plan! You will literally be missing a quarter or a third of GOD's complete Divine nature! Embracing the Material Face of GOD will open your eyes to GOD in a way that is just as rich as the Spiritual level and psychological level! It is only when you have all three levels of God Realization that you will truly know and Realize God!

The Divine Mother and the Goddess energies also give a deep and rich appreciation of the feeling nature. In the history of the Earth, what happened is when the negative ego/fear-based/separate mind took over, it caused the feeling and emotional nature to become filled with negative feelings and emotions! This then caused a process of shutting down the emotional nature, as a means of self-protection and as a means to stop suffering! Mankind not being able to recognize the true cause because of its lack of training in Spiritual psychology, just made the feeling nature of less importance and basically in a mass consciousness numbed it out! This caused a loss of love, joy, bliss, ecstasy, sensitivity, Spiritual enthusiasm, Spiritual passion, Spiritual compassion for our Brothers and Sisters and ourselves! It caused also a loss of love and enjoyment for Earth life! The integration of the Divine Mother and Goddess brings all these things back! My Beloved Readers, the Divine Mother and Goddess energies brings back now the final piece in the puzzle to regain our full "wholeness in God"!

The Divine Mother and Goddess energies bring back the profundity of the process of incarnating into a physical body into another of GOD's seven Heavens! The Divine Mother and Goddess energy brings back the proper integration of our inner child! This is what was truly meant in the Bible when it states, "to be like a child"! Not to be a victim of your inner child, but to have the wonder and joy of the inner child in the process of Spiritual mastery! Not to lose your inner child, playfulness, fun, excitement, wonder, curiosity even though you are a Spiritual master! The Divine Mother and Goddess energies help us to enjoy the process of Earth life to the hilt! Enjoying every precious second of it. Enjoying, sanctifying and appreciating the Material Face of GOD!

Lightworkers are paying their rent to the Spiritual Face of GOD and maybe the Mental Face or Emotional Face, but are not paying their rent to the Material Face of GOD. They are building the Spiritual knowledge and information banks, but are not building their psychological and earthly knowledge and information banks to the same degree. There is a subconscious belief that material energies are inferior to Spiritual energies! There is also a belief that says Spiritual energies are superior to psychological energies! Just as the negative ego overidentified with the mind over feeling and the heart! The negative ego also overidentified with Heavenly energies over material energies! These two choices were the rejection of the Divine Mother and the Goddess energies, and the Earth and its people have not recovered from this choice from 18.5 million years ago until now! By the grace of GOD, of the Masters and the Divine Mother, the Goddess energies are now finally returning to the Earth!

One other aspect of the return of the Divine Mother and Goddess ener-gies to Earth, has to do with the return of the Archangels and Angels to Earth in a more open and pronounced way! Where as the Elohim or Co-creator Gods are the "Thought Attributes" of GOD, the Archangels and Angels are the "Feeling Tones" of GOD! This is why in esoteric thought it is known that there are three distinct lines of evolution. The Ascended Master line, the Elohim line, and the Angelic line of evolution. Part of the process of Integrated Ascension is to integrate all three of these lines of evolution into your nature, even though each person is created by GOD upon one of these lines! Most on Earth are on the Ascended Master line of evolution, however, there are many who are not. It is very important, for example, if you are on the Ascended Master line of evolution that you integrate and incorporate psychologically the Elohim and Angelic aspects of your self! At the highest stages of evolution on a Spiritual level these lines of evolution integrate, blend and merge together! One of the reasons the Archangels and Angels are becoming more in the mass consciousness now is because of the return of the Divine Mother and Goddess energies to Earth!

One other interesting patriarchal ceremony in our society is how when a woman and man get married the woman is given away to the man by the father, but the man is not given away by the mother. Interesting, wouldn't you say?

Another interesting phenomena is how people throw trash on the ground. Mother Earth is a living being. How would you like it if people threw garbage on your physical body or just threw garbage and trash on the floor in your home? My Beloved Readers, it is the same thing! The Earth is a living being! Even worse, we pollute her with industrial waste and nuclear waste that enters her bloodstream and water systems, air, and the very earth itself. How would you feel if someone poured industrial and nuclear waste down your mouth and stomach? My Beloved Readers, this is what mankind has done to the Earth unconsciously! Mother Earth has lovingly said, "Forgive them GOD, they know not what they do!" However Mother Earth's physical body has become sickened by the toxic abuse of the people of the Earth!

I was watching one of the those news magazine shows and they showed how female babies were killed because they were not seen as having as much value as male babies. It was the most unbelievable thing I have ever seen. It was either in India or one of the Arab nations, I can't remember which!

Then we do see in some of the Arab nations how women are not allowed to have professions, reveal any skin, show their face, and for minor infractions they are even killed! Some of the things that are going on in this world are unbelievable!

Then we also see that when men have sex with a lot of different women they are called studs! Whereas women have sex once and they are called prostitutes! The patriarchal and macho energy that pervades our culture is unbelievable! This of course may not be the consciousness of lightworkers, but these subconscious patterns of belief are still in the deeper layers of people's subconscious minds.

Another example of patriarchal consciousness is that it is okay for older men to be with women a lot younger than them; however, the reverse is not always the case in terms of what is seen as socially and politically correct!

In the Arab world as well, the men give the orders and women must follow! This consciousness pervades a great many of the religions and cultures over our world!

Women after dinner clean up and wash dishes. Men sit in the living room socializing. How come it isn't reversed!

What men must realize is that if they don't integrate the feminine and Goddess nature they will probably just have to incarnate as a women next lifetime which will force them to learn the lesson. The lesson is to learn the lesson in this lifetime by grace, so the laws of karma don't force you to do it this way next lifetime! Better yet, learn your lessons and become androgynous! This applies to men and women. Learn to balance and integrate your God/Goddess and you will achieve liberation and achieve enlightenment and you will not have to reincarnate at all unless you choose to!

Another very interesting lens of the Patriarchy on Earth is how we have called the Ascended Masters "The Great White Brotherhood"! My Beloved Readers, why have we not called it "The Great White Sisterhood"? I bring these points up to show how this patriarchal lens has even infiltrated religions and the New Age Movement! Part of the transformation of the New Age will come in the reframing of our language to more properly describe the God/Goddess balance that lives throughout all Creation!

Another aspect that the Divine Mother and Goddess energies bring is the ability to physically manifest. This has been a real weak spot for lightworkers. They have been able to manifest on all levels but not as much physically! This has been because of the lack of proper integration of the Divine Mother and the Goddess energies. As these energies are properly integrated you will see your ability to manifest on Earth greatly increase as well! Hence, people will become an integration of a "Visionary and Manifestor"! Lightworkers are very good at coming up with great ideas, however, they are not as good in putting them into physical manifestation! As the Material Face of GOD is integrated and the mastery and integration of the Divine Mother and Goddess energies is achieved, you will find yourself becoming a master of both! Your earthly bank account will also then begin to match your highly developed Spiritual bank account, which will allow you to do more on the physical/earthly plane! You will also find all the physical things you need coming much more effortlessly and easily!

Another aspect of the return of the Divine Mother and Goddess energies will be much greater Spiritual gifts and psychic abilities. Much greater intuition, channeling abilities, and subconscious mind abilities. The eating of the fruit of the "Tree of Good and Evil" or the choice to think with one's negative ego mind, cause a greater identification with the conscious mind over the subconscious and superconscious mind. This was good in terms of self-mastery and self-control, but also cut off a great deal of our extrasensory perceptions. We are basically taught in school to use only our left brain, and there is absolutely no honoring of right brain methods of gaining knowledge and information. The negative ego hence chose science over Spiritual senses, even making decrees that the mind and five senses are all that exists! In making this choice, it basically cut off 22 of your Spiritual senses that GOD created you with! We are literally programmed by our parents and school that everything to do with our Spiritual senses is imagination and not real, and by the time we go through the indoctrination of traditional school which is basically souless and Goddessless, most of the abilities we came with have basically, systematically shut down! As we people reopen to the Divine Mother and Goddess nature, many of these abilities will open up again! For in returning, we now have the understanding that the Goddess energy integration does not mean being run by the negative ego! One is still a master of all one's thoughts, feelings, emotions, energy, physical body, and the Earth! However, one also integrates unconditional love and the Goddess energies in the process! In not being run by the negative ego and not creating so many negative feelings and emotions, there is no more need to be so shut down in terms of one's feminine nature! This will allow some of the more feminine subconscious and superconscious senses to open up. There are more masculine supersenses as well! To learn more about this read my book *The Golden Book of Melchizedek: How To Become an Integrated Christ/Buddha in This Lifetime*, which is available from the Academy! This will allow the honoring and proper integration of the Occult path to GOD and the Mystic path to GOD! In the ideal state, we need to integrate both the Occult path and the Mystic path within ourselves! Often among lightworkers there has been competition between the two, or judgment on both sides as to which one is better! Both sides are not right! Integration of both is the ideal within every person even if a person leans a little bit one way or the other because of how GOD created them or their Ray structure! Remember, the ideal is to properly integrate all seven Rays regardless of your Ray configuration. People tend to fall into patterns of Ray structure being 2/4/6, which are more feminine Rays, or 1/3/5/7 which are a little more masculine Rays. Part of the integration of the God/Goddess within is to become a master of all Seven Rays and not let the Ray configuration you incarnated with, make you overidentify with you God/Goddess nature!

The negative ego/separative mind has created a seeming separation between Heaven and the Material Universe when, in truth, they are all the same energy! It is like water being boiled and becoming steam. Water is material, steam is Spiritual. It is the same energy! It just appears different to the five senses and negative ego mind, which has created a separation which is not there! To think one form of GOD is better than another form of GOD is total illusion. It is just energy or GOD substance vibrating at different rates of speed. To the physical eyes matter appears dense. This is illusion as well, for it is not! There is space between the electrons, protons, neutrons and atoms! GOD's Divine plan is to outpicture His Divine idea into all aspects of His creation! We are incarnations of GOD who have volunteered to not only evolve back through the 352 levels of initiation, but also to do our part in creating GOD's Divine plan on the

Material Plane of existence. This is what we have contracted to do! This is our Spiritual mission and purpose. We each have a Divine puzzle piece to outpicture on the physical/earthly plane. We are not just here to do it on the Spiritual plane, or just the mental, or just the emotional plane, we are also here to do it on the physical plane! This means demonstrating God on Earth and also helping to create a Spiritual civilization on Earth that reflects a Godly/Christed/Buddha-like civilization on Earth! The integration of the Divine Mother and Goddess energies has been the last missing key ingredient to now make this full embodiment of God on Earth within each individual, which will then allow us as a civilization on Earth to embody God in terms of creating a true God society! The return of the Divine Mother and Goddess energies along with fully appreciating the Material Face of GOD, as an absolutely essential key ingredient in understanding the true nature of God Realization, will be, in my humble opinion, the final catalyst, along with learning to master negative ego/fear-based thinking and changing it to Spiritual/Christ/Buddha thinking that will allow us, society and our earthly civilization to fully realize the Seventh Golden Age!

One other very interesting aspect of the return of the Divine Mother and Goddess energies has to do with the reawakening of the Spiritual people of the Earth to the Presence of the Holy Spirit! The Holy Spirit is part of the Trinity of GOD! This Trinity is, of course, GOD, Christ and the Holy Spirit! One does not have to be a Christian to appreciate the Presence of the Holy Spirit. Whether you believe in Christianity or not is not even the point. I believe in all religions! I also believe in Brahma, Shiva, and Vishnu from Hinduism. I believe in anything that is true! Regardless of what religion you were brought up in or what you believe, the Holy Spirit does exist and can be of an absolute enormous amount of help! It is amazing to me that lightworkers do not call on the Holy Spirit more. The Holy Spirit is one of the most powerful forces in this infinite universe. Lightworkers call on their Higher Self and Mighty I Am Presence, and even the Ascended Masters, Archangels and Angels, however, they do not call that much on the Holy Spirit! This is also part of the lack of integration of the Divine Mother and Goddess energies, for the Holy Spirit is part of the feminine aspect of GOD! The Holy Spirit is literally the Voice of GOD! When you pray to GOD, it is the Holy Spirit who answers! The Holy Spirit is the answer to every question or problem you have! It has the ability to undo all mistakes on every level! The Holy Spirit is Omnipotent, Omnipresent, and Omniscient! It is probably the most powerful force in this infinite universe! A lot of people go to the Ascended Masters or Angels for answers and help, which is great! Others go to their Higher Self and Monad, or Mighty I Am Presence, which is also an aspect of GOD! However, it is also possible to go directly to the Trinity of GOD for help! Part of the return of the Divine Mother and Goddess energies is, in truth, also the return of the Holy Spirit to Earth! The Holy Spirit, of course, has always been here and never left, for it is the "Still small voice within!" However, although it has always been here, it has not always been here in Earthlings awareness! Do call on the Holy Spirit for help, for it will astound you with its love, wisdom, and miraculous powers!

Another aspect of misunderstanding among lightworkers that stems from this lack of proper integration of the Divine Mother and Goddess energies is, that they think Spiritual knowledge is better than psychological knowledge. They also think that Spiritual knowledge is much better then earthly knowledge. They actually believe that earthly knowledge does not have much value on a subconscious level.

Well, my Beloved Readers, this is another major block of negative ego faulty thinking. In this book I have talked extensively about how important an understanding of Spiritual psychology is! It is the foundation of your entire life! This also applies to a proper understanding of how to properly master yet integrate your feelings and emotions, which is part of psychology! In truth, Spiritual psychology is the foundation of your Spiritual life. If it is not mastered and properly integrated, it will not only completely corrupt one's Spiritual life, it will corrupt your physical/earthly life as well. It will affect your physical body in an adverse way and it will make you unsuccessful in earthly endeavors depending on how extensive the imbalance or lack of understanding is. In truth, the belief that Spiritual knowledge is more important than psychological knowledge is actually one of the most dangerous and disturbed beliefs of all of the negative ego, and it is one of the single biggest reasons 98% of lightworkers do not pass the advanced tests of Spiritual leadership and planetary world service. Without mastery and proper integration of Spiritual psychology and the negative ego/fear-based/separative mind not only will lightworkers not pass their lessons, the Spiritual work they are doing will become corrupted and they won't even realize it! Ponder deeply on what I have just said for it may be one of the most important things I have said in this book!

Taking this one step further, lightworkers also think that Spiritual knowledge is much better than earthly knowledge! This is equally as much a corruption of the negative ego mind! It is again a rejection of the Material Face of GOD! It is also one of the main reasons why they are unable to fully manifest their Spiritual mission, purpose and puzzle piece on Earth. It is why their Spiritual teaching and channeling remains on the Spiritual plane and never grounds itself! It never embodies into the physical body or serves Mother Earth in a complete sense. Most lightworkers don't realize that all channeling is governed by what is in your information banks; both in a Spiritual, psychological and earthly sense, from past lives and this life. If there is no knowledge on an earthly level in your information banks then you will not be able to channel helpful information that has any earthly practicality. Anyone who doesn't believe this is being deluded by the negative ego! Even the great Edgar Cayce, the "Sleeping Prophet," was told by the Universal Mind that it was his past life training that allowed him to channel the information he was bringing through! If you have no training in past lives or this life in astrology, for example, you will not be able to channel on astrology; this is a fact! If you have no earthly knowledge in your information banks because you spend all your time only studying Spiritual things or just psychological things, then you will not be able to channel anything of earthly use! My Beloved Readers, we are meant to be whole and complete on all 352 Levels of GOD like the Mahatma, not skipping the lower ones and saying only the higher levels are important. This is like saying that the upper part of the Cosmic Tree of Life is important and the lower Sephiroth or parts are unimportant. This is like saying the upper chakras are important and the lower ones are not important. My Beloved Readers, this is delusion! Do not buy into false illusionary separation of Spirit and Matter! This is why the educational system in our world is so unintegrated, for they have separated our educational system from the soul. They have separated Church and State! It is why the Earth has so much pollution. It is why our society, civilization and all its institutions are operating out of the personality and not the soul! My Beloved Readers, this all stems back to 18.5 million years ago of the eating of the fruit of the "Tree of Good and Evil" and the choice to think with the negative ego mind which chose the mind over the heart and Heaven over Earth for those who did believe in GOD! The negative ego has infiltrated every aspect of life including Psychology, Religion, Spirituality, and the New Age Movement! It creates separation, corruption, distortion, delusion, illusion, glamour, maya, and false divisions in every move it makes! Do not be deluded by the negative ego's deluded and corrupt thinking patterns. It is now time for you to develop 100% Mastery, Love and Wisdom on a Spiritual, Psychological, and Physical/Earthly level! Read the newspaper, watch the news, become socially aware, become politically aware, read books about the earthly things that interest you, and learn about the people of the Earth you respect and admire. I personally love reading autobiographies of famous people on the Earth in all areas of life! Become a master of Earth life as well. Become a master of gardening, nature, your business, economics, money, sexuality, your physical body, the arts, music, architecture, dance, culture, and the sciences. Become a master of civilization and society so you can help raise consciousness to change our world on the earthly level! If you want a quick crash course, read my book *Manual for Planetary Leadership*! Over two-thirds of the book focuses on the great philosophical, social and political issues of our times from the perspective of Spirit, the Soul and the Ascended Masters. Contrary to popular opinion, Spirit, the Soul, and the Masters are all 100% totally involved in these issues; it is just a great many lightworkers who are not! This all stems from the false separation that was made by the negative ego which mass consciousness and lightworkers have never fully recovered from! It is time to recover from this now! Become a master of Earth life. My Beloved Readers, listen very closely to what I am about to say, for it may be one of the most important things I say in this entire book! There is no feeling in the world better than the feeling of being a Spiritual Master, a Psychological Master and a Physical/Earthly Master all in proper integration and balance! In my own life, I love the feeling of moving from one level to the next. After doing my Spiritual work I love to watch the news, work in the garden, or clean and fix-up our home and the Academy! I love politics, sports, gardening, business, all the sciences, astronomy, art, music, dance, spiritual architecture, Feng Shui, sacred sites, spiritually decorating our home and garden, physically helping people as well as spiritually and psychologically helping people. I love cooking, or watching news magazine shows like "60 Minutes." I learn incredible things. I learn a lot through educational television channels and the Internet. I love mastering computer technology and having all the most advanced equipment in the Academy and Ashram. I love the science and art of wearing spiritual clothing! For Wesak I actually have seven different tuxedos I wear, some of which I have had specially made to look a lot like how the Masters sometimes dress on the inner planes. I love learning about holistic health, cultures, religions, and sociology. I like watching movies, videos, races, some of the talk shows occasionally, and learning about people. I love watching the Olympics and learning about the different athletes' lives and what inspires them. I love to study about Spiritual leadership, and the great leaders of our world in all aspects of life! Much can be gained from studying their lives and expertise. I love to master and study the many forms of healing so I can not just help heal people's Spirit, mind, and emotions, but also their physical bodies. I love studying nutrition. I love learning about things so I can raise consciousness to help heal the Earth and the society and civilization of the Earth! I love learning about the Earth so I can call in Spirit and the Masters to help heal and fix the things that are wrong! I love the feeling of actually making a difference in the world! I love manifesting Wesak on the Earth! I love writing books that actually get physically published. I love accomplishing things physically every day, not just Spiritually, mentally and emotionally. If you talk to anyone who knows me, they know that I can get more done physically than most people on the Earth. This is because I believe in "consistency"! This is the great problem with a great many lightworkers, they are not consistent. The ideal in life is that whatever you do, you do with all your bodies and all aspects of your Being! So whatever I do in life, I do on all levels, or I don't do it at all. If I do it Spiritually, then I also do it mentally, emotionally, etherically, energetically, physically, and on an earthly level! Whatever I do, I do with 100% consistency between my superconscious mind, conscious mind, subconscious mind, physical body, and the Earth Mother! With no judgement intended, people on the Earth and lightworkers tend to be very inconsistent and fragmented. The superconscious mind does one thing, the conscious mind another thing, the subconscious mind another thing, and things never even get to the Earth! They are not consistent in all their chakras, not consistent in the mastery of all their Rays, and not consistent in honoring and sanctifying the Four Faces of GOD and their four bodies in a balanced manner!

I love to watch the awards shows and study and learn from the people who are the best in their fields. I study the science of how things work, on a Spiritual, psychological and physical/earthly level. One of the biggest reasons, I humbly suggest, why I have been successful, is my learning to understand the laws that govern this universe on a Spiritual, psychological and physical earthly level. I am not satisfied with just Spiritual success and psychological success, I want and have achieved physical/earthly success as well! That is what a Spiritual master does, they are successful on all levels of GOD! They don't reject levels of GOD and say one is more important than another is; or one is lesser than another is. This is total illusion of the negative ego, yet this is what a great many lightworkers believe on a subconscious level. My job is to bust the negative ego wherever it sticks its ugly little head! My job and mission is to write a book that leaves no stone unturned, to find out where the negative ego might be trying to hide! My Spiritual passion and mission here is to bring the Light of GOD and the Light of the Holy Spirit where others have not tread and where others have not looked!

I love studying all forms of psychology, physical sciences, and the mechanics of all things. It is why I like studying the book *The Keys of Enoch*, although it is more of a science book than a self-help book! This is also why my writing is so easy to understand and practical. I am interested in making things work on Earth not just in Heaven! I love being a philanthropist to the best of my ability and help people and causes I believe in. I love trying to reform and reorganize our society along more Christed lines! My great Spiritual passion in life has been not only to bring Spirituality, Ascension, and the Ascended Master Teachings into the areas of Spiritual psychology, marriage, family, and children, but also into every area of Earth life. This is what excites me the most! How does Spirituality translate into the mental body, emotional body, etheric body, physical body, social self, environment, and our earthly civilization? This is why the next book I am writing is *The Divine Plan for the Seventh Golden Age!* This is Spirit's and the Ascended Masters' plan for revamping our civilization and turning it into Spiritual/Christ/Buddha civilization!

So my Beloved Readers, I have explained these things to try to give you a taste for the incredible richness of God's wisdom and knowledge on the physical/earthly plane! Don't just be a master of the Spiritual level and skip the psychological and earthly levels. Don't just be a master of the Spiritual and psychological and skip the earthly level. Be a full, absolutely 100% master on all levels! Educate yourself on all levels! Become a master of all seven Rays, all four bodies, all three minds, all 12 Archetypes, all 12 signs of the Zodiac, all 12 Sephiroth of the Tree of Life, all Tarot Cards, all Four Faces of GOD, your Spiritual Self, your Psychological Self and your Physical/Earthly Self! Educate yourself on all levels! Do not become so Spiritually or Heavenly focused that you are of no good use to GOD on Earth! Grounding your Spirituality into your physical body and into this Earthly world and civilization is the Spiritual battle cry and mantra for the New Millennium, The Aquarian Age and the Seventh Golden Age! Be consistent on "all" levels! Develop your talents and abilities on all levels: Spiritually, Psychologically, and in a Physically/Earthly sense! I tell you again, my Beloved Readers, there is absolutely no better feeling in this infinite universe than being a master on a Spiritual, Psychological and Physical/Earthly level! Educate yourself and build your Spiritual information banks, your psychological information banks, and your physical/earthly information banks with total knowledge and wisdom at each level! This way you will also be able to intelligently deal with every person you meet and converse with, no matter what their perspective and background! This also, my Beloved Readers, is the only way you can develop a "God Realized Full Spectrum Prism Consciousness" that is not filled with blind spots and limited lens seeing! This is also the way you will become knowledgeable and wise of both God and Goddess energies! Do not just focus on developing knowledge of God energies and not of Goddess energies! If you do this, it is you who will be the loser, for the negative ego will have bamboozled you into thinking you were realizing the fullness of GOD, and, in truth, you will have not! You will have missed half of GOD! In this existential moment and Holy Instant you have the Divine opportunity to humbly and egolessly rethink this decision that the negative ego may have unconsciously made and make a new choice and new decision right now in this moment to never ever let this happen! Do not settle for one third of GOD, or one half of GOD, or three quarters of GOD! Only accept and fully claim for yourself 100% of GOD! Do not settle for less! Become a 100% master on a Spiritual, psychological and physical/earthly level and fill your information banks with wisdom and knowledge on all three levels as well!

Another aspect of this return of the Divine Mother and Goddess energies will be the recognition that Mother Earth is a living Being, and as a race we have treated her as an inconsequential material object with no consciousness! Not only is Mother Earth a living being, Mother Earth is in a state of evolution as well! Mother Earth is taking her initiations as well. Lightworkers at times unconsciously are kind of selfish and are only focusing on their evolution and do not care about the evolution of Mother Earth! This is why I am now, and have in the past, recommended that all lightworkers when they do any type of ascension activation work, do it for Mother Earth simultaneously as they do it for themselves! Also when you care for the Earth and sanctify the Earth and clean up the Earth in an ecological and societal sense, you are helping her evolution! It is time that lightworkers start thinking less about themselves and more about a bigger picture perspective as well! I am not saying that lightworkers should not focus upon their own Spiritual growth and initiation process, but they also need to focus much more on helping other people with theirs, and helping the Animal Kingdom, Plant Kingdom, Mineral Kingdom and Mother Earth with theirs as well! All of it is GOD! If you truly are God, then it is time to start working for GOD and not for the self part of God, if you see my point! GOD is interested in evolving all parts of GOD since GOD is everything! This is why lightworkers need to focus a little more on service and a little less on just achieving initiations! I have seen Spiritual groups and Spiritual people actually competing over initiations! All of these things are corruptions of the negative ego! We have not just come here to achieve initiations and liberation for ourselves, we have come here to be of service! The Divine Mother and Goddess energies bring true compassion and caring for others! If you truly have compassion for others then how can one just focus on one's own ascension and initiation process and not want to be of service to people and this world? An incredible number of people are suffering in this world! If we all are God, then aspects of GOD are in a state of suffering and lack of realization! It is not a sacrifice to serve, that again is the negative ego. If we truly have the unconditional love and compassion of the Divine Mother and Goddess energies then we should want to be of service to help relieve suffering! The help may come on a physical, mental, emotional, energetic or Spiritual level! Too many lightworkers are floundering trying to find their Spiritual mission and puzzle piece instead of getting out there and doing something! Any form of service is better than no service at all! It is not about necessarily making money, or Spiritual vanity, or becoming famous, or having to fulfill some great Spiritual vision. Maybe it will be volunteer work. The vow of the Bodhisattva arises out of the unconditional love and compassion of the Divine Mother and Goddess energies. I am not saying everyone has to make this vow! I am saying that lightworkers need to be of service even if it is not the ideal Spiritual job the negative ego or conscious mind thinks it deserves. It is amazing how the negative ego mind gets its hands in Spiritual matters. Stop waiting for GOD and the Masters to tell you want to do, and get out there and do something until you figure it out! The time for Spiritual floundering is over! It is time for all of us to get our hands dirty a little bit! Look at the example Mother Teresa set! Living a life just focused on Spiritual growth and not on service can be a corruption of the negative ego if one is not careful! It is our responsibility to change this world and society and help the people of the world! All negative ego, competition, comparing, jealousy, envy, false pride, Spiritual vanity, greed, selfishness, self-centeredness and negative ego motivations need to be 100% cleansed and removed from our being, and true unconditional love, caring, compassion and genuine desire to be of service to people, animals, plants, the Mineral Kingdom, Mother Earth, nature, and the civilization and society of the Earth needs to be our goal, purpose and main focus. Focus on your Spiritual growth while you are doing this! Forget about the glamour and negative ego of doing fancy Spiritual projects! If they come, so be it! What is most important is to be doing something of service to people and the planet! I cannot tell you how many lightworkers I meet who have all the glamorous Spiritual ideas and never do anything but talk about them! To be honest, it is a corruption and glamour of the negative ego! If they cannot get it to the earthly plane and manifest it on the earthly plane it really means nothing! It would be better to do volunteer work where you are really touching peoples lives and/or helping the world than making one's ego feel good by talking about a Spiritual project that never happens! Lightworkers have remained to a great extent stuck on the Spiritual, mental and emotional plane! Maybe we should change their name from lightworkers to "earthworkers" and they might get more done on the physical plane! I am being humorous here, however, there is a seed of truth in that which I say! Lightworkers are overidentified with the Light and are not recognizing the Light within Matter and the Earth!

Another aspect of the return of the Divine Mother and the Goddess energies is the Mahatma energy, which is a group consciousness Being that embodies all 352 levels of GOD! Lightworkers think of the Mahatma energy as just carrying the 352nd level of GOD energy! The truth is, the Mahatma embodies the energy of the Divine Mother and Goddess energies as well, for it is just as interested in the Material Face of GOD as it is the 352nd level of GOD! I know this for an absolute fact, for the Mahatma has told me this! The Mahatma has greatly helped me in understanding the absolute Divine profundity of the Earth and Earth energies! You will not truly Realize God, my Beloved Readers, until you learn to embody God on Earth and ground your Spiritual mission and purpose on Earth! Stop trying to glamorize Spiritual projects that feed the ego but never manifest on Earth! If you cannot manifest that project quickly and efficiently on Earth then let it go and do something you can! The time for ungrounded Spirituality is over! As Sai Baba has said, "Hands that help are holier than lips that pray"! It is the Divine Mother and Goddess energies that bring to us the incredible importance of the Material Face of GOD and properly mastering but also integrating our feelings, emotions, and Heart energy! My Beloved Readers, do not stay stuck on a masculine path to GOD that never makes it to the Earth! Do not also remain on a feminine path to GOD that has no masculine energy for that will never make it to the Earth as well! It is only when God/Goddess are equally honored and sanctified and all seven Rays are mastered and equally balanced that the true balance of feminine and masculine and Heaven and Earth can be found, realized, integrated, demonstrated and fully embodied on the Earth! Don't just embody God on the Spiritual plane, for if you do, you will have missed out on three quarters of what GOD truly is! Don't just embody GOD on the masculine and Spiritual plane, for you will have missed out on a full half of what GOD truly is. Don't just embody GOD on the feminine and Spiritual plane, for you will have missed half of what GOD truly is! Embody GOD as a true God/Goddess fully in your physical body and on the Earth! Make God happen in the Material Universe not just in Heaven! If you never make it to the earthly plane, in truth, with no judgement intended, you will have been somewhat deluded by the negative ego. You will have not integrated fully the Divine Mother and Goddess energies within you! You will have rejected unconsciously one of the Faces of GOD! Do not live a life of only sanctifying a half of GOD or three-quarters of GOD! If you do this you will have blocked yourself from realizing what true God Realization really is! Do not let the negative ego delude you on this point! It will tell you that you are an exception to the rule and you do not need to be part of the Earth or ground your Spiritual mission and purpose. I ask you to consider who is reading this chapter, you or the negative ego! This is a very key existential moment in your life right now! Will you chose to embody God on Earth, or will you only embody God in Heaven! If you choose to only embody God in Heaven, with no judgement intended, you will lose it! For you will have let the faulty thinking of the negative ego confuse your thinking! You will not achieve full God Realization, this is a fact, for you will have not realized the Material Face of GOD and you will have not fully realized the Divine Mother and Goddess energies on the Earth! You will also not have fully completed your Spiritual mission, purpose and puzzle piece to help Mother Earth and her Kingdom, and taken responsibility for the society and civilization of the Earth as you contracted to do before you came into incarnation!

Very few Spiritual teachers take a stand for the Material Universe, the Divine Mother and Goddess energies! It is time we, as the collective stewards for this planet, right this wrong that was set into motion 18.5 million years ago and set it right once and for all! Spirit, the Masters, the Elohim Councils, the Archangels and Angels of the Light of GOD, the Divine Mother, the Lady Masters and the Goddess energies, Mother Earth, Pan, and the Nature Kingdom, put forth now the "Clarion Call" to Spiritual leaders, Spiritual teachers, channels, scientists, healers, counselors, and people in all professions on Earth, to hereby make a Spiritual vow in this moment "to return the Divine Mother, the Goddess energies, The Holy Spirit, The Mahatma, Pan, Mother Earth, the Nature Spirits and Plant Devas and Tree Spirits, to their proper place and perspective to correct this wrong that started in our ancient past! The Clarion Call is now sounded forth by the entire Cosmic and Planetary Hierarchy for lightworkers to make a Spiritual vow in their own lives right now to fully embody the God/Goddess energies on Earth in their own lives and to try to make a difference in this earthly world and civilization to the best of their abilities in a balanced and integrated way! It is time the Divine Mother and the Goddess energies took their rightful place in the consciousness of the people on Earth as they already are in the consciousness of GOD, Spirit and the Masters in Heaven!

So let it be Written! So let it be Done!

45

The Core Fear Matrix Removal Program

Since taking my ascension, one of the most extraordinary spiritual processes with which I have been working is a new program recently unveiled by the Spiritual Hierarchy called the Core Fear Matrix Removal Program. It is a new dispensation recently received on Earth to remove core fear.

As has been stated, there are only two emotions in the entire world: love and fear. All other emotions, in their essence, come down to one of these two. Another way of saying it is, that there are only two ways of thinking: you think either with your Christ mind or with your negative ego mind; you think either with your lower-self or with your higher self; you have either fear-based emotions and reactions or love-based emotions and reactions.

The Core Matrix Removal Program is a divine dispensation from the Creator that allows the senior members of the Spiritual Hierarchy, currently living on inner planes, to actually pull your core fear patterns right out of your subconscious mind and four-body system. Clairvoyantly, these can be seen as black roots with many tentacles throughout the body being pulled out in the same way that a gardener would pull a weed from the soil. The roots of that weed from the garden look a lot like the emotional and mental roots of core fear patterns. When these roots are pulled out and removed, as though a vacuum were sucking them right out of your crown chakra, they are completely removed from your soul records.

This work can be done by any one of the masters connected with the seven rays on the inner plane. I might suggest asking Djwhal Khul and Vywamus to help in this work, as they are quite proficient at it. This matrix removal program is amazing and has never before been available.

Being a psychologist, I find this process to be especially incredible. Most people must be in therapy for many, many years to get rid of their core fear patterns. Only a skilled spiritual psychologist can help them to do it, and even then, there are many tentacles and roots that pervade the subconscious mind from past lives, parallel lives, other souls extensions, and early childhood that no amount of therapy is going to completely remove.

This is no longer the case! The process is so extraordinary that during a workshop that I hosted on the subject, in one weekend the group of people in attendance had 45% of their core fear completely removed from their subconscious mind, four-body systems, and soul records. It is the easiest form of therapy known to humanity. Much of the work occurred during sleep. The Spiritual Hierarchy got out their spiritual vacuum cleaners and began pulling and sucking the fear out. This work is not available to you only if you attend our workshops; it is available to you for the asking. You have fear programming or you would not be living on this planet. You would have graduated long ago. Even some of the great masters whom we revere still have some remnants of fear programming.

You can try it right now as you read this. Think of a fear pattern that you have been carrying with you. Now ask Djwhal Khul and Vywamus and your own Mighty I Am Presence to remove it. If you are not clairvoyant and cannot see it actually happening, then you can feel it being subtly removed through your crown chakra.

Any time you feel your buttons are being pushed or you have a negative reaction or emotion, a fear program has been triggered. Immediately call to the ascended masters and have them remove it. Every night before going to bed for the next three to six months, I recommend that you pray that all of your core fear be removed. Also request to be officially signed up for the Spiritual Hierarchy's core fear matrix removal program. Once you have signed up on the inner plane, they will work on you on an ongoing basis without your even having to ask.

There is one extremely important understanding you must have about this process, however, 90% to 95% of your core fear can be removed, but it will return if your conscious, reasoning mind does not hold a philosophy of always trying to think with your Christ mind rather than with your negative ego mind.

The problem is that most people do not know what I am talking about when I say this. In my opinion, this is the single greatest stumbling block for disciples and initiates on the spiritual path, bar none. That is because we are now dealing with a psychological issue, not just a spiritual issue. Most people have not been properly trained in this understanding and there are very few people who really understand it in its full depth. As Sai Baba said, "God equals man minus ego." You will not recognize God until you learn to transcend the thinking of the negative ego, or lower self. It is your thought that creates your reality. All suffering is self-induced. Sai Baba also has said, "It is your mind that creates bondage and your mind that creates liberation." Through my efforts to fully integrate this understanding, I am learning how to master my mind in the service of soul and spirit. This has freed me.

A lot of sincere Spiritual seekers try to get rid of the mind, thinking it is bad. That is a grave mistake that will backfire on them most miserably. All aspects of self need to be integrated into a unified whole. The mind is not bad; it just has to be mastered and used in service of the soul. Does not the Bible say, "Let this mind be in you that was in Christ Jesus"?

As long as you learn to think properly, the core fear that has been removed will not return. Part of the reason the masters are removing core fear so rapidly is, in truth, that it is kind of an experiment. If you are living in core fear, it is like a dark cloud that surrounds you at all times. It reminds me of Pigpen, the character in the *Peanuts* comic strip who is always surrounded by a cloud of murky dust. When you are enmeshed in fear, it is hard to make progress or to see yourself clearly.

The rapid removal of the fear eliminates the cloud, and for the first time you can make clear choices. The masters, in truth, are not looking for perfection in the sense of expecting you never to have any negative emotions; that is the ultimate ideal but it is unrealistic. What they are looking for from the higher level initiates and disciples seeking ascension, is that you always consciously choose love instead of fear and attack, and that you constantly choose Christ thinking instead of negative ego thinking in every situation in which you find yourself, that you always consciously choose forgiveness instead of holding a grudge. It is intention they are looking for.

If you don't understand the philosophical basis, you don't see that your negative feelings, reactions, and suffering are all coming from your own illusionary negative ego and lower self, from fear-based, separative, selfish programming, from glamour, illusion, and maya. Instead, you blame it on other people, outside situations, and a delusionary philosophy that tells you that having all those negative reactions and emotions is normal and healthy and could not possibly be something you are able to control. You are likely to believe yourself a victim. You might even think you are creating your own reality. However, you are not applying that philosophy to your emotional body, for it does not make logical sense; the negative ego is not logical. As Master Yoda said in *Star Wars*, "Don't underestimate the power of the dark side of the force."

I would recommend that any time you become aware of an area where fear-based programming lives, then immediately call to the masters to remove that specific program. It is very important to be specific and state which fear-based program you want them to remove. You cannot just say one time, "Remove all my fear-based programs" and never ask again. It won't happen. You must continually work with the masters and continually ask them to remove the core fear patterns in different areas.

For example, you might be watching a movie on television dealing with the pain of rejection, which triggers those feelings within you. Close your eyes while watching the movie and ask the masters to remove all your fear-based programming dealing with the pain of rejection. You might be talking to a friend about death and that stirs up some bad feelings. Again, ask the masters to remove all your fear-based programs on that subject. What I am trying to say here, is that there are hundreds if not thousands and even tens of thousands of areas where core fear is stored. For example, you might be watching a television special on tribal circumcision in Africa. You could ask that all fear-based programming be removed from that experience which had traumatized you as a child or in past live. Are you beginning to see how extensive the subject is?

Sit down with your journal and make a list of all the possible core fears and negative ego programming you can think of. In each meditation, or each night before bed, ask that a particular area be removed form this life and all your past lives. If you would like to do some excellent world service work, ask that it also be removed from the collective consciousness of humanity. This is especially good to do in spiritual group meetings. That way, slowly but surely, the dark cloud in the astral plane of the planet will be lifted.

If you think of all the past lives you have had and recall that you have eleven other soul extensions whose past lives and programming are affecting you, you can see how monumental this job is. Most people take hundreds of lifetimes to do it, so the idea of removing 45% of all core fear in one weekend is extraordinary! That workshop was the first time the program had been used in a large group or for as long as forty-eight hours. Previously, it had been used only for individuals and small groups for two or three hours at a time.

The next important point is the understanding that it is not enough just to remove all the core fear; it must be replaced with core love. This means self-love, love for God, and love for humanity and all other sentient beings. Did not Jesus say that the whole law could be summed up in the words "Love the Lord thy God with all thy heart and soul and mind and might, and love thy neighbor as thyself." This is the whole law. If you follow no other spiritual practice but this, you are on the right track and you will ascend. All the other spiritual practices can speed up the process but the essence of it is unconditional love.

This is a psychological issue, not a spiritual issue, and it cannot be resolved on a spiritual level but must be resolved at the level of the problem. My book *Soul Psychology* contains 25 methods for reprogramming the subconscious mind.

The Core Fear Matrix Removal Program can also be used with children. I must add here that it is usually used by the masters on disciples and initiates rather than on people who have not even stepped onto the Spiritual path.

The main point is that if you just remove core fear and do not replace it with love-based programming, the core fear is going to return. It takes only 21 days, however, to cement a new habit, which is not a high price to pay for freedom from fear.

46

The 385 Ascension Activations and Cleansings of GOD to Ask for Before You Go to Bed Every Night for Yourself and Mother Earth

My Beloved Readers, the following list of Ascension Activations of GOD and the Masters is the most powerful and comprehensive list ever put together in one book, let alone one chapter! Every night before bed call for about one to five of them to be activated while you sleep. When you ask GOD, Christ, the Holy Spirit, your Mighty I Am Presence, your Higher Self, the inner plane Ascended Masters, the Archangels and Angels of the Light of GOD, the Elohim Councils, and Christed Extraterrestrials for these activations, ask for them for Mother Earth as well so you and she will get the activations simultaneously! If you follow my Spiritual Guidance here you will experience a spiritual, mental, emotional, etheric, energetic, physical body and Earthly transformation that will truly "passeth understanding"! You will literally be reborn and resurrected spiritually, mentally, emotionally and physically! While you are on this one year program, read my books *How To Release Fear-Based Thinking and Feeling: An In-depth Study of Spiritual Psychology* and my book *The Golden Book of Melchizedek: How to Become an Integrated Christ/Buddha In This Lifetime*! This will insure that your Spiritual Growth is balanced and integrated on a Spiritual, Psychological and Physical/Earthly level! If you trust and follow my guidance here in all regards, you will literally be a 100% completely different person in one year's time, and well on your way to not only perfect radiant health, but also Self Realization, Integrated Ascension, and God Realization!

- Platinum Net
- Axiatonal Alignment
- Ascension Column and Pillar of Light
- Balance your chakras and four-body system
- Remove all negative implants and negative elementals
- Light and Love shower
- Core Fear Matrix Removal Program to remove all fear-based negative ego programming from your energy fields and subconscious mind
- Repair all holes and tears in your aura from past lives and this life
- Remove all karma from your chakras, energy fields and your being!
- Open all your chakras, facets in your chakras
- Open your Ascension Chakra
- Bacterial and Viral Vacuum
- Ask Archangel Metatron to add Electrons to your energy field
- Anchoring of Microtron
- Baptism of the Holy Spirit
- 72 Names of Metatron
- 72 Names of GOD
- Keys of Enoch
- 72 Divine Attributes of GOD!
- Building of your Antakarana back to Source
- Ask Holy Spirit to undo and remove everything that is not of GOD in your entire being
- Tube of Light of Protection

- Ask Archangel Michael to cut all energy cords that are not of GOD from all past lives and this one!
- Complete merger with Higher Self and Monad!
- Help in being balanced and integrated in everything you do!
- Clear lower aspect of Seven Rays
- Clear lower aspect of Twelve Major Archetypes
- Clear lower aspect of Twelve Signs of the Zodiac
- Integrate and cleanse all your Soul Extensions from your Oversoul and Monad!
- Ascension Seat of the Golden Chamber of Melchizedek
- Clear your Genetic line of all Karma
- Violet Transmuting Flame
- Anchoring and Activation of Anointed Christ Overself Body, Zohar Body of Light, Higher Adam Kadmon Body, Lord's Mystical Body
- Anchor and Activate all the Fire letters, Key Codes and Sacred Geometries of GOD to Achieve God Realization and full Integrated Ascension
- Anchor your Monadic Blueprint body and Mayavarupa body
- Anchor and Activate your 330 chakras back to Source!
- Anchor and Activate your 12 strands of DNA
- Anchor and activate the Universal Christ Buddha imprint
- Balance your God/Goddess energies
- Balance your 12 Major Archetypes
- Balance and integrate your Seven Major Rays
- Anchor and activate the Light Packets of GOD from the Treasury of Light
- Remove all gray fields, astral dross, mental dross, etheric dross
- Remove all negative thoughts, feelings, emotions, bad habits and addictions
- Remove all entities from aura that do not belong there
- Cleanse all physical, etheric, astral, emotional and physical disease from the fields

- Call for the anchoring of the Prana Wind Clearing Device
- Call for the return of all Soul Fragments and the removal of all Soul Fragments that do not belong in me!
- Remove all irritations, spots and leaks in the aura
- Golden Cylinder to remove all negative energy
- Call the Arcturian Liquid Crystals to deactivate all negative energy
- Call the Arcturians to tighten your grids
- Repairing of all past life or present life emotional, etheric, or mental wounds in the aura
- Repairing of all Bodies and Chakras
- Anchoring and Activation of the Cosmic Tree of Life!
- Opening and activation of the Twelve Sephiroth of the Cosmic Tree of Life
- Opening of the Hidden Sephiroth of Daath or Hidden Wisdom
- Opening of all mind links
- Establishment of full spectrum prism seeing
- Remove the veils of Light and Time
- Rewire electrical system to partially live on Light
- Golden Bubble of Protection in your daily life from mental, emotional, energetic, and physical disease of others
- Building of your Light Quotient, Love Quotient and Power Quotient
- Anchoring of Platinum Rod by Archangel Metatron
- Acceleration of your Initiation and Ascension process
- Melchizedek Crystals and Diamonds
- Anchoring and Activation of your 12 Higher Spiritual bodies
- Anchoring of the 72 Light bodies of GOD!
- Brain Illumination
- Anchoring and Activation of the Deca Delta Light Encodements from the 10 Superscripts of the Divine Mind
- Anchoring of the Yod Spectrum
- Anchoring and activation of the 10 Lost Cosmic Rays
- Illumination of the 72 Areas of the Mind

- Anchoring and activation of the Divine Template of the Elohim
- Anchoring of the Father's Eye of Divine Creation
- Nogan Shells of GOD
- Anchoring and Activation of the Scriptures of Light
- Anchoring and Activation of the Tablets of Creation
- Anchoring and Activation of the Garment of Shaddai or Light Body of Metatron!
- Anchoring and Activation of the Super Electron or Electron of GOD!
- The Spiritualization of your Blood Chemistry
- Anchoring and activation of the "Language of Light"
- Revelation of GOD
- Anchoring and Activation of the "Coat of many Colors"
- Gifts of the Holy Spirit
- Cleansing of your Oversoul and Monad
- Cleansing back to your original covenant with GOD!
- Resurrection, Ascension, Translation, Rapture, Enlightenment, Liberation, Integrated Ascension, God Realization, Self Realization
- Anchoring and activation of the Torah Or
- Anchoring and Activation of Elohistic Lord's Body, Paradise Son's Body
- Ask to be a Cosmic Walk-in for the Mahatma
- Initiation into the Order of Melchizedek by Melchizedek himself!
- Call forth the Melchizedek Transmitting System in your chakras
- Celestial marriage with GOD, Christ, the Holy Spirit, your Mighty I Am Presence, and Higher Self
- Anchoring and Activation of the Higher Kabbalah
- Opening of the Three Seals of Creation
- Call forth your Ascension Angels to help accelerate your Ascension
- Anchoring of the Star Codes of Melchizedek
- Widening and Opening of your Antakarana
- Activation of Epi-Kinetic body
- Activation of Eka Body Activation

- Full activation of Electromagnetic body!
- Anchoring of the Sephirothic Knowledge
- Anchoring of the Divine Seed of the Elohim
- Opening of the Seven Seals of GOD
- Opening of the Gates of Light
- Anchoring of the Biological Codes for the Christ race
- Anchoring and Activation of the Holy Scrolls of Burning Light
- Anchoring and Activation of the Cosmic Ten Commandments
- Full Awakening of your Spiritual Mission and Divine Puzzle Piece on Earth
- Anchoring of the Tetragrammaton of GOD
- Anchoring of the Hidden Divine Word
- Anchoring of the Image of the Elohim
- Anchoring of the Flame of YHWH
- Anchoring of the Light Vibrations of the Sacred Names and Mantras of GOD
- Anchoring and Activation of the Ark of the Covenant of GOD
- Training in Advanced Ascended Master Abilities
- Anchoring of the Psychological Qualities of GOD
- Merger with 72 Christed Universes of GOD
- Anchoring of Light Packets from Shamballa
- Anchoring of Light Packets from the Great White Lodge on Sirius
- Dr. Lorphan and the Galactic Healers for help with any physical health lessons
- Anchoring of the Cosmic Heart!
- Merger with the Divine Mother and the Goddess energies
- Anchoring and Activation of the Twelve Cosmic Stations
- Opening of the Alpha and Omega Chakras
- Merger of the Great Flame with the Lesser Flame
- Calling forth a Matchstick worth of the Cosmic Fire
- Healing Platform to heal physical body at night while you sleep
- Spiritually Train at night while sleep

- Etheric Acupuncture
- Etheric vitamin and mineral shots for whatever you need
- Increase of your Spiritual Current
- Program the Gematrian body with geometric codes for God Realization
- Platinum Angels to live permanently in any area of your body that is weak
- Energetic anchoring in your consciousness while sleeping of the Bible (Old and New Testament), Dr. Stone's 33 Volume Ascension Book Series, *A Course in Miracles*, *Keys of Enoch*, Vedas, Bhagavad-Gita, Koran, Kabbalah Theosophical books, Alice Bailey books, books of Sai Baba, books of Paramahansa Yogananda, Dhamapada (Buddha's teachings), Edgar Cayce's books, Huna teachings, Urantia book, I AM Discourses of Saint Germain, Masters of the Far East and all others that God and the Masters recommend. Then request anchoring all books in Shamballa and The Great White Lodge as well!
- Arcturians to remove all cancer energy from you energy fields
- Removal of all Ancestral Karma
- Masters to run Spiritual Current through you all night and all day long
- Djwhal Khul to adjust your energy fields with his Holographic Computer!
- Call forth a permanent energy beam to any weak organ, gland or system in the body
- Clean all past life energy
- Help for your other 143 Soul Extensions in your Monad
- Ask that Spirit and the Masters reprogram your subconscious mind to Spiritual/Christ/Buddha Consciousness and put programs into subconscious mind
- Pray for Physical Immortality
- Complete cleansing of your Aura and Energy Fields

- Fully open your Spiritual Channel
- Open your Third Eye and Crown Chakra
- Activate your Pineal and Pituitary gland for the purpose of God Realization
- Anchoring of Divine Nectar and Amrita
- Opening and Activation of your 22 Supersenses of GOD
- Help in Physically Grounding your Ascension
- Opening of your Clairaudience
- Opening of your Clairvoyance
- Opening of your Clairsentience
- Anchoring of the Cosmic Rays
- Love Seat of Sai Baba
- Training in Seven Ashrams of the Christ while you sleep
- Call forth the Arcturian Light Chamber
- Call forth the Atomic Accelerator Ascension Seat
- Cleansing and clearing for your Soul Extensions
- Cosmic Cellular Clearing
- Generalized Karma Clearing
- Anchoring of Aum or Om Mantra
- Merger with Light Body of Melchizedek
- Merger with Light Body of the Mahatma
- Merger with Light Body of Mother Mary
- Merger with Light Body of Quan Yin
- Merger with Light Body of Isis
- Merger with Light Bodies of the Masters or Archangels of your choice
- Removal of all Glamour, Maya and Illusion from energy fields, aura, and subconscious mind
- Anchoring of GOD Mantra, Names of GOD, and Spiritual Words of Power
- Call forth the Ascension Flame
- Pray for Physical Ascension

- Djwhal Khul's Light Quotient Building Program in the inner plane Synthesis Ashram
- Golden Dome of Protection
- Anchoring and Activation of your Unified Chakra
- Call forth the Golden Flame of Melchizedek for purification
- Call for God Crystals and Seed Packets from planetary, solar, galactic, universal and cosmic levels
- Ask the Mahatma to anchor, activate and open the 352 levels of GOD!
- Anchor Light Grids of Ascension
- Call forth the Divine Mother and Goddess energies to fully anchor the Divine Feminine within
- Divine Mother and Lady Masters to become fully anchored within your heart
- Removal of all wrong motivations
- Removal of all separative thinking and energy
- Remove all lack of forgiveness, conditional love and judgmentalness
- Removal of all selfishness and self-centeredness
- Removal of all egotism
- Removal of all anger, impatience, irritation
- Removal of all fear and worry
- Removal of all inferior and superiority thinking and feeling
- Clear all future life and parallel lives
- Creation of only life hormone in pituitary gland
- Opening of Channeling abilities
- Opening of all Psychic abilities for a Spiritual purpose
- Perfect radiant health in all four bodies
- Raising of vibrational frequencies in all 12 bodies
- The perfect completion of Dharma or purpose
- Call forth Perfect Alignment with your Spiritual mate or the finding of your right Spiritual mate if you would like this in this lifetime!
- Call forth Fifth Dimensional Self or higher to integrate and blend its consciousness with yours

- Ask the Ascended Master of your choice to meld its consciousness with your consciousness
- Call forth your Higher Rays to replace or overlight the ray configuration you came in with
- Remove all darts and arrows from etheric organs, glands and chakras from past and this life subconscious or psychic attack by others that got through your protective energy fields
- Call for the Core Love to fill all that has been cleansed
- Call forth God Realization in all Four Faces of GOD
- Call forth the Removal of all the Glamours of the Spiritual Path
- Ask to fully realize your 12 Levels of Initiation
- Help in increasing the Eight Psychological Quotients of GOD
- Help in increasing the 72 Psychological Subquotients of GOD
- Ask for help in increasing your Finances and removing any blocks to Financial Abundance and full God manifestation abilities
- Call forth the full anchoring of the Mantle of the Christ
- Call forth the full anchoring and activation of your Spiritual Leadership and Planetary World Service
- Call forth and fully claim you anointing as a World Teacher in total humbleness and humility
- Call forth help in developing great Spiritual Vigilance and Spiritual Discernment
- Call forth the Removal of all your Earth Crystals
- Ask that the Name of GOD run through your electrical and energy system on a permanent basis
- Call forth the Light Rod of GOD
- Call forth Secret Rod of God of Lord Buddha
- The Secret Rod of God of Helios and Vesta
- The Secret Rod of God of Melchior
- The Secret Rod of God of Melchizedek
- The Secret Rod of God of the Mahatma
- The Secret Rod of God of Archangel Metatron

- The Secret Rod of God of the Holy Spirit
- The Secret Rod of God of your own Mighty I Am Presence
- Call forth the anchoring and activation of your Higher Light Body, Love Body and Power Body!
- Remove all limited lens seeing
- Ask for help in mastering Spiritual energies, Psychological energies and Physical/Earthly energies!
- Call forth an integration of the 22 Cosmic Rays of GOD!
- Call forth help in transcending all physical laws and overcoming all limitation
- Call forth the complete removal of all veils stopping you from God Realization
- Ask for help in healing your inner child
- Ask for help in fully opening your Mystic and Occult Spiritual Vision
- Call for help in developing a flawless character
- Ask for help in being unconditionally loving towards self and others at all times
- Call for help in developing God Purity, God Honesty, and God Integrity at all times!
- Call for help in developing a 100% efficient perception of reality!
- Call for help in learning to quiet the mind and learning to meditate more effectively
- Call forth help in perfectly balancing your Three-Fold Flame!
- Ask for help in balancing your Heavenly and Earthly nature!
- Ask for help in removing all poverty consciousness and help in programming into your subconscious prosperity consciousness
- Ask for help in developing a perfect Spiritual psychology and philosophy that is in perfect alignment with the Holy Spirit and your Mighty I Am Presence
- Ask for help in passing all your Spiritual Tests
- Ask and pray for help in transcending all negative ego/fear-based/separative consciousness

- Ask for help in developing humbleness and humility at all times
- Ask for help in transcending all negative ego duality and the removal of these thought forms and patterns from your energy field and subconscious mind
- Ask for help in learning to integrate the Heavenly Ideal with the real world or third-dimensional reality!
- Ask for help in turning any perceived negative thing that has ever happened to a positive thing by the help of GOD, Christ, the Holy Spirit, and your own Mighty I Am Presence
- Merkabah of GOD
- Matrix of Synthesis from the Mahatma
- Joy, Bliss and Ecstasy of GOD
- Call forth a Spark of the Mind of GOD
- Merger with the Universal Mind of GOD
- Merger with the Heart of GOD
- Universal Archetypal imprint of God/Goddess energy
- Balancing and cleansing of the four elements of God
- Anchor and Activate the 48 Dimensions of GOD
- Anchoring of the Cosmic Monad
- Anchoring and cleansing in the Cosmic Burning Bush of GOD!
- Anchoring of the Limitless Love and Light of GOD!
- Anchoring and activation of the Ain, Ain Soph, and the Ain Soph Or!
- Anchoring of the Cosmic Wisdom of the Ages
- Anchoring of the Cosmic Waterfall of GOD
- Anchoring of the Inbreath and Outbreath of GOD
- Anchoring and Activation of the Arcturian Plating System
- Anchoring of the Arcturian Joy Machine!
- Arcturian Healing Chamber and Revitalization Program!
- Anchor the Arcturian Spiritual Computer Monitoring System for Self-Realization
- Anchoring of the 72 Activations of GOD as described in Dr. Stone's books!

- Anchor the Sacred Ember of GOD!
- Anchor the Sacred Fire of GOD!
- Anchor the Divine Seed of GOD!
- GOD's Transmitting System
- Anchoring of the Mahtama's Transmitting System
- Archangel Metatron's Transmitting System
- Baptism of GOD, Christ and the Holy Spirit
- Anchoring of the 72 Virtues of GOD!
- Merger with the Cosmic Pulse of GOD!
- Merger with the Divine Template of GOD!
- Merger with the Ray of GOD!
- Integration of the Divine Shaktipat of GOD!
- Crystals and Diamonds of GOD!
- Book of Life of GOD!
- Seed Atom of GOD!
- Holy Breath of GOD!
- Keys to the Kingdom of GOD!
- GOD's Cosmic Book of Knowledge
- Merger with GOD Consciousness on all levels!
- Merger with the Cosmic Pyramid of GOD
- Complete merger with GOD, Christ and the Holy Spirit
- Merger with the Unfathomableness of GOD!
- Ordination by GOD!
- Complete merger with GOD's Three-Fold Flame!
- Call forth the complete building of your Light body
- Anchoring and Activation of the Elohim Scriptures
- Anchoring and Activation of the Melchizedek Scriptures
- Archangelic Scriptures
- The Mahatma Scriptures
- The Archangel Metatron Scriptures

- Help in developing your 14 levels of Love, Wisdom and Power as described in Dr. Stone's book *The Golden Book of Melchizedek: How To Become An Integrated Christ/Buddha In This Lifetime!*
- Help in building your three levels of Immune System (Spiritual, Psychological and Physical)!
- Call for help in learning to co-create with Spirit and the Masters!
- Call for help in developing a better physical, mental, emotional, energetic, spiritual, environmental and social diet!
- Ask for help in learning to integrate the Material Face of GOD!
- Ask for help in turning lemons into lemonade!
- Ask for help in learning to "Dine with GOD"!
- Ask for help in becoming the Eighth Type of Ascended Master as described in Dr. Stone's book *The Golden Book of Melchizedek: How To Become An Integrated Christ/Buddha In This Lifetime!*
- Ask to be opened to your full multidimensionality and your full abilities of multidimensional communication
- Ask for help in learning to live in the "Tao"!
- Ask for help in learning to not only understand and feel GOD, but also to Demonstrate God every moment of your life to the best of your ability!
- Ask for your current Spiritual Assignment and Assignments to be revealed to you!
- Ask for help in learning to be a better Spiritual Parent to your inner child
- Anchor and activate a complete permanent merger with GOD!
- Anchor and merger with "YHWH"!
- Open all the Petals in all the Chakras!
- Call forth an ember of the Eight Sacred Flames!
- Activation of the Scrolls of Wisdom and Knowledge!
- Activation of your etheric nadis and all your acupuncture meridians!
- Anchoring of the "Full Living Light Garment of the Christ"!
- Anchoring of the full Garment of Perfection!

- Anchoring of the Jeweled Vehicle of Ascension!
- Call forth the Light Encodements of the Mahatma!
- Anchoring and activation of the Great Central Sun!
- Merger and integration with the Light Bodies of the Entire Cosmic and Spiritual Hierarchy!
- Full Garment of the Father/Mother God!
- Infinite Garment of YHWH!
- Cosmic Divine Scriptures of GOD!
- Infinite Garment of GOD, Christ and the Holy Spirit!
- Anchoring and Activation of Heavenly Jerusalem!
- Merger and integration with "Alpha and Omega"!
- Merger and integration with "Brahma, Vishnu and Shiva"!
- Merger with the "Shekinah"!
- Merger with "El Eliyon"!
- Merger with the "I Am that I Am"!
- Merger with "Ehyeh Asher Ehyeh"!
- Merger with "Ancient of Days, The Recent of Days and the Future of Days"!
- Merger with the "Om Tat Sat"!
- Merger with "All that is"!
- Merger with "Jehovah"!
- Merger with the Cosmic Christ of GOD on all levels!
- Merger with the Cosmic Buddha of GOD on all levels!
- Merger with GOD and the Godforce on all levels!
- Merger with Allah!
- Merger with the Cosmic Oversoul of GOD!
- Merger with the "12 Cosmic Rays of GOD"!
- Merger with the "Cosmic Mighty I Am Presence of GOD"!
- Merger with the "Infinite Attributes of GOD"!
- Merger with the "Infinite Names of GOD"!
- Merger with "Godhead"!
- Merger with the "Still, Small Voice Within"!

- Merger with "Infinite Spirit"!
- Merger with the Light Body of GOD!
- Merger with the Love, Light and Power Body of GOD, Christ and the Holy Spirit!
- Merger with the Synthesis of GOD!
- Merger with the Enlightenment of GOD!
- Merger with the Unconditional Love of GOD!
- Merger with the Compassion of GOD!
- Merger with the Faith of GOD!
- Merger with the Liberation of GOD!
- Merger with the Revelation of GOD!
- Merger with the Perfection of GOD!
- Merger with the Purity of GOD!
- Merger with the Name of Names of GOD!
- Merger with the Egolessness of GOD!
- Merger with the Salvation of GOD!
- Merger with the "Ascension of GOD"!
- Merger with the "Resurrection of GOD"!
- Merger with the "Translation of GOD"!
- Merger with the "Transfiguration of GOD"!
- Merger with the "Healing of GOD"!
- Merger with the "Rapture of GOD"!
- Merger with the "Realization of GOD"!
- Merger with the "Victory of GOD"!
- Merger with the "Gratitude of GOD"!
- Merger with the "Selflessness of GOD"!
- Merger with the "Forgiveness of GOD"!
- Merger with the "Holiness of GOD"!
- Merger with the "Divine Image of GOD"!
- Merger with the "Word of GOD"!
- Merger with the "Divine Splendor of GOD"!
- Merger with the "Integrated Ascension of GOD"!

- Merger with the "Multidimensional Ascension of GOD"!
- Merger with the "Physical Immortality of GOD"!
- Merger with the "Physical Ascension of GOD"!
- Merger with the "Revealed and Unrevealed Name of GOD"!

So let it be Written! So let it be Done!

47

My Spiritual Mission and Purpose by Dr. Joshua David Stone

My Spiritual mission and purpose is a multifaceted process. Spirit and the inner plane Ascended Masters have asked myself and Wistancia (married since 1998), to anchor onto the Earth an inner plane Ashram and Spiritual/Psycho-logical/Physical/Earthly Teaching and Healing Academy! This Academy is called the Melchizedek Synthesis Light Academy! We are overlighted in this mission by Melchizedek, the Mahatma, Archangel Metatron, the Inner Plane Ascended Master Djwhal Khul, and a large group of Ascended Masters and Angels such as the Divine Mother, Archangel Michael, Archangel Gabriel, Sai Baba, Vywamus, the Lord of Arcturus, Lord Buddha, Lord Maitreya, Mother Mary, Quan Yin, El Morya, Kuthumi, Serapis Bey, Paul the Venetian, Master Hilarion, Sananda, Lady Portia and Saint Germain, and a great many others who we like to call the "Core Group"!

I have also been asked by the inner plane Ascended Master Djwhal Khul, who again wrote the Alice Bailey books, and was also involved in the Theosophical Movement, to take over his inner plane Ashram when he moves on to his next Cosmic Position, in the not too distant future.

Djwhal holds Spiritual Leadership over what is called the inner plane Second Ray Synthesis Ashram. On the inner plane the Second Ray Department is a gigantic three story building complex with vast gardens.

The Ascended Master Djwhal Khul runs the first floor of the Second Ray Department in the Spiritual Hierarchy. Master Kuthumi, the

Chohan of the Second Ray, runs the second floor. Lord Maitreya the Planetary Christ runs the third floor! When Djwhal Khul leaves for his next Cosmic Position, I will be taking over this first floor Department. The Second Ray Department is focused on the "Spiritual Education" of all lightworkers on Earth and is the Planetary Ray of the Love/Wisdom of God. What is unique, however, about the Synthesis Ashram is that it has a unique mission and purpose which is to help light-workers perfectly master and integrate all 12 Planetary Rays which is one of the reasons I love this particular Spiritual leadership position and assignment so much! For this has been a great mission and focus of all my work!

Wistancia's and my mission has been to anchor the Synthesis Ashram and Teaching Academy onto the physical Earth, which we have done and are continuing to do in an ever increasing manner on a global level. Currently there are over 15 branches of the Academy that have been set up around the world! The Academy actually first came into existence in 1996! This we have been guided to call the Melchizedek Synthesis Light Academy for the following reasons. It is called this because of the Overlighting Presence of Melchizedek (Our Universal Logos), the Mahatma (Avatar of Synthesis), and the Light which is the embodiment of Archangel Metatron, who created all outer light in our Universe and is the creator of the electron! These three beings, Djwhal Khul, and a very large Core Group of inner plane Planetary and Cosmic Masters help us in all this work.

I have also been asked by the inner plane Ascended Masters to be one of the main "High Priest Spokespersons for the Planetary Ascension Movement on Earth." I have been asked to do this because of the cutting-edge, yet easy to understand nature of all my books and work, as well as certain Spiritual Leader-ship qualities I humbly possess. In this regard, I represent all the Masters, which works out perfectly given the Synthesis nature of my work. I function as kind of a "Point Man" for the Ascended Masters on Earth, as they have described it to me.

The Masters, under the guidance of Lord Buddha our Planetary Logos, have also guided us as part of our mission to bring Wesak to the West! So, for the last six years we have held a Global Festival and Conference at Mt Shasta, California for 2000 People. This, of course, honors the Wesak Festival, which is the holiest day of the year to the inner plane Ascended Masters, and the high point of incoming Spiritual energies to the Earth on the Taurus Full moon each year! We invite all lightworkers to join us each year from all over the world for this momentous Celebration, which is considered to be one of the premiere Spiritual Events in the New Age Movement!

The fourth part of my mission and purpose is the 30 volume "Easy to Read Encyclopedia of the Spiritual Path" that I have written. So far I have completed 27 volumes in this Ascension Book Series. The Ascended Master Djwhal Khul prophesized in the 1940's that there would be a third dispensation of Ascended Master teachings what would appear at the turn of the century. The first dispensation of Ascended Master teachings was the Theosophical Movement, channeled by Madam Blavatsky. The second dispensation of Ascended Master teachings was the Alice Bailey books, channeled by Djwhal Khul, and the *I AM Discourses*, channeled by Saint Germain. My 30 volume series of books is by the grace of GOD and the Masters, the third dispensation of Ascended Master teachings as prophesized by Djwhal Khul. These books are co-creative channeled writings of myself and the inner plane Ascended Masters. What is unique about my work is how easy to read and understand it is, how practical, comprehensive, cutting-edge, as well as integrated and synthesized. Wistancia has added to this work with her wonderful book *Invocations to the Light*.

The fifth aspect of our work and mission, which is extremely unique, is the emphasis of "Synthesis." My books and all my work integrate in a very beautiful way all religions, all Spiritual paths, all mystery schools, all Spiritual teachings, and all forms of psychology! Everyone feels at home in this work because of its incredible inclusive nature! This synthesis ideal is also seen at the Wesak Celebrations, for people come from all religions, Spiritual paths, mystery schools, and teachings. The event is overlighted by over one million inner plane Ascended Masters, Archangels and Angels, Elohim Masters, and Christed Extraterrestrials. Wesak, the Books, the Academy and all our work, embody this synthesis principle. This is part of why I and we have been given Spiritual Leadership of the Synthesis Ashram on earth, and soon on the Inner Plane as well. This also explains our unique relationship to Melchizedek who holds responsibility for the "synthesis development," of all beings in our Universe. Our connection to the Mahatma is explained by the fact that the Mahatma is the Cosmic embodiment of "Synthesis" in the infinite Universe. This is also why the Mahatma also goes by the name, "The Avatar of Synthesis." Archangel Metatron who holds the position in the Cosmic Tree of Life of Kether, or the Crown, hence has a "Synthesis Overview," of all of the Sephiroth or Centers of the Cosmic Tree of Life! Djwhal Khul holds Spiritual leadership of the "Synthesis Ashram" on the Planetary, Solar, and Galactic levels for the earth! The Core Group of Masters that overlight our mission are, again, the embodiment of the synthesis understanding!

The unique thing about our work is that it teaches some of the most cutting-edge co-created channeled work on the planet, in the realm of Ascension and Ascended Master Teachings. This can be seen in my books *The Complete Ascension Manual, Beyond Ascension, Cosmic Ascension, Revelations of a Melchizedek Initiate,* and *How To Teach Ascension Classes.* Because of my background as a Psychologist and licensed Marriage, Family and Child Counselor, I also specialize in some of the most advanced cutting edge work on the planet in the field of Spiritual psychology. In this regard, I would guide you to my books, *Soul Psychology, Integrated Ascension, How To Clear the Negative Ego,* and *Ascension and Romantic Relationships*! Thirdly, I also have humbly brought forth some extremely cutting-edge work on the physical/earthly level in the field of healing, Spirituality and society, politics, social issues, Extraterrestrials,

Spiritual leadership, Spirituality and business, Goddess work with Wistancia, and of course the annual Wesak Celebrations. This can be found in my books: *The Golden Keys to Ascension and Healing, Hidden Mysteries, Manual for Planetary Leadership, Your Ascension Mission: Embracing Your Puzzle Piece, How to be Successful in your Business from a Spiritual and Financial Perspective,* and *Empowerment and Integration Through The Goddess* —written by Wistancia and myself.

Adding to this, the eleven new books I have just completed and am completing. *The Golden Book of Melchizedek: How to Become an Integrated Christ/Buddha in this Lifetime, How to Release Fear-Based Thinking and Feeling: An In-depth Study of Spiritual Psychology, The Little Flame and Big Flame* (my first children's book), *Letters of Guidance to Students and Friends, Ascension Names and Terms Glossary, Ascension Activation Meditations of the Spiritual Hierarchy, The Divine Blueprint for the Seventh Golden Age, How to do Psychological and Spiritual Counseling for Self and Others, God and His Team of Super Heroes* (my second children's book) and *How to Achieve Perfect Radiant Health from the Soul's Perspective!*

Currently I have completed 27 Volumes in my Ascension Book Series. Fourteen of these books are published by Light Technology Publishers. A newer version of *Soul Psychology* is published by Ballantine Publishers, owned by Random House, which I am quite excited about as well! The other books are in manuscript form and I am currently negotiating with various publishers for publishing rights! My books have also been translated and published in Germany, Brazil, Japan, Holland, Israel and this process continues to expand.

Spirit and the inner plane Ascended Masters have told me that because of this unique focus, that what I have actually done in a co-creative way and manner with them, is open a new Portal to God. This new portal opening stems out of all the cutting-edge Ascension Activations and Ascended Master Teachings, the totally cutting-edge Spiritual Psychology work because of my background as a Psychologist and licensed Marriage, Family and Child Counselor, and the unique ability to ground all the work into the physical/earthly world in a balanced and integrated manner. Spirit and the Masters have told me that this new Portal to God is on an inner and outer plane level, and continues to be built in a co-creative way with Spirit, the Masters, myself, and certain other Masters and High Level Initiates who are helping me on the inner and outer planes! I have Spiritual leadership, however, in spearheading this project, and it is one of the most exciting projects I am involved in.

In terms of my Spiritual initiation process as I have spoken of in my books, I have currently now taken my 14th major initiation. These are not the minor initiations that some groups work with, but are the major initiations that embody all the minor initiations within them. The Seventh Initiation is the achieving of Liberation and Ascension. The 10th Initiation is the completion of Planetary Ascension and the beginning of Solar Initiation. The 11th Initiation, being the first Galactic Initiation. The 12th Initiation, being the first Universal Initiation from an Earthly perspective. Having taken my 14th initiation, what is most important to me is that these initiations have been taken in an "integrated manner," for, in truth, the Masters told me that they are not really into Ascension, which may surprise a great many lightworkers. The Masters are into "Integrated Ascension"! There are many lightworkers taking initiations, but many are not doing so in an integrated and balanced manner! They are taking them on a Spiritual level, but they are not being properly integrated into the mental and emotional bodies or psychological level properly. They are also not transcending negative ego fear-based thinking and feeling and properly balancing their four-body system. They are also not integrating their initiations fully into the physical/earthly level, addressing such things as: Healing, Grounding their Missions, Finding their Puzzle Piece Mission and Purpose, Prosperity Consciousness and Financial and Earthly Success, Integrating the God/Goddess, Embracing the Earth Mother and the Nature Kingdom, Properly Integrating into Third Dimensional Society and Civilization in terms of the focus of their Service Mission. This is just mentioned as a very loving reminder of the importance of an integrated and balanced approach to one's Spiritual Path. The grace to have been able to take these 14 major initiations and be able to have completed my Planetary Ascension process and to have moved deeply into my Cosmic Ascension process, I give to GOD, Christ, the Holy Spirit, Melchizedek, the Mahatma, Archangel Metatron, and the Core Group of Masters I work with. I have dedicated myself and my life to GOD and the Masters' service, and I have humbly attempted to share everything I know, have used, and have done in my Spiritual path and Ascension process with all of you, my Beloved Readers!

Melchizedek, the Universal Logos, has also inwardly told me, that because of the Cosmic work I am involved with, that I have taken on the Spiritual assignment of being one of the "12 Prophets of Melchizedek on Earth." I am very humbled to serve in this capacity. For Melchizedek is the Universal Logos, who is like the President of our entire Universe. In truth, all Religions and Spiritual teachings have their source in Melchizedek and in the Great Ancient Order of Melchizedek. It is my great honor and privilege to serve GOD and Melchizedek in this capacity. This is something I have never spoken of before, although I have known of this for many, many years. I have been guided after all this time to share a little more deeply about my Spiritual mission on Earth at this time.

The Academy Website is one of the most profound Spiritual Websites you will ever explore because it embodies this "synthesis nature" and is an ever-expanding, living, easy-to-read Spiritual "encyclopedia" that fully integrates all 12 Rays in design and creation! This is also embodied in the free 140 page information packet that we send out to all who ask who wish to get involved and know more about our work! The information in the information packet is also available by just exploring the Academy Website!

We have also set up a wonderful Ministers Ordination and Training Program, which we invite all interested to read about. I am also very excited about a relatively recent book I have written called *How to Teach Ascension Classes*. Because I have become so busy with my Spiritual leadership and global world service work, I really do not have the time to teach weekly classes, as I have in the past. I firmly believe in the motto "Why *give* a person a fish, when you can *teach* them to fish!" In this vein, the Masters guided me to write a book on how to teach people to teach Ascension classes based on my work. I humbly suggest it is a most wonderful channeled book that can teach you in the easiest way and manner on every level to teach Ascension classes in your home or on a larger level if you choose. These classes are springing up now all over the globe and have been successful beyond my wildest dreams and expectations. When I wrote the book I was so involved with the process of writing it, I never fully envisioned the tremendous success it would have on a planetary and global level. Using this book and my other books, I have really done the initial homework for you, which can and will allow you to immediately begin teaching Ascension classes yourself. I humbly suggest that you look into the possibility of doing this yourself if you are so guided!

One other very interesting aspect of our Spiritual mission is something the Masters have been speaking to us about for over 10 years which is what they described as being "Ambassadors for the Christed Extraterrestrials"! We have always known this to be true! This was part of the reason I wrote the book *Hidden Mysteries*, which I humbly suggest is one of the best overviews in an easy to read and understand manner, of the entire Extraterrestrial Movement as it has affected our planet. If you have not read this book, I highly recommend that you do so. It is truly fascinating reading! My strongest personal connection to the Extraterrestrials is with the Arcturians! The Arcturians are the most advanced Christed Extraterrestrial race in our galaxy. They hold the future blueprint for the unfoldment of this planet. The Arcturians are like our future planet and future selves on a collective level. Part of my work, along with the Ascended Master Teachings I have been asked to bring through, has been to bring through a more conscious and personal connection to the Arcturians, the Ashtar Command, and other such Christed Extraterrestrial races. This year's Platinum Wesak, because of being the year 2001, will have a special connection to these Christed Extraterrestrials, and we invite you all to attend for this reason and for many others! I also encourage you to read my book *Beyond Ascension* where I explore some of my personal experiences with the Arcturians, and how you may do so as well!

Currently, behind the scenes, we are working on some further expansions of this aspect of our mission, which we will share at a later time! Wistancia has also been involved with "White Time Healing," which is another most wonderful Extraterrestrial healing modality that she offers to the public!

One other aspect of our mission deals with having developed, with help from the inner plane Ascended Masters, some of the most advanced Ascension activation processes to accelerate Spiritual evolution that has ever been brought forth to this planet. In this co-creative process with the Masters, we have discovered the "keys" to how to accelerate Spiritual evolution at a rate of speed that in past years and centuries would have been unimaginable! This is why I call working with the Ascended Masters "The Rocketship to GOD Method of Spiritual Growth." There is no faster path to God Realization than working with the Ascended Masters, Archangels and Angels, Elohim Masters and Christed Extraterrestrials! What is wonderful about this process is that you do not have to leave your current Spiritual practice, religion, or Spiritual path. Stay on the path you are and just integrate this work into what you are currently doing! All paths as you know, lead to GOD, my friends! This is the profundity of following an eclectic path, and path of synthesis! I humbly suggest I have found some shortcuts! I share this with all lightworkers on earth, for I love GOD with all my heart and soul and mind and might, and I recognize that we are all incarnations of GOD, and Sons and Daughters of this same GOD, regardless of what religion, Spiritual path, or mystery school we are on. We are all, in truth, the Eternal Self and are all God! There is, in truth, only GOD, so what I share with you, I share with you, GOD, and myself for in the highest sense we are all one! What we each hold back from each other, we hold back from ourselves and from GOD. This is why I give freely all that I am, have learned and have, to you, my Beloved Readers, giving everything and holding back nothing! In my books and audiotapes, I have literally shared every single one of these ideas, tools, and Ascension activation methods for accelerating evolution that I have used and come to understand. My Beloved Readers, these tools and methods found in my books and on the audiotapes will "blow your mind as to their effectiveness," in terms of how profound, and easy to use they are! I would highly recommend that all lightworkers obtain the 13 Ascension Activation Meditation tapes I have put together for this purpose. Most of them were taped at the Wesak Celebrations with 1500 to 2000 people in attendance, with over one million inner plane Ascended Masters, Archangels and Angels, Elohim Masters, and Christed Extraterrestrials in attendance, under the Wesak full moon and the mountain of Mt Shasta. You can only imagine the power, love, and effectiveness of these Ascension activation audiotapes. I recommend getting all 13 tapes and working with one tape every day or every other day! I personally guarantee you that these tapes will accelerate your Spiritual evolution a thousand-fold! You can find them in the information packets and on our Website. They are only available from the Academy! Trust me on this, the combination of reading my books, Wistancia's book, and working with these audio ascension activation tapes, will accelerate your Spiritual evolution beyond your wildest dreams and imagination!

One other extremely important part of my mission, which is a tremendous Spiritual passion of mine, is the training of lightworkers on earth in the area of Spiritual/Christ/Buddha thinking and negative ego/separative/fear-based thinking! These are the only two ways of thinking in the world, and each person thinks with one, the other, or a combination of both. If a person does not learn how to transcend negative ego thinking and feeling, it will end up, over time, corrupting every aspect of their lives including all channeling work, Spiritual teaching, and even healing work! One cannot be wrong with self and right with GOD. This is because our thoughts create our reality, as we all know! I cannot recommend more highly that every person reading this book, read my other books: *Soul Psychology, The Golden Book of Melchizedek: How to Become an Integrated Christ/Buddha in this Lifetime,* and *How to Release Fear-Based Thinking and Feeling: An In-depth Study of Spiritual Psychology*! I humbly suggest that these three books will be three of the most extraordinary self-help books in the area of mastering this psychological area of life. They are extremely easy to read, very practical and filled with tools that will help you in untold ways. Being a channel for the Ascended Masters and being uniquely trained as a Spiritual Psychologist and Marriage, Family and Child Counselor, as well as being raised in a family of psychologists, has given me an extraordinary ability to teach this material through my books in a most effective manner. The combination of my books on Ascension, and these books on Spiritual Psychology, along with Wistancia's book on the art of invocation, will literally revolutionize your consciousness in the comfort of your own home! The most extraordinary thing about all this work is how incredibly easy to read, and easy to understand it is. It is also incredibly comprehensive, completely cutting-edge, and totally integrated, balanced, and synthesized. It contains the best of all schools of thought in the past, present, and channeled cutting edge future understanding that is available now! I humbly ask you to trust me in this regard and just read one of these books and you will immediately want to buy the others!

One other aspect of our work and mission is our involvement with the "Water of Life" and the Perfect Science products for the healing of our own physical bodies and the physical body of Mother Earth of all pollution in the air, water and earth. This is the miracle Mother Earth has been waiting for to bring her back to her "original edenic state" after so much abuse. This is not the time or the place to get into this subject in detail; however, I invite you to check out the "Water of Life" and the Perfect Science information in the Information Packet and on the Academy Website! It is truly the miracle we have all been waiting for to help heal the Earth!

One other aspect of our work and mission is a project that the Ascended Masters have asked us to put together on behalf of lightworkers and people around the globe. It is called the "Interdimensional Prayer Altar Program"! that the Masters have guided us to set up in the Academy in Agoura Hills, California on the property we live on. We have set up a "Physical Interdimensional Prayer Altar" where people can send in their prayers on any subject and we will place them on this Altar. In consultation with the Masters, Archangels and Angels, Elohim Masters, and Christed Extraterrestrials, we have set up an arrangement with them that all physical letters placed upon this Altar will be immediately worked upon by these Masters. We have been guided by the inner plane Ascended Masters to create 15 Prayer Altar Programs in different areas of life that people can sign up for. For example, there is one for health and one for financial help in your Spiritual mission. Two-thirds of these programs are totally free. There are five or six that are more advanced Spiritual acceleration programs where written material is sent to you to work with in conjunction with these programs so as to accelerate your Spiritual growth. All letters we receive by e-mail, fax, or letter are placed on the Altar by myself or my personal assistant. It is kept 100% confidential and is an extremely special service provided by the inner plane Ascended Masters and Angels to help all lightworkers and people on Earth with immediate help for whatever they need, should they desire assistance. Other examples of Prayer Altars are: Building your Higher Light Body, Extra Protection, Relationship Help, World Service Prayers, Help for your Animals, Prayer Altar for the Children,

Integrating the Goddess, Integrating your Archetypes, Integrating the Seven Rays and working with the Seven Inner Plane Ashrams of the Christ, Integrating the Mantle of the Christ, Ascension Seat Integration, and Light, Love, and Power Body Building Program! These Prayer Altar Programs have been co-created with the inner plane Ascended Masters as another tool for not only helping all lightworkers with whatever they need help with, but also as another cutting-edge tool to accelerate Spiritual evolution!

In a similar regard, the Masters have guided us to set up a Melchizedek Synthesis Light Academy Membership Program which is based on three levels of involvement. Stage One, Stage Two, and Stage Three! Stage One and Stage Three are totally free. Stage Two costs only $20 for a Lifetime Membership with no other fees required. You also receive free large colored pictures of Melchizedek, the Mahatma, Archangel Metatron, and Djwhal Khul for joining. It is not necessary to join to get involved in the work; however, it has been set up by the inner plane Ascended Masters as another service and tool of the Academy to help lightworkers accelerate their Spiritual evolution! When joining the different Stages, the Masters take you under their wing, so to speak, and accelerate your evolution by working with you much more closely on the inner plane while you sleep at night and during your conscious waking hours. The joining is nothing more than a process that gives them the permission to work with you in this more intensive fashion! Again, it is not necessary to join to get involved in the work, and is really just another one of the many fantastic tools and services the Academy has made available to you to accelerate your Spiritual, psychological, and earthly/physical evolution in an integrated and balanced manner!

I had a dream shortly after completing my two new books, *The Golden Book of Melchizedek: How To Become an Integrated Christ/Buddha in This Lifetime*, and my book *How To Release Fear-Based Thinking and Feeling: An In-depth Study of Spiritual Psychology*. In the dream, I was being shown the different Spiritual missions people had. My Spiritual mission was the embodiment of the Holy Spirit. I clearly was shown how other people within GOD, Christ, and the Holy Spirit had missions of being more detached off-shoots of the Holy Spirit, and continuing outward from there, had all kinds of different Spiritual missions. However, mine was the embodiment of the Holy Spirit on Earth.

My Beloved Readers, I want to be very clear here that in sharing this I am in no way, shape, or form claiming to be the Holy Spirit. There is enough glamour in the New Age Movement and I am not interested in adding any more to it. What I am sharing here, which is being given to more clearly and precisely share my Spiritual mission and purpose, is that which I am here to strive to embody and demonstrate. The Holy Spirit is the third aspect of the Trinity of GOD. I have always greatly loved the Holy Spirit, for the Holy Spirit is like the "Voice of GOD"! It is the "Still, Small Voice Within"! When one prays to GOD, it is the Holy Spirit who answers for GOD. The Holy Spirit is the answer to all questions, challenges, and problems. The Holy Spirit speaks for the Atonement or the At-one-ment! It teaches the Sons and Daughters of GOD how to recognize their true identity as God, Christ, the Buddha, and the Eternal Self! In truth, there are only two voices in life! There is the voice of the negative ego and the "Voice of the Holy Spirit"! There is the voice of negative ego/fear-based/separative thinking and feeling, and there is the Voice of God/Spiritual/Christ/Buddha thinking and feeling! There is the "Voice of Love" and the voice of fear! There is the "Voice of Oneness" and the voice of separation!

I was given this dream after completing these two books because, I humbly suggest, this is the energy I was embodying in writing them and that I am striving to embody at all times in my Spiritual mission and purpose on Earth. This is not surprising in the sense that this has always been my Spiritual ideal and the dream was just an inward confirmation in that moment that I was embodying and demonstrating that Spiritual Ideal in the energy flow I was in. This is what I strive to do in all my work, be it my Ascension Book Series, Wesak Celebrations, Teaching,

Counseling, Videotapes, Audiotapes, and all my work, which is to strive to be the embodiment of a "Voice for God"! By the grace of GOD, Christ, the Holy Spirit, and the Masters, I provide a lot of the "answers" people and lightworkers are seeking! I teach people how to "undo" negative ego/fear-based/separative thinking and feeling, and show then how to fully realize God/Christ/Buddha thinking and feeling! I show them how to release and undo glamour, illusion, and maya, and instead seek "Truth, as GOD, Christ, the Holy Spirit, and the Masters would have you seek it!"

My real purpose, however, is not to just be the embodiment of the Holy Spirit on Earth, for I would not be embodying the Voice and Vision of the Holy Spirit if I just focused on this. The Voice and Vision of GOD, Christ, the Holy Spirit, and Melchizedek is that of synthesis! This is the other thing I feel in the deepest part of my heart and soul that I am here to embody! So my "truest and highest Spiritual ideal" that I am here to strive to embody, is GOD, Christ, the Holy Spirit, the inner plane Ascended Masters, the Archangels and Angels of the Light of GOD, the Elohim Councils of the Light of GOD, and the Christed Extraterrestrials of the Light of GOD. I feel in the deepest part of my heart and soul, and what I try to embody every moment of my life is "All that is of GOD and the Godforce on Earth!" In this regard, it is my Spiritual mission and purpose to strive to be the embodiment of the "synthesis nature of God on Earth!" This is why I have been given Spiritual leadership of the Synthesis Ashram and Academy on Earth and future leadership of the inner plane Synthesis Ashram that governs our planet.

The other thing I strive to do in my Spiritual mission is to embody Spiritual mastery on a Spiritual, psychological, and physical/earthly level. What most people and lightworkers do not realize is that there are three distinct levels to God Realization. There is a Spiritual level, a psychological level, and a physical/earthly level! To achieve true God Realization, all three levels must be equally mastered! Another way of saying this is that there are "Four Faces of GOD"! There is a Spiritual Face, a Mental Face, an Emotional Face, and a Material Face! To truly realize God, all four must be equally mastered, loved, honored, sanctified, integrated, and balanced! The "Mental and Emotional Faces of GOD" make up the psychological level of GOD. So, my Spiritual mission and purpose is to fully embody Spiritual mastery and unconditional love on all three of these levels and in all Four Faces of GOD! In a similar vein, my Spiritual mission and purpose is to embody self-mastery and proper integration of all "Seven Rays of GOD," not just one or a few. For the "Seven Rays of GOD" are, in truth, the true "Personality of GOD"! My Spiritual mission and purpose is to not only strive to embody all levels of GOD, but to also try and develop all my God-given abilities and Spiritual gifts, on a Spiritual, Psychological, and Physical/Earthly level, and in all Four Faces of GOD!

My Beloved Readers, all these things that I have written about in this chapter are what I strive to fully embody and demonstrate on the Earth every moment of my life, and is what I strive with all my heart and soul and mind and might to teach others to do as well!

As the Founder and Director of the Melchizedek Synthesis Light Academy along with Wistancia, with great humbleness and humility, it has been my great honor and privilege to share "my Spiritual mission and purpose" in a deeper and more profound manner at this time. I do so in the hopes that all who feel a resonance and attunement with this work will get involved with the "Academy's Teachings" and all that it has to offer. I also share this so that all who choose to get involved might join this vast group of lightworkers around the globe, to help spread the teachings and work of the inner plane Ascended Masters. The inner plane Ascended Masters and I, along with the Archangels and Angels, Elohim Councils, and Christed Extraterrestrials, put forth the Clarion Call to lightworkers around the world to first explore this work, then integrate this work, and then become Ambassadors of the Ascended Masters so we may at this time in Beloved Earth's history bring in fully now the Seventh Golden Age in all its Glory!

About the Author

Dr. Joshua David Stone has a Ph.D. in Transpersonal Psychology and is a licensed Marriage, Family and Child Counselor, in Agoura Hills, California. On a Spiritual level he anchors **The Melchizedek Synthesis Light Academy and Ashram**, which is an integrated inner and outer plane ashram that seeks to represent all paths to God! He serves as one of the leading spokespersons for the Planetary Ascension Movement. Through his books, tapes, workshops, lectures, and annual Wesak Celebrations, Dr. Stone is known as one of the leading Spiritual Teachers and Channels in the world on the teachings of the Ascended Masters, Spiritual Psychology, and Ascension! He has currently written over 27 volumes in his "Ascension Book Series," which he also likes to call "The Easy to Read Encyclopedia of the Spiritual Path"!

For a free information packet of all Dr. Stone's workshops, books, audiotapes, Academy membership program, and global outreach program, please call or write to the following address:

Dr. Joshua David Stone
Melchizedek Synthesis Light Academy
28951 Malibu Rancho Rd.
Agoura Hills, CA 91301

Phone: 818-706-8458
Fax: 818-706-8540
e-mail: drstone@best.com

Please come visit my Website at:
http://www.drjoshuadavidstone.com